Conkers

Conkers

British Twins in Nazi Germany

Ken Lambert

Design by Guy Pommares

© 072485721

To my brother Ron
and to our companions Dieter and Hans.

After seventy years, here at last,
is the memorial that I promised you
so that some may know of your courage,
your tenacity and your selflessness.

What is history all about, if not the exquisite delight of knowing the details, and not only the abstract patterns?

Stephen Jay Gould

Contents

Interior photography by Dieter Wolf, Ken Lambert
and Isabel Weeks.
Cover photography courtesy of BlueDaisyGlass.
Back cover author's portrait by Maria Elena Reggeti.

ACKNOWLEDGMENTS

With my heartfelt gratitude
to my wife Isabel, for putting up with me all this time;
and for all her help and support as I was writing down
these experiences.

And also, thanks to my friend Guy Pommares
who did the layout, proofing and cover design.

PROLOGUE

HITLER'S THIRD REICH

When Germany lost the Great World War of 1914-18 it had to sign the very destructive and humiliating Treaty of Versailles.

It lost all its colonies: Alsace went to France, Gdansk to the League of Nations, East and West Prussia and parts of Pomerania went to Poland. The German territory on the West Bank of the Rhine was then occupied by the combined troops of the victorious powers. The League of Nations administered the Saar district and its coalfields were just given to France.

Now Germany was forbidden to form a union with Austria, or to build another war machine. It was saddled with astronomical sums to be paid for reparations. These measures provided the complex ingredients for a new wave of German fanaticism.

ADOLF HITLER, AND HIS RISE TO POWER:
Today the world believes Hitler to be Satan personified, or a raving psychopath. He may have had real illusions of grandeur, but he was a product and the voice of a very hungry society at that time:

As a disappointed bourgeois artist with no political experience he existed in his Vienna flophouse without skill or a trade until he climbed on a bandwagon of European Anti-Semite German Nazis.

By 1932 he tried to take over the local government in Munich, but his rebellion failed and the attempt landed him in prison with Rudolf Hess. Together they wrote the book Mien Kampf.

One year later, Brown Shirt supporters of the young Nazi movement were forming in the beer taverns of Munich, stirring the people at every opportunity. Their leader, just fresh out of prison was a grubby Adolf Hitler, whose strong voice told the people what they wanted to hear and they listened earnestly. At that time Germany was ripe for a new commander to rise from the ashes of war.

The terrible treaty of Versailles and the economic crisis it caused created six million unemployed. The hungry masses were looking for a strong new leader to get them back to work and put food on the tables for their children: they thought Hitler was their man. If the powerful men in industry and the lower ranks of the army had not supported Hitler, he would have never made it from his prison cell to the head of the German State in such a short time.

He and his armed Brown-Shirt thugs of the SA organized mass movements, and controlled a powerful army of unions and unemployed. They always told the common people what they wanted to hear, especially propagating the destruction of Marxism and the Jews. He promised the people, that if elected to office, he would restore Germany to its original status as a mighty world power, so millions listened carefully.

The leading German industrialists and bankers felt very uneasy about this man Hitler. He held a tight grip on the unemployed masses and the unions, so they cautiously joined him and quietly funded his campaigns, supporting him in order to keep the peace in their work places and enjoy strike free production.

Hitler and his NSDAP (The Nazi Workers' Party of Germany) became a useful tool in the hands of the banks and big business.

The steel baron Fritz Thyssen later admitted as much in his book called "I PAID HITLER". Others were to follow: Bankers Emil Kirdorf, director of the Deutsche Bank, Schalt of the Reichsbank, then the industrialist Borsig, Von Strauss, Friedreich Flick and Krupp all paid Hitler's party extremely well for peace with the unions and harmony in their individual industries.

At the height of Germany's economic crisis, the political bickering and differences came to a gridlock. The parliamentary government in power just shut down and ceased to function.

The high-ranking circles of Germany's industrialists and leading opinion makers of the day pressured President Von Hindenburg to transfer the power to govern to Hitler's Nazi NSDA. They pointed out that his was the only party that was totally together and united firmly behind its leader. After all, many political figures had tried to form a government and floundered. The parties and cabinets of Bruning, Papen and Schleicher had all torn themselves to shreds trying to hold their cabinets together. They had failed; there was no party left that could form a stable government.

So the senile President Von Hindenburg was forced to appoint Hitler Chancellor on 30th January 1933.

Hitler then formed his first Nazi Cabinet. So there was a strong firm government, fanatically loyal to their beloved Führer Adolf Hitler. There was no other alternative for Germany.

NAZIS IN POWER:

So started the barbarous Third Reich. Hitler's brown terror lasted for twelve years in Germany. First the Communist Party was totally banned. Its leaders and their families forced into exile or thrown in to the early concentration camps.

But after the next election, the Nazi NSADP acquired a majority vote of 44%, so the smaller parties in the Reichstag accepted Hitler's "Enabling Act". It gave Hitler all power as Dictator. The Nazi NSDAP thus came to power quite legally, without a fight.

Hitler's SA was now strengthened into a powerful armed force of brown-shirted thugs and the army was re-organized to be led only by loyal Nazis. Hitler now had not only the political power, but also the brute force. He was unchangeable.

The unions were broken up and banned. Finally all the opposing political parties were dispersed.

Prologue

Factories, offices, schools, banks, universities, the radio, press, people, organizations and the entire spectrum of German society, were all forced into step and regimented to the "New Order" whether they liked it or not.

For this New Order to grip Germany in its iron grasp it needed strong and disciplined organization to keep a firm control.

Here are just some of the units and authorities of that New Order:

The *SA Sturmabteilungen* (Brown Shirts, armed thugs) led by Ernst Röhm they would perform the strong-arm tasks and `quiet any unrest'.

The *SS Schutzstaffeln* (An elite private regiment of Hitler's own soldiers,) members of the party wearing the dreaded black uniform of the SS.

The Gestapo, Geheime State Police (The plain clothes Secret Police,) was the most dreaded and feared of all the Nazis. Each one of their officers was a well-trained fanatical Nazi. He held the power of life or death in his hands and was entitled and able to cut across all ranks in matters of state security.

RAD Reichsarbeitsdienst (The German Work Front.)

A massive labor movement. Every boy and girl was required to serve at least a year at a work labor camp after their eighteenth birthday.

Four compulsory youth movements, for pure Aryan boys and girls only:

HJ *Hitler Jugen* (Hitler Youth) for boys 14-18 years.
DJ. *Young Volk* (Young Folk) for boys 10-13 years.
BDM. *Bund Deutscher Mädchen* (German Girls) girls 14-18.
JM. *Jungmädel* (German Young Girls) for girls 10-13 years.

By 1940 the Nazi movement exercised total control over the body and soul of all German people.

Participation in those days was compulsory. Mass gatherings, torchlight processions and party conferences were the catalysts of the nation's awakening. It was a bright day for the German "New Order". The Nazis made noises about the chosen northern Aryan race. The Führer Adolf Hitler then told the German youth they were the Aryan elite, a super race and that one-day they would rule the world.

He then began the grisly business of excising all the "inferior life"

The Jews were declared vermin. On the night of the 9th November 1938, *Kristallnacht* (The night of broken glass) Jewish people were attacked killed and robbed. Their stores smashed and looted, the police stood by and watched. On that night the German people surely lost their innocence. Later in 1941 the Jews were subjected to Hitler's `Final solution'. Millions of European Jews died a gruesome death in Aushwitz, Treblinka and extermination camps like Madjanek, Buchenwald and Dachau. It was a holocaust like no other ever known.

WORLD WAR:

Shortly after coming to power, Hitler explained his foreign policy:

> "In order to protect Germany against world powers like England, the USA and the Soviet Union it will be necessary to fragment Europe and merge them into a larger unified economic body, under German leadership. Then they would procure by force new export markets".

Hitler convinced the Nazi party and the army that the Nazitification, of new lands in the east was also very necessary.

The Nazis then embarked on a very busy plan of war preparations. Soon tanks were rolling on the new motorways that were built specially for them. Today the autobahns still form the basis of the German contemporary road networks.

In just five years Hitler recouped almost everything that Germany had lost at the Versailles Treaty. A year later the German Wehrmacht marched into the Rhineland. In March 1938 came the annexation of Austria, then after the failed Munich conference it marched again into the Sudentenland and that Czechoslovakian territory became part of the new German Empire. The British and French policy of appeasement at the Munich Conference had failed miserably.

After the Soviet-German non-aggression pact of 23rd of August 1939 was signed, Hitler and Stalin divided Europe up between them. Then in September, in very close cooperation, the German and Russian troops jointly invaded Poland. Poland's own standing treaty with France and England then kicked-in triggering the start of World War Two. England and France declared war on Germany. With over fifty million dead world- wide, it was to be the most terrible war ever known in the history of mankind.

For two years the German forces supported by their allies, marched unstopped from victory to victory. By 1942 the Nazi's controlled Europe and now in league with Italy, sought to bring Africa under their yoke.

Nazi Germany then embarked on a reign of bloody persecution, spreading, oppression and terror among the people they conquered. They forced vast numbers into slave labor camps to work in the German factories of BMW, Krupp's, Mercedes-Benz, AG Farben, Siemens, Dorner, Messerschmitt, Heinkel, and Volkswagen. The German Jews and the Jews from the newly occupied countries were sent for "Special Treatment" in the gas chambers.

Hitler broke his non-aggression pact with Stalin and invaded the Soviet Union. Eventually his advancing army came to a freezing halt in winter outside the gates of Moscow where his fortune at last changed. The Japanese, with their usual deceit and absence of diplomatic honor, sneaked in to Pearl Harbor and bombed on a peaceful Sunday morning whilst their groveling ambassadors were actually talking about a peace treaty with the US President. Without any warning or declaration of war, they attacked the U.S. fleet, awakening America the "Sleeping Giant". America now promptly entered the war against Japan and Germany.

Prologue

The British Empire, the USA and the Soviet Union now presented a massive militarily superior alliance to fight Hitler.

The defeat of the frozen German 6th Army at Stalingrad and the allied landings in Normandy on `D-Day' signaled the end of Nazi aspirations.

The collapse of the Third Reich came with its unconditional surrender on the 7th-9th May 1945. Hitler wanted to conquer new *Lebensraum* for Germany and make his nation an invincible world power. But Germany now lay in ruins, bombed to smithereens, occupied, divided and starving.

It finally dawned on the people of Germany, Nazi rule had plunged this once proud nation, into an all-time moral low point in history.

Our story starts in Munich before this war at Christmas time 1938, a happy time, when the Lambert twin boys were just nine years old.

1. HOME

The solid front door of the large old house is tugged open by a lively nine-year-old boy, dressed in a warm gray school uniform.

He trots out swinging his school satchel, running down the long front path past wide lawns that are buried under a deep blanket of snow. He slides to a halt in front of a pair of huge wrought-iron gates. Ron, his twin brother chases him shouting.

"Hey Ken, wait for me; wait for me".

Ken grins and scrambles easily to the top of the estate's front gates, then jumps down lightly on the other side and grins back to Ron, who yells,

"Wait till Max opens it with his switch from the house".

"Yes, but this way we get a free ride, come on".

There is a click and a deep electric hum and the heavy gates start to slowly swing open. As soon as the gap is big enough for Ron to slip through he runs round the front and jumps on and both boys ride the gates as they open, singing,

"Oh, any old iron,
any old iron, any,
any, any, old iron..."

They brace themselves waiting for the gates to bump on their stops. With a dull clump the gates stop and almost without a pause they start to swing close again with a creak and a lighter hum.

The boys climb to the top yelling. *"Old iron, old iron"*.

Ken yells: "Hey Ron.... I'll race you up to the corner".

The large ornate electric gates close noiselessly, but the serenity of the street is shattered by the shrill voices and echoes of the twins running as fast as they can. Ron spreads his arms out like an airplane,

"Look at me, I'm a ME-109. Brrrr... Bombs away! "

Ken almost catches him up; he too spreads his wings yelling,

"Look out, here comes an RAF fighter, and I'm on your tail...
Rat-a-tat-tat-tat-tat.... You're dead and crashing in flames, here
comes my victory roll. Brr-brr-brr".

Ron fakes his crash, finding a convenient deep snowdrift to dive into. Ken does his victory roll over Ron's body. The battle over, Ken brushes the snow off Ron's back and the twins run off in to town.

It's a cold snowy December day in 1938. Munich looks very exciting to the boys. They are free for the Christmas holidays and free from their strict and rigid boarding school in Walchensee and it's only five days to Christmas. The fresh fall of snow is still clean and white. People are busy Christmas shopping. Long red and white Nazi banners hang down the sides of most of the buildings blending in with the Christmas decorations and making the city look very festive.

The boys trot past shops with windows that are all decorated for the season. They run into an open air market past a row of stalls selling everything a boy could eat, stopping at the 'Glabberjucks' stall with the wonderful-looking desserts that have crystal clear green and red gelatin topped with a vanilla sauce. All are safely under glass looking delicious but just out of reach of their little fingers.

They trot on through the market and come to the meat section where the stalls are selling all kinds of sausage. Clouds of steam bellow from the large round copper cookers with a different smell of fresh-made sausages at each stall. All mixed with the scent of burning wood logs that are used to fire the big boilers. Ken grabs Ron's arm and tugs him to a halt,

"Ron, let's go past old fat Scholter's place:
we might get a free taste".
"Yes, his garlic sausage is yummy; come on".

They wander slowly past 'Scholter's Cooked Meats'; it's the largest sausage stall in the market with a long glass covered counter. There are rows of hanging meats and hams in string nets. But it is the large pig's head with tired looking eyes and an apple shoved in its mouth sitting on a big silver tray that catches their attention, Ken says.

"Hey Ron, what sort of people eat pigs' heads?"
"Pig head eaters..., fat Bavarian pig head eaters'.
"I bet it looks awful when it's all roasted,
its ears would go crispy, ha...
Hey, do they eat the eyes, these pig head eaters?"
"Yes, stupid, they're the tasty bits".
"Yuck, I couldn't eat pig's eyeballs, yuck".

Ron fingers out an imaginary pig's eyeball and licks his fingers yelling,

"Yum, yum, pig's bum, you can't have none.
Mm, mm tasty eyeballs".

Herr Scholter, the jovial butcher who looks just like Father Christmas complete with red shiny cheeks, slices a large ham sausage on a hand-cranked slicer. He smiles at the twins and recognizes them, laughs at Ron saying,

"Hey, you Lambert boys, you want to try some of this,
it's from Holland you know".

The Butcher gives a fat slice to each boy and throws his right forearm out with his fingers closed in a lax gesture, vaguely resembling a Nazi salute, smiles and says.

"Merry Christmas.... Heil Hitler. "

The boys munch the meat.
"It tastes good yes, don't forget to tell your cook
who gave it to you".
The boys wave and yell,
"Herr Scholter.....Vielen dank, Merry Christmas".
Then for a little fun Ron quietly says,
"Drei Liter. Herr Scholter! "
(Three Liters, it just sounds like Heil Hitler, the boys use it when they want to impress someone but not actually say Heil Hitler)
They wave, and then run off through the crowded marketplace munching on their sausage, out into the busy streets of Munich.

At Neuhauser Strasse the boys stop to watch a platoon of 'Hitler Youth' fit young boys in their winter uniforms, singing boisterously, their field packs and water bottles swinging in time to their feet. The first two boys, the biggest, are proudly carrying a pair of very large banners. The front rank is being led by a blond boy of about fourteen with a very determined look on his face, he yells at the top of his voice.
"Hey! Hey. We are Germany's future.
So don't you get in our way!"
Ron jumps to attention, puts his fingers to his nose like a Hitler moustache and gives a very exaggerated mock salute. The tail end boy notices Ron's rude gesture and points his finger accusingly. Ron grins and whispers with admiration.
"Wouldn't mind getting into that mob".
Ken says excitedly,
"Did you see the knives they all had on their belts?"
They all get them you know; parents can't stop the boys from wearing them either because it's part of their uniform.... You know, those knives are so sharp they can cut right through a ten centimeter nail".
"You would have to whack it with a hammer".
Ron adds.
"Ten, you have to be ten years old to get in".
"We could lie; we look ten; some of the boys in that platoon
look younger than us".
The twins trot on through the streets of Munich. Nowadays they play with German children and read Nazi comics. The German newspapers they look at are Nazi because foreign papers are forbidden. This is how it is in the German child's world. At school they all are made to yell,
"What luck we have a Führer! He'll tell the whole lot of them-
Czechs, Jews, Americans, Communists,
Brits. and Priests - where they can get off!"
The twins have no idea what Communists or Jews are yet.

3

The brothers wander across the bridge at Maximilian Strasse, and look down into the river Isar. A slim stream of fast running water is snaking down the center between banks of broken ice. They watch the solid stone pilings that support the bridge cut through the flow like the gray prow of a fast moving ship, the water shooting up each side of the bow. They make snowballs by scraping the new snow off the wide stone handrail and try to bomb the birds on the ice but miss.

Ron points to the park across the river where a group of boys are engaged in a ferocious snowball fight.
"Look over there Ken, look at the deep snow,
It's still thick; come on let's get stuck into them".
The twins run across the bridge into the park along the path. Ken recognizes one of the snowball fighters and yells.
"Look, there's Karl... look at his uniform, let's get him".
Karl is a thuggish boy, bigger than the rest, about twelve, with bright carrot-red hair and freckles. He is wearing a new Young Folk uniform of the Hitler Youth. He is a bully and is the Lambert brother's worst enemy, he has been in many fights with them, but never yet managed to get the better of the twins; he is just not strong enough to bully the brothers when they are together. That is until two weeks ago, when he had caught Ron on his own, just as he was leaving the public library.
Karl crept up behind him and punched him catching Ron off guard. Without Ken, Ron was no match for Karl so he took his beating and ran off knowing he would meet up with Karl again one day with his brother by his side. This is going to be their day for settling the old score. Karl bends down to pick more snow and notices the twins.
"Well if it's not the two little English shits,
what are you doing in my park, assholes?"
"Your park? How did it come to be your park?"
Ken yells.
Ron says very cautiously.
"Hello Karl, I like your uniform".
Ken goes on, laughing.
"So, Karl, are you going to eat one of those little boys trussed
up for your Christmas dinner then, ha?"
Karl yells. "English pigs".
Ken shrieks back defiantly,
"Carrot top, don't get any shit on that new uniform...
How did you get such awful colored hair Karl,
did your mother drink too many bottles of cheap red wine".
Ken ducks the expected blow that Karl sent to his head. Ron scoops up a handful of snow and throws it into Karl's face. Karl bends down to

pick up some snow and Ron grabs his chance and pushes Karl's backside so hard, he dives face first into the snowdrift.

The boys all fall about laughing. Karl, who is training to be a Hitler Youth leader, now face down in the snow and in front of all his little boys. The twins roll about laughing. Ken, not paying too much attention gets a little too close to Karl and like a flash he snatches Ken's satchel straps, grabs him in a head lock, draws out his Hitler Youth camp knife from its black metal scabbard and holds the blade very close to his eye.

Karl's face is bright red, he snaps back at Ron.

"You come any closer and I will cut this baby's face".

Ron backs off, slowly takes off his school satchel and holds it like a weapon. Ken wiggles; Karl lowers his knife to get a better grip. Ron times a swing of his satchel that's heavy with books and smacks Karl full in his face knocking him on his backside, but Karl still holds on to Ken's neck. Ron grabs Karl's wrist and bites into it as hard as he can. The knife flies into the air and Ken gets loose.

While Karl is rubbing his sore wrist, Ken bends down and tries to find the knife, feeling in the snow. Karl swings around and kicks Ken on the side of his face sending him reeling on his back, dazed. Ron takes a second swing at Karl with his satchel of books, this time the bag really connects with Karl's head with a bang and he drops like a sack of potatoes lying flat on his back stunned and disorientated. Ken yells screaming,

"Put the boot in quick, Ron! Put the boot in!"

Ron grins at his brother then stamps on Karl's face with his boot.

Karl's small boys look on in total amazement; they are silent as Karl slowly comes around and sits up. He is enraged, very red in the face spitting out snow and has a bleeding nose. Ron yells,

"Hey lad, you pick a fight with one Lambert, you have to fight us both".

Ken and Ron run off laughing and shouting.

"Karl got a kick in the head, Heil Benny Goodman".

Karl yells back defiantly hissing through his teeth.

"You two are dead, fuckers, you're in for it!"

"I'll get you two little shit-bags, you wait".

Karl Kaltenbrunner was quite used to getting the odd bash on his head now and then from his brutal father. He would often turn up at his local school with a black eye or a thick lip that his father had given him and brag about the big gang of Jewish boys he fought. He would say he was outnumbered and would show the battle scars to prove his tale. He was a big boy for twelve and could pass for fourteen, he was heavier and stronger than most boys his own age, and so it was easy for him to become a school bully.

Franz Kaltenbrunner, Karl's father, was also a big man and was at one time a laborer on the railways and a professional bare-fist boxer. He had been an active member of the party since the early days of the Nazi struggle and a master at befriending the right people.

He worked his way up through the ranks of the organization by being 'useful' with his specialty. Any outspoken critic of the party who publicly insulted Adolf Hitler would have to be punished. The word would get back through informers, then a few SA members lead by Kaltenbrunner in their brown uniforms and jackboots would pay the accused a visit at 4:00 am. Beat him up, smash his home up and knock down anyone who got in their way. No paperwork; it was all word of mouth. It was often reported as 'Putting down a Political Disturbance'.

Kaltenbrunner was very good at his assignments, and in the days of the struggling Nazi party they needed such men. He was finally given the rank of Zelenleiter (Street Leader) in the SA, a full time job with a uniform and a small salary.

He organized the civil street leaders in the district where the twins lived, supplementing his income with bribes from Jews or minor offenders who broke some of the many new rules. The Lambert twins had no idea that the boy they knew only slightly and had just beaten up had such a father. Karl lived close to the park with his father, in an apartment once owned by a wealthy Jewish family.

His father arranged exit visas and immigration papers for the family in exchange for the ownership of the apartment and its `Yiddish contents', as Karl called all the fine furniture they now lived with.

Back in the park Karl stands up, brushes the snow off his uniform and pushes a small boy roughly down in the snow. He races home that afternoon; so he can tell his father how he has been beaten up whilst he was in his Young Folk uniform by two little English shits. But what he gets instead of sympathy is another whack around his head for being beaten by two boys younger than himself.

His father then grabs his face and asks,

"How long have you had that broken tooth?"

"About a month Papa".

"Ha, we will get that tooth fixed by the Englishman, so you let the two little shits knock your tooth out did you?"

Karl thinks for a bit and nods, he has grown very fond of his broken front tooth; it makes him look tough somehow and thoughts of having regular teeth again... well, all those needles.

His father asks him if he knows where the boys live. When he tells him they find the telephone number in the book, then make the call.

Through the streets of Munich the victorious warriors run. When they stop to wait for traffic at a major road, a motherly woman tries to dab the blood off Ken's face with her handkerchief but he catches her hand.

"Oh no thank you, I want to save this; we won the fight".
Ken says proudly.

Back home at Leopold Strasse, the boys climb back over the big iron gates, run around the back of the house and burst into the kitchen all out of breath. Ron grabs a fresh tea towel, runs it under the cold tap and starts to look at Ken's head.

The Lambert's cook, a plump jovial woman in a long white apron strides over and snatches the wet towel out of Ron's hands and looks at Ken's face.

"Don't you dare use one of my best tea towels for blood.
What's he been into this time; did you take my books back to the library yet?"

Ron moves to lean on the sink strikes a casual posture as he does when he is about to lie through his teeth and says.

"Oh, hello Cook, we were walking in the park, you know, to go to the library for you, when we were set on by a platoon of Hitler Youth; they all had knives and thick sticks.... We had to fight our way out by swinging our school satchels. It's a good job we had all your cookbooks to make them heavy. We left four of them lying on their backs you know. That's why we couldn't take your books back could we Ken?"

Ken's face is blank without a hint of support.
Ron continues.

"We couldn't fight our way all through the park, could we Ken? There were twenty of them, with thick sticks too".

Cook holds Ken's face to the light.

"So who won? It doesn't look as if you two did".

"Oh, well, actually, yes we did win, a bit".

Cook pulls a face,

"You can't win a bit, you either win or you lose; Are my books alright?"

Ron proposes, grinning,

"Oh yes Cook, we will take them back tomorrow, promise".

He whispers to Ken,

"We should stick that knife of Karl's right up his own bum; see what comes out".

The Cook smiles, paying more attention to the blood spots on Ken's shirt than the cut over his eye.

"Ronald, you watch your mouth in my kitchen, you know swearing like that turns the fish bad".

"Green stuff will ooze out, all over the place". Ken says boldly.

The cook growls sternly,
> "Quiet you two, or I may just wash your mouths out with dish soap".

Ken pretends to throw up in the sink, Cook says,
> "Your father and mother won't like this one little bit. Get upstairs and get in the bath quick, dinner is in twenty minutes. Here take some ice to put on that eye. Don't you get blood on the white towels up there, you hear?"

Cook offers them a large jar, the boy's hands dive into it and take a small cake each, she gives both boys a hug and sends them up to their bath with a bowl of ice. Just as they are about to leave the kitchen, Cook says to Ken smiling,
> "How many boys were there with knives?"

Ken looks back, when Ron has gone out the door, he puts one finger up in the air and grins. Cook turns back to her sink smiling to herself,
> "Twenty HJ with knives and sticks, Ha".

Cook smiles to herself as the sound of the twin's feet scamper up the bare wooden stairs of the staff's back staircase.

The winter sun tints the branches of the old Linden trees on Leopold Strasse a warmish gold. It is a quiet street of beautiful old houses all set back in their own grounds. Imposing and dignified, they are residences of the wealthy. Number 176 is an old Victorian villa, the home of the Lambert family. It too stands solid in its own gardens and is surrounded by a high wall that has the same intricate brick pattern as the exterior of the house.

The twins' father, Joseph Lambert, is a senior official in the British consulate in Munich. He can speak and translate five languages to German and English. He met his Viennese wife when she was playing the zither at his favorite restaurant. They married and their twin sons Kenneth and Ronald were born in the villa. The Lambert's love the house and live very comfortably.

They entertain and give dinner and supper parties. It is a very valuable diplomatic skill in these troubled times to be able to arrange meetings with foreign ambassadors and dignitaries away from the formality of the British consulate. The Lambert's are gracious hosts; everyone is made to feel relaxed at their table. They are well liked by the stiff and starchy German foreign officials who sometimes dine with English and French diplomats.

The large richly furnished house opens its front door to a wide elegant hall with a curved light mahogany staircase that the twins are not permitted to use. They are supposed to use the back staircase with the staff. But sometimes on Sunday they would slide down the long curved banisters, when there were no visitors in the house.

To the right, through a carved wooden doorway is the main reception room with a magnificent glittering crystal chandelier. Heavy embroidered velvet curtains drape the huge bay windows. A matching pair of tapestry-covered divans face each other in front of the grand Delft-tiled fireplace. Palms set the tone of the room's rich Victorian opulence. On the left of the hall is a paneled neo-Gothic dining room with a long table that is often opened up to seat twelve guests when the British Consul and his wife come there to entertain German politicians.

The house has its own staff consisting of an English cook, her German husband the gardener and two housemaids. The boys' domain is the large kitchen, the back stairs, upstairs hall, the nursery, now called "the boys' study" (because they are almost ten years old). The twin's bedroom and the servants' third floor hall.

Here they can race about and be boys. But in the main and more elegant part of the house, they have to walk about quietly because they never know who may be visiting.

Ron is splashing in the bath and Ken stands at the sink looking at his face in the mirror, holding a towel with ice to his cheek. The boy's Mother, a very elegant, smartly dressed woman in her early forties comes into the bathroom. She holds Ken's head turning it gently.

"Oh my goodness Ken, you're going to have a nice black eye".

Mother opens the cupboard over the sink and starts to dab Ken's head with something out of a bottle.

"Ow.... It was Karl Kaltenbrunner, he started it".

Mother muses,

"Mm".

Ron lies, with a very hurt look on his face saying,

"There was this woman with a baby, and the Hitler Youth
platoon started to push her about. She wasn't Jewish or
anything, so we went to her rescue;
There were twenty of them, they had".....

Mother spins round and points a finger accusingly at Ron,

"No there weren't, there was only one boy and it was Karl and a
few of his little friends. His father just telephoned complaining
that you two set on him and beat him up... Did you know you
broke one of his front teeth? Did you really kick him in the
mouth with your boot?"

Ron looks down at the water and says quietly,

"Well, yes we did kick him a bit, but not very hard".

"Well it must have been hard enough to break a tooth, we are
going to have to pay his father for the dental bills.... he will
want a gold one put in there, I expect.
Goodness knows what that's going to cost us".

Ron pleads again,
    "He had that broken tooth a week ago,
    we didn't do it, did we Ken?"
Mother becomes very concerned,
    "Now listen you two, we told you to stay away from those
    Hitler people, they have so much power now.
    The police don't take any notice when they beat people up
    They just get away with whatever they want to.
    They seem to be a law unto themselves. So please.
    We don't want them knocking on our door at 4 in the morning,
    just stay away from them... Alright?"
Ron asks,
    "Mother, why don't the Nazis like the Jews?"
Mother dries Ron's hair with a towel, gives him a hug.
    "I don't know your father will talk to you about all that.
Ken gets into the bath. Mum says,
    "What the Germans do to each other is none of our business,
    so don't get involved or they will turn on us... do try to get
    along with these people; don't upset them; think about your
    father and his position at the Consulate; we must stay neutral.
    We can't afford to take sides. Our whole way of life out here is
    at stake".
Ken looks puzzled,
    "How, we haven't done anything wrong?"
Mother takes a deep breath.
    "Things are very delicate between Germany and England at the
    moment. Try to make it up with this boy Karl.
    Be nice to him; try not to rock the boat".
Mother leaves the bathroom and the boys start to clown about.

The twins are gifted with that relaxed, good-humored and slightly mischievous disposition that most close twin boys possess. They seem to be bathed in radiance. Most things in their lives are "fun" or a "Good lark". They have identical, slim bodies, smooth and tanned, with duplicate congenial impish faces, large blue eyes and chins slightly too small. Their blond/brown nondescript hair is tousled.

When they are alone they speak English to each other, but as soon as they are joined by a non-English speaking third person, they politely change to the German language. They speak their words quickly and their German has a slight English accent that some of the boys at the boarding school they attend find novel.

Ken is a child of the air, joyous, spirited, warm, merry and affectionate, the scientist, capable with mechanical and electrical things, but not as high-spirited as his brother.

Ron is the stronger-minded and the leader of the two. He is a child of the earth, guarded, requiring love, but not too ready to give it to anyone but Ken. Sometimes boisterous and slightly excessive,

Ron loves to stretch the facts just a little bit to verify his own stories. In friendly wrestling bouts Ken is often the winner but if it ever did come to a real fistfight between them, the result as yet is unknown. They are inseparable and, rarely squabble.

If another boy wants to pick a fight with a Lambert he would have to deal with both of them. Most of the time, it seems all they have is themselves. Their love and bond with each other is very solid.

2. HATE

Ken grabs a black comb, puts it under his nose like a Hitler mustache, pulls his wet hair down on one side like Hitler, and stands up to see himself in the mirror, stamps to attention with his arm out in a Nazi salute.

"Heil Hitler, Heil Benny Goodman. Ron, you know Karl did
have that broken tooth before we started on him".
Ron says quietly.
"Yes... I know... You want to join the Hitler Youth?"
Ken spins round and flicks cold water,
"We're not old enough yet, you have to be ten.
Anyway, we're British, not German".

Ron holds his hand up to shield himself from the water and gets all confidential, puts his arm round Ken's neck, jumps in to the bath, pulls him down and dunks him. Then becomes the wiser brother with his 'I know more than you do' voice.

"Look Ken, we were born here in Munich, right?
That makes us German, right?"...
"Mm"
"Father was born in England,
that makes him English, right?"...
"Mm"
"Mother was born in Austria, and Austria is now part of
Germany...
So she is English, Austrian and German... right?"...
"Mm"
"If we go back to England, we will be British...
But while we are here in Germany we are German and that's
it"...
"Mm".
"So easy to grasp when you're really clever, let's face it, I'm the
brighter of the two of us... wait, look, look".

Ron points to the gray bath water covering his groin between his legs. He grabs Ken to prevent him from leaving the bath and yells,

"Stand by for a depth-charge, fire!"

Ken holds his nose and Ron lets go a major fart that bubbles up through the water between the boys. Ken struggles to get out of the bath before he has to take a breath but changes his mind,

"Oh Ron.... Ha, you stinker, shit bum, whew".
"Got you!"   Ron laughs.
Ken points to his own groin,
"Wait,"

Ken sits down in the bath and holds his brother's neck,
>"Here comes a three hundred pounder. Fire!"

Ken farts and forces Ron's head down close the bursting bubbles, holding his head close to the surface of the water with no escape.
>"Oh shit what a stink. Oh you must have dead rats in your guts. Ho what a stink, give me air please".

The boys get out of the bath and grab their towels and start to dry themselves. Ron shoves Ken and says,
>"So, do you want to join the Young Folk, you know, try to get into Karl's mob?"
>"Yes".

Ron turns-on the enthusiasm.
>"They do some super things, camping, shooting rifles with real bullets".
>"And they all get every Wednesday afternoon off from school".

Ken says grinning,
>"But we are not old enough yet".

A big broad smile comes over Ron's mischievous face,
>"So, we will lie, we'll put our age up a bit, then say we are ten. I will work it all out for us, Heil Benny Goodman".

The boys run naked to their bedroom to dress for dinner.

They speed past Emmy the young housemaid who just closes her eyes in disgust. Ron performs cartwheels down the long bedroom hall. Ken takes a dive and does a backflip on to his bed, laughing and giggling. They are nine and a half and have no vanity. A lifetime of little privacy, dressing and showering at school has made them totally indifferent to their own nakedness. Ron puts his finger to his lips for silence,
>"Look out-here it comes again, quiet but deadly".

Ken holds his nose and Ron bends down and passes wind, Ken yells,
>"Stinker, phew.... Your guts must be rotten, oh I'm gassed, air, air, give me some air...phew what a stink".

Their bedroom is a typical boys' room: stuff everywhere. Two new single beds looking slightly out of place have just recently moved in. Mother thought it was time they slept in their own beds.

As infants they had slept in a double cot, any other arrangement would have made them wail all night and kept their nurse and everyone else awake. When they outgrew the cot they shared a small double bed.

So the boys grew to their ninth birthday sleeping in the same bed. Now some mornings Emmy the maid will wake them and they will be squashed together in one of the new beds.

Model warplanes hang from the ceiling, boys' stuff on the walls, books, model ships, and a desk that's a mess.

Ron picks up his model of a six-wheeled open Mercedes with Adolf Hitler standing with his arm raised, spins the tires and says,

"We could ask Karl if we could join his Young Folk unit. We might just get in, you never know if you don't try".

Ken adds.

"Asking him, just might put us in his good books".

The bedroom door opens and Father comes in. He is a distinguished-looking man in his early forties. He walks over to Ken and holds his head to one side, looking at his black eye. He sniffs the air,

"Phew, it's stuffy in here, let's open a window,
it smells like army barracks".

Ron lies,

"It's Ken, he has been passing wind all day".

"Not true Dad!"

Father holds his hand up for silence,

"It seems we had a phone call from the Block Leader
Kaltenbrunner, who says his son Karl was set upon by two
vicious boys from this house; is that true, did you kick him in
his face with your boot?".

Father leans close to Ken's face looks hard.

"Mm, that's going to be a nice black eye in the morning. So, the
pair of you, fighting one boy, that is not very sporting is it?"

Ken looks at his father, trying to change the subject,

"How come everybody says, I will have a 'Nice Black eye'?
What's so nice about it I'd like to know that?
It hurts. How can it be nice if it hurts so much?"

Father sits on the edge of the bed, turns on the light.

"I want you two to listen, you're both old enough to understand
what I'm going to tell you, so put your pajamas on and sit still!"

The two boys become serious and attentive as they slip in to their English striped pajamas and sit on the edge of the bed. Father, trying to reach his sons continues,

"I'm still an English registered foreigner, living here on a visa....
Now, that visa could be revoked at any time. We British must
keep a very low profile. The situation is very delicate at the
moment".

Ken feeling a little guilty,

"Would they send you back to England Father, just because we
had a fight with Karl?"

Father looks hard at one boy then the other and says.

"Who knows, they can do exactly that and worse. Do you know
the father of the lad Karl you two knocked about today is an
official in the SA? He could get my visa revoked, and he would
do it with a stroke of his pen... We could all be marked as
enemies of the Fatherland because you two attacked a Hitler
Youth, whilst he was wearing his uniform. It's the uniform;

insulting anyone wearing one is a very serious offence today.

They consider your assault on the boy as an attack on the Nazi Party. Not good form boys, not very clever".

Ken slides over close to his father and says.

"So, who are 'they' Father?"

Trying to steer the talk away from their fight. Father grasps both of the boys' hands, looks them in their eyes.

"They, my little lads, are the Nazi Party, they have control in Germany at the moment. It's people like Karl's father who now hold a great deal of power over Jews and foreigners like me. It was he and his gangs of SA who went out and smashed the Jewish shop windows and beat up their elderly men; all for what? Policy, Nazi Policy, whatever that is".

Ron shrugs his shoulders in disbelief. Father catches his skepticism and grabs his chin with his hand, looks him in the eye, then he puts a hand on each of the boys' shoulders.

"Ronald, Kenneth, you both must understand.

We have to be very careful. I could be deported and if I were, it would be me going alone; you boys and your mother would have to stay here. We must get our exit visas and leave as a family, and stay together.

Kaltenbrunner's thugs have the power now, they do just what they want, all in the name of the Nazi Party".

Ron asks in an offhand way,

"Dad, we're not Jewish or anything are we?"

Father looks at his boys and shakes his head.

"No... We are Protestants, if anyone ever asks you that, remember that our whole family is C-of-E, Church of England, and we have no Jewish blood in the family, or Jewish relatives at all. Come on, get dressed and come down to dinner. By the way we don't have any Jewish friends either, no Jews ever comes to this house. You both remember that".

He smiles, giving them both a big hug. When their Father has gone through the door Ron whispers.

"Well I'm glad we're not Jews, I'd hate it if we were Jews".

Ken thinks a bit and says,

"I don't think we have ever seen any Jews, have we?"

Ron grins and says.

"They will be just like their posters I suppose, you know, fat ugly with pointy beards and figure six noses"

Mum, Dad and the boys are all seated at the dining room table. Aunt Inga comes into the room and takes her place. She's a spinster, a plumper version of her sister, the boys' mother.

Emmy, the housemaid, arrives with a large white soup tureen, sets it down and starts to serve. Cook comes in with a silver platter with two roast chickens and carves them. The meal gets underway. Emmy serves vegetables from covered silver dishes. Aunt Inga looks hard at Ken, who is sporting a plaster, a thick lip and a black eye. She shakes her head and smiles a little.

"My my, you look as if you've been in the wars.
Did you fall down the stairs?"
Mother complains.
"They have been fighting with Kaltenbrunner's boy. He's in the Hitler Youth".
Aunt Inga looks at Ken with a wink,
"I hope he looks worse than you".
Ron looks up and grabs his chance to ask,
"Father, can we join the Hitler Youth?"
Mother almost chokes on her food and turns to her husband,
"Joe, tell them, tell them to stay away from those people".
Father points with his fork and says firmly,
"You're not joining any Nazi Youth group. So you two just stay away from them, they are a bunch of troublemakers. I don't want these people picketing this house. That's all we need, is a bunch of yobos standing outside our doors in Jack Boots".
Ron quietly,
"It's alright; we're just trying to get friendly with Karl"
Ken chimes in,
"We can't join until we are ten anyway".
Aunt Inga looks up and over to the two boys,
"You should let them join the Hitler Scouts if they want to. Boys like that sort of thing: camping, tying knots; I've seen them on the news at the cinema".
Father says very firmly,
"Inga, what you see on the news is the Hitler Youth.
Our boys are too young to take part in that sort of thing".
Aunt Inga says flatly,
"Well, it's not if, it's when; membership is compulsory now. They just haven't had the manpower to enforce it. I read the papers too.... The boys will have to join whether you like or not, compulsory is compulsory nowadays, and they all look to be having a grand time anyway".
Ron and Ken glance at each other with a sly wink. Mother sees them and snaps back sternly,
"You're not joining; until you have too and that's final".
Father says quietly,
"Well if it's compulsory, I will look into it. We can't break any

local laws, can we?"

The boys are very pleased. Ken nudges his brother.

Ron asks,

"Dad, can Karl come and play billiards with us?"

Father looks up and nods,

"Yes but tell him not to wear that damned uniform".

Mother who is trying to find a way to keep the peace says,

"Ask him if he would like to stay for dinner, boys, tell him to bring his sister or someone nice".

Aunt Inga smiles to herself and says,

"This will be an interesting evening, I know who Kaltenbrunner is. He's the *Zellenleiter,* He's the official in charge of a whole block, a civil leader. I wouldn't miss this evening for anything in the world".

Mother and Father nod together. Emmy, the housemaid picks up the dishes, reacts to the boy's smiles, pulls a face and runs her thumb across her throat. She is a ruddy-faced local country girl about seventeen who's not been long off a Sussex farm. Being unnoticed she shrugs her shoulders and points her finger at the boys.

Ken pokes his tongue out at Emmy. She pokes her tongue slightly and fast at each boy and leaves with the dishes, giggling to herself.

The next day, Ron and Ken are walking past a row of small shops. Karl and a much older SA man are standing guard outside a Jewish dress shop. Karl is dressed in his new uniform, his feet apart, arms folded trying to look very stern and adult.

A large Star of David and the words 'Kauft nicht bei Juden' (Germans don't buy from Jews) is crudely painted in white letters on the dress shop window. Karl is looking very pleased with himself, at being a part of such an important guard. He hands out leaflets to people as they pass by.

His older comrade is a tough looking SA trooper in a brown uniform who is in tight control. Karl had pleaded with his father for two days to let him stand next to the SA patrols outside the marked stores. It was the SA's task to turn the public away from Jewish stores and persuade them not to buy from Jewish shops or businesses: Nazi Policy again. Ron gives Karl a stiff salute.

"We heard you were here, what are you doing?"

Karl looks at his fellow guard and sneers at Ken.

"What do you think, we're making sure traitors don't buy from Jews. If they do we take their names".

Ron smiles as sweetly as he can and says.

"Karl, can we join your Hitler Youth unit?"

Karl, embarrassed,
> "Ha, Osterkuken! (Easter Chicks), come back when you're both
> ten years old".
> "We are ten, aren't we Ken?"

Ken nods vigorously, and offers,
> "Well you could come to our house and play some billiards or
> snooker, stay to dinner with us if you like".

Karl smiles,
> "All right, but you two should go now, can't you see I'm on
> duty. This is no place for children...

The twins turn to leave and Karl warms yelling,
> "Hey, English, where did you get that black eye?"

Ron stamps to attention and tries a Nazi salute again.
> "A good friend gave it to him". He yells.

Karl and the SA trooper laugh at Ron's effort. Some people start to
approach the store, more with curiosity than with the intention of actually
buying anything. The two guards get out their notebooks and pencils then
shout at them.
> "Good Germans don't buy from Jews.
> If you enter this Jew shop, we will take your names and report
> you".

The people hurry past the shop as Ron peers in to the open door.
He sees a scared husband and wife behind the counter. The SA man grabs
Ron by the scruff of his neck and pulls him out of the doorway.

At this time it was easy to get in trouble, not only Jews were getting
arrested; anyone who protested about anything was at risk and could be
called an "Active Political Dissident". Parents who would speak out
against the Nazi party at their dinner table were often turned in by one of
their own sons obediently reporting his parent's slur or aspersion to his
Hitler Youth leader.

The German people now had to be very careful whom they talk to.
A slight joke or an offhand remark about any Nazi leader may be
overheard and reported back by a network of block leaders and informers
to the Gestapo. Then a 3 am visit by the SA, beatings and arrests. No
trial, no duration of sentence given, the perpetrator would be placed in a
concentration camp for his 'Protective Custody' usually for 'The
Duration'.

Jews and their families were easy and popular targets. It was taught
in schools and written in the Nazi press that Jews arrested for crimes
against the state would be deported to a new state called Zion to build a
new country abroad for themselves. A national lie, proved by history.
Trumped up charges ranged from 'Creating Political Disturbance', to a
new very current offence covered by the 'Inter-Racial Sex Laws'.

These laws stated clearly that it was an offence for a Jew to have consensual sex with a blond haired blue-eyed Aryan girl. Racial sex offenses were popular with the Gestapo because they made the Jews look bad. It was good copy for the newspapers creating more hatred towards the Jews who were already unpopular with the masses. Charges were rarely explained to the Jews arrested.

Entire Jewish families just disappeared; their property was confiscated and they were never heard of again. No one ever asked questions. Concentration camps were filling up; new camps were being built as fast as they could drive the slave laborers who were building them. A neighbor and his family would just disappear and no one would ask questions. Most people would think.

"They must be Jews, sent off to their own country".

The twins witnessed an incident one afternoon that left a profound and lasting scar on their memory. It brought the fanatical hatred the German New Order had for the Jewish people to a sudden and very vivid realization to them. As the boys were trotting home one afternoon from the library they turned a corner in a nice well-to-do neighborhood and a commotion on the street stopped them in their tracks.

They saw a small crowd of onlookers watching Jewish people being forced into a large army truck by strong looking men in black leather overcoats and gray hats. A distinguished looking Jewish man with his gray beard all bloody from a bleeding nose is protesting loudly,

"There is a mistake!" he shouts, "We should not be on your list!
We were told we would not have to go, if we paid the
Zellenleiter... We have always paid him on time he said we
would not have to go if we paid! And we paid, always we paid".

Two of the men in the black leather coats grab him and try to heave him on to the truck but he is quite overweight and not easy to move. Ron nudges a woman in a green coat standing in the crowd and asks.

"Excuse me, what have they done?
Why are those men being so nasty to them?"

The woman looks down at Ron with a tone of disgust and sneers,

"They are Jews... I don't know what they've done.
But I wager they have swindled someone".

Four of the Gestapo men close around the protesting Jewish elder, one of them clubs him from behind with the butt of a pistol and he slumps to his knees. His family helps the men lift him into the truck.

Ken looks at Ron and says,

"They are Jews... Poor buggers, what've they done
to be treated like this?"

The woman spins around and says,

"They know what they did, so they are being deported. Him
over there, the Zellenleiter, he read out the order. They can

only take one case each with them, so hang about, there will be some nice pickings when he sorts all their stuff out".

Two small dark haired girls crying, each carrying a large heavy case get roughly shoved up onto the truck and their cases thrown up after them. A boy about eleven years old comes out of the front door carrying a heavy case, he has a fixed look of hatred on his face and he is defiantly taking his own time.

One of the men in a leather coat yells at him. "To get a move on" The boy just steps up to him with a gesture that he wants to whisper a secret, the man bends down to hear what he has to say and the boy grins then spits in his ear. He receives a whack around his head and gets shoved on his way, sliding across the sidewalk tripping he falls to his knees.

The woman in the green coat sneers,

"You two boys wait about for a while, the police will be handing out their property soon, that boy is about your age, you may find something of his that fits you".

Just then more men come out of the house with boxes and lay them on the sidewalk. The Jews choice belongings, furs, silverware, good china, cameras, and binoculars are all loaded on to a smaller truck for disposal. The Jewish family stand in the truck and watch the man in the black leather coat start to read from his clipboard.

"As a District Leader with the Police Department the confiscated goods that were the belongings of these filthy Jewish traitors will be distributed to you people who have long been exploited and cheated by them. Don't take the furniture, kitchenware or bedding, it has to stay in the house".

The small gathering of women step forward and push their way in to the house.

The back door of the truck is slammed closed and it drives away.

The twins just stand on the sidewalk sadly watching people coming out of the grand old Jewish house carrying armfuls of clothing, vases, boxes of china, pictures and paintings in frames. The woman with the green coat appears at an open upstairs window and yells down.

"Hey you two boys come on up here, front bedroom!"

Ken shakes his head but Ron grins and says,

"Come on, it's all right, let's just have a look".

The twins push past the front door and see the house is being ransacked. People raking through open drawers, women holding up dresses in front of themselves to see the fit. Ron calls to Ken,

"Look Ken, the boy's room".

The twins stand in the doorway peering in. The small room is untouched. Boy's books are neatly stacked on shelves, Boy Scout camping photographs on the dresser, skis and ice skates hang on the wall. On a table in one corner a beautifully handmade puppet theater that is obviously in the process of being assembled with all its puppets hanging neatly on their strings. A fat woman carrying armfuls of clothes tries to shove her way in to the room but the boys push her back. She makes for one of the other bedrooms.

Ron opens the closet door to see the Jewish boys clothes all neatly folded and hung, good jackets and long warm overcoats, shirts folded and stacked on shelves. A writing desk with a stack of schoolbooks and homework that has just been worked on, still with the pages open, is waiting to be finished.

On a small shelf on its own there is an expensive leather violin case hanging on a brass hook under the shelf. There is a matching leather music case. Ron looks at Ken and mimes playing a violin. Ken nods sadly. By the window a small brass telescope sits on a wooden tripod and there is a chart of the stars and moon nearby.

"This boy has a lot of things, the best of everything".

Ken sadly says,

"He is a very neat boy, look how everything is put away, not like our study"

Just then a burly man pushes past Ron almost knocking him over and grabs the telescope and its stand and throws them on the bed, then very quickly piles up most of the boys' valuable things pitching the violin and its music case into the pile. He gathers up the bed cover like a sack and makes off with the bundle. Ron and Ken are in tears they just run out of the house and down the street.

After a while they stop breathless, Ron says,

"Why Ken? Why do people just take all their things?

What did the boy do to have all his things just taken like that?"

Ken says quietly,

"And where do you think the Jews were being taken?"

Their questions weren't answered and it was a week before the boys could stop thinking and telling everyone about their experience in the ransacked Jewish Home. They tried to look forward to Christmas but there was a sad look on their faces every time someone would talk about Jews. They had just had a taste of what it's like to be a Jewish boy, but their naïveté and juvenile ignorance still did not connect the Hitler Youth or the Young Folk with the Anti-Semitic New Order.

3. CHRISTMAS

Christmas shopping with Mum and Dad cheered the twins up. It is a very exciting time for them. Whenever the family went shopping in Munich on a weekend they would always end up at the model train shop that sells the Hornby and Marklin electric trains. It had the most magnificent setup of model electric trains running as a display: it was a boy's dream. Both boys are sure they want to be model railway engineers and work in a train shop when they grow up, or open their own model train store. Then they will let the boys who come into their shop operate the controls and run the trains themselves.

So it is always the highlight of the day and the last place visited. Mother and Father would usually take the boys into the shop and go off for a coffee across the street, leaving the boys to gaze at the trains with all the other boys and talk to the engineer who actually built and ran the great setup.

The twins know every track in the store and had been looking forward all day to seeing what had been added to the set-up for the Christmas Special display. But when the twins tried to pull their Father across the road to go in the train shop he shook his head.

No, today they were Christmas shopping and their father said they couldn't go to the Train Shop because it would be very crowded and they were running out of time. They still had to get the Christmas tree and they wanted to get there before it got too dark so they could sort out a good tree. Father explained this, disappointment showed on both boys' faces. Ron nudged Ken when he pulled a face and gave him the sly signal, a part of the twins own language that boys knew between them, two sharp taps on the back of his hand, it meant,

"I want to tell you a secret in private".

They walked sharply on ahead and Ron whispered,

"Trains, Trains.... We are going to get a train set for Christmas.

That's why they don't want us in the train shop".

Ken's face beamed,

"Oh really Ron, do you think so?"

Ron nodded his head very slowly, grinning

"What larks we will have Ken".

By late afternoon the family arrives at a big compound in the Tierpark on the east bank of the river Isar. A section is all fenced off, full of Christmas trees and decked out with long red and white Hitler Youth Flags. It is being run by a platoon of teenage boys in their HJ uniforms.

A fun time buying a huge Christmas tree from the troop. Energetic strong young boys in uniforms carefully bind the tree up, sawing off the lower branches and slicing a few centimeters off its bottom.

Two lads march the tree out of the compound holding it over their heads, singing. As they march by the twins, they both jump to attention and give the tree bearers a Nazi salute. The two Hitler Youths carrying the tree yell out
"Heil Hitler".
Mother sees the enthusiasm her sons have for the Hitler Youth and nudges her husband; they both look on in dismay. The teenage H.J. boys tie the tree on top of the car and fasten a small paper swastika to its peak that hangs over the back of the car. The biggest Hitler Youth boy stands to attention gives a smart salute and yells,
"Thank you and a Merry Christmas, your contributions will be very appreciated by the National Socialist Party, Heil Hitler".
Father nods, raises his hand slightly in a polite gesture.
Mother watches apprehensively as her sons take total delight in supervising the whole process. As soon as the Hitler Youth boys return to their compound, Father rips off the little swastika flag and stuffs it in his pocket.
Sitting in the back seat of the car Ken decides to try to bring up the subject of him and his brother joining the Young Folk again,
"We saw Karl again today; he was handing out leaflets outside the library".
The boys watch their parent's faces and see the negative reaction they expect. Ron nudges his brother and whispers.
"Later Ken, it's not a good time just now".
"Well you don't get anything if you don't ask, do you? You have to ask, don't you?"
Ken mutters loud enough so their parents can hear. Father leans over to the back seat and says quietly but sternly,
"It's not a good time, not at Christmas, not now".

Setting the tree up in the living room is a whole household affair. In Europe, it's a tradition that the servants join the family for the Christmas celebrations and share the joy of the tree, then sit down with the family in the big dining room for the evening dinner. Cook and her husband Max the gardener struggle in to the living room with a large wooden barrel that was cut in half years ago and has held Christmas trees up for many years. Its red paint is starting to show its age.
Setting the tree square and making it secure and adding all the water it can drink until Twelfth Night is Max's job. When he has finished he falls back in a soft armchair with a large stein of beer to watch the tree get trimmed. There's lots of fun and good cheer. In the kitchen the housemaid Emmy and the boys wrap small gifts to go under the tree. Ken grabs Emmy's arm,
"Come on Emmy, let's build a snow man".

Emmy is suddenly a little girl again; she squeaks with delight as she disappears into the pantry and comes out with a large carrot. She holds it up for the boys to see. Ron teases,

"What's that for; the snowman's thing, Ha?"

Emmy laughs out loud,

"No stupid, it's for his nose, Ha Ha".

The two boys and Emmy still wearing her long white apron push a big snowball around the front lawn making the fat body of the snowman. When it is complete and the big round head gets lifted into position Emmy sticks her carrot in its head for the nose and Cook comes out with one of her husband's old hats and two potatoes for its eyes. There is lots of fun and shouting.

At six-o-clock on Christmas morning, Ron is the first one up. He jumps onto Ken's bed and shakes him until he awakes,

"Happy Christmas brother, come on, let's go downstairs and see what we got for Christmas".

The boys creep downstairs to the living room door. The big old box lock on the door is locked.

"Shit, they did that last year too". Ron says.

Ken sleepily tries the door handle,

"They did say not to come downstairs till 8am".

"It's only six o'clock"

Ron says looking at the old grandfather clock in the hall,

"What are we going to do for two hours?"

"Sing, let's sing, come on let's sing carols as loud as we can and wake them all up".

The boys sing, their squeaky voices echoing through the house,

"Good King Wenceslas looked out on the feast of Steven
When the snow lay round about deep and crisp and even
Brightly shone the moon..."

Mother and Father appear in their dressing gowns holding out their arms smiling, waiting to embrace the boys in a good morning hug and a kiss for Christmas morning, even if it is only 6am. Father unlocks the living room doors and says smiling,

"Don't open anything until we are all in there".

The boys pick up the brightly wrapped packages and read the labels, feeling the weight, Ken points to a pile of identical size boxes marked, 'To Ron and Ken' placed deep under the tree, he grins,

"Trains"

Ken was right: There was a train set under the tree and it was a big success: it took Father and the twins until lunchtime to set it up in the boys' study. Mother smiled and said,

"Come on Joe, get them downstairs for lunch. I don't know

who the trains were bought for, you or the boys".
Dad glances at the twins saying,
"Well these things are not that easy to set up".
Then he looks to the boys for support, Ken shakes his head saying,
"Yes they are, piece of cake, easy to put together and run.
We know how, don't-we, Ron?"

Late afternoon on Christmas day, the living room is warm and comfortable and the family are all sitting around the big fire. The house looks very festive. The Lambert family hold Christmas very dear with their English traditions. Dad is on the couch reading aloud from a new boy's book. Ron is lying on the rug in front of the fire flipping through the instruction book for the train set; Ken is on the couch leaning on his Dad.

Mum and Aunt Inga are knitting. The big Christmas tree is trimmed and the little lights twinkle. The radio has the BBC London tuned into "Carols from Westminster". They had just heard the King's Christmas broadcast, a very British tradition.

This year because of Hitler's rise to power it was a very cautious one, talking about the dark horizons of Europe. Hoping that the upcoming Munich conference is successful.

But the clouds of war may be gathering for England.

Outside in the deep snow, waiting under one of the big old Linden trees is Karl. He had been there for a quarter of an hour, waiting, looking through the iron railings and plucking up his courage to knock at the big oak door. "They did say come around for dinner and play some snooker or billiards".

But the thing that stuck in his young mind the most was what Ron had said, when he had sarcastically asked about Ken's black eye.

"A good friend gave it to him".

They must like him a little bit. Earlier that Christmas day he had wandered past the cinemas in the center of Munich; the UFO-Post was showing 'Auf Wiedersehen Franziska' with Marianne Hoppe:

A stupid love story. He didn't care for those mushy films and he had seen 'Ride for Germany' and 'Stukas' three times because they were free for boys under sixteen. So he thought of the twins' invitation.

The Lambert house looked so warm inside with all the lights on, the decorations, the Christmas tree and the fat snowman on the lawn.

It seemed a big contrast to his own apartment this Christmas, stinking of cheap cigars. His father was entertaining some fellow junior officers and a few handpicked young ladies.

He gave his son some money and told him to make himself scarce and go down to the local beer hall where there might be some entertainment, beer and Christmas dinner. But Karl had found himself standing and looking through the windows of a very happy family and longed to be a part of their Christmas. "Well they did say come any time".

He had stood outside there twice before but had never plucked up the courage to knock at the door. Eventually he says to himself,

> "Come on Karl, they can't shoot me, and if I stay out here much longer I will freeze my balls off, so here goes. They can only throw me out".

He carefully arranges the two small posies of flowers he has bought at the station for Frau Lambert and her sister and pushes the big white china bell.

The living room door opens and Emmy appears, showing a maiden's flush, she dips a little curtsy.

> "There's a boy here to see Master Ronald and Master Kenneth, Sir".

Father sits up from his book,

> "On Christmas day?"

Mother and Father exchange glances, Mother says calmly,

> "Well, show him in Emmy".

Emmy leaves and reappears followed by Karl clutching Christmas bouquets. He looks very smart in a new Young Folk uniform. He greets Father formally with a steep head nod and a click of his heels and then offers his flowers to Mother and a small posy to Aunt Inga. The two ladies graciously accept them. Mother notices Karl's knees are very red from his ginger complexion and the cold outside.

> "Go over there and warm yourself by the fire boy; you look frozen stiff".

Karl is very impressed with the richness and warmth of the Lambert home. He is very polite and a little over-formal, wishing everyone a Happy Christmas. He has taken great care with his own personal grooming. His ginger mop of curly hair is well plastered down. He has even ironed a crease in his uniform shorts. Ken, Ron and the whole Lambert family make him very welcome and Father eventually brings the conversation around to Karl's favorite topic, the Hitler Youth.

> "I'm twelve now, and a Young Folk Leader".

Karl boasts, but Father, knowing how to get on his good side says,

> "Twelve, oh I would have thought you were older".

Karl smiles and mumbles on.

> "The Hitler Youth are training leaders like myself as fast as possible, ready for next spring".

Father asks with genuine concern.

> "What's happening next spring then?"

Karl smiles, and smugly says,

> "We expect the membership to grow very fast".

"Why is that Karl?"

Father is beginning to worry. Karl is now in his glory, he turns his back to the fireplace and puts his left thumb into his belt as he has seen Hitler do so many times on the newsreels at the cinema, then he places one hand up on the mantel. He isn't going to miss this opportunity to tell his story. He addresses the whole room.

> "Next year the movement is clamping down on non-joiners, lads ten to thirteen in the Young Folk and boys fourteen to seventeen in the Hitler Youth. There are lots of them out there. They need new leaders; that's why I was trained. I am going to form a Young Folk unit at a boys' private school".

Father glances at his boys,

"What school will that be then?"

Karl smiles and shrugs his shoulders,

"Oh, I will go wherever they send me".

Ron whispers,

"I wonder if it's our school."

Karl boasts,

> "You know that our Youth leader Baldur Von Schirach said in our brotherhood there shall be no generation gap, Youth must be led by youth..."

Karl realizes he has the undivided attention of the room, something he is not yet used to, so he continues, his mind racing for something really profound to say. He blurts out.

> "Our flag means more to us than death. I was born to die for Hitler and Germany. I will too gladly, if I'm given the honor".

Ron and Ken exchange glances. Father asks how his father is and not to forget to send the dental bill to him. Emmy opens the door her face all-beaming.

> "Christmas Dinner is served, everyone....
> A very Merry Christmas to you all".

Karl jumps up and looks about for his hat and coat, as if he is about to leave. Father puts his arm round the boy's shoulder.

> "Karl, please, do stay for dinner; we have a place set for you, haven't we Emmy?"

Emmy nods vigorously beaming a broad smile, Karl is flattered and splutters his thanks. They all follow Emmy in to the dining room that is decorated for Christmas with laurels on the long table, Karl is shown to a place next to Emmy who chats away making him feel very important.

It's a very traditional English Christmas Dinner. Father carves the large turkey. Cook slices the big ham, serves the roast potatoes, Brussel-sprouts, green garden peas and cranberry jelly. Fat and colorful Christmas crackers get pulled with a bang spilling out the paper hats. Karl eats like a peasant, enjoying the feast.

Joseph Lambert looks at his sons and feels the admiration that the boys both have for the Hitler Youth. He whispers to his wife,
"I just can't see them running around and marching up and down with swastikas on their arms".
Mother nods and says,
"They must find it a very attractive movement,
they are bright active boys, that sort of camaraderie
will appeal to them, they don't know what Nazism is all about
yet, all they see is the camping and the outdoor fun and games.
Joe we will all have to get to England soon".
Father thinks and vows to himself to get his whole family out of Germany after Christmas as soon as possible. He does not want his boys growing up in the Nazi system.

When Karl has devoured his fill and everyone else has finished, Father jumps up and with a grin, dims the lights. Max, cook's husband, enters with a large English-made Christmas pudding all flaming with burning brandy; the blue flames still alight on the plates as cook serves it.

Emmy, sitting next to Karl, hangs on to his every word gazing into his eyes when he speaks, making him feel very important.

When everyone is sitting back feeling full, Ron and Ken nod to their father, then sneak off out of the room. They are going to entertain and sing, they have been rehearsing an old English comic vaudeville song they heard on one of cook's gramophone records.

After a while the sound of a small banjo strumming is heard and everyone looks to the large sliding doors. The doors open and Ron and Ken make an entrance dressed in rags like a pair of street tramps with big red noses. Ken strums a small banjo,

Ron bangs a tambourine. Everyone applauds and cheers. As Ken strums, Ron does a soft-shoe shuffle. His baggy pants are held up with very springy red suspenders. They bounce up and down as Ron does his funny walk. Ron and Ken sing in English cockney accents.
"Oh, any old iron, any old iron,
any any any old iron, you look a treat,
walking down the street, you look all nipper,
from your napper to your feet,
dressed in grey, dressed in green,
with your father's old green tie on,
Oh, I, wouldn't give you tuppence,
for your old watch chain,
old iron, old iron.
Oh, did'l did'l dum dum,
did'l did'l dum dum
Dar did'l um dum, dum dum".

Applause, they all clap and cheer, Ken keeps the strumming going as Ron does his funny walk, bouncing his pants up and down again. Emmy and Karl are getting very friendly. She hangs on to Karl's shoulder. Karl keeps pushing her away shyly. Ken and Ron start to sing,

"*Oh, Aunty Nelly,*
had a fat belly
with a red pimple
on her bum".

Father interrupting
    "Please, not that one tonight; it's Christmas".

Ron does a funny little walk, the boys respond to the applause from everyone by taking big exaggerated bows.

Father claps and picks up Mother's Zither, then takes it over and lays it on her lap,
    "You boys get cleaned up, Mother will play
    and we will sing some nice Christmas Carols".

Carol singing around the fire to the accompaniment of Mother's Zither makes for a warm Christmas feeling. At the end of the evening, Karl gets up to leave. He wishes everyone goodnight, stands to attention, puts his left hand in his belt as if to give a Nazi salute, but changes his mind and just waves goodbye.

Emmy the young maid comes in with his coat and hat and they both leave. When they get into the front hall, Emmy gets hold of Karl's hand, looks quickly left and right and tries to kiss him full on his lips. Karl is very surprised and pulls away shyly.

Karl and Emmy stand looking at each other, they hold hands, gaze into each other's eyes for just a short moment. Emmy looks to see if the big doors to the living room are closed and that they are alone. Sounds of Carol singing are heard faintly. Karl pauses for a moment confused and not aware of what is expected of him. Emmy picks up his hat and coat and walks him to the door, kisses him hard on the lips. It's a long kiss.

The twins sniggering makes Karl look toward the living room doors. Ken and Ron are peeping and grinning at the kissing couple.

Karl glares at the boys and points his finger at them, then smiles at Emmy and allows himself to be gently pushed through the door. Karl strides out into the cold night air. He hums to himself resolving to be nice to Emmy. Yes, she is all right, he had felt a very odd feeling in the pit of his stomach when she kissed him,

He had never felt that before, but then he had never been kissed by a young girl before. What shit-bags those twins were to spy on him, he hated that, it made him feel so silly, them watching him. So he resolved to teach them some respect for his uniform, he will be avenged soon. And he put that at the back of his mind for later.

One evening the boys are in their beds. Father comes in and sits on the edge of Ron's bed. He looks serious,

> "You know, there just may be a war. The British Prime Minister Neville Chamberlain is trying to make a peace pact for Britain. Adolf Hitler doesn't want war with England. But it just may come to that".

Ron sits up on his elbow,

> "What happens to all of us if there is a war Father? Will we all go back to England?"

Father pulls his bed covers up,

> "Yes most likely".

Father tucks the boys in and kisses them both,

> "I'm making arrangements for us all to go to England. My exit visa is the only one that has come through, you two and your Mother's are all being delayed for some reason".
> "Can't we just get up and go; we're British?"

Ken says cheerfully. Father nods,

> "I am. All your exit visas may just be taking a different route through all the red tape. Or, it could be that I will be the only one allowed to leave Germany at this moment".

Ron looks into his father's eyes,

> "Is that why they are holding up our visas? Why don't we just go?"

Father shakes his head,

> "We wouldn't get past the first check point without exit papers, they wouldn't let us on the plane. It could well be that... I may have to go first, then you two and your mother can come later, but we will all stick together if we can".

Ken smiling,

> "Like glue Dad, like glue".

Father nods, kisses each boy goodnight, and turns out the light as he goes, leaving the bedroom door slightly open. After a few moments, Ken sits up and turns on the light again.

He stares at Ron looking for answers.

> "Ron, do you think we will all stay together?"

Ron shrugs his shoulders, puts a finger to his lips for quiet,

> "Sh, Listen... "

Ron gets out of his bed, turns the light out and beckons Ken to follow. The boys quietly creep out of their bedroom, along the upstairs hall and sitting on the steps they slowly descend the stairs one by one.

On the stairs just out of sight of the wide-open living room doors, they listen to the conversation of their parents, hearing their father's voice,

"I told them to be prepared for a family split up for a while".
Mother's voice sounds almost desperate,
"Joe there has to be a way, we can all stay together".
Father's voice gets softer, the boys creep closer to hear,
"Jenkins, you know the Englishman from the transport
department, his children were born here too. He couldn't get a
visa to get them out either. They're not letting any Germans
born to aliens leave at the moment. It may be different when
this peace thing is signed".
Mother says very concerned,
"Did he just go to England and leave his family here?"
Father almost resigned says in a whisper,
"No he was picked up and put on a plane to England. His wife
and children went to their German grandparents in Stuttgart".
Aunt Inga gets up to leave, Mother says,
"Well, we should just go; let's just pack up and go".
Father says quietly,
"I could go, but you and the boys would not get past the gates
at a border without exit visas and they are not granting then to
anyone at the moment".
The boys scramble back upstairs into their bedroom, jump into their
beds and turn out the light.
Ron stares at the model warplanes hung from the ceiling thinking.
Looking for some assurance Ken says.
"Well it looks as if we stay here, if there is a war".
"We want to stay at school here, don't we?"
"I hope so, we hate it there in London, all that rain, no deep
snow, no skiing".
"So, you and I stick together, right Ron?"
Ron says with that big-brother voice,
"Like glue, old chap, like glue".
Ken jumps out of his own bed and into Ron's. Ron gives Ken a big
hug, then turns over and pushes him out of bed with his feet. Ken gets
back into his own bed and starts to sniff as if to cry.
Ron whispers again in his big-brother voice,
"Come on Ken, don't be such a big cry baby. Whatever way it
goes, we will stick together, you and me, right?"
Ken sniffing, "I'm cold".
"Oh come on in then, you're such a baby".
Ron opens his blankets, Ken jumps out of his bed and into Ron's,
arms, they snuggle down under the covers and cuddle up tight for
warmth, and each other's protection. Ken whispers,
"Ron"
"What"

"If there's a war, will we have to fight the British... will it be like the last war, soldiers shooting each other for years, bombing and killing all the time?"

Ron whispers,

"Shh, go to sleep, don't think about it".

"If I don't think about it, war still might happen, right. Will they use gas again?"

"I don't know, but we will be alright.

We will look out for each other won't we?"

Then Ron whispers,

"Keep your cold feet off me and don't wiggle about. Every time you move I get a cold draft down my neck".

"Good night"

"Don't let the bed bugs bite".

The last week of the boys' Christmas holidays passed very quickly. Most of their time was spent re-routing the tracks of their new train set.

It's a bright clear crisp January morning and the bedroom door bursts open, Emmy bounces in, opens the heavy drapes and the boys wake up.

"My, you two look nice and cozy in there, that's the way to keep warm. It's school for you two today. Max is driving you all the way to school, did you know that?"

Ken knowingly grins,

"Seen Karl lately?"

Emmy smiles, closes the closet drawer, with a bunch of boys' underwear clutched to her breasts, wistfully turns round, throws them onto the empty bed,

"Karl is very nice, but he is only a little boy".

Emmy packs the boys cases, trying to hold back her giggles. Ron notices her embarrassment and nudges Ken in the ribs,

"We saw you in the hall kissing Karl on Christmas night, didn't we Ken".

"You little pigs, were you spying on us?"

Outside the front door of the house, in the crisp cold air the cases are being loaded into the big old Bentley. The boys are dressed in their private boarding school uniforms. Mother, Father, Aunt Inga, cook and the two maids are all bustling about loading the car. Father pulls Ron to one side, takes him in the house on his own, then into the study and shuts the door and gives him a large brown envelope,

"Here are your passports and a check for this year's fees.

Hand these in when you get to school".

Father pulls a flat red tin bound with black tape from the drawer in his desk.

"Here is some money in this tin, hide it outside the school as soon as you get there, and don't tell anyone about it except Ken. Trust no one. It's for emergency only. Keep the rubber tape tight to keep the water out. Bury it so that it is standing upright, so that if any dampness tries to get in, it will be saved by the lid. It's for you and Ken. You look after him. I know you're the strongest. Remember, we love you both very much".

Father puts the flat pipe tobacco tin in Ron's back pants pocket, securing the button and gives him a big hug and kiss.

"Keep that button on your back pocket done up now. Don't lose it. Make sure you both know where it's hidden".

Ron nods all tearfully. He feels it may be the last time he will see his family when they get to the door Ken runs to join them. Ron says.

"We will see you again, won't we Dad?

You won't go to England without us will you Dad?"

Father shakes his head and hugs both of the Twins.

On the driveway outside the house the Bentley is loaded and ready. There are big hugs all around; Mother and Cook are both in tears. Max closes the doors and the car drives off with the two boys' faces looking out of the rear window. Ken says to his brother,

"We shouldn't be leaving, should we? Not now".

As they drive through Munich Ron locks the doors and takes out the flat pocket-shaped tin can his father gave him and shows Ken. It's a "Prince Albert" American pipe tobacco tin with a flip top. Ron peels off the rubber sticky tape, carefully sticks it to the wood frame of the window, opens the tin and shakes out a wad of money: All new notes, he lays them out in piles: US dollars, French Francs, German Marks and Swiss notes all folded to fit snugly into the can.

The money smells of his father's pipe tobacco. Ken says,

"So where did you get all this; is that what Dad wanted to see you in the study for?"

Ron carefully replaces the money in the tin and wraps the rubber tape around the lid, puts it back in his back pocket and buttons it up and says,

"Yes, Dad gave it to us to hide in case of emergency, this lot should get us to England if war comes...

"I wonder who Prince Albert is."

Ken looks out of the window,

"Do you think there will be a war Ron?"

"Most likely, but I hope not".

4. SCHOOL

Lindenburg College for Boys is a large rambling Gothic estate. The old mansion was once the baronial home of a German Count. In its three hundred years as boys' school, buildings have been added for classrooms, studies and dormitories. A gymnasium and a great hall was added to match the original style of architecture, solid and permanent.

The school stands overlooking the edge of an alpine lake in its own beautiful park. It looks like a very old English private school from Hampshire, transplanted and dropped into the mountains of Rauchenburg Bavaria.

Its academic traditions and scholastic reputation are not very distinguished. No one famous was ever educated here, but it has provided the rich of southern Bavaria an exclusive private boarding school, a rare thing in 1939. The dormitory college educates wealthy persons' sons from age eight to eighteen and almost guarantees that a privileged student will get into a decent university.

Reich Minister Dr. Bernhard Rust was appointed Minister of Science and Education five years ago in 1934. Since then there had been many changes, there was a time when the subjects of political science and propaganda would never have been allowed in the curriculum. But in 1939 the old school turned gradually to embrace the new Nazi controlled education system and now reluctantly steers the minds of its young students towards the *New Order*.

The Nazi higher education authority has issued the school a new set of principles; they are being applied to the boys slowly, so as not to send a shock wave through the old structure.

Under the bright new Swastika blood banners their old school is now a Nazi school. Like all the rest of German youngsters, the boys now belong to Nazi youth organizations; the Nazi party supervises the films and books they are allowed to see and read.

The boys' young lives now belong to the Nazi State. The pupils have little knowledge of a world outside of the German borders, they read and believe the Party controlled newspapers and books. The Hitler Youths magazine the "HJ" and its comic pages are sought-after and read voraciously by the boys. The front-page motto says.

"Adolph Hitler, who totally controls the youth of today, can call himself Lord of the future".

Dr. Rust the Reich Minister has ordered:

"Boys brains must not be burdened with subjects that they do not need and will most likely forget. It has been the custom at most schools in Germany to attend school six days a week with only Sunday as a holiday. Well that's now changed... Saturday is now Reich Youth Day".

To the boys' glee and joy, Saturday school has been canceled. Saturday is now a "HJ Day". Since membership in the Hitler Youth has become compulsory the boys' free time would soon be all taken up with Reich approved Youth activities.

The first day of term is a crisp sunny day. The lake is frozen but not safe yet for skating; the pupils are arriving from their Christmas holidays wearing gray blazers with school badges on their breast pockets and their names on big paper ID labels.

With their gray shorts, school ties, caps and long gray cloaks, they all look very English climbing out of chauffeur driven cars and hired buses. The junior schoolmasters in their black academic gowns act as greeters and traffic wardens. Every one of the maintenance and ground staff, regardless of their position in the school, is expected to turn out on the "First Day of term". The staff is all dressed in long dark green aprons to put on a big show for the parents, helping to get all the bags and trunks off the cars and into the school's main building.

The boys' 'First Day' is one of the few times in the year that Max, the Lamberts' family gardener, puts on his chauffeur's cap and uniform to drive the boys to school. Their father feels that the sons of an English Diplomat should arrive well. The twins shake Max's hand and a master in a long black gown waves the old sedate Bentley out of the driveway.

Inside the oak gothic reception hall the grand stairway is teeming with boys all in the same uniform, carrying cases and trunks. In the center of the hallway a group of small new boys are sitting on their cases looking lost and sorry for themselves. A young master with a kind face, in a black academic gown climbs up a few stairs and blows his whistle and shouts,

"Look at the big board to see where you're supposed to go....
Look for your accommodations on the big board....
All your names are up there.
We want all boys undressed and in gym kit for medical examinations in the Great Hall now, now, now.
Don't forget to bring your registration envelopes from home".

Ken and Ron push their way through a crowd to the big notice board. They search for their names. Ken finds the list they are on and shouts to Ron,

"We are in Two-A-Lower, dorm six".
"Smashing", yells Ron, "it's close to the school; look, here's Hans. Get him over here".

Hans is a fair-haired sprite of a boy with big bright intelligent blue eyes; lightly built and the same age as the twins. Glasses sticking out of his breast pocket, his shirt totally out of his pants, socks down around his ankles. His tie is loose and his jacket is wrongly buttoned: he looks a mess. He smiles when he spots the twins and says with a slight accent, that gives away his aristocratic breeding.

"Hello, you two, Oh Ken, we will all be able to tell the difference between you two now, and where did you get that lovely black eye?"

The boys all shake hands, Hans leans over close, smiling, and whispers,

"Heil Benny Goodman - I got two new Jazz records with my Christmas money. I hope they are not broken. The trained apes at the station just threw my case on the rack.... Are we in the same..."

Ron butts in,

"Yes old chap, they can't split up the terrible trio. Dorm six.... Do you want a hand?"

Hans nods, Ken and Ron start to clap their hands together in applause. Hans laughs,

"Ha, ha, very funny, ha ha. Hey, I can't wait to play you these new records they're awesome! It's total pure decadent American jazz and it's so decent, you should hear Gene Krupa the drummer".

Hans taps the side of his case. The three boys chain-carry their cases between them, pushing and shoving their way through the crowd, stepping over the new boys. Hans is being dragged through at the rear, hanging onto his own case.

It's the second term for all three boys so they know their way through the echoing hallways to the back door. As they approach the rear doors a group of lost new boys are looking over bits of paper trying to find their rooms. Ron yells,

"Mind the wet paint, coming through with wet paint".

The young first year boys scatter out of the way, looking around to see what had just been painted.

Outside of dormitory six, its doors almost hidden in a deep snowdrift, sits a bear of a boy about eleven years old. He sits astride on his upturned case that has been set down on the only patch of dry sidewalk. His mop of blond curly hair looks as if it hasn't been cut for a month. He has steel blue eyes and a healthy outdoor tan and is immaculately dressed. Sitting to attention with a wooden clipboard on his knees and a thick fountain pen in his hand. He looks up and holds his hand up with the authority of a senior but in the short pants uniform of a junior. He looks at the boys' nametags. Pulling the lapel of Hans's jacket closed.

"Greetings, scumbags, did you all have a nice Christmas?
Good, it looks as if I am to be your senior boy this year. I'm
your dormitory monitor. Dieter Wolff is the name and
discipline is my game. Aren't you a bunch of lucky lads?"
Ron replies defiantly,
"Well isn't that so nice for us, I think
I will vomit all over Hans here".

Hans looks disgusted as Ken opens the neck of his shirt and
pretends to throw up in it. Dieter with scorn says,
"You two are totally disgusting; you must be brothers".
"Twins," Hans volunteers, "And I bet you can't tell
them apart when that black eye clears up".

Ken leans over and points to their names on the board. Dieter looks
at Hans, who is even more disheveled from his rush, dragging his bags
through the school. Dieter pulls the last bit of Hans' shirt out of his
shorts, grabs him by his lapels and yells.
"So, your parents haven't taught you how to dress yourself at
home yet then.... We will soon sort you out.
Kenneth, you can come with me to get our fire extinguishers..."
"Ken... I don't like being called Kenneth".
"You Ronald, are in charge of clearing the snow off the door
and path. Please keep the snow off my case".

As soon as Dieter turns his back, Ron pokes his middle finger in the
air at his back.

The twins and Hans grab the three beds closest to the big stove in
the center of the room. There is a bustle of activity, as beds are being
made.

The dormitory of 2A lower is one of ten identical units that were
erected close behind the school: solid wood buildings put up by German
craftsmen thirty years ago. It's a long room with twelve iron beds on each
side, each bed has its own foot-locker for which a private padlock is
permitted. There is also a small standing wardrobe that the boys are not
allowed to lock.

A small room with a lockable door is at the front end of the
dormitory. This is for Dieter the class Monitor; his little bedroom has a
boarded-in ceiling, it is a private place, it gives him stature and authority,
but it had to be earned by a combination of scholastic and athletic
achievements.

The roof of his little room supports all the boys' travel cases and
trunks stored in neat piles, with the largest on the bottom and the smallest
on the top. At the far end of the dormitory is a cement-floored shower
stall with six big shiny copper showerheads and a row of smallish un-
walled toilet basins with scrubbed wooden seats. One wall has a sloping

copper urinal trough with a flush pipe running over it. All the brass and copper fittings have the look of years of polishing by little hands that have been punished for some small infraction.

In the center of the dormitory there is a big wood-burning stove set on a cement slab. Long scrubbed wooden tables run lengthwise down the center with benches to accommodate twenty-four boys. The walls are painted sensible light gray with the ceiling and upper parts of the walls that boys can't reach, painted white. Across from the Monitor's small room is a steel-lined bunker for stove wood, it too showing years of polishing. Large airy windows run down both sides of the room.

The boys bustle about trying to sort out their things.

Clothes go in the lockers, the twins have little to stowaway, one aluminum soap tin for the two of them to hold the good soap, the school soap is dreadful, toilet articles, a shared comb and hairbrush but they have a new toothbrush each.

Ken hides his secret diary inside the big old teddy bear in his footlocker. Innocent as it is, the diary is full of his own opinions about the people around him. He writes something most days, in English for security.

There is a buzz of activity as the boys tear down last year's posters, stick up photographs on the inside of their locker doors. A pile of a books and magazines newly arrived from Munich sit in a neat stack on one of the scrubbed tables.

Ron grabs the top paper. Ken points to an announcement on the back page of the *Pirmasenser Zietung*, It is a notice from the Mayor of Munich, and the twins read it.

> "*It has repeatedly been observed during funeral services that the dead are buried or cremated in valuable clothing, some even newly bought. I consider it a duty of all good German citizens to omit all unnecessary pomp and use a simple shroud for funerals. - The Mayor*".

Ken pulls a face flipping through the pages looking for pictures,
> "So Ron, what's a shroud?"

Ron laughs,
> "It's what they put on the people when they're dead, it's a sort of death shirt".

The boys get undressed and into gym gear. Dieter grabs one boy, who is putting his gym shorts over his underpants and says quietly but with authority,
> "Not today boy, no underwear on today. No socks no shoes, we are having an examination by a Doctor. No time for pants or socks. The Doctor gets eight seconds to do a really thorough medical assessment on each of your puny bodies. So, let's go, let's go, go, go".

Dieter lines the boys up and marches them out bare footed and shivering across the snow-covered yard and into the school.

The Great Hall has long tables that have been set up at the stage end. Lines of boys wait to see the doctors.

It's a medical production line. Karl Kaltenbrunner dressed in a new brown Hitler Youth leaders' uniform is ushering boys, instructing them to drop their shorts and walk from table to table naked to be examined by the team of medical people in white coats. Ken spots Karl at the front of the hall and points over to where he is bullying the small boys to get in line.

"Look who's here Ron... how the hell did he get into here ".

Ron pokes Hans and whispers.

"Look, that's the shit-bag who gave me this black eye.
Wait until he sees us. Oh, will we be in for it".

The rows of naked boys get their hearts listened to, ears and mouths peered into. Heads right, cough. Heads left, cough.

As Ron Ken and Hans run from the tables they pass Karl. He looks down at their naked genitals and sneers,

"Hey, well if it is not the little Lambert boys. I heard you two
were here. I see the English side of your family showing with
your little dinkies down there, ha".

Ron snapped back with the most devastating lie he could think up at such short notice, in a soft and confident voice he says,

"Emmy, our maid, told us that you were a bit of a limp-dick-
non-performer in the love department".

Karl turns nasty and angry, he shouts,

"Liars... you will get it and you won't know
when it's coming, assholes. Move on there,
get back in the line now, move, move".

The naked twins march back to retrieve their shorts swinging their arms in jerks like wooden soldiers, making faces at Karl as soon as his back is turned, laughing and giggling. As the boys march across the great hall they are not aware that Karl has turned and is following them grasping a meter-long wooden ruler like a sword.

Ron bends down to pick up his gym shorts. Karl, with a well-aimed swipe, whacks Ron so hard across his bare backside. The crack echoes through the hall and the hard wooden ruler snaps in two. Ron's yell causes the doctors to turn their heads. Ken in a flash grabs a piece of the stick from the floor and using it like a blade thrusts the jagged broken end into Karl's upper leg with all his weight. Karl yells but ignores the wound and chases Ken, who runs naked and slides through the exit doors out of the Great Hall into the snow.

Karl catches up to Ken, who is now trying to scramble bare footed up a snow embankment. He grabs him by his ankle and rolls him in the snowdrift, then presses his face into the ice with his heavy boot on his neck and takes furious whacks at him with the remaining half of the stick.

Seconds later Ron appears running at full speed and pounces on Karl's back pulling his hair trying to bite off his ear and punching the side of his head as hard as he can. It takes three masters and a Doctor to stop the fight and separate the two naked brothers who are viciously punching biting and kicking every part of Karl's body they can get at, using all their strength in a spirited, brutal and ruthless attack. Karl sits up from the floor bleeding from his ear and nose yelling,

"I'll get you two little English shits".

Two strong masters hold onto Karl and the naked brothers run off, grabbing their shorts as they slide across the Great Hall singing,

"Oh, any old iron, any old iron,
Any, any, any, old iron,
Karl looks a treat, walking down the street,
he looks all dapper from his napper to his feet,
dressed in brown, all around town,
With his father's old black tie on.
Oh... we wouldn't give him tuppence
for his old watch chain, Old iron, old iron.
Didle didle dum dum, didle didle dum dum,
dum didle dum dum - dum dum".

As they all trot back to the dormitory Hans says to Dieter,

"Oh, I really wouldn't want to get on the wrong side
of the Lamberts, I thought they were going to tear Karl to bits,
what if the masters hadn't stopped the fight. The way those two
were going at him, they could have killed him for sure".

Dieter grins and says,

"I should have stopped it".

Ron whispers to Dieter and winks,

"Pick a fight with one Lambert and..."

At 2 am the dormitory is a quiet buzz with boys in deep sleep. Some of the toughest boys by day whimper quietly at night, it's when they miss their home and loved ones the most.

Ron gets out of his bed and tugs on Ken's arm and puts his hand over his mouth to stop him from yelling out. Without a word the boys pull on their overcoats and creep out of the dormitory with their boots in their hands. They sit on the front steps and put on their boots, Ron whispers,

"We have to bury the tin Dad gave us. Look,
I've borrowed Dieter's Camp Knife, come on".

Ken follows Ron out into the chilly winter night. They make their way to a big old Chestnut tree on the edge of the school grounds. Ron cuts a round hole in the grass under the snow with Dieter's camp knife, takes a newspaper out of his pocket and spreads it out. He scoops the soil into the newspaper, buries the can of money deep, making sure it is stood upright. He then pours the soil back into the hole, pats it all down and marks the spot with a notch in the tree.

"Can you remember how to find this?"

Ken nods and says,

"How did you get Dieter's knife?"

Ron smiles with his 'I know more than you' look.

"I crept in his room and slipped it off his belt while he was asleep".

"Ron, you're very sneaky, did you rig for silent running?"

"Mm, but he leaves his door open. Let's get back I'm getting cold".

The boys cover the fresh soil and make their way back to their beds and slip Dieter's knife back in its place. Outside it starts to snow lightly covering all traces of their secret hole.

A math class is in progress in the home classroom of 2A upper and the master, Herr Rosen, is writing a math problem on the blackboard with squeaky chalk. Rosen is in his forties, Jewish and looks it. He has managed to slip through the net of the early anti-Jewish sweeps of the schools when the Nazis tried to weed out all the Jews from the German education system. The school Principal, Dr. Tolling, is a kindly old scholar and would not hear of firing his three Jewish teachers or expelling the Jewish students. He hates the Nazi party and all their thugs. The school being far from the big cities has fallen through the cracks in the New Order. Rosen spins around from the blackboard,

"So, that's ten problems by tonight. Oh, those who are in the Young Folk and have to go to the Heim, do just one problem, you can go as soon as you're done"..

The Heim, is the 'Young Folks' and 'Hitler Youth' duty room, it has its cupboards full of books and board games. There is a small pile of army picture magazines called 'Signals' which display photographs of the glorious German Army in action. The walls are covered with posters of aircraft and ships, and also tent instructions.

A large picture frame with 'All the knots a Hitler Youth should know' is nailed on the wall, some of the more complicated knots have been undone and the cords dangle down because no one knows how to re-tie them. There are two large worktables with chairs. Four boys are noisily playing Skat-cards with a small crowd watching.

Every Wednesday afternoon boys of the HJ and DJ have their meetings and then sit around at four pm and listen to the "Heimabend" the radio hour that is broadcast just for the Hitler Youth. The radio is an official Volksemphanger (People's Receiver). It can only receive the German Nazi propaganda stations and no other foreign stations. It's switched off as soon as the 'Youth Radio Show' is over.

Most of the boys are in uniform except Hans and the twins. They are sitting at a table with Dieter, who is in his DJ uniform and has now been accepted into the trio's tight circle of friends as a sort of older brother and defender.

All four boys are wearing earphones, and are listening to Hans' jazz records that have been re-labeled "French Language Exercises". Dieter has his back to the door and is really into the music, tapping the table with his fingers like drumsticks.

The 'New Order' is changing the school. One of the many new `Directives' to come down from the head's office is that Dieter, Karl and the other school monitors now have to be called 'Sergeant' and hold that rank in the Hitler Youth. Herr Strote strides through the open door. Karl slides over to meet him and cannot wait to tell. He nods to the record player and noxiously whispers,

"Herr Strote, sir, those are not French language records, they're American Jazz with the labels changed".

Herr Strote looks at the table. Dieter is not yet aware of Strote's gaze. Strote walks over behind Dieter, slaps him around the head sending the headsets flying. Dieter spins around ready to kill.

Hans quickly turns off the record player. Dieter sees the large balding Strote, and slowly sits down. He notices Karl grinning behind him. Herr Strote speaks to the room, fingering his round solid gold lapel badge that shows he is a senior member of the NSDAP (the Nazi party) and proud of it. He ignores the record player and barks,

"Who has collected for Winter Relief before?"

There is no response from the room, he continues.

"No one? No one? No one at all?"

Herr Strote picks up one of Hans' records and looks at the label,

"There is a reason that I don't smash this foreign decadent trash…. I will be nice to you boys today.

It's winter relief time and you are going to sell for me. There will be a collection box, a tray of flags for each boy. You must get twenty pfennigs for each flag you sell".

Strode looks at the three boys without uniforms, fingers Ron to stand up,

"Where are your uniforms? And why are you at a meeting, on parade not dressed properly, aren't you proud of them?"

Ron quietly explains,

"Sir, we are not old enough to be members yet".

Strote, ignoring the answer, picks up an English book that is lying on the table, 'Just William'. He looks at Ron.

"Are you the twins who speak English?... Good.
Germany needs translators. We will have influence in England, soon".

He draws a figure seven with white chalk on the blackboard,

"Now, we will talk about the origin of the Swastika and the reason it was adopted as the symbol of National Socialism. Number seven is a lucky number. In 1918 when the Führer was in hospital wounded half blind from having been gassed, by our own troops, I might add. The first thing he saw as the Army doctors took the dressings from his eyes was a stone swastika over the door, a good luck charm".

Strote joined the 'sevens' together and drew a swastika on the board. He becomes very serious as he explains,

"Our Führer simply reversed the crosses and produced a true swastika. Later it was known as the Hitlerian swastika, turned aslant, and then adopted as the party symbol. It symbolizes the eternal sign of the unstoppable wheel. The word 'swastika' although of Indian origin is purely German. Emperor Charlemagne used it in his crest and had it embroidered on his royal robes. You boys must respect this emblem it's the symbol of our Fatherland and you will defend it with your lives".

He folds his arms and gazes around the room of quiet boys. No one has any questions. His gaze falls upon the twins and Hans,

"You three go to the matron. Get yourselves in uniform, we need every boy we can get out there selling. If they haven't got uniforms for you at least get yourselves proper armbands... Don't come back here without them. Go!"

It's a hot and sultry day and the train slowly pulls in to Munich Station. The carriages are crowded and the boys have had to stand all the way. Dieter marches his dozy little platoon into the center of the station. Hans and the Lambert boys are still not in HJ uniform, they are just wearing armbands marked 'Winter Relief Fund' over their gray school uniforms.

Each boy has a tin box for money and a tray of flags. Ken gets placed in position by a platform passenger gate. As the people pass through, Ken sees to his dismay that they are all wearing Relief pins.

A Hitler Youth about fifteen in his uniform comes through the gate carrying three empty flag trays and swinging three heavy money cans. Ken dismayed yells,

"Hey, did you ride the train just to sell pins?"
The HJ Boy laughs

"All day, this is my third trip, ha".

A cold voice behind Ken causes him to turn around. A boy dressed in a Hitler Youth Leader's uniform about sixteen years old hisses,

"This train has been sold by my lad, what do you want here boy?"

Ken notices the Special School's badge on the sergeant's right pocket showing his successful completion of the Reichsführerschule and thinks to himself,

"You don't get those badges unless you're a real shitty Nazi fanatic".

The sergeant's boy holds up his three cans with pride,

"Look, Sergeant Steiner, three trays again".

Sergeant Steiner boasts.

"See this; my boys travel and collect. Well done boy".

Steiner slowly turns to Ken, walks around him, pulls out his shirt, leans over and sniffs his jacket,

"What school uniform is this then, don't you rich boarding school boys ever wash? You smell like a Jewish whore in heat".

Ken makes an effort to explain,

"I had a..."

Before Ken has a chance to say more than two words, Steiner brings his hand up with a well-aimed back-handed whack across Ken's face, sending him flying on his backside, his tray and empty can rolling down the platform.

"You speak only when you are spoken to private school boy".

Dieter picks up the rolling can and he helps Ken pick up all his scattered pins. The HJ boy and Steiner laugh in the background. Ken has blood running down from his nose.

Steiner grinning smirks,

"See, the school sergeant he is just as grubby, groveling there. No wonder his boys look so dirty, what a bad example he sets".

Dieter smiles at the cadet sergeant, walks over close to him. He is taller and bigger than the cadet takes hold of his hand as if he were going to shake hands saying,

"Hello I'm Sergeant Wolff, and I'm telling you to keep your nasty manicured hands off my boys.

Or I might break a few of those pretty little fingers".

Then he squeezes the Sergeants hand with all his strength. At first Steiner tries to squeeze back but Dieter had the hold first. He is stronger so has the advantage; he puts on more pressure making the sergeant wince and fall to his knees. Steiner glares as they walk off to another part of the station. He shouts, his adolescent voice squeaking with rage.

"I am going to put a report in about your insulting behavior sergeant Wolff... It's not good discipline".

In the gymnasium the boys from the second year class are dressed in an assortment of gym wear; half of them have red sashes the other half are in yellow. They are split into two equal teams. Dieter with the red team, Karl with the yellow. Herr Rosen strides into the gymnasium dressed in running shorts and an undershirt.

He has a trim figure and is in good physical condition, for a man of his age. This surprises most of the boys who have only seen him in a suit with his academic gown. He blows his whistle,

"Who knows the game 'Wolf'?"

One or two boys put up their hands. Karl and Dieter get the boys lined up, one team at each end of the large gym. The twins and Hans are on Dieter's team. Rosen grabs Hans around his waist, lifts him off his feet, and then tucks him under his arm and strides around the gym.

"The object of the game is to rush your opponent, pick him up off his feet, then yell "Wolf."
His feet must be off the ground when you yell "Wolf". Then he's out of the game; he must retire off the field. Remember it's a game, not a platoon fight".

The two equal teams stand in line across the gym. Rosen blows his whistle; both teams charge. Boys sort themselves out with opponents they think they can tackle, victors yell "Wolf".

Rosen blows his whistle again and they all stop.

Dieter and Karl sort the teams out back at their starting ends of the gym. Rosen calls for silence.

"Now we all know what it's all about, I want to hear some blood curdling yells. The object is to scare the pants off your opponent, so let's hear some war cries".

The teams line up again. The whistle blows and the two teams charge screaming and yelling. The noise from sixty-eight boisterous charging boys is too much for the smaller lads, who turn tail and run for their lives. A true combat ensues. As the boys are lifted off their feet, yells of the victory cry "Wolf". Those who have been defeated are cheering on those who are still struggling. The whistle blows; Rosen counts the victims and declares a draw. But Dieter and Karl are still at it, struggling. The whistle blows again; Dieter and Karl break off their private struggle, pushing each other away. Rosen blows his whistle,

"Running on the spot, begin... up, up, up, up".

As the trio trot their way back to the dormitories across the school grounds Ron says,

"How do you think Rosen gets away with it?"

Hans walks in front of Ron, and walking backwards facing him says,

"What do you mean, getting away with what, what is it he is getting away with?"

Ron puts on his 'I know more than you do' voice and says,

"He is Jewish, that's what he's getting away with. Jews are not supposed to be teaching in Aryan schools....
I'm very glad we are not Jewish".

On Saturday at the back of the school grounds, the second year nine-year-old boys are being marched into a playing field. Rosen blows his whistle for a race the boys love, he yells
"Roman chariots: small boys only for the charioteers".
The boys cheer and quickly form themselves into teams of six.
Three boys in a line link arms. Two strong boys behind them bend down and grip the waist belts of the three in front. The two outside front boys wear their leather cross-straps loosely; these are used as reins for the charioteer who stands on the backs of two boys in the rear and ride them, one foot on each of their inside shoulders. Racing the length of the soccer field Dieter's team with Ron, Ken and Hans come in third. Karl's team comes in first and takes a victory lap around the field.
The boys all hot and exhausted pile into the showers, singing as loud as they can. Their shrill adolescent voices almost shatter the glass windows. Dieter flicks Ken's backside with a wet towel,
"Ow!" Ken yells,
"Hey, next month, you two could join my platoon in the
'Young Folk', we can use some new good men".
Ron makes a sour face, so Dieter gives him a friendly push in his back. Ron slips on the wet floor and plops down onto his naked backside. All the boys laugh. Ron says all disgruntled,
"We don't want to join your Hitler Youth, we are supposed to
be school boys, not fucking Storm Troopers".
Dieter is totally taken aback by that unexpected answer and yells,
"Shut up... Just shut up".
A silence falls over the changing room: no one had ever said that, especially not to a sergeant. Ken holds his hand out to give Ron a hand to stand up. Dieter goes all official,
"It's only because I think of you Lambert's as personal friends
that I don't report you two for very severe punishment. I am a
sergeant in the Young Folk now. I hold this rank; some boys
have been locked up for a week for saying less you know"...
Dieter lightens up,
"Ho, Come on let's get to supper; I'm hungry".
Dieter puts his arms around the twins, smiling, he lifts them both off their feet and carries then over to the changing room. All the boys laugh. Ken looks at Ron and raises his eyebrows, with a "don't let's push him too far" look. Ron understands very well; they have pushed Dieter as far as they could, for today.

It's a wet and dreary Monday afternoon and as on most wet days the schoolyard looks empty. A small Gestapo staff car and a SS truck have just arrived outside the school's front door. Boys start to peer out of windows and stand in doorways to watch the scene.

A squad of SS guards in long green rubber coats and steel helmets have grabbed the Professor, Herr Rosen the teacher and five Jewish boys and are roughly escorting them into one of the trucks. They all look very scared.

A small group of students ignore the rain and wander toward the truck but keep their distance and watch quietly. Karl in his new uniform stands at the tailgate of the truck and throws cases up to the boys. Ron and Hans join Dieter and Ken in the crowd. Hans, all out of breath says,

"They've arrested Herr Rosen and Professor Tolling".

Ken points,

"Yes, they are all in the truck".

"What did they do?" Ron whispers.

Dieter pushes his way to the front of the small crowd.

He looks back sympathetically,

"Nothing...poor shits... They're all Jews, the Headmaster has
been arrested because he didn't report them years ago".

Dieter spins around, looks at Karl, very hard and points.

"But I know who the hell did... It was him"!

Karl overhears the questions, strides over and addresses the group.

"Nowhere, they're not going anywhere, just to Munich. Jews are
not allowed in our schools, (raising his voice) He knew what he
was doing. He's a traitor for not reporting them years ago".

Ron asks,

"What about the boys, what did they do?"

Karl snaps back,

"Nothing, they're just Jews. They'll be sent home, they have
their own Jewish schools to go to".

Dieter says quietly:

"Did you report them to your father?"

Karl nods,

"Certainly. It's our duty; it's the law. We will get a new
headmaster now, one who we can all look up to, and one who
will lead us into the New Order. Not a Jew lover either, like
him".

Hans asks,

"Will this new Headmaster be some relative of yours then?"

Karl walks over very close to Hans and grabs him by his collar as if to bash him. Hans yells very confidently,

"Go ahead asshole, hit me, and see how long your father holds his job.... You and your old man will be back digging shit on the railway where you both came from".

Karl drops him, turns around and sees Ken grinning at his brother, then catches him unawares with a smack around the side of his face with the flat of his clipboard. Ken drops to his knees holding the side of his face. Karl goes back to the Captain and salutes.

The car and truck drive off. All the boys in the small group wave goodbye sadly. As the platoon walks off, Dieter trots along and catches up with Hans and the twins. He puts his arm around Hans' shoulder,

"So, Hans, tell me, what's all this about Karl's father?
Why did he back down from you like that?"
Hans grins,
"My Dad, is his father's Colonel, in the stinking black pig brigade, you know, the shitty SS".
Dieter laughs
"Ha, now I see why he has to be nice to you, So you'll have to join the HJ, then".
"That, or get the shit beaten out of me again".
Ken looks up,
"Again?"

A reluctant nod comes from Hans. Dieter puts his arms around all three boys and gives them a big bear hug,
"We four are going to be best friends, right, right?"
The four boys all smile and shake hands.
"We are going to look out for each other... Right?"
"All for one and one for all...Yes".

The four take off running down the path laughing, they weren't thinking about their Headmaster or the Jewish boys, they were concentrating on making sure they stamped in every puddle trying to splash the boy running next to them. Hans slips and sits hard on the ground, the boys run up alongside him and jump in to the puddles next to him and soak him.

5. WAR

That spring term passed and the school slowly evolved and fell in step with the 'New Order'. At the end of the term the twins' Mother and Father thought it would be good for their sons to be out of Munich and away from the city. They were very worried about the fights in the streets, their problem with Karl and the influences of the Hitler Youth movements.

So the twins were sent to what their father thought was a private non-Nazi farming summer camp for boys not too far from Munich near Starnburg on the Starnburger Lake. They were only one hour's drive away so if the family exit permits came through they could grab the boys and get back to England quickly. But the times were changing very fast.

Although it was a fee-paying camp it still came under the boot of the New Order and was run by the State Youth Services (The Hitler Youth). It was a healthy summer for the boys; they worked on the farm in the mornings, then hiked, swam, and did sports and Hitler Youth programs in the afternoons.

They returned home for the last weekend of their summer holidays looking well fed, fit, tanned and happy, but with very little knowledge of what was going on in Munich or Europe.

It was decided the twins were mature enough to take the train back to school for the autumn term by themselves. Their Mother and Father saw them off at the station.

As they were saying goodbye and getting warm hugs and kisses, Father pulled Ron to one side and whispered in his ear,

"You still have all that money buried in the tin?"

Ron grinned and nodded.

Ken had overheard and whispered,

"Yes, only we know where it's stashed, it's our secret".

"Have you spent any of it yet?" Dad said softly.

Both boys grin and shake their heads. The father winks at his sons and picks them both up together in a close three-way hug and whispered

"If you get sent to a camp or farm, don't forget to take the money tin with you".

The people of Germany at this time in history were living in information isolation, completely blocked off from news and radio programs from the rest of the world. All newspapers and radio stations were in the very tight censorship clutches of Dr. Goebbels and his Nazi Propaganda Ministry. It was forbidden and a serious offence to listen to foreign broadcasts. Powerful Nazi transmitters jammed most of them.

Ken and Ron pick up a newspaper someone had left on the train seat. The paper is from Karlsruhe. The boys spread the paper out in front of them. Ron says, "They don't let us read this stuff because most of it is lies anyway... Look".

Ron reads out the headlines of the newspaper DER FUHRER.

"WARSAW THREATENS BOMBARDMENT OF DANZIG!
AGITATION BY POLISH TROOPS, ARCH-MADNESS!"

> "I don't believe this shit, why would Poland want to start a war with Germany? It says here that the Poles are killing the German families and driving them off their farms".

The boys are unaware that Hitler has made a pact with Stalin, a Nazi-Soviet Non-Aggression pact to divide up South Eastern Europe between them so that Hitler gets Poland and other South Western territories and Russia gets the small Eastern countries. Hitler had to make the German people, most of whom did not want to go to war, believe him. So with a great speech he said to Germany on the radio and in newspapers.

> "In order to survive as a nation, they must prevent the circle blockade threatened by England and its allies".

Hitler then notified his Generals that,

> "This is precisely what lost us the last war".

> "So if Germany dominated Eastern Europe as far down as the Black Sea, we would be the strongest and most powerful nation in Europe. The food and raw materials so vital to our very existence would then be in our own territories".

It was accepted. That's the way it's going to be. Hitler has said so. No one dared to oppose him. But Hitler needed an excuse to invade Poland. So he and his Nazi Propaganda Ministry created one.

The day after his big military birthday celebration, Hitler's newspaper 'Volkische Beobachter' said,

> *"Our German Army, is for us, the shield and security for peace, a German Peace that will provide for a powerful people its necessary rights".*

So followed a charade of lies and set-up incidents along the Polish border. All were reported in the Nazi newspapers.

The 'Volkische Beobachter' had headlines....

"THE WHOLE OF POLAND IN WAR FEVER!
1,5000,000 POLISH MEN MOBILIZED.
POLISH TROOPS TRANSPORTED TO GERMAN
FRONTIER. CHAOS IN UPPER SILESIA!"

5 War

POLISH TROOPS SHOOT GERMAN FAMILIES"

The 'Borsen Zeitung' headlines proclaimed,

"COMPLETE CHAOS IN POLAND"
"GERMAN FAMILIES FLEE FOR THEIR LIVES"

There was not a word about the fact that the German Forces had been mobilizing for at least eighteen days and massing all along the Polish borders. On Friday the 1st of September 1939 Hitler told his people that the German Army had "Counter Attacked" and had responded to an attack the Polish army made across the German border; a flagrant lie proven by history.

German troops, tanks and aircraft led by their armored divisions massed across the border and drove deep into Poland. Just two days later on the 3rd of September 1939, England and France honored their treaty to come to Poland's aid and declared war on Germany. World war two had started.

The Great Hall is buzzing with anticipation. The whole school is seated and they have just finished an unusually good lunch. Rumors are flying about war, even the staff that have been moved up on the stage are whispering among themselves. The new replacement teachers, who have been selected for their Nazi ideological convictions over their scholarly qualifications, look very young and fit.

Ken nudges Ron to look up to where a teacher is wheeling a large console radio to the center of the stage and whispers to his brother,

"Hey look, they're going to play us some swing. I hope they play some Benny Goodman; (shouting) Hey play us some Benny..."

Ron quickly puts his hand over his brother's mouth and shuts him up. The teacher looks at his watch and holds up his hand for quiet. He turns up the volume. The German national anthem plays. All the school stands up, holding their arms up in a Nazi salute. A stern voice booms from the radio,

"This is the Bavarian Broadcasting System with a direct proclamation from Berlin..."
"This day the 3rd of September 1939 we present the Führer of the German Reich... Adolf Hitler".

A gasp ripples through the whole school. There is a long pause. The great hall with hundreds of boys falls totally silent. Hitler's voice starts very quietly, almost a whisper, so quiet that the master steps forward and turns up the volume control,

Hitler speaks...

"Great Britain has, for centuries, pursued rendering the peoples of the world defenseless against its policy of world conquest whilst it built its empire. They have claimed the right to attack and destroy any State they deem dangerous to them.

The British Government, driven by the warmongers, whom we know from the last war, have now declared a state of war on us, Germany and our people... We are, therefore, at war with Great Britain, its Empire and France".

The German anthem plays and the boys sing 'Deutschland Uber Alles' holding their right arms up in a Nazi salute, then two verses of the 'Horst-Wessel' song. As the singing drones on and on and the boy's arms get tired they rest their arms on the shoulders of the boys in front of them.

The room is stunned by the news. Doctor Weiss, the new headmaster, turns off the radio and walks to the edge of the stage. Ron takes a deep breath and whispers to Ken,

"That's it, you and me, we will be sent to England I reckon".

The twins look at each other for some other explanation.

Weiss stands with his arms folded waiting for silence. Doctor Weiss looks like a Prussian Officer with his hair cut too short on the sides, and a fierce stare. He steps to the edge of the stage and gives the room a grudging lopsided smile a half smile that the left half of his face doesn't even participate in; it is more like a half leer. Doctor Weiss shouts triumphantly,

"That was the voice of our Führer, Adolf Hitler... "

Let's salute him with a triple.... The whole school yells,

"Sieg Heil... Sieg Heil... Sieg Heil".

The boys all cheer. Dr. Weiss holds his hand up for quiet,

"I am Dr. Weiss, this is my school now. The previous headmaster allowed the good name of this school to be smeared by harboring Jewish teachers and students".

That state of affairs has been corrected. You are all my boys now... Our Reich Youth Leader Baldur Von Schirach has sent a personal message to me and this school. I will read it to you'.

He fumbles with a wad of papers, and clears his throat.

"You stand in your youth next to one another with the same rights and the same duties. There is no special Hitler Youth for the poor or the rich. No Hitler Youth for secondary schoolboys and girls, or for young workers... There is no Catholic or Protestant Hitler Youth. In our group everyone, who is of German blood, belongs. Before the flag of youth, everyone is the same".

Weiss then drones on about the Nazi seizure of power on the 30th of January 1933 and finally exalting the birthday of Adolf Hitler on the 20th of April 1889.

The hall buzzes with excitement, the older teachers on the stage look at each other in dismay. Ron grabs Ken's hand and whispers,

"Don't lose sight of me, we must stay together".

"What are we going to do Ron, where will we go?"

Ron smiles confidently at his brother and puts his finger to his lips for silence; he nods towards the stage where Weiss is about to continue. Dr. Weiss takes a deep breath,

"Our Führer Adolf Hitler said...

"Every Boy must march, suffer hunger and thirst,
be able to sleep on the bare earth, endure all privations
cheerfully, and be a fighter and a soldier
from the moment he is sworn into the Hitler Youth".

He looks around the eager faces that are staring back up at him,

"Very soon this school will have a one hundred percent
Hitler Youth and Young Folk membership. We will now all
reaffirm our oath to our Führer Adolf Hitler.... Attention".

The school stamps to attention with their right arms extended. Weiss with a passion in his voice yells....

"Captain Mitter".

A bust of Hitler is carried to the center of the stage, then Captain Mitter leads the whole school as they recite the oath,

"I swear before God, this solemn oath,
To give to the Führer of the German Reich Adolf Hitler
the Commander in Chief of the Hitler Youth, Total
obedience, and in case of any danger, should I be given the
honor. To be ready, to give up my life.
Sieg Heil, Sieg Heil, Sieg Heil".

Weiss steps forward and plants his feet astride,

"Now the New Order has at last come to this school.
It's better late than never. So, we the staff, have some
adjustments to make to the school's curriculum".

He takes a pace back, scowls at the school as if he had forgotten something, then yells,

"Whoever serves Adolf Hitler the Führer, serves Germany,
Whoever serves Germany serves God".

Then with his half smile he waits for the hall to go quiet, he grins a phony smile showing all his teeth saying,

"As from today, but strictly confined to the school grounds,
you all have a four day holiday! Dismiss".

A wild cheer rips through the great hall, the boys file out. Ken and his brother look very worried as they make their way to the big notice board in the school front hall. Ken says,

"What's going to happen to us Ron?
Will Mum and Dad come and get us?"

Ron grabs Ken's shoulders and whispers,
        "Let's not do anything stupid.
        But we will have to run alright,
        we are enemies of Germany now,
        let's see if we can get home, Mum and Dad
        will have to get out too, we should all go to England together...
        Let's get the money tin
        and bugger off out of this place, come on".
They push their way through the crowd to the board with all the new
orders that have just been freshly posted. There is nothing on the board
about them.
        Ken says.
        "Well there wouldn't be would there?"
Ron just shakes his head. Dieter spots the twins and pushes his way
through to the front using his height and rank, he reads aloud,
        "Our classes are now called platoons. We can't eat unless our
        total platoon is all-present. This place is going to be just like the
        army. See, we can't even talk in the dining room".
Hans joins the group, reading,
        "Up at 5 am, March to the showers with just a towel,
        all of us marching bare bummed naked,
        will that ever look funny,
        a bit chilly around the little things, ha".
Dieter studies all his new responsibilities. Ken looks worried,
        "Ron, what's going to happen to Mum and Dad?
        What's happening to us?"
Ron grins with an 'I know it's alright look'.
        "Come on, don't worry about it;
        they can't shoot us we're underage".
Ken thinks a bit, grabs Ron's arm and says,
        "So, how old do you have to be to get stood-up
        in front of a firing squad then?"
        "Sixteen at least".
Soon the little group of boys are totally focused on the big notice
board and are listening carefully to Dieter as he reads out all the new
orders. Ron grabs Ken's sleeve and quietly leads him away. Their strides
getting faster as they hurry down the busy hallway, pushing and shoving
their way past the young first year boys who seem to be running about
like confused ants. Ron says,
        "Ken, whatever happens we stay together... Right?"
        "Yes, where are we going Ron?

"Money tin first, some kit and then
we get out of this place, come on!"

The twins start running hard as soon as they are out in to the school field. At the foot of the big old chestnut tree Ken looks around and yells,
"Ron, are you going to dig it up now...
Someone might see us?"
"It doesn't matter if they see us,
we won't hide it in the same place again will we?"
Ron digs up their flat tin with a table knife he took from the dining room and then they run off to the dormitory.
The long room is empty when they burst in; Ron takes charge again, grabs Ken's Teddy bear and throws him the tin,
"Here stuff this in your Teddy, make sure that secret zip is
closed properly, it's not a secret if it's open".
In seconds Ron grabs their two rucksacks and places them side by side on the bed, he quickly packs each one with, socks, shirts and a warm jacket in each bag, throws a new pair of socks at Ken and says,
"Put these on and your hiking boots, come on quick
and stuff the Teddy in your bag. Let's move, move, move!"

The twins fill their water bottles and stroll out of the dormitory causally, making their way around to the edge of the grounds, keeping well away from the main gate then quietly hop the fence and slip into the woods, unseen.
As soon as they are out of sight of the school buildings they break into a light trot. After about fifteen minutes Ken stops and breathing heavily says,
"Hang on a minute Ron. What way are we going? "
Both boys fall down on the soft moss around the base of a big old tree and lay back looking up into its branches. Ken seems to want some reassurance,
"So, Ron, what way are we going then?"
"I don't know, we need a compass. I know downhill is north
and we must go north to get to Munich, so we go downhill for
now...
That'll be when we've had a rest".
"Munich is over sixty kilometers from here Ron,
we should try to find a station...
We didn't say goodbye to anyone did we, Ron?"
"How could we? It would have given the game away".
Both boys lay still looking up, getting back their breath, after a few moments Ken says,
"We don't have any food do we Ron?"
"No".

"So?"

"So we will get some, when we are hungry won't we?"

"Where".

"I don't know where, we will steal or buy some, don't be such a big baby… I won't let us starve will I?"

Ron brightens up and points to a tree saying,

"Look see, the dark side of the trees, well that's the north side and so we know where we are going, don't we?"

"We do?"

"Yes we do, if we go north, that way, we must come to a road eventually and we can hitch a ride to the next village, alright?"

The boys keep walking for two or three hours stopping to sip at their water bottles. As the woods start to thin the boys hear the rumble and grind of heavy trucks straining up steep inclines ahead. Ron brightens up and says,

"See, I said there would be a road down there, we may be able to get a lift, come on Ken get your bum in gear!"

The soft leafy ground gets steeper as the boys run and almost slide down toward the road. They stop in time and hide behind a rock outcrop. The road is just ahead of them and they see a convoy of army trucks slowly making their way down the hill. Ken whispers,

"Let's lay low and wait until they've passed".

But Ron jumps up and yells,

"No, come on, let's go, we can get a lift, they think we are on their side they don't know we are English do they, come on!"

Both boys scamper down the steep embankment on to the road and stand watching the trucks slowly rumble past them. Ken shouts,

"It's a Wehrmacht Alpine Patrol on maneuvers".

Ron yells

"Hey Sir, can we get a ride please".

"Hey wait for us!"

As the traffic backs up, the trucks slow down to a trotting pace. Ken and Ron run behind a truck and the infantrymen hold out their hands for the boys to grab, then pull them up onboard. The soldiers are in a good mood because it's the end of their patrol and they are going home to their base. Ron grinning asks a soldier with a friendly face what towns they are going to go through.

"We only go as far as Weilheim", he said

"So just what are you two boys doing so far out here?"

Ron thinks for a second, then his face lights up and he lies as convincingly as he can saying,

"Oh we are on a Young Folk, Self-reliant Test, we have to get to Munich any way we can, so this is very nice of you to give us a lift like this".

Ron had heard Dieter talk about the older boys doing these tests. The soldiers seem to believe them and give them some chocolate.

The trucks drop the boys off in the center of Weilheim and rumble off out of the village. The twins look about them, there are few people about so they feel very conspicuous, Ron points across the center square,

"Look there is an Inn, let's see if we can get something to eat there".

The twins eat their fill of goulash soup with extra helpings of potato pancakes. A fire is cheerfully burning in the huge fireplace and two older local farmers sit at a scrubbed wooden table playing cards gripping tall seines of local beer. Ron approaches them smiling politely.

"Excuse me sir, but is there a train station in this town?"

One of the old men smoking a pipe looks up and studies the twins and says,

"So where do you two boys want to go on the train then".

Ron is taken aback for about a half a second and lies with confidence again,

"Ho, we are going to a Hitler Youth Camp in Munich".

The man with the pipe said,

"Where?"

"Where what sir?"

"Where do you two want to go in Munich, it's a big city?"

Ron was taken aback but only for two seconds,

"Oh, we are all meeting at the Hauptbahnhof".

The men nod and the one with the pipe looks up at the clock,

"There is a train for Munich in an hour and twenty minutes, the station is just down the road, on the left".

As they walk into the station the twins are totally relaxed. They have to wait an hour for the ticket booth to open.

Ron says to his brother,

"You wouldn't think a war had just started, everything around here looks so very normal".

The twins are unaware that four heavy built teenage boys from their school have just arrived and are creeping up behind them. Four pairs of strong hands grab them and quickly lock steel wrist cuffs on to each of the twin's arms. The cuffs are chained to a metal belt that is round the waist of one of the senior boys.

Dieter arrives with a grin, followed by Karl smirking. Dieter gives the twins a bear hug and says,

"I've come along to make sure these thugs treat you two fairly, and don't knock you both about".

Karl pushes his way in to the group and says,

"It's alright, it's just that the Captain wants to see you both to sign something".

Not very much is said on the truck journey back to the school. Dieter is trying to be as cheerful as possible. The older boys keep talking about the two nine-year-old runaway twins. Outside the school's main building Karl becomes much warmer and takes the steel belt and clips it around his own waist and says,

"Come on you two I have been ordered to take you to see Captain Mitter, it's all right, just some papers to sign and they want to take some photographs of your ugly faces".

Dieter says,

"Don't look so worried, you will both be back tonight... Come on".

The boys follow Karl down the corridor. Ron sees the worried look on Ken's face,

"It's all right, he said we will be back tonight. Isn't that right Karl?"

"Yes, but we have to see Captain Mitter first, he has the train tickets".

"Train tickets?"

"Shh..., quiet now!"

Captain Mitter's office door is open. Karl stamps to attention, at the threshold,

"Heil Hitler, Captain, the Lambert brothers".

"Well bring them in, bring them in sergeant".

Karl tugs on the chain and the boys come sheepishly through the door. Captain Mitter finishes sealing a big brown envelope, smiles and says,

"Well I hope you both enjoyed your little excursion, what were you both thinking about, running off like that?"

Ron grabs his chance and blurts out,

"Captain, er, we thought we would both be stood up against a wall and shot, Sir, you know because of the war with England".

Mitter roars out laughing,

"Ha, we don't shoot little nine year old boys, do we sergeant? We would like you both to join us here and be a part of our brotherhood, ha, so no more about that, foolishness, alright?"

The Captain smiles, and sits down behind his desk, the boys nod in agreement.

"Were you two born here in the Reich?"

The boys nod again; Mitter smiles,

"Good, then there will be no problem".

Ron breathes a sigh of relief,

"Are there any Jews in your family?"

"No".

"Did you know any Jews, or did any Jews ever come to your
house?"

Both boys shake their heads. Captain Mitter lowers his voice almost
to a whisper.
"So what religion is your family?"
Ron almost shouts'
"We are all C-of-E sir, Church of England; we are both very
Protestant. We were both christened in a proper church…. I'm
not sure which one but I know our Mother would know… Sir".
Mitter is slightly taken back by Ron's outburst and smiles saying.
"Good, so we will need to get you registered properly in
Munich. So all three of you should be back here tonight".
Ron asks,
"Why do we have to be chained like this sir?"
"It's regulations. The sergeant here will take you down to the
registration office. We will get you both Whitewashed Aryan
Certificates".
"Give Dieter your packs he will look after them for you, then
you will all be back here in quick time, no chains".
Karl has a very self-satisfied smug look on his face. Mitter gives him
the rail passes. He salutes and with a gentle tug on their chain pulls the
boys through the door.

Ron and Ken feel very embarrassed on the train to Munich with Karl
who grins, holds up the chains to show them to the conductor and tells
him that they are his prisoners. Ron glares and says,
"Why did you have to say we are your prisoners like that?"
"Well until you get those white-washed papers sorted out you
are".
"What do you mean white-wash papers?"
Karl taps his small attaché case and says,
"I'm not allowed to talk about this, but everything there is to
know about you two is in here".
Ron gets very friendly,
"Come on Karl, let's have a look. Aren't you just a little bit
curious to have a look too?"
"I can't, even if I wanted to. The file is all sealed up".
Ron gives Karl a tug with his chain,
"So what about these white-wash papers, what are they?"
"Well this is all I know, they are certificates of Aryan Purity or
something… You know, pure white, very non-Jewish".
The boys sit back look out of the window and think about their fate.
Ron thinks to himself:

61

"They will soon be done with this interview and
we will have time to look around Munich and
see what our Father has to say about us being in chains.
Mum and Dad may just pull us out of this school
now that it has gone all stupid and Nazi".
Ken looks out at the green countryside as it rushes by and thinks:
"They will put us in separate concentration camps
with no food. Then when we are half-dead, flog us
and send us back to England. Or tie us to a post
and flog us until we just faint....
I'll have to remember to pretend to faint
after the first stroke of the whip".

6. STATE WARDS

The Gestapo headquarters resembles an art museum with its big marble steps. Quite normal looking people are coming and going through the unguarded front entrance. A big swastika flag hangs down the front of the building. Ken looks up and thinks that there must be a new one put up there every day and I bet they send the old ones off to the minor government buildings like the post office.

Karl strides in and the echo of his boots on the hard stone floor makes him sound military; he feels very important in his uniform.

A SS Corporal in his late forties is sitting behind a big marble reception desk. He leans toward Karl,

"So sergeant what can I do for you and your young charges?"

Karl, his pride swelling at being called a sergeant by a SS man blurts out,

"Prisoners, they are here for their documentation".

"So what sort of documentation? They don't look like Jews; are they Jews?"

"Oh, no sergeant. Aryan purity examination".

Karl leans into the SS sergeant and whispers,

"Their father is an Englishman".

The sergeant opens a drawer and picks out a brass disk with a large letter 'E' stamped onto it. He pushes back the big brown envelope across the shiny marble desk and with a slightly annoyed look waves them away and says,

"You will have to see the Brown Sisters. Go back out of the front doors, turn right then into the courtyard to door 'E'. You will need this disk to get in there, Heil Hitler".

Ken fidgets and says,

"Karl asks him if there is a toilet here".

Karl spins round and hisses,

"Not now".

Karl stamps a smart salute, picks up the disk and envelope and marches his prisoners back out of the front door. They turn into the arched courtyard and are confronted by a pair of ornate gates that are made of scrolled wrought iron and very secure.

Karl shows the SS. Guard his brass disk and holds up the chains from his waist. The guard opens the gate and points to the left side of the small courtyard,

"Door 'E'....They will open it when you get there".

The guard picks up a telephone and dials. As they walk diagonally across the cobblestone courtyard the boys notice they are surrounded on all sides by iron doors. Each door has an identical narrow observation slit.

Just before the boys arrive at the door marked 'E', it opens revealing another SS Guard in a black uniform he nods them to come in.

They find themselves in a small bare room with another iron door. In the wall at the side of the door is a small reception window. Karl starts to babble to the guard who cuts him off with a tap on his shoulder and points to the reception window, then strides through the door leaving Karl alone in the room with the boys.

Ken grabs his crotch and hops up and down and says,

"Karl I have to pee really very badly".

Karl spins him around with the chain,

"Well you will just have to wait, won't you"?

On the little sill under the window there is a push button labeled 'Push once only'. Ron tries the iron door he has just come through; it's locked. He hums to himself,

"Any old iron, any old iron, Mm....Old iron".

Karl pushes the button. They hear a faint bell ring. After a while a stern-looking woman dressed in brown robes like a nun comes to the window and opens it and holds out her hand smiling.

Karl hands her the envelope and the brass disk. He starts to explain, but she stops him up with a finger to her lips and closes the window. She opens the brown envelope and starts to read every page smiling and nodding. Ron strains to see through the window, gives up and whispers,

"She must be one of the Brown Sisters".

Ken asks, "Is she a nun?"

Karl walks the boys away from the little window and out of earshot of the Sister, then says,

"No they look like Nuns, but she is an SS woman".

The 'Brown Sisters', a name they earned in Poland kidnapping Aryan-blond looking babies for the Lebensborn project, are the female counterparts of the SS.; a wing of the Youth Service. They are usually mature, hard-women whose uniforms are long dark brown cassocks with white piping, a white collar, a cape, a gray apron and a nun-style head dress, hence, the nickname 'Brown Sisters'.

They are taught racial criteria by which Nordics can be infallibly distinguished. They were given the dubious title of 'The Physiognomic Brigade' and were qualified to make the decision (by interview and physical examination) establishing legally, if a child or an adult was pure Aryan. Racially Valuable Children, especially boys, were needed for adoption to boost the lopsided male German population depleted by the 1914-1918 war.

When the Sister is finished reading every sheet of paper in their files, she looks up and smiles at the boys. She gets up and opens the steel door saying:

"All three of you come with me".

With her near ankle-length skirt and short paces, she seems to glide down the polished corridors that smell of repeated waxing. She speaks without turning her head as the boys follow,

> "You will have to wait for a while, there is a lot going on down the hall...Twins are you, mm, good-looking Germans too....You will call me Sister, that's my rank in the Youth Service, is that understood?"

Karl yells,

> "Yes Sister".

As they follow the Sister down corridors and stairs they seem to be going deeper and deeper, the dim low ceilings have dusty pipes running with them. Ken thinks they look like the building's intestines. As they turn the corner Ken spots a toilet and bursts through the door. Karl tries to hold him back with the chain yelling,

> "No not yet".

"Oh Karl I have to go now, or I will do it all over the floor".

The Sister waves her finger at Karl and all three boys go into the toilet. Ken runs to a cubicle, close the door; Karl and Ron stand close to the door to allow Ken to take the slack in the chain.

Then with a big sigh, relieves himself in the toilet staring at the brass pipes and steel fittings thinking; they have been polished every day and the room is so clean you could eat your dinner off the floor.

Feeling a lot better now the boys resume their journey following the skirts of the Brown Sister deeper and deeper into the basement. The corridor is stacked with baggage of all kinds and a lot of canvas kit bags with labels.

They hear voices of people and children crying as they come to a large room that seems to be crammed with hundreds of people and a lot of children. A small table has been set up just outside the wire cage door that is locked and has a big square key. Sitting at the table is a fat SS guard with two slimmer ones, all of them armed. The fat jailer stands up when the Sister arrives.

She hands him a slip of paper and turns to the boys and says,

> "You won't be too long in here".

Then looking at Karl she says,

> "You will have to stay too".

Karl looks at the Sister with total disbelief, she nods firmly.

The guard reaches under the table and holds out a kit bag to Karl,

> "All three of you, empty all your pockets on to the table, put your bootlaces, belts, knives and caps in the sack. Write your names on the label".

The Sister stands there looking and watching the boys put all their things on the table. The guard swipes the contents of the boys' pockets into the sack. Just as the Sister turns away to leave, Karl asks her,

"Please Sister, what about unlocking the chain. The key is in the envelope".

She turns to him smiling and shakes her head. The doors open and the boys are pushed through.

There are more people in the room than they thought. There are no windows so the only air has to come through the steel wire door. Ken says,

"There's not enough air in here".

All the wall space has been taken with people sitting shoulder to shoulder, their backs propped up against the rough brick wall. Babies are crying to be fed or changed.

The room stinks of unchanged babies. Ron whispers to Karl,

"Where's the toilet?"

An older man sitting close to them points to a row of steel buckets in the corner, Ron says,

"Shit, no wonder it stinks in here".

After an hour the steel gate is unlocked, the fat guard starts to read out the names of all the women with babies. They leave and the door is slammed shut again. The sound of the babies crying drifts away down the corridors and up the stone stairs.

The concrete room is quieter now with little groups of people huddled together whispering anxiously in their own languages. Ken whispers,

"This place is full of foreigners, Dutch, French, all sorts".

Karl moans,

"It looks as if I'm the only purebred German here, I shouldn't be locked up, because I'm just a guard".

After a while the steel gate is opened again and names of older married couples are called. They leave. Ron asks an older man how long he has been down here,

"About three days I think, but that's a good sign. If they feed you, it means that you're going to be kept in here. If we don't get fed, we can assume we are only visiting".

The three boys grab a spot vacated by some of the women and sit down with their backs to the wall.

Because of the chains, Karl is in the middle. The telephone rings, causing the people to look hopefully towards the door, waiting for the fat man to call a name or two. But after a short quiet conversation he motions to his guards and they all leave. As their footsteps fade to the end of the corridor there is a 'clunk' and the cell and the passage get plunged into darkness.

It's total darkness; not a chink of light. There is a murmur of conversation and a general rustle as the prisoners' settle down for the night. Karl whispers in the darkness,

"It's not fair, why should I be kept in here? I'm just the escort".
Ron laughs out loud,

"Ha, if they lose the key, you will have to stand against the wall
with us and be shot".

A gruff voice from the other side of the room yells at them,

"Shut up and get some sleep, the lights are not off for very
long".

Karl sleeps the sleep of the ignorant lying flat on his back. Ken and
Ron sit up, Ron whispering his theory about what was going to happen
to them.

"There are so many people like us; it takes time".

Ken starts to sniff, and is trying to hide his fear,

"Why would they shoot us Ron?"

"Shh, no one's going to shoot us, try to get some sleep".

"So Ron, why isn't Dad banging the doors down to get us out
of here, do you think Mum and Dad are locked up somewhere
like us too?"

Ron leans over Karl's sleeping head and puts his arm around his
brother's shoulder,

"Look Ken, there's two answers. If they send Mum and Dad
back to England, they will send us too, or if they don't they
don't, so there is not much we can do about it to night anyway
is there?"

"Ron that fat SS guard is a nasty bit of work. We don't want to
get on the wrong side of him, do we?"

The brothers eventually fall asleep sitting up.

The following morning the lights are switched on and there is an
exchange of latrine buckets by prisoners from other cells while the armed
guards stand in the doorway. Then large steel fresh water canisters with
tin mugs attached to their handles by small chains are dumped in the
center of the room. This is the only sustenance that has come to the cell.

The people quietly and slowly stand in line to take their early
morning drink of water. Ron notes their numbers are thinning out. Two
new Dutch inmates have arrived since the boys arrived. Karl sits watching
all this, fuming and boiling with anger. His breathing becomes fast and
panicky. He stands up and shouts to the guard,

"Sergeant, like you I am a sergeant, an escort to these two boys
here. We have been here over twenty four hours and had
nothing to eat yet".

The fat sergeant stops and spins around, strides into the cell barging
past people, pushing them out of the way. His face very red, he yells in
Karl's face:

"Boy, you are lucky. You are so lucky not having anything to
eat. The poor shits in the cells below were fed this morning but
they are to be shot in three days.
So shut your face and try to behave like a sergeant.
Just wait, you three will be out of here soon".

That evening the guards go off as usual and the lights get turned off.
Ron says,
"I wonder what the man meant about the poor people
downstairs who are going to be shot?....
Well at least it means we are not getting shot".
The next morning new guards arrive and after the bucket swapping
and fresh water routine, Karl being very polite asks the new sergeant what
are the chances of getting some food as this was the third day they hadn't
eaten. The Sergeant looks at his clipboard and says,
"You three are up for showers this morning so you will
be on your interviews today. That's what usually happens".
Then pointing at the boy's handcuffs asks Karl,
"Do you have the key?"
Karl shakes his head. The sergeant bellows out a laugh that echoes
down the hallway,
"Ha, what an escort, you will learn the hard way,
always keep a spare key in your own pocket. Come here".
The sergeant pulls a small key out of his shirt pocket and unlocks
Karl out of his belt.
The three boys get marched to the showers and stand in line with
men women and children, as the lineup for the showers gets closer to the
sound of running water the fat sergeant orders all of them to strip,
"Leave your clothes where they are in the corridor here, they
will be all disinfected before you put them on again".
Ken and Ron have stripped as much as they can but the chain from
each boy's wrist is preventing them from removing most of their clothing.
The fat sergeant appears and whacks Ron round the ear,
"Why are you not undressed? You three shy ha?"
Ken holds up his hand showing the man the chain, he laughs and
reaches into his pocket for a key and unlocks the chains off their wrists.
They have a hurried lukewarm water shower with strong smelling
acidic soap and a wad of soft pine wood shavings to use as a sponge then,
dress in their clothes now smelling of disinfectant they are re-locked to
Karl's belt and escorted with dripping hair by the same Brown Sister to
an office on the second floor. They stand outside the door shivering,
waiting. The light in a box on the door flashes: 'Enter'. Ron and Ken
look at each other, and follow Karl and the Sister.

Karl skillfully opens both of the double doors at the same time, makes a smart entrance, thumps his foot on the thick carpet and salutes,

"Heil Hitler...The Lambert brothers...Sister".

Senior Sister Hartman a stern looking woman reads the boys' file.

She doesn't look up from her papers. The boys look around the clean, Spartan office. Karl falls out of his stiffness.

The sister tips the key out of their envelope, hands it to Karl and gestures to him to unlock the boys' cuffs.

The boys rub their wrists and Karl blocks the doors standing feet apart. The junior Sister stands on one side of the desk. Senior Sister Hartman is a hard-looking woman and obviously of a much higher rank than the first Sister. She wears a white bonnet with a big white bow under her chin and no gray apron. She leans back in her chair, looks at a file in front of her, and casually says,

"Lambert, Lam-bert, what nationality is that?"

Senior Sister Hartman holds her hand up as if she didn't want an answer. She leans back and takes off her glasses,

"You two boys are very lucky, do you know that? Don't stand there so stiff. Sergeant, bring that stool over for them and give them a towel to dry their hair".

Karl brings the long stool over and both boys sit down facing the big desk drying their hair with the pure white fluffy towel.

"Let's get the formalities out of the way first.

Sister Rothe here and I will examine you both, to see if you're fit for Aryan Certification. Now, are there any Jewish aunts or uncles in your family?"

The boys shake their heads, and Ron gets up as if to ask a question. The Sister holds up her hand as if to say not yet,

"When we have finished our interview I will tell you both about your parents. Did any Jews ever come to your home or did you or your parents know any Jews?"

Ron puts his hand up, the sister nods,

"Herr Rosen our math teacher at school is a Jew but they took him away".

"Any Jews outside your school, what about your father's friends?"

The twins shake their heads. Sister Rothe reaches down for a black attaché case, puts it on the desk and opens it. She takes out a large protractor and comparing notes on a clipboard, measures the boys' skulls, looks at their teeth and takes a small board with different colored glass eyes fixed in rows and compares them with the color of the boys own eyes. She calls over to Karl,

"Get them to strip".

A look of total horror falls over both of the boys' faces.

Karl smirks and walks to up to them, Ron holds up his hand as if to say, thank you we don't need any help. Both boys strip off their clothes down to their underpants.

The Sister measures their waists, chests and necks, noting it all down in her book. She nods to Karl who's standing behind them. He pulls down the boys' loose underpants. The Sister looks at their genitals, makes notes, and waves a finger to the boys who grab their underpants and quickly pull them up. Sister Rothe hands the clipboard to her superior officer Senior Sister Hartman, who glances at the papers and smiles at the boys,

"Well it seems as if we have two young Aryan Germans here; good stock too. Mother from Vienna fathers English, both of you born in Munich, blond, blue eyes.

Germany's hope for the future...you both can get dressed now".

The boys jump back into their clothes. Senior Sister Hartman sits back in her chair and thumbs through the file,

"It says here that your father and mother were sent back to England three days ago.

This was done very quickly for their own safety.

It seems your father was mixed up with some people who did not have Germany's best interests at heart. Your mother's sister Inga Pierce has been sent back to Vienna".

Ken and Ron look at each other. Ron starts to raise his hand to ask a question, he gets cut short.

"So what's to become of you two abandoned boys now England has declared war on us, eh?"

Ron slowly raises his hand again. The Sister nods impatiently,

"Sister, can we write to them?"

"Ha, no boy, this is war. We don't write or pay visits to the enemy, ha, wait until we have won this war".

Karl smirks in the background. Senior Sister Hartman turns very serious, looks at her papers,

"As from today you are both wards of the German Reich, many boys would want to be in your shoes.

The school fees will be waived; a regulation allowance will be generously given to you as pocket money, providing you both behave yourselves. You're too old for adoption; you will stay at your school. You're twins I see...how old are you both?"

Ron puts his hand up again,

"Nine, almost ten Sister".

The Sister gets slightly warmer,

"We will expect to join the `Young Folk' on your next birthday. I'm going to look out for you two....Now look at these".

Sister Rothe hands the boys their Certificates of Arian German Nationality. She turns cold and official and says,

> "Note the numbers on the top of the page. They are your Aryan certification numbers. You will never forget them, I assure you".

Ron holds his hands up for a question, the Sister nods.

Ron, looking at the nameplate on the desk, then at Karl he says,

> "Senior Sister Hartman, what about those boys who want to beat us up for being English?"

Senior Sister Hartman, stands up and bangs the table with the flat of her hand making everyone jump, she yells shouting,

> "You're not English, you're German. What are you boy?"
> "German, Senior Sister Hartman, German".

Hartman sits down and smiles,

> "Good, now I'm going to read to you what I have written on your reports...then we will be all done here".

She finishes writing, blots her signature with a rocking blotter, leans back and adjusts her glasses and starts to read,

> "The twin Lambert boys have advantageous Nordic traits, their physical appearance is a harmonious blend of Nordic,
> Germanic and British types. They are therefore pure Aryans".

She smiles at her wordage, looks up at the boys saying,

> "Well congratulations, young Germans, from now on there will be no more chains. Now before these papers are legal we need one more signature on each certificate and photographs".

She turns to Karl and tosses him the key,

> "Sergeant, do you know the Lebensborn head office on the Herzog-Max-Strasse? It used to be the old headquarters of the Jewish Community".

Karl nods,

> "Well take them over there and get the signatures, ask for Sister Schafstaller. I will telephone her about you. She knows what to do....That's it,
> Heil Hitler".

Ron blurts out,

> "Thank you Sister, we have been here for three days and haven't been fed a bite to eat. We are very hungry".

She smiles,

> "Well you must eat, you should have eaten before you came here. We are not a restaurant".

She looks at Sister Rothe,

> "Get the boys fed a proper meal before they leave".

She tosses Karl the key to the chains and he unlocks them. Sister Schafstaller waves them away.

The boys eat a hearty lunch in the SS. staff canteen then make their way across the city with a spring in their step and arrive at the cinemas on the Herzog-Max-Strasse.

The new film at the UFA-Palast is posted outside 'Auf Wiedersehen Franziska' with Marianne Hoppeand. Ron points out to Karl the films are free to boys under sixteen,

"We could see 'Stukas' and 'Ride for Germany'."

Karl shakes his head. The Kursaal Theater on Kaufinger Strasse is showing a film about Frederick the Great. Karl asserts his rank and says,

"Forget the cinema".

They find the Lebensborn Headquarters. There are a lot of girls waiting around the reception area, blond girls not like the usual Bavarian women who tend to be short, stout and darkish.

These were blond, tall, very Nordic looking, real Aryans.

Karl pushes his sealed envelope across the counter at a pleasant woman. He asks for Sister Schafstaller.

They get sent down in to the basement. Her office is like a large white medical room and has a surgical couch in the center. Sister Schafstaller opens the sealed envelopes and while she reads the files the young male assistant takes the Lambert brothers photographs.

The Sister asks the twins to wait outside for a moment while she talks to Karl. After a few moments Karl pokes his head out of the door. Grinning, he asks the boys to come in.

Ron is asked to stand by the radiator. Slyly, Karl slips a handcuff around Ron's wrist; the other end is already locked onto a heavy steel bracket supporting the hot water pipe of the radiator.

Ron starts to pull at the handcuffs and shouts to Ken to run.

Ken takes his chance and jumps over the desk scattering all the papers and makes for the door but Karl takes a flying leap and tackles him round his skinny waist, they both crash to the floor. Karl grabs Ken in a neck lock and forces him back on to the couch. The Sister lifts up the backrest, turns Ken around so his legs are running up the backrest and his head is flat on the base of the bed. Ron yells,

"What are you going to do? What are you going to do to my brother? You, hey you brown witch, leave him alone".

Karl straps Ken's ankles to the head of the couch and puts a pillow under his head then holds on to his skinny shoulders while the assistant gets a firm grip on Ken's feet. The Sister looks over her shoulder at Ron shouting, strides over to him, thrusts her fist toward his face and says threateningly,

"You shut up...another word out of you and you will get a taste of my stick, hard across your backside. We are not going to hurt him...Just shut up. We can make this easy for you both, or we can do it the hard way and the hard way will hurt. It is going to be done, so shut up!"

The Sister pushes a steel trolley with a white cloth covering the top close to the couch. Ron yells,

"Black Pigs!"

She turns around pointing at Ron,

"Do you understand? Shut up".

She then starts to set out her instruments, putting small shiny parts together. Ron strains to see, pulling at the handcuffs.

She looks at Ken and smiles,

"Now just keep still, we have to put some little numbers on your foot. If you move about, it will hurt very much. Relax, keep still and it will all be over very soon".

Karl holds onto Ken's shoulders. Ken's left foot is tied tight with straps and the assistant holds onto his right foot. Ken just gives up and stops struggling. She pulls off his boot and sock and paints the sole of his foot with some yellow liquid.

The Sister checks her papers, sets the tattoo needle to its maximum strike depth of 5mm, and starts the tattoo pen buzzing.

The first number is deeply tattooed on the instep of Ken's left foot; Karl covers his mouth with a small white face cloth muffling his screams. Ken screams in pain again, this time through his nose gasping for breath.

He falls into a state of unconsciousness just as the last of the eight numbers are deeply engraved. Ron's yelling subdues, pulling on the handcuffs but he gives up and sits on the floor.

When the Sister is finished she wipes Ken's pink bloody foot and admires her penmanship. The straps are undone and a big white plaster is put on his foot. Ken is sat up, his head lolling over to one side. Smelling salts are waved under his nose. As he comes around and wakes up he suddenly feels the pain and grabs his left foot crying out:

"Oh, shit that hurts so much. Oh, Ow,

You fucking bits of black shit".

The assistant looks at Ken. Glaring, he strides over to him.

Ken holds his face, eyes closed, to receive the expected blow, his face all screwed up, teeth clenched, waiting.

"Go on, let's see how strong you are, asshole.

You can kick little boys...Go on, have a go.

give me a good whack, no charge, it's free".

The assistant just laughs and walks over to Ron where Karl and the Sister are waiting, expecting a big struggle. Ron just holds his hand out for the key to the handcuffs. Ron says quietly smiling,

"It's alright, I won't struggle. I don't need a pair of un-trained thugs to hold me down either".

Karl hands him the key. Ron unlocks himself, walks over to Ken and gives him a big hug, then jumps on to the couch, lies down and puts his feet up to the top of the backrest. He picks up the little white towel, rolls it like a sausage and sets it between his teeth.

The Sister does her job; Ron bites hard on the towel and screams through his nose as Karl holds on to his feet.

Outside in the corridor Karl smiles and tries to explain to the twins,
"Well congratulations to our new Germans, I had no way of knowing that we were going to be put through all this tattooing stuff and be kept without food so long. We now have to get back to school as soon as possible".

Ken snarls,
"Well, how come you didn't get your foot done then?"

Ron and Ken hobble down the school hall with a crutch each. They stop outside the classroom. Each boy has his left boot in his hand. Ken stops Ron from opening the door,
"Oh, Ron, how long will it hurt like this?"

Ron looks at an imaginary watch on his wrist and smiles.
"Mmm, until tomorrow, at about one-thirty".

Ken answers,
"Not before that! You were very brave".
"You would have done the same if I had been first".

Ken says doubtfully,
"I would?"

The boys enter the classroom and quietly hobble to their desk.

A new young master watches them struggle to get settled down.

He walks over to them and says,
"I'm Herr Weigland, your new math teacher. Welcome Back. You're the Lambert brothers, I presume. What did they do to you?"

Ken lifts his foot to show his plaster as Ron leans forward and gently peels it off. The very swollen instep boasts Ken's new numbers. The class quietly gathers around to see. Dieter says horrified,
"Did it hurt?"

"Yes, a lot" Ken says with quiet conviction.

Dieter gently holds Ken's foot for the class to see and says,
"Wow do we all get these?"

Weigland sends the rest of the class back to their seats.
"No, there will be a school announcement about this at assembly on Monday. You will all know about it then..."
"You two go to your beds. I will order some cocoa and a pill to take away the pain".

The boys get up and hobble painfully to the door. Karl enters smiling,

"Whose next girls?"

The class looks at Karl with apprehension; Weigland waves Karl to shut up with a sharp finger movement and shouts after the twins kindly,

"Keep those feet dry, No showers...Hans, Dieter: you two go and get those new German Wards of this school some aspirins and hot chocolate. You should be very proud to be their friends."

7. JUNG VOLK

The whole school is singing the German National Anthem in the great hall, the boys with their arms raised in Nazi salutes.

Ken, Ron and Hans are not singing. The school sits down for their meal. The food is particularly good today and there is a festive atmosphere. All the teachers' tables have fresh flowers.

Blood banners and flags have been hung. A tall bust of Hitler in bronze is set at the side of the stage. Large Hitler Youth banners drape the main wall. The boys eat in total silence. When the meal is finished Dr. Weiss stands and slowly walks to the edge of the stage, folds his arms and waits for the last knife and fork to stop clattering. He places a hand to his ear, listening.

"Silence, that's good, every meal we eat, we will eat in total silence, understood? Good. You boys are a very superior collection of young students, now that we have weeded out some Jews and inferiors.

Each one of you Pure Aryans are the future of Germany. Be proud of yourselves, your school and Germany. Every day we start fresh. Be true to the bread of the Fatherland and our people will live forever".

"Now, first I want to introduce some new faces to you all. Captain Mitter, my second in command. Teachers, Herr Strote, Herr Weigland, Father Flanner and Matron Frau Claria.

These new teachers are not just teachers, they are physically and spiritually 'Masters of Life'...The other teachers you already know. New Hitler Youth Sergeants Karl Kaltenbrunner, Gunter Swatz and Dieter Wolff, they all hold rank and will be obeyed without question, is that understood? The others you already know".

He looks at the matron, who nods back at him,

"Now I hear the Hitler Youth and Young Folk uniforms have arrived. The gray suits, caps and school badges you are wearing have been banned as from today. Hitler Youth or Young Folk uniforms will be the dress code from now on, you will all receive them as soon as they can be issued...the cost will be charged to your parents.

Two sets will be issued to you then a third set for parade best. To destroy or damage them will be considered a gross insult to the Fatherland and will bring forth-harsh punishment to the offender. At no time will you be permitted to wear civilian clothes".

A murmur rumbles through the school that Weiss permits without chastisement. He stands looking at the boys; when he gets his total quiet he says,

> "Books Of cultural decadence and false ideas of freedom were
> banned and indeed burned way back in May 1933 because they
> were considered unworthy filth. We have found copies of these
> books in the libraries of this school. They will be burned
> together with the old school uniforms in one fire.
> A complete list of banned books is posted for your attention.
> Next week, anyone found with these books will be punished. I
> want all of this harmful and undesirable literature by anti-
> German writers and the gray clothes you are all wearing burned
> on an enormous bonfire. We will start making the pile today".

A cheer led by the new teachers on the stage rips through the school. Ken looks at his brother and whispers,

> "I didn't know we had dirty books in the libraries".
> "They're not dirty books they're decadent books".
> "What's decadent?"

The murmuring and whispering quiets down and Dr. Weiss holds his hand up for silence and smiles his half leer.

> "Now, I have something very pleasant to announce. Will the
> twin brothers, Lambert R and Lambert K. from platoon 'Two
> A Lower', stand up on the table, and let's have a good look at
> you both".

Ron and Ken are very surprised; they struggle to their feet very apprehensively, then onto the table. Dieter and Hans help, passing their crutches up to them. Ron looks at Ken,

> "Now what?"

Weiss says warmly,

> "These two young German-born brothers have
> been abandoned by their British father and Austrian mother.
> But we want them… Germany needs them.

They are now wards of the state. They have just been awarded their Certificates of German Aryan purity; they are therefore, racially pure German… We salute them both. Congratulations pure young Aryan Germans, welcome to the strongest brotherhood in the world!"

Dr. Weiss starts to clap, the staff joins in, and then the whole school joins the applause. Dieter beams a smile, helps them down and winks at the twins handing each boy a copy of Hitler's book, 'Mein Kampf'. Ron holds the book in the air and all the boys in the hall cheer. Ron yells, "Heil Benny Goodman".

Then he looks to see who has heard, but only Hans understands the slur and laughs out loud.

Ken Looks to Ron with the look that says 'Question?' Ron nods back and Ken whispers in his ear,

"They didn't go to England without us did they Ron?"

Ron shakes his head,

"You don't believe that for one moment...Do you? ".

Ken smiles and shakes his head; he just wanted what he believed confirmed by Ron. Dr. Weiss holds up his hand again,

"Let us not forget our new members, the league of Young German Maidens, Frau Claria's fresh breeze of young flowers".

Weiss points over to a table of twenty young blond girls aged from fourteen to eighteen, all dressed in brown and white uniforms. There are cheers from the bigger boys. Doctor Weiss continues,

> "Here is a new order that hasn't been posted on the board yet....As from today, all sports and outdoor activities are being increased by three hundred percent. Heil Hitler".

A wild cheer goes up. Dr. Weiss and the teachers leave the hall.

The boys come up and pat Ken and Ron on their backs with warm congratulations. All this adoration goes slightly to Ken's head.

He tries to return the salutes. Ron is not too keen and is very skeptical.

They get carried out on the shoulders of Dieter and Gunter. Ken leans over to his brother,

"What larks Ron, what great larks".

Ron grins and mimes, "Heil Benny Goodman".

The cheering boys carry the twins on their shoulders out to the corridor through to the big notice board in the front hall.

It has the list of banned writers from all over the world. The boys get lowered to their feet. Dieter thumbs through the pages and the lists of names, he gasps,

> "Look, Albert Einstein, Ernest Hemingway, Jack London, Thomas Mann, Karl Marx, H.G. Wells, Marcel Proust, Emile Zola; and Look Ken, Mark Twain your favorite...It's stupid, stupid, stupid".

Ken looks and sadly thinks,

> "I didn't know Mark Twain wrote any dirty books. I will have to make a copy of all these in my diary".

HJ belt buckle

HJ field compass

HJ knife with sheaf.

Young Folk at a Nazi book fair.

Jung Volk camping out.

It's 5am and dark outside, Dieter bangs a steel bar on a large empty 88mm-artillery shell case and it rings like a great bell.

He yells to wake the boys as he strides down the center of the dormitory, naked except for a towel around his waist. A few boys sit upright still stunned. Some boys keep on sleeping even through the racket of the bell. Dieter marches down the row of beds lifting the foot of each one and then dropping it with a bang. He pulls the bedclothes off the curled up boys. Some fall sleepily out of bed and curl up on the floor. Dieter shouts,

> "It's five o'clock you lazy lot, it's Monday morning. Stand by your beds! Stand by your beds! Strip naked, towels in your left hands... Come on out of those wank-pits and on your feet".

When all the boys are in a two lines, one on each side of the room, their towels in their left hands, Dieter marches to the door and yells,

"Good, quick march: left, right, left, right".

The whole platoon marches to the showers. One boy still has his shirt on. Dieter grabs him,

"Come on, you don't put clean clothes on until you have washed your smelly bodies. Get it off, into the showers, left, right, left, right".

The boys are marched into the showers. Dieter adjusts the water temperature of the main control and yells,

"Soap the armpits, soap up under your bums and dinkies and don't forget behind your ears".

They all get dressed in their new Young Folk uniforms; Dieter adjusts the boys' scarves and cross straps. Each boy makes his bed and stands at the foot of it. Dieter waits until he is totally satisfied that they are correctly dressed in their new uniforms with their beds made properly before he marches them all off to breakfast.

The boys enter the great hall, it looks different.

All the senior boys that are over fourteen are now dressed in the Hitler Youth winter uniforms. Dark blue long pants that are laced at the ankles, a blouse and a ski cap of the same material, cross straps and belts with the camp knife on the left side of their waist. On their left arms they wear the red and white striped swastika armbands.

The younger boys ten to fourteen are all dressed in Young Folk uniforms almost the same but with short pants and an 'S' rune badge on their left upper sleeve in place of the swastika. The whole room smells of new uniforms. Ken touches Ron's hand,

"Look at us, what do we all look like? Does this mean we are in the Hitler Youth now? Can they just put the uniform on us, just like that, we're not ten yet!"

Ron whispers back,

> "No, we are in the Young Folk, bloody cannon fodder that's what we are, bloody cannon fodder".

Ken lowers his voice,
    "Well, they might have asked us if we wanted to join.
    They didn't even ask. So, we're in right?
    When do we get the camp knives and badges then?"

Ron puts his finger up to his lips,   "Shhh".
It's a good breakfast, a big plate of hot porridge, sticky buns that are stuffed with slices of sausage. Big white jugs filled with steaming hot chocolate. The whole room eats in silence. The only sound is the clatter of crockery.
    After breakfast, the usual flag ceremony and singing of the national anthem, the school marches through the echoing stone corridors to their classrooms. The sound of marching boots has changed and become more military sounding since all the boys in the school have been issued with two pairs of new boots each. Their civilian boyish shoes have all been put away at the bottom of their lockers.

    After a party meeting at the Racial Office Dr. Bernhard Rust has issued an edict to the youth and all of Germany's educators:
        "The Jews are our misfortune. Racial instructions are to be taught to all ages in all classrooms".
When the twins' platoon arrives in the classroom, there is no teacher so the boys talk among themselves. Dieter and Gunter set up three large charts with flip over pages. The first picture is a profile of a Jewish-looking man who has a large hooknose and a stoop. The door opens and Herr Strote strides in.
    He's a large balding man with a brutish face. Gunter jumps up and shouts…
        "Attention… Heil Hitler. Good morning Herr Strote".
    The class all jump to their feet, Strote says quietly,
        "Heil Hitler. Soon, we will all be saluting like this.
    All in good time. You will all be taught".
    Strote looks hard at Gunter and flings his heavy coat onto his desk. Gunter runs and grabs it and hangs it on the back of the door then comes to attention again,
        "Yes sir, I will teach them how to salute properly".
    Strote sits himself in his chair and puffs out his chest,
        "Now, you boys, be true to the Fatherland
        and our people will live forever.
        So, here are some never to be forgotten people you will be
        hearing about in my class. Nibelungenlied, Faust, Egmount,
        Schiller, Siegfried, Wagner, Beethoven and Mozart. But first".

Strote struts over to the boards that have been set up and slaps one
with a pointer stick,
"Jews, who knows a Jew?"
He looks around the class with a sneer,
"No one knows any Jews? No, you had one teaching you last
week… Jews have not been legal citizens in Germany since
September 1935. They should not have taught in this school.
They are members of an inferior alien race".
Strote wanders over to the window, gazes off outside and says,
"You know the Cuckoo is the Jew of the birds.
A Jew looks a bit like a Cuckoo. Its hooked beak is like the
hook of a Jews nose. Its feet are small and unsteady that's why
it can't walk very well on the ground. The Jew does not walk
well either; he stoops and wrings his hands a lot. An Aryan
walks upright and proud like an Eagle, a true winner".
Strote spins around and points to a boy and yells.
"Wouldn't you be ashamed to buy from a Jew? Yah!"
He regains his composure and continues.
"Racial science has proved they are not like us…
So what are the differences?"
He doesn't expect an answer. He flips the chart over and bangs it
with his pointer again, making the boys jump. The chart has pictures of
Jewish noses and exaggerated profiles of Jews with round shoulders. He
pulls the front lid off a glass case that is standing on the desk revealing a
variety of wax noses and ears. Strote turns around and points at Hans.
"You boy, how can you spot a Jew?"
Hans looks blankly, Strote ignores him, points his finger at Gunter.
Gunter grins, stands up and walks around the class with a stoop, sways a
lot, wringing his hands in wild gestures. The boys all laugh. Strote smiles
and waves Gunter back to his seat. He points to Hans, who then stands
up grinning saying,
"They wear a big yellow star sir".
The class laughs; Strote smiles and strides back up to his charts.
"Yes, not bad, but now they are shaving off their beards, trying
to pass as humans. When Jews shave their faces for the very
first time in their lives, they get a bad razor rash and that my
lads is what gives them away".
"Black coat and always-good shoes. The young Jew boys stick
to their father's side, girls always walk behind their men… Trust
no Jew, he will stab you in the back for the price of a glass of
beer. Watch for their noses, just look and you will see they are
shaped like the upside down figure six. That is a sign of their
Jewishness… Jews are very different from us, look".

Strote returns to the blackboard and writes,
"There are three classifications of man:

Ourselves	- Nordic
Subhuman	- Slavs
Antihuman	- Jews."

Strote spins around and throws his chalk at a boy who is staring out of the window,

"Jewish blood is not the same as ours. It's unhealthy to mix the blood. Can you imagine a German Nordic beauty like this..."

Strote flips over one of the charts revealing a full length photograph of a young Nordic girl, her long blond hair covering just one breast of her naked body. There are gasps of amazement from the boys as Strote continues,

"...going with and being sexually consumed by a dirty smelly antihuman Jew like this"?

Strote flips his chart over again. On the next board another full-length photograph of a naked male Jew, fat and very hairy, with black hair over most of his body, standing in a stooped ape-like posture. Strote takes on a look of total disgust.

The caption on the photo reads 'Jewish Antihuman' Strote sneers,

"Can you imagine your own sister being ravaged by this filth?
This is why we have race laws now, to prevent the likes of this antihuman buying the virtues of this beautiful young thing.
They do have a taste for our Nordic women. The rich ones try to buy them as mistresses".

Dieter puts his hand up to ask a question, Strote nods,

"Sir, where do they take the Jews that have been picked up by the SS?"

Strote walks over to Dieter leans too close to him,

"They are not picked up, they are asked to report and they do".

Strote closes in on Gunter; Gunter stands up. Strote walks around. "How old are you boy?"

"Just fifteen last week sir".

"So, you're old enough to know where the Jews go?"

"Yes sir, well, the young and fit go to work camps,
Families and old people go to Madagascar to a new all Jewish State, called Zion, Sir".

Strote nods in approval. Dieter puts up his hand again. Strote raises his black eyebrows and nods. Dieter stands up,

"Why Jews, Sir, why not the Lutherans or the Catholics?"

Strote says firmly,

"Lutherans and Catholics are real people,
they are practicing a religion, real people, like us...

Judaism is not a religion, it's a foul dirty race of anti-humans,
   like a higher breed of talking apes".

Strote flips the page on the easel to reveal a photograph of a young
naked teenage Jewish boy in his early adolescence. The caption on the
photograph reads 'Jewish Boy age 13'. His beard is just starting to grow.
Young boyish hair on his legs and under-arms is just sprouting. He stands
bent over his eyes cast down.   Strote using his pointer taps the
photograph on the young lads circumcised penis.

   "Look, how they mutilate their boys' manhood with
   circumcision when they are babies, this is a way of knowing a
   Jewish male".

Strote strides over to Gunter, beckons him to take off his shirt and
shorts, and then tells him to stand up on a chair in his underpants and
new boots....He points at Gunter with his stick,

   "This boy, aged just fifteen, is a striking example of Nordic
   purity. Look at the difference between him and the Jew Boy.
   Gunter is tanned, fit, stands upright and proud. He has fair hair,
   blue eyes, and a strong body. He will grow into a beautiful
   German. No facial or under-arm hair yet, that's as it should be.
   That will come in his late teens or early twenties. The Jew boy's
   photograph was taken on his thirteenth birthday. You see how
   mature his body is, look at all the black hair he has. On his
   chest his back, he is maturing very early just like apes. It's the
   racial difference; they are different from us. You can see he will
   grow into the ape like posture and shape of his father in the
   first picture".

Strote taps Gunter on his crotch with the pointer and laughs.

   "Ha, don't worry I'm not going to ask you to show your fellow
   classmates your uncut manhood".

The boys all laugh, Strote smiles saying quietly.

   "Gunter, it's your duty to our Fatherland to sire at least five
   babies for Hitler as soon as possible".

The boys react to Strote's observations, snigger and giggle.
Gunter blushes as he puts his shirt back on.

   "Nordic men and women are superior beings,
   don't you ever forget it".

Strote smiles and looks hard at the class, laughs out loud as he thinks
of a joke, smiling he points to Gunter,

   "Gunter, what do you think the shortest measurable unit of
   time is?"

Gunter grins and shakes his head. Strote glances around the class.
Ron gingerly puts up his hand. Strote nods to him. Ron takes a deep
breath and stands up,

   "The time it takes for a grade school teacher to change his

political views in favor of the Nazi Party, sir".
Strote laughs out loud and bellows,
"Yes…Ha, you know what side your bread is buttered.
So listen and remember all of you, it is your duty to report to
your sergeants any Jews you see, or know of.
No report is too small or too trivial. Keep your ears open, I
want to know about anyone who makes the slightest remark
against Germany or our Führer Adolf Hitler, my private door is
always open –
Heil Hitler".
Dieter grins and swings a friendly fist at Ken's head, but misses. He
motions them to sit down around him. When he has their attention he
pulls a notebook from his breast pocket.
"Mutprobe, have you heard of the Mutprobe?"
The three boys nod and Ken says,
"I thought we had to do that when we were fourteen, for the
HJ".
Dieter smiles and shakes his head,
"Oh no the Mutprobe is a test of courage for you JungVolk, if
you all pass you will be entitled to wear the camp knives, belts
and buckles. So you three are going on a route march and
navigation test, you will be going out in the forest on your own.
You three will have to elect a leader among yourselves. I will
give you your orders before you leave."

The seasons in the high alpine country change quickly. The
springtime passes into a warm summer and the boys find themselves
being trained with new and exciting challenges. The twins enjoy the Field
Craft Training. Small groups of boys, with one of them elected to be the
leader, are sent alone deep into the forest. Their assignment is to find a
prize, usually edible, that's in a tin and has been placed at a location in the
woods. The twins and Hans have learned to use maps, compasses and
pure navigation to find their way and to pinpoint their position in the
forest.
On a damp thundery Saturday morning the platoon stands in
line outside their hut, Dieter asks,
"Who's elected to be leader for your Mutprobe?"
Ron grins and salutes.
"Well Lambert here are your orders and a compass. Don't lose
it. I've signed for it, see you in three days boys".

The twins and Hans set out on their three-day Mutprobe test
enjoying their newfound confidence, wandering deep in the woods out of
the control of their leaders. It's their first three day tramp around the lake,

Ron is designated as the navigator. The field compass he carries is an expensive army issue instrument in its own leather case, worn on his belt. A matching leather map-case makes Ron feel like a true leader.

Overnight rations in their bread-bags: blankets, groundsheets, warm jackets in their rucksacks and spades, canteens and water bottles on their belts, the three looked like little alpine soldiers in short pants.

During the past few weeks, the boys had been measuring off their footsteps, seeing how many paces it takes to cover ten meters. They had come to the conclusion that a comfortable cross-country stride was eighteen paces in ten meters or one thousand eight hundred paces to a kilometer. Ron says.

"This is the point that will be the start of our first compass bearing to our next point, let's rest here".

Ken takes off his boots and socks and wades into the lake,

"Wow, this water's bloody cold, when do we eat, I'm starving... I wonder if there are any fish in this lake".

Ron says,

"What does it matter if there are fish here, we don't have a fishing rod or bait? Now, we have to go one kilometer south to a tree that has been struck by lightning".

Ken looks skeptical as he puts on his socks,

"I think it is going to rain... a lot".

Hans chips in,

"Yes I would say we are in for a good wetting, we should each pick some dry sticks while we can, keep them dry, for tonight".

The boys' scramble about picking up a pile of dead wood twigs and Ken wraps them in his ground sheet, making a big bundle.

"If I can carry the bundle upside down we will have a fire tonight. Hans, find some dry grass or moss, we should all fill our pockets and keep it dry".

Ron takes his first bearing with his compass and nods to the boys to follow. They barely go half a kilometer and it starts to rain, heavily. Ron drapes his ground sheets around himself while Ken and Hans share one. They plod on, Ron counting to himself, stopping to wipe the rain off the glass face of the compass as he takes a reading. As they get close to one kilometer Ron yells,

"We have to spread out or we may just miss this bloody tree. Look out for a tree that has been struck by lightning, and don't lose sight of me. You two will have to keep your eyes on me. I have to watch this compass....Don't lose me, spread out".

The rain is so heavy now the visibility is down to about two trees and Ron is walking holding the compass out in front of him.

After what seems to be a long time Hans yells out,

"Here it is, I found it, look over here".

The big old tree had been struck by lightning some years ago and is hollow. Inside the boys find a round large biscuit tin with surgical tape sealing it. Under the cover of Ron's cape Ken and Hans carefully peel off the tape and open the tin.

It has three large bread rolls; some chocolate biscuits and three large sausages cooked wrapped in greaseproof paper and a new map.

The boys make their camp in the rain using one groundsheet as a makeshift tent and Ken's bundle of dry wood as a backrest. They devour their supper of bread and sausage, and share out some of the chocolate biscuits. It is still raining hard when the boys huddle up together and try to get some sleep. Hans says, "Ken is soaked right through, but his wood is dry in his groundsheet, he should be squeezed in between us, look he's shivering, let's get him in the middle of us and we can keep him warm".

The boys shuffle around so that Ken is squashed in between them for warmth. Ken shivers and snuggles down under the blankets and says, "Mmm, that's better. If it stops raining wake me up and I will light a fire".

Ron starts to laugh,

"Anyone want soggy peas? I've got a pocket-full".

The rain gets softer through the night and the boys are too tired to talk. They just fall asleep, soaked through and through.

Bright sunshine squints through the wet dripping trees and awakes the boys. Ron jumps up and starts to sort out their wet things,

"Come on, we should make a big fire and dry out".

The boys sleepily crawl out of the sagging makeshift tent and stretch their arms feeling the warm sun.

Hans produces a coil of stout cord from his rucksack,

"Let's put up a line, to dry out all our things".

Ken shivers saying,

"No, let's start a big fire first".

The burned out hollow trunk has had numerous campfires set in it and is a big natural fire pit that's been burned out over the years. Ken piles his dry sticks and the moss from their pockets and soon there's a big fire blazing away. The warmth of the fire and the morning sun creates a cheerful mood in their little camp and the boys joke as they peel off all their wet clothes.

The line is set; pants, shirts, socks and underwear are strung out to dry. The boys sit around the fire naked trying to cook their potatoes on sticks, Ken whispers,

"Is yours done yet?"

Ron tries to stick his fork into his blackened potato to see if it is done, but it falls off the stick into the fire,

"Shit, look what you made me do now".

Hans says,

"Best to leave them in the ashes, I'll bet they will take at least an hour to do properly".

Ron rakes his potato deep into the ashes sending a shower of sparks into the air swirling towards Ken's naked body; he leaps up yelling,

"I suppose you know all about cooking potatoes Hans?"

"Actually, yes I do, we should have boiled them before we left and all we would have to do is warm them up in the ashes of the fire. Raw ones will take about one and a half hours to cook properly all the way through".

"So why didn't you tell us this before we left the school?"

Hans grins,

"You didn't ask."

"So next time we boil them first."

"I don't mind them a bit on the raw side".

Ken takes a nibble at his blackened potato. The sun gets stronger cutting through the trees warming their little camp. The boys eat and stretch out on their ground sheets to warm themselves and dry out. They fall asleep in the warmth of the fire and the sunshine.

Hans Kardorff, the twins' closest friend, is the son of a very proud SS Colonel, a true Nazi. Hans is the Colonel's only son and one of his life's biggest disappointments. At the Christmas dinner in the regimental officer's dining room some of the Officers had their wives and grown children at the table. The boys over ten years of age were all in uniforms. Hans' father had bought him a Young Folk uniform and told him to be sure to have it on when he came to the Regimental Dinner on Christmas day. Well Hans lived up to his father's disappointment and showed up in his old gray school uniform. He complained that the Young Folk uniform didn't fit very well and there were no badges or insignia sewn on the shirt yet.

It was a great loss of face for his father. He was very glad the boy was at that boarding school, perhaps they could make something out of him. Hans was a Mummy's boy, but his mother died when Hans was six, she might have turned him into something. Hans wasn't what his father had in mind as Germany's hope for the future.

He wasn't at all athletic, hated all outdoor activity and was only happy when he had his nose into a good science or chemistry book. He disliked the military, found it very hard to keep step when being marched.

He seemed to have two left feet and had a habit of swinging his arms a half pace out of time with the rest of the platoon, so he was a target and would get yelled at. Then he would fall to pieces and cry. His strong glasses gave him the air of a bookworm.

The greatest love in Hans' life was his passion for American Swing. He had five very precious records of Benny Goodman, Glen Miller and the guitarist with a finger missing, Django Reinhardt.

He steamed the American labels off the records and saved them in his family photo album, it had few photographs but lots of pictures of swing stars and the bandleader Benny Goodman. American swing music was banned at the school so he replaced the original record labels with labels that said 'French for beginners' and 'English Conversation'. His old electric record player had a special modification Ken built to plug in four pairs of headsets with the main loudspeaker turned off.

He would sit around with his friends and listen to jazz with the French books open as if they were all learning a foreign language.

Few knew any better. Ron and Ken liked Hans because under that untidy and disheveled exterior was a very bright and clever little scientist, and he needed protection because he was totally incapable of defending himself against the smallest boy in the school. He was also right about the potatoes, as the boys found when they chewed on the raw charred remains of what was left of them.

Hans is the first to wake up; they have all slept for almost two hours naked in the sunshine. He sits up staring at the twins who are still fast asleep; Ron curled with his head on Ken's chest and Ken holding on to his brother's waist. Hans is amazed just how alike the brothers are and how they look even more identical lying there naked in the sun. Four identical feet, hands arm and legs, he had never looked at them before like this, it was hard to tell who was who.

The rest of the trip goes fairly smoothly, the boys following the clues they find in the tin. The map eventually leads them back to the lake and to the school. They make their report to Dieter and give him the empty tin. Dieter beams at them,

"Fifteen kilometers, not bad for your first solo overnight, did you keep dry?"

Ron digs Ken and says,

"Well no, but we made a nice fire in the tree".

"Well you had better get in the showers".

"It's Heim tonight and your awards".

The twins grin, Ron and Hans go off to return the compass and gear and Ken says,

"See you both in the showers, I'll warm them up".

Ken arrives at the sodden desolation of the empty showers.

He turns on three of the heads to let the warm water run through. The smell of damp, mildew and antiseptic is mixed with the tinge of metal. He wanders along the row of seat-less bowls looking for the cleanest one to sit on. He sits and his eyes wander around. Scabrous graffiti with naughty phrases are scrawled on the walls despite constant erasure and dire threats of severe punishment from the authorities. The large bathroom is bleak, cavernous and chilly with its sloping cement floors that are always very slippery. Sitting there, Ken wonders where it all goes when he flushes the toilet.

Steam is billowing from the showers. Ron and Hans burst in. As Ken gets up from the toilet Ron yells,

"Let's get soaped up quick before his stink reaches us".

The three boys enjoy the hot water and soon forget about the smells, yelling obscene jokes and piling ridicule on each other. Dieter enters,

"What's all this noise? You Lambert's,

clean this place up...toilet basins too".

When the boys arrive at the Heim that evening they find Dieter and Captain Mitter sitting at the table. In front of them, lined up like soldiers are the three new camp knives still in their greasy brown triangular wrappers. Three belts with cross straps and the Hitler Youth belt buckles, all gleaming.

A few words from Captain Mitter about wearing them with honor then Dieter stands up and presents Hans and the Twins with their awards. Younger boys who have yet to earn their knives gather around to feel how sharp they are, and to watch their names and numbers get deeply stamped into the handles. Dieter supervises the fitting of the belts, the position of the knife and the adjustments of the cross straps. Ron says.

"Well we are in now, horrible little Nazis all three of us."

Dieter frowns and points a finger at Ron, who knows he has pushed Dieter as far as he can for today, and shuts up.

On Saturday night, in a field behind the school the pile of uniforms and books have been stacked with broken desks, old chairs and other burnable bits of junk. Then it is all doused in petrol.

Karl, who is in charge of the whole operation, is trying to get the less than enthusiastic crowd to sing, but only a few of the boys from the school turn out to see the lighting ceremony.

So when Karl throws the lighted bundle of rags onto the petrol soaked stack of books and old school uniforms, there isn't much of a cheer. Then as the clothing made from wool and cotton catches fire a cloud of black smoke chases away most of the spectators.

Dieter, Hans and the twins sit under the big old chestnut tree at a safe distance and laugh at Karl's puny efforts to make the burning into some sort of occasion.

Karl thought that everyone would turn out to watch the biggest bonfire the school had ever had, so he didn't issue an order to attend. He wished he had, he knew his occasion was turning into a flop, so he went scurrying about trying to round up as many small boys as he could and ordered them to watch. When the flames were at their highest there were only twenty or thirty onlookers. The darkness hid the failure of Karl's occasion and no adult teachers showed up at all.

On the annual three day trip to Munich, Dieter's platoon visits the Science museum, art galleries and they attend a political parade where they need a lot of Hitler Youth to show off to the press.

The platoons are housed in a school gymnasium with two hundred other boys all under fourteen from Munich and its suburbs. In total charge is a very staunch Nazi Matron, Fraulein Knoll. She has a short haircut and a scrubbed ruddy face with rosy cheeks. A strong buxom Russian-looking woman, she is immaculate in her white uniform as she herds the boys from breakfast to the hall or out naked to the bathrooms for showers. She clips the boys around their ears or gives them a smack on their bare bottoms if they talk or stray behind. Her voice echoes in the tiled halls and showers with a screech that could shatter glass. The boys have a nickname for her; they call her 'Fraulein Kristall', Miss Broken Glass.

One boy, a local student who is regularly supervised by the woman, tells Ron and Ken that when Munich had its first air raids back in June, she went to pieces in the shelter during the bombing and spent most of the raid in and out of the toilet.

Every day there is an air raid practice drill just to see how long it takes to get six hundred boys into the shelters.

During one of the drills Ron makes up a little plot with Ken who nods to Dieter to look inside his jacket. Dieter says,

"What's that?"

"Red carbon paper".

"Carbon Paper, what's that?"

"You know it's used to make copies on the typewriter- It's for the toilet in the shelter."

Ron replaces the toilet paper in the air raid shelter with the red carbon paper and Ken unscrews the red light bulb in the little 'Air Raid on' sign, the sign that's switched on only during a real raid, and sticks a wad of silver paper under the light bulb.

When the sirens wail the next day for a real air raid most of the boys in Dieter's platoon are delighted. They laugh and giggle as they walk fast to the air raid shelter. They don't care that the RAF is bombing the BMW works. The word is around about the carbon paper in the toilet.

When all the boys are in the shelter deep underground, Fraulein Knoll counts the heads, then slams the big iron doors shut and turns the switch for the 'Air Raid On' sign to light up. There is a flash and all the lights go out, a cheer goes up from the darkness in the shelter. Fraulein Knoll feels her way down to the toilet and shuts herself in. As the sound of the bombs falling on Munich starts to rumble and shake the shelter the boys start to sing and shout---

"No butter for our eats,
Our pants, they have no seats,
Not even paper in the loo,
Hitler- we don't know why we follow you?
Tommy in the RAF, please don't drop your bombs on us,
We're young German school boys, we don't want war or fuss,
Berlin's where you ought to be, to make old Adolf duck,
Drop them on his bunker and make him eat his muck.
They're coming for you Fraulein Kristall.
They're coming, they're coming, they're coming"

When the raid is over and the iron doors are opened all the boys stream out, but instead of running out in all directions, they all hang about at the doors waiting for Fraulein Kristall to emerge. When she does, she's her old self again shouting at the boys to get out of the way. But this time her face and hands are all crimson red from the die of the carbon paper she has used in the toilet. All the boys fall about laughing. She shouts even louder because she is still unaware of her own red face.

8. CONKERS

Three winters pass into the warm springtime of 1942 with little real news of the war filtering through to the boys at Lindenburg College. They hear only what the 'Youth Hour' wants them to hear.

The Lambert brothers have grown and are now almost twelve years old. Foreign radio stations and newspapers are forbidden, so the boys find out about the news anyway they can sometimes listening to the illegal radios at night under the teachers open windows and whisper to each other about what is going on in the rest of the world. The whispers spread through the school ear to ear. The pro-Nazi boys embellishing the German victories and the traitors (None Nazis) boast the advances of the Allies.

Their mornings are filled with school subjects followed by vigorous team outdoor sports activities in the afternoons. Weekends the boys work on local farms or go out on campfire cookouts, adventurous field trips, war games, where they learn infantry tactics and how to plot the position of the other platoons with maps and compasses.

One afternoon Dieter and the twins wander in to the large hall and notice a small crowd of boys gathered around the notice board. The excitement is caused by a charts and new orders. Dieter using his height and rank pushes his way through the complaining boys.

He studies the board for a bit then reads aloud.

(1) New Maneuver Sport for all boys.

(2) Close formation drill.

"Well we do plenty of that already".

(3) Taking cover, camouflaging, staying hidden

"That's new. Look at all this stuff…"

(4) Indian club throwing for accuracy.

"Ha, Clubs, they mean the peaceful sport of throwing grenades for accuracy".

Dieter looks about him to see if any one who matters overheard. Ron makes his way to the board and points saying,

"Shit look at the distances we are supposed to march now; for us, age eleven to twelve years old ten sodden kilometers in a day! Marching in full equipment with sodden great packs on our backs...when are we going to get time to do all that shit?!"

Ken sighs,

"Look at this one 'Cross-country and endurance running…'

What's endurance running, run until you drop dead? "

Ron points at the list of special training courses saying it is compulsory for every boy to take at least one and earn a badge.
Ron says,

> "Look Ken you'd better take the 'First Aid Medical' course, one of us should know about that doctoring stuff. It might come in handy if we get into a war zone".

Ken smiles,

> "They give you a badge too, look 'Feldscher' (Field Surgeon)"

Hans arrives and says,

> "Feldscher...Feldscher...isn't that just a bit medieval, they had them as doctors in wars way back in seventeen twelve. They killed more of the poor bloody wounded than they saved ".

Ken shrugs,

> "Well while I am learning to sew you lot up I won't be doing any long marches, and at least I will get to wear a Red Cross badge if I pass".

Ron puts his arm around his brother,

> "You will pass. Ken loves patching people up don't you? He would like nothing better than to put stitches in someone's open and painful cut".

Ken pouts quietly,

> "There's nothing wrong in wanting to help people who are in pain is there?"

Ken passes his First Aid course, earns his badge, and is presented with a small medical kit that gets mostly used to treat sore feet and blisters from the boys extra marching.

Ron wins an Advanced Navigation Map-craft badge. Dieter laughs,

> "One twin will be able to get us all lost and navigate us to fall in to a ravine; and the other can patch us up if we are able to crawl out".

Despite Dieter's sarcastic remarks, the twins take a keen interest in the all the outdoor wilderness survival training.

The survival training is very comprehensive. The boys learn how to live off the land, make fire without matches and trap small game for the pot. Ken practices putting a few stitches in the live rabbits before they are killed for the stew.

They are taught what you can or cannot eat that grows in the wild.

They learn that a hand-full of Acorns has just as much nutritional value as a pound of hamburger but they have to be boiled a few times to get rid of the bitter toxic taste. A tin mug full of Pine needles, chopped and boiled into a tea, and then left to seep for five minutes, contains more vitamin C than two fresh-squeezed oranges.

Grasses, chewed and spit out are rich in protein. It's all out there, they are taught to live off what they can find and survive.

The three-week intensive course ends with a test in the form of a short survival march. Each boy is given a map and an objective deep in the woods. He has to live alone and off the land for ten days, running trap lines for small game and birds and eating the plants and roots he finds on the way.

The survival course is the first time the twins have been split up, so it is especially hard on Ken who always followed Ron's leadership.

On his third day alone Ken comes to a river. He is so hungry he just sits looking at the emergency food package that is sealed and not supposed to be eaten; the instructor's voice rings in his ears:

"If any boy opens the seal on the emergency food package too early, he will lose points, you don't know what sort of country you will be going through so it's a test of your own self-discipline"

Ken is now faced with the real prospect of living in the wild on what he can find to eat. He has set seven rabbit snares using all the fine wire he was given and has spent the afternoon stuffing his bread bag with the odd fistful of wild asparagus, the young fiddle tops of bracken ferns and bulrush roots. Peering under the large leaves of the burdock plant he finds its small tender young leaves. With his bread-bag now crammed almost full of greens he starts to explore the banks of a small river.

There is a large bed of stinging nettles. He had learned all about stinging nettles, how nutritious they are after the sting has been boiled out of them.

"I must cut a big stick to beat down the old nettles; I need a stout digging stick anyway to dig for roots"

In a little clearing by the river, he prepares to light a fire using a flint stick he has carried on a leather bootlace around his neck (the flint stick is a strictly forbidden item on this exercise; the boys are supposed to make fire without matches or lighters).

So with some dried moss he carries in his pocket he tries to light his fire. He makes a small ball out of the moss and sheltering it from the wind with his knees, strikes the flint stick with his camp knife. A shower of sparks shoots everywhere except in to the ball of moss, he scrapes the flint again and again, no flame.

"The moss must be damp!"

He rummages through his bread bag and finds a folded piece of school notepaper. Unwraps it sheltering it with his open jacket from the damp moisture laden wind.

There, in the paper is a flat compressed block of very dry cotton-wool that Ron has stolen from the infirmary,

"That's the best stuff to catch a flame from a flint stick, if you
keep it dry". Ron had said,
His brothers' words in his ear, Ken takes a little, and pulls it in to a
little square blanket and folds the rest up to keep dry.

This time he winds the leather lace around his finger to get a better
grip on the short flint stick and strikes hard and true with the top edge of
his knife. The sparks shoot into the cotton and it smolders into a small
blue flame. Quickly he starts to blow into the tiny smoldering wad and
then as if by magic, it bursts into flames. Soon there is a cheerful fire.
The warmth puts him in a better mood.

When the flames have died down and the fire is safe to leave, he
goes off to look for a thick stick. He cuts himself a stout pole and sits
down and sharpens one end, burns it in the fire embers to make it hard
for digging out roots.

But now to attack the tall stinging nettles, he imagines he is a lone
Knight swinging his stick left and right like a two handed sword; slashing
and cutting the heads off the attacking dreaded yellow hoards from
Mongolia. He's winning, he is the victor, and he has killed hundreds,
chopping them down, clearing a section of the stinging plants.

After a while he sits down exhausted wondering how he was going
to pick the young plants he has exposed without getting stung. Cutting
some large burdock leaves to protect his hands from stings he gingerly
cuts the young nettles' tops until he has a good pile. He then chops them
all up finely and crams them into his mess tins.

As they boil on the ashes of his fire he adds more, pushing them
down and adding water. After a half an hour of boiling he turns his
vegetable stew out on his tin canteen.

A large blob of dark green twisted leaves and stalks, he sniffs them:
they smell terrible. Slowly he cuts into the green soggy mound and takes
a fork-full tasting it, a little bitter but not as bad as it looks,
"I wish I had some bread...and sausage", he thinks.
Mmm this is not that bad".

In a few moments it is all gone, he is still very hungry, he wondered
if there are any rabbits in his snares yet.

Ken starts to backtrack over the path where he had set his snares.
Nothing, not a bunny to be seen anywhere. His senses become more
acute. He smells the live pine of the trees and the dead pine on the
ground. Plenty of rabbit droppings and at one snare he sees rabbit prints,
but they have walked around his trap. Then it dawns on him.
"Oh the scent, they can all smell my stink,
I have to wipe my scent off the wires".

Ken revisits his snares, wipes the wires with dandelion leaves and
resets them. Disappointed, he makes his way back to his camp up the
river. He picks the odd bulrush and chews on its roots.

Using his groundsheet on a bed of bracken, he rolls himself up tight trying to get to sleep but hunger and the odd ant keep him awake. He lays just watching the fire embers die slowly and stares up into the stars. There's the Big Dipper with its pointers, so that must be the North Star, and underneath on the horizon is north. So if it were winter, the Big Dipper would be upside down. There's the Northern Crown. Oh would I love a long sausage just now.

My there's a lot of stars out there, I bet Ron can see the same sky. I wonder how he's doing,

I bet he has still got his emergency rations and will bring them back as instructed, unopened. If I open mine I would never hear the last of it; he would never stop reminding me how I had to open the packet. So what will I eat tomorrow? Hope there's a fat rabbit or hare in one of the traps. Have to move on at midday tomorrow, up river. I wonder where the nearest human is. My, so many stars up there.

It is just getting light and it starts to rain as Ken wakes up. He feels stiff and cold and pulls the ground sheet over his head. After a while he hears a munching sound. Without moving he opens his eyes and sees a young hare, no more than two meters from his head. He just lies there watching the animal eat its breakfast.

"All his food is around here, he hasn't got to go far".

"There has to be something to eat around here. Now if I could grab it".

He slowly starts to climb out of his bedroll, but the hard ground sheet is noisy against the dried ferns and the young hare bounds away a few paces without looking back.

Ken reaches for his stick thinking, if I can bash it just once.

As he stands up the hare spots him and runs off, Ken chases after it. This is when he finds out just how fast a hare can run.

Running at full speed crashing through the wet laurel carrying his stick like a spear he bounds yelling. The hare gains speed and is losing him. As if a last desperate effort Ken flings his stick like a spear and in doing so trips on some roots falling and sprawling and rolling into a growth of ferns. He looks up hoping he hit it, but it had bounded off to a safe distance and was only interested in chewing on some young clover. Ken looks at his grazed knees and elbows then notices the very young Fiddle Back Ferns pushing their way up through the soft undergrowth. He picks some of the young and most tender ones putting them in his mouth,

"Mm, not bad, these don't taste that bad,

Mm just like apples".

He crawls on his hands and knees picking just the young fresh seedlings, putting them in to his mouth one after the other, sometimes spitting out the odd bit of soil or those that have grown too stringy and tough. Soon he is full and has had enough of eating young ferns.

Feeling a little better, he packs up his camp and starts to retrieve his traps. The first five are empty. As he approaches his sixth trap he knows he has caught something. Lying flat trying not to be seen, he spots the small hare caught by its neck. Got you. Ha, dinner. Ken grabs the animal by its shoulders and with a mighty twist turns its head around like a doorknob. It kicks out its back legs and then stays still.

He hangs the hare up by its front legs as he has seen Dieter do. He gingerly places his ear to the animal's chest to see if it is really dead. Taking his camp knife he carefully cuts the stomach skin, hocks his finger inside and cuts slowly down. Suddenly the hare's guts just fall out and hang there. He pulls on them and they plop down onto the ground.

Ken thinks.

"I must get the bladder out before it spoils the meat".

So gingerly he removes the bladder without spilling a drop.

Skinning was easy. Then he cuts up the meat into small bits for his pot, keeping the two hind legs to roast over the fire.

Ken's dinner tonight is the hare, and lots of greens. All that tastes very good too, especially when you're hungry.

In the morning he strides off to the next part of his objective, his traps hanging on one side of his belt. When the sun is directly above him Ken feels it must be about midday and he is feeling very hungry again. He stops, finds a good place to camp and sets his traps. Spotting a rabbit hole he sets one around one entrance that looks as if it has been used lately. There is nothing he can find to eat so he decides to make his way back to his camp and wait for his traps. The open meadow he is traveling through has very little cover so he decides to get closer to the small wooded glade; the words of his wilderness survival teacher keep ringing through his ears:

"Lambert use Splatter vision! Splatter vision!"

Splatter vision is scanning the horizon expanding your field of vision looking for the slightest movement.

'Focused listening hard' he cups his ears and listens in different directions...'What was that?'... With his ears still cupped, he swings slowly from left to right. He can hear the nasal snort and squeak of a hare....There it is again, that's the noise they make when they are in a mating frenzy. He cups his ears and peers left and right scanning the ground ahead of him and gets a fix on the sound and now a direction...

'Stalking' He thinks about the lessons and how he took almost fifteen minutes to stalk up on Ron once in a wood, but Ron had not heard him until he touched him on his back.

Ken starts to move to where he hears the sounds coming from, moving each limb slowly maintaining complete control of his body deliberately whistling like a bird to cover the soft sound of his boots placed very carefully on to the damp under-grass.

Very slowly stalking, feeling the soft breeze in his face and altering his course so the gentle wind blows at him, from the direction of the dinner he is trying to stalk.

He stops and ducks down, listening by cupping his ears, yes it is a pair of hares not too interested in the world outside their mating. He grips his stick tight thinking he will try to get close enough to whack it rather than throwing it like a spear.

"If I throw I know I will miss. Hares can dodge a spear,
no dinner".

He is getting very close, now the long grasses hiding the pair of hares so he slows down moving like the grasses all around him. He can feel the strain in his legs and arms and the tension of his slow and careful movements.

Ken freezes still for a moment; he can see the hares through the long grass, a big buck and two small females.

Very slowly he raises his stick to a striking position, takes a slow but very deep breath and leaps in them, and strikes the big male hard across its head, then turns and chases the two females swiping the nearest across her hind quarters.

He quickly turns back and grabs the stunned buck, twisting its neck then dropping it to return to the female who is coming back to life and starting to get away he grabs it and wrings its neck too. The other hare has dived into the dry brush and lives to tell the story.

That evening Ken is so hungry he eats both hares roasted over his fire. He goes to sleep that night feeling full and much better about the survival test. Tomorrow, he would check his traps; he was bound to get something by morning.

At the end of the ten days it was obvious that some of the boys didn't do that well. They had eaten their emergency rations and were almost ready to drop with exhaustion and exposure, but the twins came through looking fit; they had both eaten well and learned to survive without touching their emergency packs.

April 20th. 1942 is Hitler's birthday. The whole school is lined up for the morning daily Flag Ceremony in the Great Hall. Boys over fourteen are all dressed in their Hitler Youth uniforms, the younger Boys are in Young Folk uniforms. The whole school is standing in platoons (they used to call them classes) ready to reaffirm and re-swear their oaths to Adolf Hitler.

Hands at their sides, fingers pointing down, and raise their right arms three fingers pointed to the ceiling. Ken keeps his fingers crossed on his left hand. They all turn and face Hitler's bust. Mitter barks and the boys restate their oaths to Hitler and then all lower their hands. Mitter smiles at the new first year boys then at the rest of the school,

"Now let's show the new boys what comradeship and brotherhood triple sounds like".

Hundreds of boyish voices shout in unison,

"Sieg Heil.... Sieg Heil.... Sieg Heil"

The school all clap and sing the Horst Wessel song, stamping their feet to keep time and adding a little more drama to the occasion.

The new boys file down to the floor and the older boys pat them on their backs and congratulate them.

Ron looks at Ken, whispering,

"Heil Benny Goodman, Swing Heil".

It is a hot spring afternoon and Dieter is drilling the platoon on the playing field behind the school. Marching left, right, Dieter is relentless and performs every move himself with his platoon. After an hour, the boys look hot and tired. Dieter yells,

"Come on, left right left right, swing your arms from front to
rear, left right, don't bend your arms at the elbows, dig your
heels in and widen your pace, open your legs, you've got
nothing to drop yet, Ha,
You've got nothing to drop yet....Left turn.
Don't you think that's funny? No perhaps not"

Sergeant Dieter Wolff is now fourteen and is crashing through puberty. He is almost a man, not quite full grown but at that curious intermediate stage when the changes of nature instead of producing a gangly monster, fashion for a year or two a replica of male perfection, slightly reduced in scale. He is a good-looking boy who boxes and is good at fighting, wrestling and most sports. He has a shock of blond curly hair and bright kind blue eyes.

He keeps a brotherly look-out for Hans and the twins. The four have formed a very strong friendship.

Dieter has just discovered girls and is totally smitten with one in particular. She is new to the school, a pretty blond girl named Hanna. A fourteen-year-old member of the BDRM, Band Deutsche Madchen (League of German Girls).

Twenty-four of them have just arrived and under the watchful eye of their leader Frau Claria, they have just been attached to the school to take over the domestic burden and relieve the adult staff for essential war duties. They are the female counterparts of the Hitler Youth.

Hanna and Dieter have exchanged many smiles and glances in the dining hall. Although no words have ever been spoken between them, there is already an understanding. Well there is as far as Dieter is concerned.

So having passed his first little note to Hanna this morning at breakfast, Dieter is feeling very good and has been thinking about her all through this sweaty drill. Dieter glances at his pocket watch; the boys are all out of breath hot and flushed with the hot sun.

"All right, we have another half hour to go yet but we will take it resting under that big tree, keep low and out of the way.

Dismiss, let's stay out of sight in the shade".

The boys all cheer quietly and undo the buttons of their shirts and pull them open to get cool air over their hot torsos.

They flop down on the soft grass in the shade of a big old chestnut tree, and take deep gulps from their water bottles. Ron and Ken roll down their heavy socks and kick off their boots to let their toes feel the cool grass in the shade.

Laying there dreamily Ken notices that the number tattooed on his brother's foot has turned from black to blue, he looks at his own; it too is dark blue. He remembers it was black when it was first put there three years ago and wonders if it will ever disappear altogether.

There is a murmur of approval from all the boys as they shed their shirts and boots to cool off.

The twins, Hans and Dieter are lying on their backs looking up into the tree's massive canopy of branches. Ken nudges Ron,

"Has anyone ever made conkers out of the chestnuts they have here?"

Dieter looks up inquisitively,

"Conkers, what are conkers?"

Hans joins him,

"Yes what are conkers?"

Ken and Ron stare at each other with a

"I don't believe they don't know" look.

Ron and Ken jump up and face each other as if they are going to fight a duel. Ron takes an old conker out of his pocket. (It's a chestnut, brown and shriveled with a bootlace running through its center and a knot underneath to stop it coming off the lace).

Ron starts to twirl his conker over his head and says,

"This is the challenge like this".

Ken says,

"And this is the way we accept the challenge".

Ken draws a conker out of his pocket, holds it out in front of him swinging like a clock pendulum. The twins now have all the boys' total attention. Ron explains,

"We take turns trying to smash each other's conkers.

If I smash his conker, I win.

I'm the challenger, so I get first strike.

He must hold still, and the cords must be of equal length".

The boys crowd around to get a closer look. Ron adjusts the length of lace to match Ken's. Ken holds his conker out at arms- length and says,

"If he misses, it counts as a strike, then it's my turn".

Ron leans forward and steadies Ken's slightly swinging conker.

Taking up a dramatic strike pose, his right hand holding the string, his left holding his conker high over his head, Ron turns to the small group and says quietly,

"This one is already a 'fiver' that means it has destroyed five of his conkers, a true old soldier".

Ron takes aim and whips his conker down with all his strength.

The conker strikes with a whack. Ken recoils and examines his conker for cracks, and yells,

"Ha, not broken. Now it's my turn".

Ron now holds out his conker, so with equal vehemence Ken strikes Ron's conker. This strike and counter strike routine continues until Ken, with a massive whack, shatters Ron's conker, sending bits flying like glass. A cheer goes up from the boys.

Ken triumphantly holds up his conker,

"This, is now a twofer, a twofer".

Ron quietly remarks with a shrug,

"Mine used to be a fiver".

Ken picks up a fallen green chestnut shell, cuts it open with his camp knife, takes out the shiny brown chestnut, holds it up to the platoon,

"If you drill a hole through it, and dry it, then it's a conker".

Some of the boys scramble about picking up chestnuts, stuffing them in their pockets...Hans points over to the school...

Karl is striding toward them dressed in his new Hitler Youth Leaders uniform and sees Dieter asleep, with his platoon all-lolling about in the shade. He kicks Dieter's boot and shouts disapprovingly,

"Sergeant Dieter Wolff, what's this, slacking off? You lot are scheduled to be drilling for another fifteen minutes yet... Come on, on your feet, get your platoon in line and give me twenties and fives to the lake move! Move! Move!"

Dieter bustles about getting his boys in line, most of them are half-asleep, putting their boots on. Finally the dozy platoon get themselves in some sort of line. A few of the boys have laced up their boots, some of them are carrying their shirts, most are in bare feet. Karl shouts,

"Come on Sergeant get them going and give me twenty and fives.

Get dressed properly you lot. Put your shirts on.

To the lake quick march, left right, left right.

Don't look back at me... look to your front...
Swing your arms from front to rear, left right, left right".
Ken imitating Karl's coarse working class accent shouts,
"Don't bend your arms at the elbows...
Open your legs, you've got nothing to drop yet!"
As the platoon marches off, Dieter counts twenty paces, and orders..."Down". The platoon drops down and does five fast push-ups. Then they march another twenty paces and do another five push-ups. After a while Dieter looks around because they are getting very close to the lake. Karl waves them to keep going, Dieter gets it and yells grinning,
"He wants us to march right into the lake...Let's do it with style boys...Heads up, left, right, left right...watch out for Hans, he can't swim".
The whole platoon marches along a short wooden jetty that runs out into the lake. The boys, with broad grins, march right off the end, into the lake.
There is lots of fun in the lake with Dieter making a big show of saving Hans from drowning although he is in shallow water.
Then the platoon marches back to school, all wet, their boots squelching in time to Ken's singing the Auntie Nelly song in English. Ron translates and they get great laughs from the boys.
"Oh, Auntie Nelly, had a fat belly,
with a red pimple on her bum,
Oh, Auntie Nelly, had a fat belly,
Stick-a-pin, in the pimple, on her bum,
Bang!....Yuck. Ha, Ha".
They have lots of fun as all the platoon know when to yell "Bang", having sung it many times before.

Another year passes in to the summer of 1943. The brothers are thirteen and their hormones are raging as they near the brink of puberty.
One afternoon they are strutting out along a school path when Hans passes them going in the other direction. He does not stop but just waves. The brothers turn their stride and grab hold of him.
"Hey, Hans, what's your hurry, where you off to?"
"Nowhere".
Ron says with a grin,
"Ha, no one goes at that speed going nowhere".
"I can't tell you. It's a secret".
Ken gets close to Hans and whispers in his ear,
"You can tell us Hans, we are Ken and Ron".
Ron gets all friendly and puts his arm round his shoulder,
"Come on Hans we are your best friends,
you can tell us everything".

Hans starts to hurry along. The boys catch up with him, one on each side and turn the pressure on. Ken says,

"Come on Hans, please, tell us?"

Ron tries appealing,

"Hans we will just stick to you, wherever you're going, so you might as well just tell us".

Hans says reluctantly,

"All right, but it will cost you twenty pfennigs each".

Ken says inquisitively,

"Hans, we're broke. What are we paying for anyway?"

Hans stops, looks each way to make sure he's not overheard and whispers,

"To see a naked lady! I'll pay for you two, but I want it back, forty pfennigs with interest".

Ken and Ron stop and look at each other. Ron grabs Hans's neck. Ken grabs his arm. Ron earnestly,

"You're joking, a real woman naked? Totally naked?"

"Yes and some boys get to touch them".

Ken smiles,

"What do they touch?"

Hans grins. The boys let him go. Hans makes a cup movement with his hands at his own chest. Hans says.

"You know the senior boy Erik, well he is acting in this show but I know he is in for a big surprise... Ha and he doesn't know a thing about it yet".

Ron looks at Ken then at Hans he demands,

"What surprise?"

Hans just smiles and says,

"You will see soon".

Ken and Ron look at each other, they all grin and the boys follow Hans to the back of the school to a small ground-level window at the rear of the boiler house. Hans taps on the window. It opens and the voice of an older boy growls,

"Three marks".

"Gerhard said, three for one mark". Hans lies.

The voice inside replies,

"No he didn't. Three marks".

Hans pleads,

"I've only got one mark".

"Oh come on in then".

Hans fumbles in his pocket; the money is passed through. Hans slides in through the window feet first, then grins at the boys as he slides down the steel coal chute.

Ken and Ron follow, sliding down the chute. When their eyes get used to the darkness, they see they are in a large boiler room packed with boys. The main wide staircase is acting as an audience bleacher. The big doors are blocked by a mass of small boys on the stairs. Ken, Ron and Hans scramble up on top of a pile of empty boxes to get a better view. A coal bay is empty, except for an old couch that is covered with a white sheet and is bathed in a red glow from one of three rusty tin cans above containing red lamps. The effect is quite eerie.

A buzz of excitement runs through the room, Ken and Ron nudge each other and rub their hands together in anticipation. Ken whispers to Hans,

"So, have you been here before?"

"Twice".

Ron laughs

"My, you're a dark horse, fancy you not telling us".

Two of the older boys remove the steel chute and close the black-painted windows. There is an excited whisper buzzing through the group of boys as they wait in total darkness for the show to start.

From behind the big old boiler Gerhard Knoll steps out, walks into the light and holds his hands up. The room gets quieter. Gerhard is an Italian-looking boy of about seventeen, short, stocky with longish hair. He is wearing a top hat and a large bow tie. The jacket is too big for him, but it completes his 'Master of Ceremonies' outfit. He is not a student but a maintenance worker at the school and looks it. He speaks in a rough working-class accent.

"No cheering or shouting, or she will go away.

The first boy who whistles or shouts gets bashed, by Peter and Erik over there".

Gerhard points over to his two big money collectors that are armed with long sticks. Gerhard says quietly,

"If there is too much noise we will be discovered. Then we will all be in the shit. See me after to buy cigarettes and booze".

He looks around the crowded boiler room and tries a phony smile saying.

"When the show's over, don't all leave at the same time".

Gerhard goes back behind the big boiler...There is a buzz of excitement from the boys.

A scratchy squeaky phonograph record of Eastern Arab-sounding music wafts out and a hush falls over the audience of wide-eyed boys...The music gets a little louder and the light clicks off, leaving the room in total darkness....The pit-a-pat sound of bare feet running across the room in the darkness heightens the anticipation. There is a whisper, 'Now! '.

With a click, a red light comes on and bathes a very young slim girl, scantily dressed in a transparent eastern Arab costume. The effect is very dramatic. Breathy gasps from the boys drown out the music for a moment. The dancer starts to dance moving rhythmically and very seductively around the couch, shedding one of the many veils.

She continues to frolic and shed veils until she is down to her transparent pantaloons and little jacket. Very quietly a little tambourine starts to tap from behind the boiler.

Peter, one of the boys who was taking the money at the window, appears dressed in a pair of flimsy eastern pantaloons topped with a red sash. His pantaloons that are almost too transparent and slightly small for him are tied at his ankles. He wears a small red fez hat on the back of his head. Standing in the center of the stage with his arms folded over his naked upper torso he looks like a blond godlike eunuch standing guard in a scene from the Arabian nights, he tries to keep his boyish face looking tough and stern...

The exotic dancer starts to wind herself about the boy, she smiles and Peter, takes off her little jacket and throws it to Gerhard behind the boiler.

Peter the blond eunuch looks blankly forward but is clearly getting quite disturbed. The dance is choreographed to seduce him. Only the red light hides his rosy flush...She undoes her gold-edged bra...Holding the straps out but not letting the bra drop, she turns her back on the audience and drapes the bra about Peter's neck. Then she pulls herself in tight to him.

The surprised boy's arms fall to his sides partly with shock and partly with sheer embarrassment. She turns around to the audience and for a brief moment they see her full bare breasts... The gasp from the boys causes Ken to look around and realize just how many young lads are crammed in the cellar, all of them, like himself, had never seen a naked dancer. Quickly she grabs Peter's hands from behind her and places them over her breasts like a human bra... This prompts more gasps from the boys... They both sway and move to the music, Peter's hands still holding her breasts with his cupped fingers... Peter grins at the audience, causing a ripple of laughter.

After a while, she takes one of his hands and puts it on her gold belt. With a spin and a twist she spins away from him leaving him holding the flimsy breakaway pantaloons.

She is now totally naked with the exception of a bright red jewel stuck fast in her navel.

Spinning around Peter who is slightly stunned, she turns around into the audience. Dipping to allow the boys in the front row to gently touch her breasts. Our blond eunuch looks shocked; he drops her pantaloons on the bed. He just stares at the girl as she wiggles and snakes toward him. She grabs him around his neck and pulls his head face down into her bosom, takes off his little red hat and tosses that on the bed. The boys all laugh and giggle…

Nature gets the better of the blond eunuch's self-control and he grabs the dancer by her buttocks and in a bear hug, sexually thrusts himself at her… Titters ripple through the gathering of boys. Then with the experience of a club stripper she easily frees herself and sits Peter down on the couch.

He just sits there, trying to hide his throbbing lower parts. It is impossible to hide his excitement and a huge bulge shows through his almost silky costume.

The dancer wanders back into the audience stepping over seated boys, inviting them to touch her breasts and blond maidenhair. Making her obligatory circle of grabbing boys she runs back behind the boiler.

A few moments later the main white lights click on to find a room full of stunned little boys. The dancer has gone and Erik the young eunuch just sits on the bed very flushed totally amazed having had the most unexpected experience of his young life.

Hans leans forward and looks at the twins and asks,
  "Well, was that worth the money?"
The boys all nod, Ken smiles,
  "It was the most amazing thing we've ever seen".
Hans points to Erik at the edge of the couch,
  "Look, I know he didn't expect the girl to do that sexy stuff to
  him. Gerhard told me he was asked just to stand out there with
  his arms folded looking stern… Wow! Look he's, still got a
  hard on".
With squeaks of delight the boys leave the boiler room chatting, feeling they really had their money's worth. Hans reflects wistfully,
  "Did she ever have a beautiful pair?
  Perfect shape but I didn't see her thing".
Ken asks inquisitively,
  "What thing is that then?"
Hans looks puzzled,
  "You know, her thing, she's supposed to have a pad with a slit
  in it… where ours is".
Ken whispers with authority,
  "Hans, she only has a pee hole there, to pee with".
Hans, starting to raise his voice in frustration,
  "So, where does a man put it when he puts the sperm stuff in
  her for babies?"

Ron knowing, quietly,
"It goes into her through her belly button, that's where…
That's where babies start growing just like rabbits. She had it
blocked off by that jewel. Take out the jewel and there's a hole
for the man's dick".
Ron with his, I know more than you do voice,
"How else would they do it? I didn't see a place, except for the
jewel".
Hans, getting bored with the subject,
"She has a slit, I've seen my sister's when she was twelve. She
has a pad with a crack….Don't forget you two owe me seventy
pfennigs, I must have it".
Ron laughs,
"For that money you would think they would have done it all
the way. He should have put it inside her for all that money".
Ron says,
"I bet he thinks about her little tits tonight when he's in bed
wanking off, ha".
Ken starts to do cartwheels and runs back to the group,
"I wonder what's for supper. I'm starved.
I hope it's not fish, I hate how they do fish here".
Hans moans,
"If it's pork sausages and cabbage, you two can have my
cabbage".
Ron opens his pocket and feels inside,
"Old Gerhard Knoll must have made some money. Did you see
how many boys were in that place?
She had nice tits, I wonder what's inside them?"
Hans grins,
"Milk. I wonder if it ever goes sour, ha…
But it was a good show, wasn't it".
Ron says,
"Mm, Hans knows more about this sex stuff than any of us. He
can wank-off quicker, better, and shoot father than anyone else,
but I still think babies come out of ladies' belly buttons".
Hans smiles knowingly,
"She has a slit, and that's where the boy's dick and sperm goes
in and babies come out, I saw it in a book".

Ron and Ken sing,
"Oh, Untie Nelly,
had a fat belly,
with a red pimple on her bum,
with a red pimple on her bum".

The three boys walk on chatting and pushing each other about.

Ken puts his fists up inside his shirt and makes two breasts and wiggles his backside like an exotic foreign dancer yelling.

"Hey that eunuch boy Peter had a huge dick,
I mean it is really a big one. I've never seen one that size.
Do you think he would get it all inside the girl?"

9. BROTHERS

It's a warm summer afternoon. Ken is standing with his back to the big tree trunk, hiding. Ron passes unaware of Ken's presence... Ken jumps, grabs Ron by the neck in a playful wrestle. Both boys tumble and roll about, their new Young Folk uniforms getting covered with dust and leaves.

Ron gets the better hold and ends up kneeling on Ken's upper arms sitting on his chest. Hot and out of breath, they seek the cool shade and soft grass under the canopy of the big old chestnut tree. They flop down staring up into the branches. In the distance they can hear boys' voices singing. Ron turns over on his back, puts his hands behind his head and stares up into the branches and says quietly,

"You'd never know there is a war on, would you?
It's so peaceful here... Ken what side do you feel you're on?
Dad's English. We are being trained to fight the English.
The English are supposed to be our enemy".
Ken looks sad,
"I don't want to fight anyone".
Ron shrugs his shoulders,
"We will have to fight when we are old enough.
The British, the Americans; what about the French
and the Russians? That's what we are getting trained for,
it's not the bloody Boy Scouts we're in".
Ken gets serious,
"We have to stay English... English first, Ron"
Ron sits up and looks at his brother,
"If we're there, you know, at the front, right in the fighting,
you just can't say, Excuse me, I'm sorry. I can't do this,
I don't want to fight. You can't just not fight.
If you don't kill them, then they will most certainly kill you.
Or someone like Karl will shoot you in the back
for cowardice or as a deserter".
"That's fucking war that's how it works.
And we have just taken an oath to obey Hitler and his gang".
"Well it doesn't count for me,
I had my fingers crossed in my belt".
Ken excited,
"So did I, so did I".
Ron grabs Ken's hands and looks him in the eyes,
"So for us, the oath hasn't been taken, right?
So why don't we make our own?"

Ken asks,
    "Shall we swear?"
 Ron nods with enthusiasm,
    "You and me, let's make our own oath. Let's swear,
    just you and me: a brother's oath".
Ron thinking,
    "Yes, I've got it, take my hand and say after me"...
    "I swear by my own life"
Ken repeats.
    "To remain true to England and Father".
Ken repeats.
    "To play the Nazi Hitler Youth games".
Ken repeats.
    "But if this war comes to killing".
Ken repeats.
    "We will hide until it's all over".
Ken repeats.
    "Look out for each other, with our lives".
Ken casually turns his nose up,
    "That's a bit strong…"
Ron earnestly and getting serious,
    "Do you swear? Say it, say it properly!"
Ken shouting,
    "On my life, I vow, Ron, on my life".
Ron smiles and pushes Ken over, rips a handful of grass and thrusts it into Ken's mouth. They hug and roll into a wrestling bout, enjoying getting their uniforms all grubby and covered with leaves. Ron sits up and feels in his breast pocket and pulls out a small flat tin, Ken looks on intrigued, he whispers,
    "What's that in there?"
Ron smiles and opens the tin and takes out a whole new fat yellow cigarette and puts it under his nose and sniffs it like a connoisseur of fine cigars,
    "It's French, the finest they tell me".
He puts it between his lips and with a match from the tin lights it and starts to puff the smoke, blowing clouds over to Ken.
Ken holds his hand out to try,
    "All right, but don't make the end all wet".
Ken takes the cigarette, and holding it underhanded like the film stars he's seen. He sucks in a lung full… Then starts to cough and splutter saying,
    "Oh Ron, how can you suck on this thing, here you do it".
He hands it back to Ron, who grins and says,
    "Want to see smoke come out of my nose?"

He sucks in some smoke and blows it out of his nostrils; Ken pulls a face looking hard at his brother's nose. Ron is looking a bit green but he puts up a good front saying,

"Want to see it come out of my ears?"

Ken falls back laughing, Ron nods with assurance.

"All right, listen, you have to put your hand on my chest and when I nod you have to push gently, alright?"

Ron stands up and faces Ken, grabs his hand and places it on his chest, sucks in smoke and nods. Ken pushes on his brother's chest, watching his ears. Quickly Ron takes the cigarette and lightly touches the hot end on the back of Ken's hand.

"Ow, Ow, you shit bag, that bloody hurt".

Ron laughs so hard his face turns red, then a little pale.

He suddenly runs over to the bushes and throws up his lunch. Now Ken is laughing so hard he falls on the ground and rolls over yelling,

"Oh, look at the great smoker, let's see you puff smoke out of your bum Ron".

It is a rainy afternoon, and all outdoor games are canceled. The H.J. Heim is crammed with both Karl's and Dieter's platoons, the room smells of damp boys all trying to pursue useful indoor activates with games and books.

There is a line of boys waiting for their compulsory spoonful of cod liver oil. Served by the school nurse, it is always followed by the weekly issue of licorice roots cut to the size of cigarettes.

The licorice treat is supposed to take away the oily taste and keep the boys natural functions regular. The boys suck on them like cigars, a treat for arriving at the Heim on time.

A colored poster on the wall shows two good looking blond fit young men, stripped to the waist with shovels in their hands and claiming that every boy should serve his year as a member in the R.A.D. (Reichsarbeitsdienst), a compulsory labor service each boy has to serve at seventeen. The caption boasts,

"We strengthen body and soul".

Another poster shows a hand clutching a money collecting can for "Winter Relief" on the fifteenth and sixteenth of October, with the declaration, "Workers collect, Workers Give".

There are posters of tent instructions showing how the waterproof tent quarter each boy carries on his pack as a marching rain cape can be all laced together to form one large bell tent for ten boys. There is a wooden board with rope knots tied and stuck showing `Knots every boy should know'. Stacked in one corner are poles with rolled up flags and banners.

There are no toys, just books, mostly sitting un-touched they should be read during the long "Comrades Evenings" The titles read:

Life Stories of German War Aces, The Infantry Marches on, Aviator's Nest in the Elder-Bushes, The Book of German Colonies for the Young, Peter the Soldier-Boy and Sister Clair at the Front.

Dieter and his three lads are sitting at a table and are all wearing headsets and nodding in time to the faint jazz music.

A box of records that have been relabeled with French for beginners is open next to the record player. All the boys are in uniform. Ken writes in his diary,

"Ron smoked his first and last cigarette.
Made him very sick, Ha, he looked ill,
I tried it, very shitty, tastes like burned rubber, yuck!"

Captain Mitter comes into the Heim looking smart in his Hitler Youth leaders' uniform, he looks young, slim and very fit, every inch a Nazi. Mitter barks,

"Now then, attention".

The room clatters to attention, as boys who were lolling about on the floor stand up. The Jazz fans stop their record player and stand up. The two sergeants, Dieter and Karl, step forward and stand each side of the Captain. He goes over to a small blackboard,

"First the big news: this school will be a part of a Youth Rally in the Sports Stadium in Munich. Our Führer
Adolf Hitler will be speaking so we must all be at our best. I know you won't let us down. Who has seen the Führer in person before?"

There is a buzz of electrified whispers rippling around the room. The Captain takes his moment to shuffle through his papers as the boys' chat among themselves. He nods to Karl who raps on his desk yelling,

"All right, no one has seen him, let's keep it down, quiet".

The Captain opens his folder,

"I have never seen him either. Directly after the rally the school will split into its platoons and there will be a cross-country march, each platoon has a final objective…. Arriving at the Munich Sports Stadium".

He starts to write on the blackboard,

"Two armies: one blue, one green".

Captain Mitter holds up a fistful of rope sashes, either blue or green,

"Platoon one, with Sergeant Karl Kaltenbrunner is the green army, and Sergeant Dieter Wolff is the blue army.

The object of this battle is not to fight, but to seize the colors of the opposing army using field craft, map reading, stealth and good leadership".

Mitter starts to pass out the rope sashes, as he explains:

"The platoon leaders will see me for maps, compasses and sealed orders… That means they are not to be opened until you all get to your designated starting points.

Go and get packed ready… There will be a full inspection at 5 P.M. Slackers improperly turned out will miss supper; Dieter and Karl see me now. The rest of you, move… Come on move what are you standing around for, come on? move, move, move!"

Boys scramble about putting away board games and books on shelves, not daring to leave the Heim untidy for Mitter to see, he shouts above the din,

"We leave at dawn at 5am, on the dot".

The doors to the dormitory burst open as a mass of boys' rush in. Ken and Ron fit small packs to themselves, water bottles, straps, fitting a folding spade in its belt. Dieter checks how boys' boots are done-up; he rolls blankets and shelter quarters tight for the boys who have not put their kit together well. Then he comes out of his little room with a cardboard box and hands a new pair of socks to every boy.

Just before supper Dieter looks at the clock on the wall, blows his whistle and shouts,

"Platoon… Stand to!"

The boys jump to attention as Captain Miter comes through the door. Dieter steps forward and snaps a smart salute,

"Heil Hitler, platoon two ready for inspection, sir".

Mitter followed by Dieter strides around the room picking at odd flaws in the field marching gear. Ken says under his breath,

"I hope we get through this time. I'm starved. I can't go without supper tonight".

Mitter stops at Ken, opens his backpack and removes his Teddy Bear, holds it up for the whole platoon to see. Mitter smiles,

"What's this, the platoon mascot?"

The boys all laugh. Ken rolls his eyes, takes a big sigh.

Mitter strolls down the room holding on to the Teddy Bear then nods with approval,

"Well done, Platoon Two A Upper, well done, Sergeant Wolff take them off to supper. Remember, five A.M. in the morning; get a good night's sleep… Goodnight. Heil Hitler".

The whole room shouts,

"Good night; Heil Hitler".

Captain Mitter tosses Ken's teddy bear over to Ken with a smile. The boys cheer, and then shuffle in to a line to be marched to supper.

It's 5am., still cold; dark and very damp, Dieter's platoon is standing in three ranks outside the barrack.

They have packs and gear on, ready to march off. Dieter is checking each boy's equipment, hoisting a pack up, twisting a blanket roll, and tapping water bottles to see if they are full. Each boy has a blue length of rope as a sash and a small blue wool strand tied round his right arm tucked in his pocket. Ron shivering says,

"Brr, why couldn't he have done his inspection inside?
It's cold enough to freeze the balls off a bloody brass monkey out here. Brr... And why shorts why can't we have long trousers like the HJ?"

Hans loudly,

"Yes, why do we have to wait here?"

Ken moans,

"If I have to walk with all this shit on my back for very far, my body will shrink down like an accordion".

Dieter says as he looks at his pocket watch,

"Shut up, Mitter said he might meet us here be here. We leave in two minutes".

Ron still grumbling,

"I bet Captain bloody Mitter is still tucked up nice and cozy in his wank-pit. He will arrive two minutes before the train leaves on his motorbike, I bet".

Dieter pushes the boys into a line,

"You Lambert's have got big mouths. Since you have so much wind, you two can carry the flagpoles. Keep them dry in their cases until we get off the train. Get up in the front of the platoon, both of you... Move".

Dieter hands Ron and Ken two heavy long flagpoles with the precious flags rolled up in their black cylindrical cases and wave them to the front of the platoon. Dieter yells,

"Anybody wants to piss... Now's the time.
We don't stop for piss heads or nicker wetters
and don't do it up the wall in the shower, use the toilets".

A few boys run back into the dormitory. Hans pushes and shoves to move up to the front of the platoon and get alongside between his friends.

Karl's platoon is first out of the school gates. Dieter's platoon follows keeping the regulation one hundred meters back. The last boy has a strip of round glass reflectors that are strapped to his belt as a traffic warning, it glows red from the school lights.

The whole school, plus one thousand six hundred boys from other schools are all on the march.

Dieter is marching at the side of his platoon. Ron, Ken and Hans are in the front row. After an hour marching through a fine mist along totally deserted country roads, they get to the outskirts of the local town. The sun comes up and warms the boys. The platoon stops for a little traffic at a crossroad.

Whilst waiting for the order to march again the sun catches the steam from the hot damp bodies of a tight group of young boys.

Trucks pass full of singing boys all on their way to the station. Hans yells,

"Dieter, how come we walk and they get to ride in trucks?"

Dieter smiles,

"That's because they're all riff-raff and we are the cream of the cream".

The special train is crammed full of boys, from all over Southern Bavaria, singing as loud as they can so as to drown out the orders shouted by their organizers. The twins and Hans sit on their kit in the corridor, there are no seats left. Ron opens a sliding window and peers out down the platform,

"Come on you lot, get up here or you will miss the free goodies, look".

Coming down the platform is a large steel wagon being pushed by four young girls in brown and white uniforms. They are handing out buns and filling the boys' tin mugs with a lemonade like drink.

"We have ace positions here, hold on tight, they can't miss us here". Ken yells.

The crush and clamber to get a bun and a drink of weird-tasting lemonade substitute turns out to be useless as the girls run out of their stock before they get anywhere close to the boys' window. There is a great shout of dismay from the train as the girls turn back to the exit. Ron consoles himself with a swig from his water bottle as the train jerks forward.

"Our mountain water tastes better than their phony lemonade; it's probably all made from chemicals anyway"

It's two o'clock in the afternoon and the large sports stadium is packed with twenty two thousand boys and girls in HJ uniforms. Companies of the tall SS all in black are Hitler's own color guard. Dieter's and Karl's platoons have been standing in the space under the concrete bleachers for four hours waiting for the disorganized marshals to get everyone into position. Finally they get the signal to march into the stadium.

Dieter gives Ron the signal to unroll their banners, then leans over and says to the front row banner bearers,

"Keep them clean, I don't want to see a mark on them...

They march into the bright sun of the day. In the center of the arena is a large podium with rows of high ranking uniformed officers sitting in very uncomfortable-looking seats. Senior SS, Army, Navy, commanders all in their order of seniority are sitting in the sun. The fat 'Golden Pheasants', the high-ranking political leaders of Munich and Bavaria, look very red stuffed into pristine gold braided white uniforms that are too tight. The Platoons reached their assigned places in the stadium and sit down on the grass to wait for the show to start.

Dieter passes around his little brass telescope for some of his boys to see but Hitler isn't there yet. A presentation of sports units performing very tight intricate maneuvers and stylish exercises, thousands of boys and girls all moving together as one dressed in white vests and gym shorts.

When they finish they all run out using all the exits. A clear young voice barks out from the public address system,

"Attention, on your feet for our district leader,
Bannführer Dieckhoff"..." "Attention"

(Bannführer is a "Bann" leader with the rank of Major-General)

All eyes turn as the drums get louder echoing around the stadium. The boys' scramble to their feet, platoon leaders shout to make straight ranks. Bannführer Dieckhoff is a very tall man. Looking very stern he flicks the microphone and its pop echoes through the stadium. Standing with his arms folded looking around as if to notice every last boy and girl in the square, he waits. He gets the absolute silence he expects very quickly. He steps forward, his voice echoes around the packed stadium,

"To our new young members of this Bann Welcome.
Our Führer Adolf Hitler has created a Bann in which all
Germans are brothers.... The world's strongest community...
For most of you the next few days will be your first camp out.
You will earn your badges, belt buckles and camp knives".

He then drones on about the glorious achievements of the German Army and of the new and secret weapons that are going to win the war for us. He finally winds up saying,

"Be proud of your Banners and Flags, guard them well.
To abuse them will be an insult to the Fatherland...
Enjoy your march.
We salute our Führer Adolf Hitler with a Triple.
Sieg Heil Sieg Heil, Sieg Heil, Sieg Heil".

It is getting quite dark now and a battalion of crack SS in their black uniforms tramp in and give a show of clever marching.

Their demonstration ends with a formation of a living swastika that rotates, then every man in the black battalion ignites a flaming torch. The stadium lights are dimmed, making the living flaming swastika more spectacular.

After a while the swastika starts to fall apart with the torches going out one by one. To save SS the embarrassment of the swastika falling apart as the flames die, there is a fanfare of trumpets and spot lights light up the podium and takes every one's attention to the youthful but tubby figure of 'Shir'. (nickname for Baldur Von Schirach, leader of the HJ).

His speech is boring, telling us he will expect us all to swear like our fore fathers the Knights of the Holy Germanic Empire an oath of obedience to Adolf Hitler. Then goes on to tell us that the slogan for the Hitler Youth is "Youth for the Führer" and that there is only one ideal race and that's The Germanic race where the Horst Weasel song came from, how Horst Weasel was a martyr and what he said, before he fell shot dead on the barricades in 1930.

"If a Red pokes you in the eye, blind him.
If he breaks one of your teeth, tear his throat out.
If he wounds you… You kill him".

Then he droned on about his ancestors who signed the American Declaration of Independence (his mother was an American).
He ends his speech by saying
"The Führer is God-like"
And he promised Hitler loyalty to the grave.
"The flag stands higher than death he yells".
Baldur Von Schirach leads the stadium in a thunderous triple
"Sieg Heil".

Thousands of boys and girls let out a cheer and yell so loud that a boy could not hear his own voice: A sound that hurt their ears.

A moment that no one in that arena will ever forget. Stepping to one side Reichsführer Von Schirach introduces Adolf Hitler.

Hitler takes three paces forward and stands with his arms folded, just looking. Every boy and girl feels his gaze and is sure he is looking straight at them. He stands for a long time just waiting for quiet, sometimes looking at his papers that are on a small table on his left side. Finally twenty two thousand boys and girls hushed. He starts to speak very casually, man to boy quietly, about his own hard-driven youth. Steadily turning up the tempo and raising his voice,

"You my Youth" he shouts, "Are our nation's
most precious guarantee for a great future".

Hitler promises, Law and order, a sense of purpose and challenges the youths to believe in themselves.

"Remember" he bellow's… The single boy is nothing;
the community is everything".

He mesmerizes everyone from his staunch followers to his most zealous critics; we are all captivated. He is not afraid to tell the Nation what they wanted to hear,

"We deserve to rule the world". He says.

Creating frenzy of nationalistic pride that came close to hysteria. For a longer time that we thought was possible, we all shouted, all of us. Hitler stands there drinking in all the cheering and yelling. He raised his hand, only slightly and the crowed hushed.

"Remember my youth.... A German boy must be slim and
slender. Be swift like a Greyhound, tough like leather and as
hard as Krupps Steel. Then one day you will rule with me under
the glorious flag of German National Socialism".

We all sing the national anthem and the grand march-past starts.

A large fanfare band with their trumpets drowning out the boyish shouts of the sergeants. The military band of the Flying Hitler Youth, leads marching down the long strip in front of the podium.

The proud elite section in their Luftwaffe (air force) blue uniforms are led by a tall drum major with a long silver mace, followed by a line of fifty long drums, twenty large cymbals and thirty brass fan-fare trumpets. Then a full brass band appears, led by twenty-four handpicked blond youths all the same height, carrying their flags and banners. The sound of the trumpets and the brass band in the stadium is awesome. The thousands of youthful voices all cheering sends a chill through the twins.

There is a long drum roll, then the band strikes up the Hoist Weasel song, Germany's second national anthem.

Everyone sings their hearts out as they march past the podium and see Adolf Hitler.

Ken looks at his brother and sees tears welling in his blue eyes. It is infectious. He too takes a deep breath and tries to hold back the tears of pride. Ken yells at his brother and Hans,

"Look at them up there on the podium watching us Ron... Us,
superior German boys Ron... Ha, some lark Ron, some lark,
ha, Heil Benny Goodman Ron, Heil Benny..."

He becomes aware of his own insults to Hitler and shuts up,
Ron yells through his tears,

"Dieter will march us off... We march for Dieter,
not Adolf bloody Hitler".

Ken looks at the faces around him. His heart is pounding with excitement. Who heard the slur? No-one, everybody is electrified by the occasion.

Ron and Hans are also aware of this new pride and have that determined look, waiting to jump when Dieter orders.

Finally Karl marches his platoon off, his face beaming as he sees his father in the back row, on a side stand.

Calm confidence shows in Dieter's face as he waits to time his orders just right. Dieter's whole body is being stirred and fed by the heavy drumbeats and the clash of cymbals. Now it's his turn to march his little platoon past the raised platform with Hitler and his gang taking the salute. Dieter turns, a smart about-turn and faces his platoon, (An unheard of move for a parade) and shouts… His voice breaking yet still being heard above the band,

"Let's show them how we can march, boys…
Heads up. Feel proud. We are the best they have here today.
You're all marching for me now, not him.
There's no riff-raff in our platoon, is there?
*So… Boys of Lindenburg College Platoon… By the left…
quick march… Left, right, left, right".*

Ron looks up to make sure his flag is not twisted around his pole. He sees that Ken feels pride too. As Dieter's platoon marches past the podium, they swing into a pace with unison and precision they have never known in their marching before. This is the first time they have marched to such a large band and hundreds of drums. The beat holds them all together.

Hitler stands smiling. Each boy can feel his gaze, eye to eye. Captain Mitter is smiling. He stands with all the other masters and officers from the school in front of the podium, but only whilst their school marches past Hitler. As the platoon gets to the edge of the stadium they approach the block of hundreds of young girls. Dieter grabs his moment to show off to the girls, and looks at the sea of healthy scrubbed young maidens, his eyes searching for Hanna. He shouts so the girls can hear, grinning mischievously,

"Left, right, left, right… Swing your arms from front to rear… Don't bend your arms at the elbows,
Dig your heels in, and open your legs wide… You've got
nothing to drop yet… Ha, they have nothing to drop yet,
heads up, left, right, left, right".

The girls all giggle and smile. The boys smile too. Dieter grins.

They march out of the stadium and make their way back to the Theresienwiese Park for something to eat. Dieter yells,

"Not far now; just two kilometers.
We get hot chocolate, buns and a chat to a platoon
of the pretty BDM (League of German Girls);
they will be there waiting. I might see Hanna again".

They march through the city in the long column of singing Hitler Youth from other districts. People stop and wave to the boys as they march past. Buildings are hung with flags and long banners. As they reach the gates of the park, a Policeman in a long green rubber coat directs Karl and Dieter's platoons to their position in their section of the park. Groups of Young Folk and Hitler Youth have already arrived and are sitting on the ground. Banners and flags give the place a festive feel.

Other groups are still arriving; some look as if they have been marching all night.

A Hitler Youth officer in smart uniform strides over to Karl and Dieter salutes and barks orders pointing to tables set up with refreshments by the League of Young German Girls.

The teenage girls in fresh white uniforms are busy coping well with the task of feeding masses of hungry boys. Each boy gets two extra-large jam-filled buns, a lump of black bread and his own tin mug full of hot chocolate and his water bottle filled. Back in their positions they eat. The park is now jammed full of Hitler Youth units all waiting to be marched back to the station.

At the station the boys pile in to an already full train, Dieter yells,
    "How can they expect us all to get in here... It's so packed".

The train pulls out of Munich station full of tired hot boys all squash together and after fifteen minutes chugs into a siding and stops. A railway guard with a metal megaphone walks along the side of the train announcing that they will be stopped in the siding for six hours. He warns the boys not to get out of the train and wishes them a Good Night. The boys settle down and eat whatever is left of their rations and try to get some sleep. Dieter's platoon stretch out on the floor of the corridor in a mass of arms and legs packed like puppies and are lulled to sleep by the singing.

So tired that sleep comes very easy. At eleven thirty the lights in the train go out and the Air Raid Sirens start to wail. Ron tries to open the door but it is locked fast.

Someone yells.
    "All the doors are locked; we have to stay on the train".

The boom-boom of anti-aircraft guns start thumping away then the sound of the railway yards to the north of them being bombed.

Few of the boys panicked they just covered their heads with their blankets and laid on the floor.

Ron put his arms around Hans and Ken to stop them from bolting for the doors. Some of the bombs were very close and shook the train. Then suddenly the train began to move off with a jerk. There was a muffled cheer from the boys and they heard the engine trying to pick up speed as fast as it could, its wheels spinning then slowing down as the wheels griped the rails. Soon the train was out of the railway marshaling yards and speeding south out of Munich leaving the bombing sounds behind them. The boys' cheers got louder as they uncovered their heads and started to sit up. Soon nervous singing started again this time more from relief than amusement. An even louder cheer went up when the very dim war time lights came on.

At 8am the train slowed in to Starnberg station, this wakes everyone up. There is a strong odor of hundreds of hot sweaty boys still damp from the fear and terror of last night's Air Raid.

A three-kilometer march into the countryside and Dieter yells,

"We haven't far to go now, big pork sausages and apple strudel with jam for breakfast".

The two platoons arrive at a farmer's field. The boys flop out with fatigue. Karl and Dieter open their sealed envelopes.

Each sergeant walks off in a different direction to read his own secret routes and maps. Then they carefully stash them away in their pockets. Karl shouts to all the boys,

"Come on, both platoons stay here for two nights to rest up. On your feet, let's get camp made. Lay your shelter quarters over here, ropes and laces here, tent poles over there".

The boys take off their packs and pile all the equipment in separate piles. Karl orders,

"Four tents with fourteen bodies in each. Dieter, you grab two strong lads and lace all the quarters up. You've done it before. Let's get some tents up that don't leak. Hey and Sergeant Wolf just sent the Lambert brothers over there to dig the shit pit".

A group of boys runs past Karl and he grabs two of them by their cross straps,

"You two get rocks or bricks for the fire, the rest of you gather dry wood, lots of it".

"And don't break down fences!"

Dieter yells,

"The quicker we get done the quicker we eat".

Karl joins Dieter,

"No one eats until we get the tents up, and the shit pits dug… Move, move".

The individual tent quarters that each boy carries get laced together to make four big tents. All the tent poles, tent pegs and cords have been evenly distributed throughout the boys' backpacks. Soon four tents go up. Each boy in the platoon has his own bread bag and water canteen. The vegetable ingredients for the evening meal are carried between the boys in their bags: A fire is built and a field stove is made out of local bricks and rocks. A big meal is soon cooking.

Ken and Ron dig a hole for the latrine. Ron takes off his boots and puts his socks on his hands as gloves. Ken is very disgruntled,

"Why us, why do we have to dig the shit hole?"

Ron offers a little comfort,

"Well it's because Karl likes us so much. It's his way of getting to us… Still, it's better than having to fill it in after it's been used by everyone, yuck".

Ken sits down and watches his brother work saying,

"If we let Karl annoy us, if we let him see that we are pissed-off or angry at him he will have won and will he ever gloat. We should just ignore him just let's pretend he just isn't there and bollocks to the shit-bag Karl".

Ron shakes his head.

"That's where you are wrong…
Let him see we are both pissed off and
then he will feel he has got one over us".

Ken brightens up and digs the soft muddy clay and changes the subject.

"So Ron, what did you think of the show in town? Did you see how tall the Flying HJ were? Will they all be aircrew and pilots? They all looked very intelligent".

Ron puffs working his spade,

"It's the uniform, take them out of that uniform and
they will look as stupid as us. Come on, it's your turn to dig.
Take your boots off and use your socks as gloves".
"Ron my feet ache so much".
"Come on, take your boots off, the mud feels
so good through your toes".

After a while both boys are knee deep in a mud hole with the mud squashing through their toes and their socks on their hands.

Digging away the latrine is quite deep. Ron is aware of a trickle of water coming down the wall of the pit.

He looks up to see a boy pissing in the pit. He yells.

"So what the bloody hell do you think you're doing?"

Ken picks a fist full of wet mud and throws it at the boy's crotch.

"How about letting us finish the digging
the sodding hole first, asshole"

The boy tries to pick the mud out of his shorts saying.

"Hey, Karl told me to do it here,
and he said to piss on your heads"

Soon all the boys sit down to eat hot stew with lots of thick sausage, bread and a big slice of apple strudel each for dessert.

That evening the boys sit in a large circle around a big fire singing cheerfully. Dieter, Hans and the twins are all having a good time. A few of the bigger boys led by Karl run and jump over the flames of the fire. It's a bigger boy thing to be able jump over the immense campfire without catching themselves alight.

Some of the tired boys drift into the tents to get their heads down. Hans draws the first watch for the night guard. He is given Karl's watch and the spear, a flagpole with the flag removed.

It looks very vicious, with a polished brass bayonet styled point. He gets closer to the fire, putting more wood on to cheer himself up.

Inside the tent, the big ground sheet is spread on a fat pile of soft bracken. Each boy has his own blanket pinned up one side with oversized brass safety pins, like a sleeping bag. The boys sleep with their heads into the center pole. They joke and chatter about yesterday and the big parade. Ron yells,

"Did you hear about the woman who had
wooden tits and plywood sex organs..."...

Dieter loudly interrupts boyish giggles,

"Settle down, it's another long hard day tomorrow.
The next boy who speaks will stand extra guard duty,
Goodnight. Oh, when you go on guard duty try not to step
on your comrade's faces. And if it rains, guard duty is canceled.
But don't let the fire go out. We need it for breakfast that's if
you want hot chocolate in the morning".

The boys are all wrapped tight. Ken looks to the top of the tent, it's just visible in the candlelight night and backs in closer to Ron. Ron who is half asleep automatically snuggles closer. The boys draw on each other's warmth. Ken whispers,

"Ron"

Ron turns over and nods,

"What?"

Ken whispers,

"Do you think Hitler is bonkers and off his rocker?"
"Shhh, you will get us shot".
"He looked very mad, angry and sort of nutty to me, I think he
would step on you like a bug and kill you if you got in his way".
"Shhh, go to sleep Ken".
"This is a good lark, hey Ron, a good lark".

Ron nods, turns his back and pushes back to get closer. The shuffle is reactive, each boy packing close for warmth. Ron whispers

"She got drilled and screwed into".

Giggles ripple around the tent muffled by the blankets.

Outside the tent Hans is by the fire, sitting with the spear in his hand and peering into the darkness. Looking left, then right... After a while the sound of a soft footstep makes him turn around instinctively, pointing his spear in the direction of the oncoming figure. It's Karl in his underpants. Karl whispers,

"You alright? Don't look so scared, it's only me, hey, give me
my watch back, you go in and get your head down. Get some

sleep, there's nothing to steal out here. I'm going to have a piss. Tomorrow is going to be a hard day for all of us".

Hans doesn't need telling twice,

"Good night, thank you sergeant".

Hans comes quietly into the tent. The Lambert brothers have made his bed for him. He snuggles down in his space and pushes in close to Dieter for warmth.

The next day Karl, Dieter and their two little armies march off in opposite directions, across meadows of knee-length wet grasses that wash their bare shiny legs as they trudge forward. They all quietly sing, with their heads bent, gripping the straps of their packs tight.

"*Wenn der Kuckkuck lacht in gruner Fern*
Kuckkuck- Ho-la-la-"
"*When the Cuckoo in the greenwood sings-*
I hear the voice of a thousand springs
Cuckoo-Ho, la la.
Like you I will the burden bear.
When duty calls, my courage is there,
Your cry of cuckoo, beautiful and bright,
Will fortify and set me right.
Clear-eyed and full of trust I see,
Ahead, around, and over me...
Like Siegfried, I will rise up straight
To open the German Golden Gate".

After three hours they stop to rest, the boys all flop out on the side of the road a few of them complain about the lack of food. Others complain about the hardship of the long marches.

Little Willie is swaying oddly and looks as if he is about to pass out. Beads of sweat drip from his boyish chin. His hair is soaking wet with perspiration.

Dieter grabs him by his shoulder straps and holds him still,

"Are you alright or are you faking this boy?"

Willie's head wobbles, Dieter takes his monkey (Knapsack) off his back and pulls his shirt off and wipes the sweat from his skinny body.

"You have got yourself all over heated, lad"

Dieter sits him down gently and using his shirt, fans him as a boxing second would do. Ken takes his own shirt off and passes it around the platoon getting a little water from each boy's bottle to dampen the shirttail and then he cools off Willie's body with it. Dieter holds up Willie's knapsack.

"Who will carry Willie's monkey?" he asks.

No one volunteers Willie looks around pleading. Dieter says,

"If we don't carry it we will end up carrying Willie himself, so I

126

will tote it for a few kilometers but I want some help…
Alright?"

Ken opens his first-aid kit and attends those who have problems
with their feet. He yells to Dieter,

> "Look Dieter… These boys feet are all blistered, we should
> stop by a stream, wash our feet and put on the extra pair of
> clean socks, get everyone to dry out their boots and put on
> some of this antiseptic foot powder".

Dieter nods.

Ron and Dieter spread out a map and take turns sighting landmarks
with the compass. Then they trudge on through wide, hilly countryside
and Willie's knapsack gets passed around the platoon each boy taking his
turn to carry it.

They get to the given location that is marked on their map. Ken
climbs a tree and retrieves a tin can containing the fresh orders. The
platoon all cheer as they open the can and share a large packet of Swiss
chocolates then they start to read the new maps.

Dieter's new pristine map takes his platoon along the edge of a river.
Ken and Ron are lagging behind at the rear end of the platoon. The boys
are forced into single file on a narrow bank.

As the platoon marches under a bridge, the boys shout to hear their
own echoes. Ken shouts,

> *"Oh Auntie Nelly, had a fat belly,*
> *and a red pimple on her bum".*

Ron joins in,

> *"And a red pimple on her bum".*

The echoes ring around and around until the platoon comes out
from under the bridge the other side. Ron catches up with Ken and dives
at him grabbing him in an arm lock trying to throw him to the ground.

Ken reverses it and heaves Ron in to the muddy bank yelling,

> "Ow… That hurt asshole".

A wrestling bout starts and is joined by Hans and Dieter in a free-
for-all. The rest of the platoon tries to pull the wrestling bodies apart so
lots of boys end up in the mud on the riverbank.

After a few moments the boys are so covered with mud they can't
stand or grip hold of each other. Dieter sits up in the mud and tries to
blow his whistle but he is laughing too hard. Eventually most of the
platoon discard their clothes and backpacks and end up swimming in the
river and washing the mud off their clothes.

The sun comes out from behind the clouds hot and bright so the
boys all lay out to dry themselves.

Dieter looks at the Lambert brothers laying naked on their backs and
sees two identical boys, strong with well-toned wiry bodies and says,

> "Have you two ever had a real fight with each other?"

Ken and Ron look at each other, grin and shake their heads. Hans says quietly,

"I have never seen such a perfectly matched pair; it would be a pure fight, we should get the boxing gloves on you two one day, neither of you would have the advantage. You are both the same weight and height and have the same strength. It would be a battle of the minds".

Dieter stands up and grabs each of the twins by their arms,

"Come on let's see who's the strongest of the two of you; let's see who can wrestle the other to the ground first".

Ken looks at his brother and gives him a look that both boys know. They face off to each other like a pair of professional wrestlers growling and trying to grab each other's hand, making circles, crouching working closer and closer to Dieter, then Ron yells,

"Now!"

Both boys turn and jump on to Dieter crashing him to the ground. The surprise worked and knocks the wind out of him. Ken grabs him with a full arm lock around his neck pulls him back from behind. As soon as he is down, Ron jumps on him sitting astride his legs and chest, his right arm in the air clutching a fist-sized rock ready to strike at Dieter's head. Dieter yells,

"All right! All right...

What you going to do with that rock, kill me? Wow!

Remind me not to get on the wrong side of you two!"

The twins laugh and let Dieter stand up, Ron says quietly,

"If anyone ever starts a fight...

Well they had better have eyes in the back of their head".

Later that afternoon dried and refreshed with clean dry socks Dieter's platoon picks their way slowly through a wooded slope looking for Karl and his green platoon.

Dieter's navigation has been very accurate so they know they must be close to their opponents by now. Dieter spots one of Karl's boys running down into a gully. He stops, drops to the ground and signals for silence. Waving to the platoon to lay flat he whispers,

"No knives, pass it on, we just need to

break their green wool armbands to win".

The orders are quietly whispered around the platoon. The twins open their packs and take out a pair of thick winter socks that have a fist-full of round pebble rocks shoved into the toes; formidable and sneaky weapons. They hear Karl's voice shouting in an argument over some map-reading point.

Dieter splits his platoon into two and sends half of his boys around the rear to make his attack a total surprise. When the platoon is ready and in position Dieter signals his lads to take off their field marching gear and packs. Quietly they slip out of their equipment.

Karl's tired and unsuspecting platoon is huddled in a hollow clearing, arguing about map coordinates, they still have all their packs and field gear on, with no guards posted. Dieter gives a signal with a wave of his arm and a short blast of his whistle.

The blue army swoops down charging, yelling, jumping on their opponents; pulling them to the ground and ripping off their green wool armbands to render them neutralized. The surprise attack works.

Ron and Ken work as a team; bashing any boy with their socks who stands up to them. Some, seeing how effective the swinging socks are, just pull off their own wool armbands and hand them to the twins. It is all over in a few minutes. Most boys worked in pairs. There are some bloody noses and boys with crushed pride.

It takes Dieter and three other boys to hold down Karl who fights like a tiger. He has laced thin wire through his wool armband, so it is hard to remove, but Dieter and his platoon have clearly won the day and are the victors.

Karl, who is a very poor loser, yells about the sneak surprise ambush. Ron and Ken discreetly empty the rocks out of their socks when no one is looking.

It takes six hours to march back to the college. As Dieter's platoon gets close to the school and it starts to rain. The boys are showing signs of being on their feet in the open for three days. They are wet through, muddy and bedraggled. Dieter cries out,

"Come on, let's show them we are not tired or short on discipline. Heads up, swing your arms, we are home now. Let's march into this school like Dieter's men. Left right".

Dieter picks up the pace and the platoon starts to march as if they haven't ever been out of the school. Ken, Ron and Hans start singing as loud as they can,

"Oh Auntie Nelly had a fat belly
with a red pimple on her bum,
with a red pimple on her bum...
Bang".

As they march through the main gates and past the front of the school building, they pass Captain Mitter talking to Dr Weiss on the steps. Captain Mitter comes to attention and salutes the muddy group. Dieter returns the recognition and salutes.

They arrive at their hut at last, so tired they feel like dropping on the spot. Before Dieter dismisses them to the showers he says

"I don't want any of this muddy gear on the clean floors of the dormitory. Leave your boots and wet clothes outside here, strip off and into the showers quick. We will march to supper nice and clean... Dis-miss".

Packs, water canteens, straps, belts, wet shirts, boots and socks all plop on the cobble path outside the hut. Naked boys run into the showers and sing, happy

Voices rise through steam as the boys enjoy their first hot shower in three days. Dieter moves about looking at the boy's blisters.

"I'm going to get some plasters and disinfectant from the Medical Room and patch up some of these battle trophies. You lot, get all that gear outside stowed away when you're dried off".

Ken and Ron are drying themselves off and singing as loud as they can, their voices echoing in the steamy shower room,

"Auntie Nelly, had a fat belly
and a red pimple on her bum,
and a red pimple on her bum"

Karl enters; he is covered in mud and is very angry, he screams,

"What's all this stupid noise about, and why is all your gear still outside in the wet?"

Karl takes off his muddy jacket and throws it hard at Hans. It hits him full in the face. Ken and Ron just stand there singing defiantly. Karl takes off his very muddy socks and slowly rubs them into Ron's face. Ken comes up behind him and kicks Karl hard in his backside. Karl spins around and punches Ken full in his face with a straight left that takes the boy totally by surprise it lands very hard. Ken reels back banging his head heavily against the wall and slides plopping to the floor unconscious. Ron pushes Karl in his chest and yells,

"Look what you have done, asshole!"

Karl takes a wide swing at Ron's head; Ron ducks the fist that whizzes over his head. Ron attacks, his fists flying madly, throwing punches at anything he can hit, most of them missing. Karl is two years older than the twins and he uses his bulk and height.

The blows that Ron land are totally ineffectual. Karl covers up and dances around. His time in the boxing ring is showing. Like a prizefighter he dodges and punches a left and right, then like a flash catches Ron with a heavy blow on his jaw. Ron's hands drop; he reels back leaving himself wide open.

Karl moves in, grabs him by his hair and lays punch after punch on his body and face. Ron's screams echo in the locker room. Han's yells,

"Someone go and get Dieter… Quick!"

Hans jumps up on Karl's back and tries to put his arms around his chest in a futile effort to stop the beating. Karl reaches over and grabs Hans's head and pulls him over his shoulders laying him out on the floor punching him just once full in his face. Hans lays still totally dazed.

Ron grabs the moment and tries to crawl under the bench for cover but gets dragged out by his foot. Karl's rage is now totally out of control. Furious punching as fast and as hard as he can, sitting astride Ron's chest and punching his face from left to right.   Ron tries to cover his face, his screams repeating with each breath. The attack goes on and on until Ron is almost out of voice. Two other boys pick up a wooden changing-room bench and charge Karl with it using it as a battering ram.

They succeed in knocking him off his balance but only for a moment. Ron's screams are now just heavy breaths with no voice left. Karl quickly regains his position over Ron's chest grabbing his ears and is about to smash his head into the cement floor when the door bursts open. Captain Mitter yells,

"No sergeant! No! Just stand still!"

10. PETER'S DISPATCH

Mitter grabs a towel, puts it around Karl's face from behind and pulls his head back to stop the beating... he yells,
"Stand over there sergeant and calm down".
The Captain enlists the help of the boys to lift Ron and Ken up and lay them both out on benches. Ron's bloody face has a cut lip that is bleeding badly. Ken is still unconscious. He comes around when someone dabs him with a wet sponge and cold water. Dieter runs in and is told to get the boys to the medical room.
Captain Mitter orders Karl to the office.

That evening the Lambert brothers and Hans are sitting up in the white painted beds of the infirmary looking much bashed about. Ron's face is so swollen he is hardly recognizable. Dieter comes in with a tray and three bowls of soup and some big chunks of bread. Dieter laughs as Ron tries to feed himself. Dieter takes over with the spoon.
"Do you two ever look terrible; see what happens when
I turn my back for a moment, all three of you start fights".
Ken shakes his head in protest.
"Ha, Ha, I know, I've heard the story ten times.
Karl's been sent to some training school for Youth Leaders...
We won't be seeing him for a while.
So, are there any nice nurses in here then?"
Dieter gets a little closer and peers at Ron's face,
"You two look awful, how do you feel?"
Ron just nods slowly trying to crack a smile. Dieter hands Hans his glasses. Hans, nursing his own black eye and split lip says.
"Thank you, if Karl had done that to me, I would be dead,
very dead, I couldn't take that kind of a bashing".
Dieter grins and says,
"Karl's very sorry, you know.
He has sent you both some Swiss Chocolates,
I am keeping them safe for you three".
Ken asks through his swollen lips,
"Is he coming back to this school?"
Dieter shakes his head and shrugs his shoulders, Ken painfully nods his head and holds his thumb up and says,
"Ron's got four stitches, I have two".
Dieter says grinning,
"That will keep you two quiet for a few days".

The war has been going badly for Germany and the boys at the school know that Germany's days are numbered and the New Order is fighting for its life.

Today is April 20th 1944 and Hitler's birthday. The Lambert boys will be fourteen in four weeks. Dieter makes sure they all are dressed properly, with clean boots, before he marches them to breakfast in the great hall. Today there will be speeches and oaths so everyone has to look his best.

Just before they go through the large carved wooden doors in to the Great Hall Dieter whispers to the twins and Hans,

"You three will be sworn into the Hitler Youth today.

I have put in good reports for you. Don't let me down".

After a better breakfast than usual Dr. Weiss steps forward to the edge of the stage. He stands looking around and gets the silence he expects.

New flags and banners have been hung; the bronze bust of Adolf Hitler has been centered on the stage. Ken whispers,

"They should put wheels on that thing or someone will drop it one day and end up getting shot for treason".

Dr. Weiss looks at Captain Mitter, who walks forward to join him. Weiss starts speaking very quietly,

"In a moment Captain Mitter will read out a list of names.

If you hear your name, quietly make your way down to the front of the stage here and stand still".

He nods and Dieter marches into the center of the stage proudly bearing the school Hitler Youth banner with the motto "Blut und Ehre" (Blood and Honor). The large red and white swastika banner edged with a silver fringe is on a black and silver engraved pole. Captain Mitter calls out a list of names and boys start to shuffle down to the front of the stage.

When Captain Mitter calls the names of the twins and Hans, Dieter gives them a wink. Dr. Weiss looks down at the group of little boys in their Young Folk uniforms, he sees some of the boys are over fourteen and are growing too big for the uniforms. Weiss speaks in a kind and fatherly voice.

"I have had very some very good reports from your superiors and some fair reports, but you have all passed the tasks set for you so you have my sincere congratulations. This is your last day in the Young Folk. You are no longer Pimpfs (young boys) today you can take the Sigrune off your left arms and replace it with the Hitler Youth Swastika armband.

But remember when you put on the armband of the Hitler Youth, you are a member of a brotherhood that bears our Führer Adolf Hitler's name. Now all childish behavior stops. You will prepare yourselves for military service. From now on you may have to give every afternoon and all day Sunday to Hitler Youth Duties.

Those of you who are used to going to church on Sunday will give it up. You don't need the church now; you can discard the old bourgeois prejudices. You will be busy with far more important duties…"

Dr. Weiss now address's the whole school.

> "My remarks are now made to the boys leaving the Young Folk and entering the Hitler Youth… Do you want to join the strongest brotherhood in the world and become a Hitler Youth?"

The group all yell,

> "Yes Sir"
>
> "Then step forward and grasp the school banner that has been consecrated by Reichsjugendführer Baldur Von Schirach for this school. On this standard you will swear your oaths".

Solemnly Dieter calls the school to attention and leads the singing of the National Anthem and slowly lowers the sacred banner down from the stage. The boys gather around it and grasp a handful of the silver edge with their left hands. The twins wink at Hans.

The flag is big enough for the boys to form a semicircle. They raise their right hands three fingers up in salute. Dr. Weiss leads them in the oath. As they bury their fingers in the cloth of the flag the twins and Hans cross their fingers in defiance. They say'

> "I swear before God, this solemn oath.
>
> To give to the Führer of the Reich Adolf Hitler,
>
> The Commander in Chief of the Hitler Youth,
>
> total obedience, and in case of any danger,
>
> be ready, to give up my life.
>
> Sieg Heil, Sieg Heil, Sieg Heil".

Each boy marches up on the stage and receives his HJ armband and a handshake from Captain Mitter and Dr. Weiss. Out in the corridor Dieter gives each boy a hug,

> "Well you are all in the HJ now and you three not yet fourteen. When you are in uniform you can stay out on Saturday nights until nine PM, if you are on duty you can stay out all night. You see, people will now treat you as adults".

Ron opens his brown paper bag and looks at the armband,

> "Are they all the same size?"

Dieter grabs Ron's left arm, draws his camp knife and starts to carefully cut off the old Sigrune badge, the last symbol of the Young Folk, then slips the armband up Ron's arm and sets it square,

> "It will need three stitches to hold it in position".

Dieter repeats the service for Ken and Hans; smiling he says,
   "You know I feel this is an act of
   close friendship to put these on for you".
Then he leans close to them and whispers,
   "I know we all hate the HJ and Adolf fucking Hitler
   but we have to put on a good show, don't we?"
The boys all smile and give artificial Nazi salutes. Ken Laughs,
   "So if these uniforms make us look older, will we
   get to squeeze a few young ladies, ha, I hope so".

Ron Laughs,
   "Ha, we haven't ever kissed one yet, so when do we get
   to make some babies for Hitler? When do we get all the
   badges and belt buckles? Yes, yes we look older, just like
   Hitler's young cannon fodder"

The war is getting closer. The boys at the school are hearing a lot more war news. Some of them keep secret maps of Europe and plot the war's progress; a practice strictly prohibited.

Their Hitler Youth civic duties are demanding more than half of their school time. Their assignments take them into Munich, where they serve as messenger boys on bicycles during the air raids. They work at issuing and distributing monthly ration cards to the public and serve station duty on the platforms, as not very diligent eyes for the SS, looking for deserters, runaway slave labor workers and Jews. They also have guard duty, guarding the freshly bombed houses and apartments from being looted.

Some of the older boys have been trained to man the anti-aircraft guns. Now almost sixteen, an older Dieter has grown a blond baby mustache. He is still the sergeant, but his group has grown to include the first platoon since Karl had been packed off to an officer cadet training camp.

Dieter's control of his fifty lads is firm but most of his boys know that he is not a true Nazi and at least half of his boys are just going through the motions, doing what they have to stay alive and survive the war. The punishment for rebellion is quick and harsh, so they all tag along.

It's raining hard outside. Ron and three other boys, damp from the rain, creep along to the end of a corridor past the upstairs bedrooms to a short staircase that leads to the loft storeroom.

Ron taps three long and three short quiet knocks on the door. After a few moments it opens and the boys slip inside. They pick their way through trunks, boxes and old disused gym equipment. Sitting in a circle on a pile of old window drapes just under a dusty attic dormer window are Ken, Hans and Dieter.

Ken is reading from a battered dog-eared copy of a sexually explicit book called "Arab Lovers and their tales". Its plain cover has been replaced with a new label 'French for beginners'. The new arrivals settle down quickly and melt into the shadows. Ken looks up and moves himself to a more comfortable position and asks the new boys,

"Have you heard any of this?"

The boys shake their heads. A ripple of excitement rings around the boys as they nudge each other and giggle. Ken opens the book.

"While I'm reading, no comments, no questions, it's best to close your eyes; let your imagination run free".

Dieter grins, lays back and covers his face with his cap.

Ken flips to a bookmark,

"I'll start this chapter again".

The boys shuffle and get closer and more comfortable.

One boy asks.

"So what is this book all about"?

There's a buzz of excitement as Ron puts his finger to his lips for quiet. Ken starts to read,

"She said to the boy, so, you're only sixteen, could I, lad, belong to anyone but you? She swiftly casts aside her veils, removes her clothing and appears as naked as she was born. Her body is as white and fresh as new snow. Her perky little breasts stand firm.

Her golden hair falls gently over her shoulders and her deep violet eyes smile as she peels off the boy's soft shirt.

The Princess is soft and white; she exudes a scent of fine amber. He takes her in his arms, probes her intimate flower and finds she is still a virgin".

Ron holds up his hand, trying to poke his finger into his tightly rolled fist. Dieter grabs his coat and spreads it over his lower body, looks to see if anyone is watching and slides his hands under his coat and down inside his pants and closes his eyes.

Ken continues reading:

"His hand roves over her lovely limbs and neck. She places his youthful member into herself, holds his bottom with both hands and pulls him into her as hard as her strength would muster. Her pain and pleasure race with both their heartbeats.

Then, so weary of their passions, they fall asleep in each other's arms, drunk with joy, naked on the silk, laying in the warm night air under the stars".

Ken is distracted from his reading by Ron creeping over close to Dieter, so he reads the last page again. Ron stands up and puts one finger to his lips for hush and points to Dieter's hand working his erection under his coat.

Dieter now has his jacket over his face and is in a sensual world of his own, totally unaware that Ron is standing over him. Ron grins and carefully peels back Dieter's shirt. Ken reads on. At first Dieter is not aware of the exposure and continues his pleasure. Hans can't hold back his giggles and sniggers.

Dieter looks up and instantly realizes everyone is watching, he laughs, throws off his jacket and jumps up, his shorts and underpants fall down around his ankles. The boys all laugh.

"Will that go right up inside a girl, all of it inside?"
Ken asks,
"Dieter, in the book, how does he know she's a virgin?"
Dieter pulling up his shorts,
"We are all virgins, all of us. None of us has ever been with a
girl, so we are all still young virgins.
When you have actually put your little thing inside a girl,
you break it open, then she's not a virgin, nor are you,
she's lost it so have you".
Ken getting frustrated,
"So what breaks on the boy?"
Dieter smiles,
"Nothing breaks on a boy, he just has to put it
inside a girl to lose his virginity".
Ken still frustrated,
"Well what does it look like before he loses it in a girl?...
Is it up inside us ready to come out?
You know, when we do our first girl?"
Dieter laughing,
"You three should be wanking yourselves off by now,
it makes it grow bigger you know".
Ken says hopefully,
"Does it really?"
Ron gets up and looks out of the window says to Dieter,
"So Dieter, how often do you wank-off then?"
Dieter giggles,
"Oh about two or three times. I started on my thirteenth
birthday".
Ken says,
"Three times a week; how do you find the time?"
Dieter laughs out loud,
"Oh no, three times a day".

Hans's grumbles,
>"It all sounds very boring to me. I would rather eat
>than do the sex stuff, any day".

The boys all leave; Ron and Ken are trailing at the rear. Ken makes a jerking movement with his hand, points at Dieter and says,
>"Dieter the big wanker".

As the boys go off to supper Ken walks close to Ron, nudges him and says confidentially,
>"Is it true that if we wank-off three times
>a day like Dieter said, it will grow larger?"

Ron smiles,
>"Well mine isn't getting much bigger".

Ken stops and looks Ron in the eyes,
>"How many times a day?"
>"Twice"

Ken looks shocked,
>"You, twice a day? You never told me, can you come and
>everything...?"

Ron nods and grins, Ken says,
>"Fancy you not telling me that you wank-off, can you shoot
>stuff... All I get is a thrill but nothing comes out".

Ron points his finger accusingly,
>"So... you do wank off, you didn't tell me either".

Ron pulls his right trouser pocket open and shows Ken the tip of his erection poking through a hole in his pocket.
>"Pocket snooker".
>"No, pocket billiards, ha".

Dieter's platoon is lined outside the school office to hear what duties they have next week. Hans is now sporting adult army issue steel-rimmed glasses. All the boys are wearing the same uniform: black boots, gray socks, black cord shorts, brown shirts, a summer cap, the blood red armband with a white square and a swastika, belts, cross shoulder straps, badges and a black neck scarf tied with a brown leather scarf knot.

Dieter gives the twins extra white armbands with the words 'Ordungs-Dienst' (Control Service) in black letters. Dieter reads to his platoon from a clipboard,
>"Today, the Lambert brothers here are going to Munich on
>messenger duty for three days. The rest of us have farm work.
>At least we will eat well on the farms".

A cheer ripples through the ranks. Dieter pulls the twins away from the rest of the section and puts an arm over each one of the boys shoulders like a big brother and warmly says,
>"So, Munich, three days for you two.... Will you be all right?

Ron and Ken nod and shrug their shoulders, Ron says smiling,
    "If we get killed, we will come back and tell you"
    "Seriously, I have authorized each of you to draw six days'
    food rations from the cook house, don't expect them to give
    you any in Munich, we have more to eat here than most people.
    As soon as you get there, report to the station messenger office,
    grab good bikes and steel helmets".
    "If you have to ride through an air raid, don't forget to wear
    your steel helmets... all right.... Good luck".
Dieter, the twins and Hans all shake hands warmly and Dieter strides
back to his platoon,
    "Sad news now.... Paul and Gunter from the sixth platoon were
    killed by a bomb on their 'Flack Helper' duty at the railway
    yards last night. They were helping out on an 88mm antiaircraft
    battery, all their details are on the board".
A group of sad little boys gather around the big notice Board in the
Great Hall silently reading about the heroic actions of the two fifteen year
old Hitler Youth 'Flack Helpers' from their school. They continued to
pass the ammunition on the 88mm anti-aircraft gun while they were
wounded, fighting bravely for the Fatherland and finally died when a
bomb struck close to the gun emplacement.
    The twins cycle through the bombed out areas of Munich, picking
their way through rubble-strewn streets. The air is acrid and smells of
burnt rubber. They pass gangs of old men and women clearing the roads
of debris. Smoke from fires drift across the road and falling ash looking
like snowflakes settles in their hair. They ride into the station that's full of
tired looking soldiers lying around on their kit, just waiting for trains that
may or may not come. The restaurant is closed and boarded up.
    Ron notices an old sign still hanging on one hook.
          FOR PUBLIC HEALTH REASONS TURKS AND
          ARABS ARE NOT PERMITTED TO REMAIN
          MORE THAT TWENTY MINUTES IN THIS
          RESTAURANT
    "You know **what's** wrong with Arabs and Turks?"
Ron whispers.
    "No," Ken answers.
    There are SS patrols at most platform gates checking passes and
papers. Gestapo Agents in plain clothes walk around in pairs looking at
everyone.
    Tucked away in the corner of the station they spot the Messenger
Room. The twins go into the office, where six other HJ boys and a few
Young Folk are sitting playing cards or marking up their small maps
copying from the large one on the wall. The big map is all blotched with

red marks showing roads that are closed to traffic due to bomb damage. In the background, through a wire cage is the radio room that is buzzing with incoming messages.

Ron and Ken try to find good-fitting steel helmets, but they are all too big.

Peter, a pleasant fresh-faced boy about fourteen in a HJ uniform, hands Ron and Ken some white rag from a torn bedsheet and shows them how to pad out their helmets so they stay on and fit better. Peter says,

"They're all the same size, you know".

He then takes them over to the sergeant who shows them the big map marking the roads that are closed due to bomb damage; they mark up their own maps and bring them up to date. Peter smiles, comes over to them and asks,

"Will tonight's raid be the first time you two have been out in the rain?"

Ken whispers apprehensively,

Will there be a raid tonight then?"

Peter answers,

"I expect so".

Ron politely,

"I didn't think it was going to rain, I didn't bring a cape".

Peter smiles,

"Not the wet sort of rain, it will rain hot metal when our eighty-eights start firing at the Lancaster bombers tonight".

Ron looks concerned,

"They wouldn't send us out in a raid... Would they?"

Peter nods,

"Always... I'm Peter by the way".

The boys all shake hands. Peter senses Ken's fear and puts his arm around his shoulder and says:

"You two will be alright, you're too young to die.

Ha, and no-one ever dies on their first night duty".

For two days the boys get bored. There are no raids and only a few messages to deliver. But on the third and last day the wail of the air raid sirens start, the sound sending a chill through the air. The messenger boys react and exchange anxious looks. They gather up their cards and casually relocate themselves under the big strong steel table that's been built as an air raid shelter. The thumps of the anti-aircraft guns make the boys jump and duck quickly under the table. Peter beckons to Ron and Ken,

"Here they come, stay here until you get called, put your helmets on".

The sergeant starts to stuff envelopes with messages and yells,

"Areas 8... 12... and 24".

Three boys jump forward and take the envelopes. They stuff them in their belt pouches, tug on their helmet chinstraps and go out into the streets. The Sergeant leans over the counter,

"Area 5… Urgent… Peter, it's yours".

Peter crawls from under the table, takes the envelope, stuffs it in his pouch, gives the boys under the table a smile, and leaves.

The bombing gets closer and more guns open up. The sergeant gets under the table and the frightened little boys cling together, crushing to be in the center of the table, where they feel it's safer.

There's a loud crash and a 28cm splinter of steel rips through the roof and sticks into the floor like a stumpy arrow. It glows cherry red, flames and smoke come from the wood around it.

The sergeant yells "No" as a small boy moves to get a closer look, he pulls the boy out of the way gets out from under the table and pores water over it from a fire bucket then looks up at the small hole in the roof. The bombs come closer again and the boys under the table peer out wide-eyed and fearful, huddling closer together. Their steel helmets looking far too big for them. Ken shaking with fear, points to the steaming fragment of steel,

"Shit, wow, if that thing hit you, you would be very dead… would this table stop that? Will the steel of this table hold if we took a direct hit Ron"?

Dust flakes down like gentle white snow and the boys flinch at each bomb blast. Ron starts to sing nervously,

"Oh, any old iron, any old iron, any old iron".

The sergeant smiles at Ron's singing, then looks at all the boys, each one terrified, each one hoping he won't be the next to be called to go out in the street.

The telephone rings and the sergeant props the phone under his chin and scribbles a note. The Lambert brothers are called, he holds his hand up as if to say, stay there and joins them, sitting under the table himself.

He asks,

"Do you two know Brienner Strasse at Konig's Platz? It's less than three streets from here".

Ron and Ken nod their heads. Ken smiles as the bombing stops and then the anti-aircraft guns stop firing. Everyone breathes a big sigh of relief and start chattering nervously. They kick the still-hot lump of a shell fragment that's stuck fast in the floor. The Sergeant stands up and looks at his papers saying.

"Well you two get over there. Peter Swatz is down… Do what you can for him".

Ron says firmly,

"What do you mean, he's down?"

Sergeant with indifference says,
"He's been knocked off his bike. I don't know any details.
Take the first aid kit with you and do what you can for him.
But this is very important, get his belt and pouch...
If he still has the message, one of you stay with Peter,
the other deliver it...
Read it first; don't go riding about in the rain.
If the message is out of date or frivolous,
well you just use your own judgment... Go".

Ken and Ron start to the door, tightening their helmet chinstraps.
Ken picks up the small first aid kit and clamps it on the rack on the rear
of his bike. Both twins feel very scared as they go through the door and
into the station.

The brothers ride their bikes at full speed through the streets. The
sounds of anti-aircraft fire and bombs are not too far away. They wear
their scarves over their faces to try and keep out the dust and smoke. The
over-sized helmets wobble on their heads as they pedal. The streets seem
to have a different feel now that an air raid is in progress.

They arrive at Konig's Platz and look about for the downed boy
Peter. There is not a living person to be seen on the street. They ride
slowly around the traffic circle looking left and looking right. Ken points,
and they see Peter sitting up against a lamppost. His cycle is lying at his
feet. Peter's jacket and shirt have been ripped open and his light brown
shirt is black with his blood. His chest has a vicious wound starting at the
shattered collarbone that is protruding through his shirt and running
down to his lower breast. A steel shrapnel fragment has torn through
flesh and bone. Blood and air bubbles are gurgling out of the dark hole
hot and frothy.

A small line of blood is dribbling from his mouth. The boys offer
him some water. He takes the moisture, sips and smiles.

Peter whispers,
"My back hurts, I think it came out of my back".

Ken looks behind him and sees a rip through his shirt at his back,
two of his ribs are sticking out. Ron says to Peter calmly,
"We have to get you to an aid station".

Ken makes a wad from the first aid kit and gently places it on Peter's
chest, he tries to pull the jacket over the dressing, but as Ken touches
Peter he lets out a gurgling scream and says painfully,
"Oh, no, please don't".

Ron gets up and looks around,
"I'm going to the aid station, you stay with Peter".

Ron jumps on his bike and rides off very fast, Peter looks down at
the river of blood that's running out from one leg of his shorts, watching
it run in pulses, he whispers,

"I'm dying aren't I... look at all this blood?"

Ken answers softly,

"No, you're not dying. The bleeding has stopped, mostly anyway, you may have a cut lung, a little blood goes a long way, and it always looks worse than it is".

Peter starts to slide in his own blood. Ken sits down and takes him in his arms, resting his head on his lap. Peter whispers,

"Get my mother, she knows what to do...

Oh, am I going to die, I don't want to die".

Ken glances down. The pool of blood is completely surrounding them. Peter's lifeblood is gurgling out in slow pulses running out both legs of his shorts fast.

The 'All Clear' sirens sound their long wail marking the end of the raid. Ken tries to comfort Peter,

"My brother Ron will be here soon with the ambulance.

He can ride like the wind".

Peter starts to nod as if to go to sleep.

"Peter, no, don't go to sleep, you must stay awake".

Ken shakes Peter to wake him. His head wobbles and he says,

"Oh, oh I... I feel cold and dizzy. Tell my mother I love her the best... I'm so tired".

Ken starts to cry, tears well up, then run down his face,

"Peter, I'm sorry, please don't go to sleep. They will be along soon. Peter, don't go to sleep, please".

Ken looks at Peter's staring eyes. They don't blink. Ken puts his ear to his mouth and gives him a shake. Peter's head wobbles to one side and a great gurgling breath escapes. His eyes are still looking at Ken, sad and hurt, tears all building up. Ken, sobbing, tries to sit him up,

"Oh, come on Peter, don't die, don't you die on me...

Oh, shit I've killed him. I shouldn't have shaken him so hard.

Oh Peter I'm sorry, Peter... I'm so sorry".

Ken looks at Peter's face. The sad look seems to have changed to one of peace. The tears are still welling up in his eyes.

As Ken places his fingers gently on Peter's eyelids and slowly closes them, the tears spill out and run down the dead boy's face. Ken is still sobbing and holding onto Peter when a small open truck arrives. Ron is in the back with his bike.

The driver jumps out and runs over to Peter and puts an expert finger on his neck. He turns around without saying anything, goes back to his truck, lifts off Ron's bike and drives away. Ken says quietly,

"Ron, he's gone... He's dead, Ron".

Ron, trying to hold back his tears, sobbing,

"He looks as if he is asleep to me, are you sure he's dead?

Where's his pulse... I never find it on anyone".

Ron tries to find a pulse on his wrist and his neck. Ken sobs.
> "He's dead Ron. He said we should tell his mother
> he loved her the best. Oh Ron, he's dead".

Ron removes the boy's belt and message pouch. An Air Raid Warden arrives, helps Ron lift the dead boy off of Ken and lay him out on the ground. The Warden writes all their names in his notebook.

Ken leans over to see what the man is writing,
> "Don't forget to tell his mother his last words, he said 'He loves her the best'. His name is Peter Swatz... Oh Ron let's get back, I feel sick".

Ron opens Peter's pouch and takes out the message, leaving bloody finger marks all over the envelope. He reads the first line, then with total disgust reads it out aloud. The Warden looks over Ron's shoulder and reads with him,
> "Birthday shit. Some asshole is sending
> birthday party invitations in priority pouches...
> How can they do that, what stinking assholes?"

He folds the bloody sheet, puts it in Ken's pocket that's already soaked in Peter's blood. Ken folds Peter's hands across his chest, and pulls his jacket closed as if to keep him warm.

The Air Raid Warden looks at Ken's bloody uniform,
> "Make sure you report this to your superior officer...
> You two had better get back".

The man holds Ken's shoulder,
> "Are you alright, is that all his blood?"

Ken nods, looking at his own body; he is covered in Peter's blood. The Warden takes Peters bloody HJ pass out of his shirt pocket saying
> "Go then, I will take care of him,
> I won't forget to tell his mother about his last words".

They see Peters' pool of blood has grown so large it now reaches the road and is running in to the gutter.

Ken is still all bloody, as both boys enter the office. The boys that are sitting around gasp and recoil. Ron carefully places Peter's belt and pouch on the counter as Ken puts the bloodstained message next to them....

The sergeant looks at the boys,
> "Where is he?"
> "Peter's dead".

The Sergeant looks them over and picks up the pouch,
> "You two all right?"

Ken nods. Ron pushes the message form to the sergeant, who reads it. Ron upset, blurts out,
> "He died for a fucking birthday greeting.
> Some asshole sent birthday shit in the pouch".

The sergeant, looks at the clock and reads the message form,
"I'm going to write a report about this.
This is gross misuse of the messenger service".
"I will want you two to sign it before you both leave, all right?
We must do this for Peter; he was a nice boy…
Now take that belt and pouch out to the toilet
and wash off all that blood and hang it up to dry".
The twins wander out to pick up Peter's bike. The streets are dark
and they take it slowly until their eyes get used to the total blackout.
People's voices can be heard long before they are seen. Little yellowish
green luminous Winter Aid badges bob past, pinned onto people's
jackets. Some are small and round, some in the form of Messerschmitt
pursuit planes, some picture gulls in flight. In the total darkness the
phosphorescent buttons stop people from bumping into each other. Ron
stops and looks at Ken with the paraffin oil lamp off their bike,
"You crying Ken?"
"A bit"
"Thinking about Peter?"
"He was so nice; why him, why did he have to get it?"
"It's just the luck of the draw; it could have been you or me".
"Ron, we have to get out of here; we have to run away and hide
somewhere or we're going to end up dead".
Ron puts his arm around his sobbing brother as they walk on.
"We will, you see; we will get out of here soon".
Ken shakes, trying to hold back his sobs,
"Yes Ron, let's run away, before one of us gets killed".
In the school dormitory that night the other boys watch with horror
as Ken and Ron undress, plopping their bloody clothes into a bucket of
cold water. Dieter asks,
"Whose blood?"
Ken says quietly,
"A boy, just like us: Our friend Peter".
As the memory of the boy's death comes back, Ken sobs.
"He died in my arms, *(sob)* for nothing, just for nothing, *(sob)*.
Oh Ron, let's take a shower".
Stripped down to their blood-spotted underpants, the twins pick up
the bucket and make their way to the showers. The platoon looks on with
sadness as they watch. Dieter, who is not too sure how to handle this
dreadful news, tries to take his mind off the situation by rinsing out the
blood soaked clothes.
In the warm water of the shower Ron says.
"We have to get out of this war Ken; you know,
Dieter, Hans and us, we've got to run away somewhere".

146

Ken adds,
   "It's not even our fucking war Ron.
   What are we doing here?
   I don't want us killed for fucking Hitler".
   "Fuck the war".
   "Fuck Adolf fucking Hitler".

The boys start to sing quietly and nervously,
       "Oh. Auntie Nelly
       had a fat belly,
       with a red pimple on her bum,
       with a red pimple on her bum,
       ho, ho and jump on her toe."

11. PREDATORS

The school's, two large covered trucks are being loaded with boys dressed in clean HJ uniforms and a platoon of girls from the BDB (*Bund Deutscher Made*, the female counterparts of the Hitler youth; girls ages range from 14 to 17). They are all loading banners, drums and flags into one of the trucks to go to a parade in Munich.

Dieter spots the girls and nods to the twins and Hans to get in the same truck with them. Long benches each side of the vehicle provide seating. Flags and drums are stacked down part of the center gangway. In the front end, there are the young girls. Some are sitting on the bench, some on the floor with their backs to the knees of the girls seated.

Dieter, Hans and the twins sit directly across from the girls. Dieter pretends to be very engrossed in his clipboard, concentrating and turning pages. The six young girls sitting across from Dieter start giggling and nudging each other. They are looking, smirking and staring at Dieter's crotch. Singing starts and Dieter is flapping his knees, opening and closing them to the rhythm of the tune. His baggy shorts with the open legs are showing the girls that he is not wearing any underwear. Still keeping up the pretense that he is unaware of his exhibition, he turns to look out of the window behind him.

As he swings his body around, he lifts his knee very naturally.

A roar of laughter comes from the girls. Hanna is the very pretty girl with blond braids that Dieter has had his eye on for some time. She yells across to Dieter,

"Hey Dieter, it's all hanging out there!
Don't you boys ever wear under-panties?"
One of the other young girls yells,
"Are you fishing for Catholic Priests Dieter?
They will love that little sausage".
Hanna, laughing,
"Oh, they don't know what to do with it at his age.
It's all wank, wank and wave it in the breeze…
Have you just discovered you've got one Dieter?"

Dieter is now very red; his little exhibition has backfired on him. He yanks himself around, leaps across the truck, grabs Hanna's face firmly and gives her a long kiss. A shout and a cheer rips through the truck. Hanna, instead of pushing him away, isn't going to miss this opportunity and wraps both her arms about him and holds him tight in a long kiss. There are louder cheers and more whistles from the truck.

The rest of the girls grab him and hold him down. Dieter is not putting up any resistance. From out of a pile of groping giggling girls, an arm holds up Dieter's black corduroy shorts triumphantly. They are quickly snatched by someone and whisked down the line of girls and hidden out of sight. As the truck slows down and stops, the screams and laughter are almost deafening.

Dieter sits up and looks frantically about for his shorts. The truck has stopped and the occupants hear Captain Mitter's voice outside and see him through the trucks rolled up side windows. Captain Mitter bangs on the tailgate shouting,

"All out, all out, get over there by
the old memorial for the photograph".

The boys and girls start to pile out, jumping down laughing.

Dieter is at the back of the truck pleading to the girls to give him his shorts back and searching the giggling boys before they jump off the truck. As the last boy jumps off Captain Mitter appears at the tailgate and sees Dieter without his pants and smiles saying,

"All out, don't forget your hats".

Then all the girls yell out in unison,

"And your shorts!"

The platoon all laugh, Dieter is left inside feeling very foolish. Finally when the photographer is ready with his group shot Captain Mitter shouts,

"Come on Sergeant, don't be shy, come on out and have your
photo taken".

The whole platoon roars with laughter. By now everyone knows the about Dieter's missing shorts. The Captain throws them to Hanna who runs over to the back of the truck and stands there inviting Dieter to come out and get them in full view of the waiting platoon.

There is a second roar of laughter as Dieter shouts at Hanna, but she just stands there holding them out about six paces from the back of the truck. Eventually Hanna tosses Dieter's shorts to him. The Captain sits in the center of the group and nods to the photographer as Dieter comes running out buttoning up his pants.

Captain Mitter with a broad smile yells,

"Who stole the sergeant's shorts?"

The whole group laughs boisterously. 'CLICK' and the photographer gets his photograph. They are all smiling, except Dieter, who is still doing up his buttons. A great photograph.

It's a quiet Monday afternoon. The traffic at the Message Office in the Station is light, with nothing much happening. There are too many boys there with little for them to do. Ron and Ken are playing cards with four other boys and the sergeant comes over, looks at the cards to see who is winning, he nods,

"You six, leave your belts and pouches on my desk and get over
to the station Gestapo Office. Ask for Cadet Sergeant Steiner.

He phoned; he needs some observers.
Be careful of him, he's a nasty little Nazi".
The sergeant looks hard at Ron,
"And Ron, you and your brother watch your mouths; don't give
him a chance to whack you. He is very quick with his fists.
Wash your hands and tidy yourself up, clean your boots, look
smart, tuck that shirt in".

The Gestapo office looks like any other but for the large portrait of
Adolf Hitler on the wall. The ironclad door with a small barred window
looks out of place in the old station. An older Gestapo plainclothes
Captain is on the telephone. Ron waits for him to put the telephone
down, salutes and asks for Steiner. The Captain waves them to the iron
door. They pull hard on the heavy door that swings open with a soft
squeal. Ken taps Ron's hand and whispers,
"Old iron, old iron".
They go through a narrow corridor past small holding cells on each
side and come to a door that opens to a large concrete room with no
windows. In the center are two scrubbed tables and some strong steel
chairs. Two bare bulbs hang shedding not quite enough light. Sitting at a
gray tin desk is a very young SS Cadet, Sergeant Steiner. He has blond
short hair, pale cold blue eyes, and a baby face not yet old enough to
shave. He stands up and is taller than any of the messenger boys. His
black uniform includes long jackboots of good calfskin polished to a
professional shine, a belt, cross strap and a small black leather pistol case
on his left side. On his desk is a black cap with the hated skull and cross
bones death-head badge. On his left arm there is a bright red swastika
armband. He sets his cap very square on his head and struts over to the
boys. With an aura of evil and cruelty, he stands looking at the line of six
slightly grubby little boys. Steiner says in a coarse dialect,
"What's this? What army do you dirty
little shits think you're in; theirs or ours?"
Ken recognizes him as the Sergeant who whacked him around the
face the day he was trying to sell flags, he also knows Steiner hasn't
recognized him yet. Ron says, stepping forward,
"We were..."
Ron doesn't get a chance to finish his sentence. Steiner fetches him
a backhanded whack across his face. It was so unexpected and so fast that
Ron sits down hard on a chair behind him. Ken instinctively steps
forward. Steiner sneers,
"You want some too...?"
He turns to Ron,
"You will get up off that chair and you will speak
only when you're spoken to and not before, understand?"

Steiner paces up and down in front of the little line of frightened boys. He stops at Ken and leans close to him, sniffing his chest, then his armpit.

> "Next time you come on duty in my office smelling like a
> Jewish bitch in heat, I will have you stripped naked and
> scrubbed raw, then washed down with a fire hose... Do you
> understand?"

> "Yes Sergeant Steiner".

Steiner turns to his table, scoops a pile of whistles, then turns back quickly as if to catch someone making faces behind his back,

> "We are going out onto the station platform today to search
> and hunt for vermin".

Steiner walks over to Willie, the smallest boy in the line who is a head shorter than the rest.

> "What vermin are we looking for boy...?"

Steiner flicks Willie's ear, then tries to flick his other ear. Willie dodges the second flick and says,

> "Rats sergeant?"

> "Not rats boy... worse than rats... Jews.
> We are going Jew spotting. If you see a Jew,
> you blow three blasts on these whistles.
> They won't be wearing their yellow stars today.
> They will be dressed mostly in black, with good boots.
> Children stick close to their parents.
> The men may have a barber's rash because they shaved
> their beards off for the first time in their lives.
> It shows and it gives them away. The father of the family
> will always be clutching a small case as if his life is in it".

Steiner is more relaxed as he drones on about his favorite subject, hunting down Jews. He throws his hat on the table and turns smiling, then says smugly,

> "A train will pull in here at ten hundred hours today to drop off
> wounded. It was not scheduled to stop in Munich at all, so, it is
> our advantage. Will the passengers be surprised? Ha, yes they
> will be very surprised. They think the train is going all the way
> to Vienna non-stop; they will all be in for a jolt.
> So, on Platform three at ten hundred hours. The train will come
> in; the SS will get all the non-military people off.
> They will all have to go around the checkpoint, and then back
> on the train... Less a few Jews, with a bit of luck".

He jumps up from his chair full of his own enthusiasm.

> "So, our job is to spot the Jews that the SS miss.
> I'm very good at it. If you see one, or a family with it's young,
> blow your whistles: three blasts hard. The SS know what to do.

If the Jews run away, don't give chase.
The SS or I will shoot them. Just lie flat on the ground,
and then you won't get shot yourselves. Any questions...?
No, good".

Steiner hands each boy a whistle on a black cord. He walks up and down his little squad tidying scarves or shirts, setting the boys' caps square.

As he stops at Ron and Ken, there is a glint of recognition as he looks from one boy to the other.

"Do I know you two from somewhere?"
Ken and Ron shake their heads, and Ron says,
"Don't think so Sergeant Steiner".

Steiner places his boys the length of the platform. He holds out a big 'T' shaped key for Ron and Ken. Steiner gets very close to the brothers, they can smell his lavender after-shave lotion, it is obvious that he doesn't need to shave yet. He grabs Ron's sleeve,

"You two brothers?"
Ron and Ken nod,

"Mm, I know one of you from somewhere... Now listen, I
don't trust these railway people. Most of them are Jew lovers.
They have orders to check that all the toilets are vacant and
lock them before the train gets into the station. They never do,
so we will do it for them. Go to the back of the train and work
your way through.
Use this key to unlock the toilets, every one...
If Jews are hiding in one, go to the nearest door and blow your
whistles. Don't forget to lock the toilets up again; oh look
under the seats too... I want that key back because I've signed
for it".

The brothers walk down the length of the platform as the train pulls in. The SS yell for all the non-service passengers to get off; lots of people and bustle. The boys slow down as soon as they are out of sight of Steiner. Ron looks at Ken,

"What a little shit-bag he is, what a nasty little asshole".

Ken whispering,

"Did you hear him, he said 'A family with its young' just like
they were cattle, what a nasty little twit". Ron looks at his
brother and says.

"Well their supposed to be vermin aren't they"?

He stops short of agreeing with himself as he usually does, thinks a bit and says,

"Well are they vermin or people, what are we supposed to
think?"

Ken stops and grabs Ron's arm, looks over his shoulder left and right to see if anyone is listening and says.

"Ron we know they are just people being hunted, for what? What harm have they done to us, they are just people with a different religion; are we going on that train to turn them in?"

Ron pulls his arm free of his brother's grip and whispers.

"We will be stood against a wall and shot if we don't turn them in. Aiding Jews to escape is a capital offence nowadays you know".

The boys work their way through the train. There are wounded military in bunks four high, looking very young. Blood bottles swing from the roof and boiled washed bandages hang out to dry.

Ron opens the first toilet; a nurse is rinsing out bloody towels. He shuts the door. The next door has the sign 'In Use'. Ron taps on the door... There is no answer. He inserts the key very quietly and slowly opens the door.

A fat Major, a Doctor with medical insignia on his uniform is fast asleep, sitting on the toilet with his pants around his ankles. They move on. The next carriage is almost empty, except a few old folk who get up and leave when the boys enter the car. It has lots of luggage piled everywhere. Ken grabs Ron's arm,

"I hate this, they're just people, oh Ron, what are we doing? Did you see the way those old folk looked at us?"

Ron whispers,

"Ken, it's our uniforms that scare them"

Ron nods, and points to the door of the next toilet. It too has a sign 'In use' showing. This time Ron doesn't knock but quietly inserts the key and opens the door.

Crowded and cramped in the small space is a group of very surprised and terrified Jewish people. Two men, their wives and four small children are all squashed into the tiny space. For moments, both parties just stare at each other. Ron is the first to move; he puts his finger to his lips with a look that says

"I won't tell, if you don't".

The pleading smile on the mothers' faces causes Ken to look left and right anxiously to see who is watching. The old lady sitting on the seat has the same pleading look. As Ron goes to slowly close the door, they hear whispers of thanks and deep sighs of sheer relief. The old lady gets up, grabs Ken and gives him a big hug, speaking in a language the boys don't understand.

The brothers continue through the train. The next toilet has another family of Jews hiding, two of the children are sobbing loudly and Ron puts his finger to his lips, smiles and quietly closes the door.

The railway guard is standing at the next toilet door, a big fatherly man. Spotting Ron's T-shaped key, he realizes what the boys are doing. He takes a pace to block the door and places his hand on Ron's shoulders, shakes his head. Sounds of a child whimpering and adult voices hushing the children to be quiet come from the toilet door. The guard looks Ron in the eyes, shakes his head and says,

"There's no one here who's going to harm the great German Reich today".

Ron winks at the guard,

"There are families back there too".

The Guard nods knowingly,

"Yes, but you're not going to use those whistles today; you're not the SS, are you?"

The boys shake their heads, so does the guard. The guard gives each boy a rub on the head and a friendly pat on their backs.

Suddenly they hear the distant crack of two pistol shots and a terrified yell followed by an agonizing scream that echoes through the train station. Ron and Ken look at each other. People are hurriedly re-boarding the train.

Ron starts to move toward the door, but the fatherly old train conductor grabs Ron's cross-strap and holds him fast.

"Wait, we don't want to go out there yet, do-we?
Just let the excitement settle down for a bit".

They hear Steiner's voice shouting for everyone to get back on the train. The guard gives Ron a shove and says goodbye.

The boys make their way to the door and as people pass them they are strangely silent and grim, looking at the twins with hate and loathing.

Ken and Ron hurry down the platform and stop when they see a young Jewish man lying in a curled up fetal position clutching at his stomach. His long black overcoat soaking up a large pool of blood that was running down the platform on to the rail lines. His face distorted into a death grin, showing he had died in great agony.

They spot Steiner waving to them to get a move on. Ken and Ron rejoin the group and give Steiner back his key.

The sergeant is looking very pleased with himself as the six boys march down the platform towards the big gates and spot a Jewish family handcuffed to the railings; a father, mother, a boy about twelve and a girl of eight who is crying. The father is trying to console her. Willie whispers,

"Steiner spotted them himself, arrested them with his little black gun. But it took the two big SS guards to chain them up like that".

Willie motions up the platform, he is all worked up and scared spluttering says.

"Steiner shot the young Jewish boy up there, just as he was
running away, well he wasn't really running away, but it looked
as if he might so Steiner just shot him, twice in his stomach".
Ron shakes his head.
"What a nasty little shit Nazi. Look at these poor sods;
what's going to happen to them now?"
Steiner struts up to Ken and Ron, boasting:
"I spotted them. They didn't bother to pull the threads out of
their boy's jacket, where he had his star ripped off...
The dead Jew was running away, I yelled at him to halt twice,
he understood all right, he didn't think a boy of sixteen would
shoot him; he was escaping and I have my orders".
Steiner then says with total indifference:
"You know, we had a report that there were two
other families on this train. You didn't see them did you?
They must have jumped off before the train got into the
station... Did you two check the train properly?"
Ron and Ken say,
"Oh yes, Sergeant Steiner"
Ken whispers under his breath, "Yes, asshole".
Steiner looks hard at the twins quizzically. The SS guard unlocks the
Jews from the iron railings and Steiner forms them up in line shouting in
his squeaky adolescent voice that echoes in the station.
Processions of boys escort the Jewish family. The mother and father
hold onto each other; the children close behind. Steiner with his pistol
drawn is walking behind the father. Ken and Ron at the rear carry some
of the family's meager baggage. Ken says in a voice loud enough for the
Jewish boy to hear,
"Why don't they try to run? There's no chains on them".
"He wouldn't shoot that pistol in this crowd".
Ron shakes his head,
"Oh yes he would, Steiner would love another chance to shoot
another Jew. They sense that, that's why they're not trying; he
shot the young man on a crowded platform, and its only luck
he didn't hit someone in the crowd.
Steiner stands at an open cell in the station complex. The family
walks in; he slams the door shut, locks it and puts the key on a small shelf.
Ron looks at Ken and nods to the shelf. They all walk through to the
interview room where Steiner quickly grabs the telephone and dials a
number. The boys sit down at the table; some bring in chairs from the
main office. Steiner speaks on the telephone.
"I've got five Jews Herr Major, all off the trains.
Yes sir, I spotted them...
Yes sir, they are here, locked up here sir...

I had to shoot one of them…
Oh yes sir he was a Jew and he was running away.
Sir, who do I call to have the body picked up?
Oh, me, sir? You want to see me…
I will be right over sir. Oh yes sir!
I'm on my way now sir… Heil Hitler".
He puts down the telephone, looking very pleased with himself.
He yells at his little squad of boys,
"You lot get this place cleaned up; they need me at Gestapo
Headquarters, and lock up the front door when you leave and
put the key through the letterbox".
Steiner grabs his hat, places it squarely on his head, salutes and
strides out. The boys hear the front door slam. Ron glances in to the front
office; it's empty. Ron says to the rest of the messengers,
"Looks clean enough to me, let's go".
The other boys don't need telling twice; in a few seconds they are all
gone. Ron goes through the motions of locking the door as the last boy
leaves. He grabs Ken's arm as they trot across the station,
"Hang on there, we have to go back, to let the Jews out".
"What… They will shoot us for sure".
"Don't worry; they won't know it was us, will they".
Ron makes very sure all the other boys are out of sight and they both
double back to the Gestapo office. Ron has left the door unlocked, they
slip back in.
"See if you can find a big screwdriver or a knife".
Ken replies,
"What for?"
Ron yells with a sense of urgency in his voice,
"Do it Ken, just do it".
Ron and Ken start to ransack the drawers and cupboards. Ken holds
up a long army bayonet,
"Look Ron, what I've found!"
"Good"
Ron grabs the bayonet, takes the key from the little shelf and goes
and lets himself through the steel door that leads to the cells. Ken closes
the drawers and cupboards to hide their hurried search.
Ron unlocks the cell door; the family draws back when they see the
bayonet in his hand… Ron starts to hack at the old wooden door from
the inside of the cell, tearing great chunks of wood out of the doorpost.
The family starts to realize what he is doing and smile nervously. As
Ken closes the door in its locked position; it swings open, then he wipes
the key on his shirt and replaces it on the shelf. Ron almost has to push
the family out saying.

"You people get on the same train, they won't search it again,
and it leaves in a few minutes".
The families all shake hands with the twins. The Jewish father gives
the boys a big hug, with tears in his eyes says,
"Tell us your names so we can pray for you".
Ron smiles and answers
"Sorry, no names, just go and catch that train".
Ken tells them to,
"Walk proud. Don't look so scared, or it'll give you away".
They grab up their bags and just before they leave the Jewish boy
takes two large brightly colored glass marbles out of his pocket, his prized
possessions and offers them to the twins. They accept them smiling, and
they all each shake hands.

The family goes through the door and disappears into the crowded
station. Ken puts the bayonet in its scabbard and places it back in the
desk drawer. He grabs a Gestapo date stamp and stuffs it in his pocket.
Then makes the place look as tidy as possible, leaving the door unlocked
but closed behind them. They hurry across the platform to catch their
train back to School. Ron says,
"If they catch those Jewish people and they tell the SS that we
let them go, we are very dead, you know that. Aiding Jews to
escape, what were we thinking about?"
Ken grabs Ron's arm,
"Listen to me, the Jews were in there when we left, and all the
boys saw us leave with them didn't they, we locked the doors,
alright? We must keep our story correct. I will say you locked
up. I know I put that bayonet back in the drawer exactly as I
found it".
The twins sit in the compartment waiting for their train to start,
looking up and down the platform and keeping a sharp eye out for
Steiner, Ken very worried says,
"Ron, what will we do, they will know it was us
who let the Jews out, all the other boys were gone"?
Ron answers in his 'I know more than you do voice',
"Ken, Ken, listen to me.
I'm going to tell you what happened.
One: We cleaned up. I went through the door first.
Two: You turned out the lights and locked the doors.
Three: We walked away with the other boys.
The Jews were locked up when we left.
That's how it happened and we will just,
well, stick to that story, all right?
The Jewish father could have had a big knife up his shirt.

They weren't searched were they?
And Steiner doesn't have any of our names does he?"
Ken nods,
"I wish this train would get moving".
Ron looks thoughtful,
"I hope that family gets away all right".
"It's a shame they get chased and hounded like animals.
Dieter told me they get packed off to Poland to some big
camp there and a lot of the old and sick ones just don't arrive.
They die in the cattle trucks. Isn't that awful?"
The train pulls out with a jerk and both boys breathe a deep
sigh of relief. Ken whispers in Ron's ear,
"We have to get out of all this Ron. You know, run away".
Ron looks at his brother and nods slowly.
"Where would we run to, we'd have to find somewhere to go"?
"You could make one of your plans Ron, we could live in the
woods, or work on a farm for food and sleep in their barn".

It's a fine day. The twins are wearing their bathing slips with towels,
sitting in the shade of the old chestnut tree. Ron is lying on his back and
Ken is sitting up against the tree and has been writing in his diary and is
sobbing deep whimpers with tears in his eyes. Ron notices him and asks,
"What's up brother?
Shit, Ken those are real tears.
What's the matter old chum?"
"I have forgotten what they look like, Ron…
Mum and Dad.
We don't even have a photograph or a snapshot.
I wouldn't know them if I met them on the street.
Ron, I can't see their faces...
I've forgotten what they look like".

It is early and the damp morning mist is still hanging close to the
ground it's almost obscuring the targets that are set up three hundred
meters at the end of the Army firing range. Dieter's platoon is lying
around on ground sheets. On the far side of the range, targets are being
shot at by another platoon.
The veteran army sergeant is decorated with medals from past
campaigns, and he has a black Iron Cross hanging from his neck. With
his tough craggy face he looks old enough to be most of the boys'
grandfather. As he moves about it is obvious that he has a metal leg, the
boys can hear it click as he paces over to the table that is set up with a
K98 rifle, stripped of its parts. He holds up the rifle and beckons Ron to
come up to the table and stand next to him.

The Sergeant picks up the rifle, spinning it as if it were paper.
"This, boys, is a soldier's 'bride', his wife...
You boy, what's your name and how old are you?"
"Lambert Ronald, fourteen, I will be fifteen............"
"I can teach you to fire this thing, but will you kill a man with
it?"
He leans in with his face close to Ron's
"Will you? It's very easy to shoot at paper targets, when your
only concern is the kick in the shoulder when it goes off,
but to aim at a man's gut is something else".
The sergeant limps over to Ron and grabs him by his collar, pulls
out his shirt from his shorts and pushes the blunt end of the rifle bolt
into Ron's exposed naked stomach, hard, making him wince. Then turns
him sideways showing the platoon his waist,
"A British 303 bullet won't stop here. It will go right through,
not clean, but on its way it will tumble over and come out here
and take some bits of hipbone with it. No one can do a thing
for you...
If you are transported to an aid station, you will hurt every
meter of the way. Then while you wait to get some attention,
you will die slowly in the worst agony you can imagine. So keep
your silly heads down. Don't stand up under fire. Most young
soldiers get killed in their first action because they just don't
keep their heads down".
The boys hang on to every word, their faces white and horrified.
"So, do not die for the Fatherland. A dead soldier is no good to
anyone. He can't shoot back. Death is very painful and stupid.
You are fourteen with lives to live.
If you see the enemy in your sights, shoot him first, or
he will surely kill you... You, put this back together".
Ron deftly reassembles the weapon. The sergeant limps away as the
boys sit down in silence. Ron says quietly,
"This is getting too bloody serious, are they going
to send us to fight the Russians? We are shooting
real live ammunition this afternoon,
and throwing live grenades".
Ken whispers to his brother,
"Ron, we have to get out of this place, soon".
The military training is stepped up. Dieter's platoon has now swelled
its ranks; his boy's ages range from fourteen to sixteen. Training to shoot
the K98, 8mm rifle, and the small 7.9mm pistol, they are constantly
stripping and cleaning the weapons until they can do it blindfolded lying
on their backs.

The next day they are marched to an army grenade throwing range. Here they are taught how to throw live stick grenades. They had thrown many dummy grenades the same weight and length in schoolboy competitions and most boys were able to hit a two-meter target. But the real thing feels quite different. When the seal is broken and the wooden box is opened the deadly stick grenades look clean and new looking. Knowing they could kill, the boys handle them with great care.

The top looks like a can of milk and the bottom of the handle has a screw cap, a wax cord with a porcelain ball to pull out before it is thrown.

The platoon stands behind a waist-high wall of thick concrete.

The instructor yells,

"We all stand up, throw the grenade,
wait and watch where it falls, then get your stupid heads
below the wall, or you just might get it blown off. Watch".

The instructor unscrews the bottom cap, with one move he whips the handle and the ball flies out. He tugs it and throws it overarm, some of the boys duck and he yells,

"Stand still! Just wait till it lands".

The grenade lands on its target and all the platoon duck down, some boys putting their hands over their ears.   Bang!

There is no flash. The instructor laughs, pointing to Dieter who is clutching his crotch.

"Yes he knows… Next time hold on to your balls,
the blast will hurts them, more than your ears… ha".

Each boy throws two stick grenades. At the end of the session they all have throbbing headaches and Ron says,

"Shit do my balls ever hurt; and my ears feel
as if they have driven sharp nails into them".

Hans chirps in,

"Did you hear the shrapnel whiz over our heads, I'm not
throwing one of those unless I have a thick wall to hide".

Ken says quietly,

"Did you see the other side of that little wall? It's all pitted up
from the fragments that's hit it. It has chunks knocked out of it
you could hide a large potato in".

The next part of the course they learn to fire a very effective anti-tank weapon, the flat nosed Panzerfaust (similar to the American Bazooka). Shooting at a burned out old tank, the boys are being taught to work in squads of three. Ron, Ken and Hans, wearing oversized army steel helmets are crouched in a small slit trench. Ken and Ron fire their weapons and hit the target, but Hans is sitting as low as he can get in the corner of the trench in a puddle of water, his knees drawn up under his chin shivering, his whole body shaking. Clenched fists pressing against his ears, he is crying and sobbing,

"Oh, I can't do it. I can't stand the bang.
It scares the shit out of me. I can't hold that thing".
The Army sergeant with a limp leans over and takes the Anti-Tank
Panzerfaust away from the boys. Then pointing at Hans he shouts,
"German boys don't cry. You, crybaby, what's your name?"
Hans starts to scramble up out of the trench. As soon as the sergeant
can reach him he grabs Hans by the scruff of his neck and drags him out
and onto his feet and starts to shout with his face close to Hans's ear.
"I said what is your name boy? Name, name, name?"
Hans still sobbing, his glasses all covered with mud blurts out,
"Kardorff sergeant, Hans Kardorff"
"Well Kardorff, you will stand next to every boy who fires a
Faust today, and when it's your turn you will enjoy it. You will
fire not one, but three.
Do you understand boy? Do you?"
Hans sobbing nods,
"What, I can't hear you boy, what did you say?"
"Yes, sergeant, yes".
The next team of three boys jumps into the trench for their turn to
fire the anti-tank weapon and the sergeant makes Hans stand to the side
and slightly to the rear of the firing line. Just as the boy is about to fire
the weapon, Hans cups his hands over his ears.
"Hold your fire" the sergeant yells.
The boys freeze,
"You, Kardorff put your hands down on your sides.
You're supposed to be there to get used to the bang.
Now stand still, Fire!"
The boy fires and Hans almost jumps out of his skin. His glasses fall
in the mud and he bends down to pick them up,
"Stand up straight. Leave the glasses where they are;
next three boys in the trench and fire".
Hans is made to stand there, close to the Anti-tank Panzerfaust as
all the boys in the platoon take their turn firing the weapons.
After the last boy has fired the sergeant walks over to Hans,
"You, Kardorff get back in the trench quick".
Hans jumps into the trench. It's now like a mud bath after forty or
so boys have jumped in and out.
The sergeant leans over and places the long weapon under his arm
in the right place. Hans is trembling like a leaf, his hands are shaking, teeth
chattering. He yells out,
"I can't see anything, without my glasses".
Ron grabs Hans's glasses, washes them off in a puddle of muddy
water and fits them onto Hans's face.

"Fire you little asshole, or I will stick that thing
right up your backside and pull the trigger".
Hans closes his eyes and fires. Painfully and with pure terror Hans
fires his other two shots. The shots go wide, nowhere near the target. The
sergeant steps forward again, grabs Hans, drags him out of the trench and
throws him down in the mud,
"I'm looking at a dead piece of shit, a useless coward.
It's not just your worthless life that will be spent,
but the lives of your comrades too".
The sergeant turns to the platoon,
"Take a good look at this one.
Be aware that he is the weak link in your group.
He's the one that will crack up in the face of the enemy.
He may cost you your lives one day".
Hans is still sobbing as the platoon marches back. Ken says,
"Don't worry, we will all be out of this place soon".
"I didn't hit the target because I couldn't see anything,
my glasses were all smeared up".
"Don't worry about it, you won't have to fire one again".

12. THE OATH

It is a very hot day and Dieter's platoon has been weeding between the rows of carrots all afternoon. It is backbreaking work, pulling long choking weeds that have a clump of soil at their roots. They bang the loose soil off with their boots, then swing the weed and throw it to the cart on the footpath. Most of the boys have become good shots and manage to get most of the weeds in or close to the handcart.

Ken taps Ron on the elbow and nods over to the cart and whispering says,

"Look whose back... Just look at his new uniform".

Karl sporting the new uniform of a Hitler Youth Oberscharführer (2nd Lieutenant) is talking to Dieter. After a few moments they both stroll off to the school in deep conversation.

As soon as they are out of sight, the boys stop work and take long swigs from their water bottles. Ron takes his shirt off and lies flat on his back between the rows of carrots saying,

"Well he won't be fit to live with, now that he's a new officer".

"Well at least he won't be our sergeant, we still have Dieter looking out for us, don't we?"

Ron says,

"Wake me up when it's suppertime,

I'm not doing any more of this shit today".

The rest of the platoons sit down in little groups, keeping an eye open for Karl's return. Just as Ron is dozing off, a long weed with a clump of wet muddy soil around its roots sails over and lands on his bare chest with a thump. Ron and Ken sit up with a start, sees a group of boys at the end of the row of carrots falling about laughing and pointing at Ron. One boy is pissing on the roots of a second clump of weeds getting ready to throw it. Ken yells back at them,

"Look at those dirty shits, peeing on them first before they chuck them at us... Hey, watch it, we may just come over there and make you drink your own piss, assholes".

Ron pulls a long weed and aims it back at their assailants and yells,

"Come on, let's get them, Ken let's get the shits".

Very soon there is a war raging, weeds and carrots sailing in long arcs with most of the platoon on to Hans and the brothers.

At the height of the battle a whistle blows a long shrill blast, freezing the boys mid-fight.

It's a whistle they have never heard before, a new whistle with a different sound. Karl its owner takes the whistle out of his mouth and yells,

"Stand still. No one moves. Stand still, all of you".

Karl strides into the field looking around at the spent weed bombs and carrots, most of them piled near Hans and the twins. Ron says.
"Where's Dieter?"
Karl brushes the question aside with a wave of his riding crop.
"What is it with this platoon? You can't be trusted
to work for ten minutes on your own".
Karl marches over to Ron, looks at his muddy chest,
"You, take your brother and Hans over there
and stand to attention by the cart.
The rest of you get this mess cleaned up, now.
Move! Move! Move!"
The three run over to the cart and stand stiffly to attention.
Karl paces over swishing his crop, smacking the side of his new long jackboots, he leans in close to Hans,
"Show me your hands".
Hans holds out his hands for inspection. Karl aims a swipe at his hand but Hans pulls his hand in and the blow misses.
Karl then strides over to Ken and taps his hands with his crop. Ken holds his hands out for some of the same but this time Ken is not quick enough and the crop whacks Ken's open palm. Ken is not slow to yell out,
"Ow, Ow, that's not official punishment.
You're not supposed to do that to us".
Ron turns to Karl and Karl pushes Ron away with his crop,
"Stand against the cart".
Karl hisses through his teeth.
"Well I should really thank you two little shits
for my training and promotion… But I'm not going to.
Instead I am going to set an example here and now,
for the platoon to see.
You three drop your shorts and lean over the cart
and get ready to receive official punishment".
Slowly the boys start to undo their belts and lower their shorts.
"Come on, get a move on, underpants as well".
The rest of the platoons work away feverishly, keeping an eye on Karl. He takes his new strange whistle out again and blows it,
"The rest of you come over here, I want you to watch this.
Learn from it. We must have discipline".
"'A unit without discipline is not a unit.
So, we will make an example of these three".
The boys are bent over the cart, bare bottoms looking pink, waiting for Karl. The rest of the boys gather around.
He turns to the platoon,
"Four strokes for each boy".

Hans yells out,
"We didn't start it; it's not our fault".
Karl walks over to Hans and lifts his face up with his riding crop,
"Not your fault? You mean, not your fault 'sir'?
Say it".
Hans, his face screwed up with Karl's leather crop yells,
"Not our fault, sir".
"Right, you will get an extra two strokes
just for having a big mouth".
The three are lying over the cart and Ron looks sideways to Ken on the far end. It is his turn first. Ron thinks:
"I hope he doesn't cry, we don't want to give
this shit the satisfaction of seeing a Lambert cry".
Karl takes careful aim and brings his first stroke down hard. Ken's head rears up as he takes a gasp of air with his mouth wide open but then he takes the other three strokes gritting his teeth without a murmur. Hans takes his six just blinking at each stroke.

Ron wonders: how he can do that. It must be very strong willpower. Karl waits behind Ron, looking at the red welts showing up on the other two boys' backsides. Karl takes his aim and brings the first stroke down as hard as he can. Ron grits his teeth thinking:
"'Oh shit that hurts! Oh," as the cane crop lands on his upper
leg. "'Ow! That one was low".
Karl waits measuring his stroke, smack. Smack. Karl then steps back and yells,
"Come on then, get dressed, so, what do you say?"
Ron smiles, and each boy says in turn,
"Thank you Oberscharführer Kaltenbrunner, thank you".
Karl grins as the boys return to the field he yells,
"And no sitting down on the job... Ha, the next time you sit
down you will remember what discipline is, remember we must
have discipline".
The three make their way back to the fields; Ken starts a cheerful and loud conversation to let Karl know that his punishment has not upset them. Ron quickly catches on and draws Hans in to the chatter and they all laugh and giggle as they pull weeds with new vigor, Karl notices and blows his new whistle then yells,
"Stop talking! Shut-up, get on with your work in silence".
The boys all glance at each other grinning knowing that they're little intrigue got to Karl.
"Silence!"
Grins are exchanged as the boys start to quietly sing.

It's a very early spring Sunday and a day off, the weather is unusually warm so that afternoon, the four boys go swimming; just diving in and out, as the water is still quite cold. They plop down at the end of the wooden jetty. Dieter sits with Ron, Ken and Hans who are sunning themselves in their bathing slips, lying on their stomachs. Ron says,
    "Well, are we going to run away?"
Each boy nods in agreement. They sit closer together and Hans rakes around in the dirt and finds a fist-full of small pebbles, sorts out five of equal size and starts a game of 'fives'. (Fives is a boy's catching game played on the ground with five small rocks and the player's hand with his fingers spread out). The real purpose of this game is to get four boys in a tight huddle so they can have a secret meeting without looking suspicious or being overheard.
    From a distance it looks like an innocent boys' game.
Ken asks,
    "Where do we go, what do we eat?"
Dieter looks out at the lake,
    "It had better be soon".
Ron suggests,
    "We could make for the farms, stay out of sight in the
    high country. Then when the Allies arrive, surrender
    only to the Americans or British".
Hans says,
    "What if it takes years, how will we eat?"
Ken looks at Dieter,
    "You have a problem Dieter...
    you look old enough to be a deserter from the army".
Ron shrugs his shoulders,
    "A crutch and a gamy leg... No you need an official
    dated wound label, shit, they shoot deserters".
Ken stands up suddenly as if he has a brain wave,
    "Messengers, we will all be messengers".
Ken starts to pace up and down on the small platform,
    "Yes... It will work... We will all be messengers.
    If we are challenged, we can say we are on an important
    delivery service... We can get all we need from the station
    office. We have already got a Gestapo date stamp".
Ron sits up and catches the enthusiasm with his new idea,
    "Or... We can spend the summer hiding in the mountains
    and the winter in the City of Munich".
Hans looks very skeptical,
    "Winter in Munich, that's nice.
    So what hotel will we be staying in then?
    I hope it has a Mountain View".

Dieter gets up thoughtfully, walks over to Ken and puts his arm around his neck in a friendly arm lock,

"Yes it would work. We need belts, pouches, proper ones,
date stamps, form and envelopes. Yes it would work".

Dieter looks at the Lamberts, and then gives them a big bear hug.

"You two bloody geniuses, work out what we need.
Ron, you work out one of your plans. We will steal all we need.
I will schedule us all on Station duty on the weekend.
They never bomb on weekends... We will rob them blind, ha...
Let's all make a pact. Let's all swear on it, come on".

Dieter brings all three around him, they all grasp wrists in a circle. Ron slowly turns over his brother's hand and says,

"Wait, we should all become blood brothers.
You know, mix the blood, all four of us.
A blood oath not to be broken".

Ken looks over at Hans,

"What about you Hans? You used to be very keen on Hitler".

Hans nods and shakes his head,

"I used to believe all that Nazi shit. But since I lost
my brother Max and we have lost Paul and Gunther.
Who's going to be next?
Germany can't possibly win this war, trying to beat
the world now; it's so stupid. I don't want to die...
I haven't even done it with a girl yet, so fuck Hitler.
I want to survive and I want to know what it's like
to do a girl before I die".
"It's got to be better than wanking off
with soap in the shower all the time".

Ken smiles,

"Yes this rotten wartime soap. It really burns down
the pee-hole in the old dink, if you go at it too hard".

Ron waves Ken to shut up and says dryly,

"Hans, I assume that means you are with us".

Hans nods vigorously. Ron rakes through the pile of clothes on the deck, draws Ken's camp knife from his belt because it's always the sharpest in the platoon, wipes it on his shirt, bends his forearm up and slowly draws the sharp blade across his arm until a little trickle of blood runs. He then hands the knife to Ken who makes his own cut. Dieter follows, and then offers the knife to Hans.

Hans looks horrified at the blade, shakes his head and hands the knife back to Dieter and offers up his arm for him to cut, turning his face away. Dieter makes the cut for him. The four boys hold their arms in a circle showing their trickles of blood. Hans has gone quite pale looking at his own blood. Ron whispers quietly,

"Everyone has to take a lick of everyone's blood to be true
blood brothers. You just need to taste don't suck it all up.
Dieter, you first, then us, then Hans…"
Dieter grabs Ron's arm first and licks a little of his blood, then Ken's
arm and licks about the same amount. And so each boy tastes the blood
from all the four blood brothers' arms. The oath is established. They all
join hands. Ron says to everyone,
"Anybody want to say anything, now's the time".
Dieter gets very serious. He grabs all the boys' arms together and
holds them so the blood mixes. He makes his oath with the boys all
repeating each line.
"We swear on our lives, best friends, this solemn oath.
We will never, even under torture, or threat of death, betray
each other. We will not fight this war of Germany's.
Try to surrender to the Americans or British.
On our lives, this we all swear".
Ron rubs his hands together,
"Well that's it then, we are all out of this place".
Dieter pushes Hans into the water and then dives in after him. Ron
looks hard at Ken,
"We still have our own brothers' oath,
the one we made years ago, you and me, right?"
Ken holds out his hand,
"Shake on it again Ron".
The brothers stand up and shake hands very violently.
Ken hugs Ron and wrestles him into the water. The boys are young
again, splashing and making a big deal about saving Hans, who's still a
non-swimmer. Dieter looks at the three,
"Just us four, no one else.
It has to be a secret, just us four".
The boys all nod and shake hands again.

On the night of 15th of March 1944. The aircraft assembly lines in
Stuttgart, to the northwest of Munich, are the first targets for the R.A.F.
The city of Munich is the second target.
The air-raid sirens sound, then the dull quiet lull before the local
anti-aircraft guns start booming.
Ken and Ron, now fourteen years old have been given more
important assignments in the Hitler Youth Messenger Service. They have
just finished delivering their wads of letters and meet to share a thick lump
of sausage; the twins sit shivering in a deep shop doorway. Ken hacks
thick slices off with his knife while trying to keep the rain off their cold
dinner. Ken says in the best French accent he can muster,
"Sorry we don't have any plates or serviettes".

"It's all right Ron smiles, try to handle
my half of that sausage with your left hand"
"Why" said Ken,
"Well, you use your right hand to wipe your bum don't you?"
Ken looks at Ron with his right finger stuck deep in to the sausage.
"Oh, my Mm... It's a bit late now, here, we're brothers,
we have the same lick don't we?"
The boys soon finish off the meat and Ron gazes up at the shop's glassless windows and says.
"At least these windows have been blown out,
we're not liable to be cut up by flying glass here, are we?"
Ron and Ken huddle in the doorway, sitting with their knees drawn up under their chins. Shrapnel from the 88mm anti-aircraft shells that are bursting over their heads falls about them like rain, but sound like thousands of little bells, tinkling on the sidewalk in front of them.

First the RAF pathfinders drop their marker Magnesium flares that descend slowly on little parachutes and light the streets up like daylight. The sharp shadows of the buildings sway and wobble as the flares swing like pendulums on their tiny parachutes.

Then bombs start exploding on the other side of the river. The boys hear them getting closer, so they squash tighter in the doorway. Looking up at the heavy iron arch over their heads,
Ken, who is trembling so much his teeth rattle, says,
"I wish we had put on our tin hats".
"'You said there wasn't going to be a raid".
"So... So I was wrong, I couldn't know everything, could I?"
The bombs get much closer and louder. Ron puts his arm around his shaking brother and they glare at one another in pure fear and terror: Bang! Bang! Bang! Bang!
"Oh, they must have been three hundred-pounders".

A new wave of bombers drones overhead, this time dropping showers of small fire bombs that don't explode, they just crack and fizz setting fire to collapsed apartment houses that have been reduced to piles of broken brick and furniture by the first wave of bombers.
"Let's stay here. There's nowhere to go. Fuck, the shit is coming
down like rain, look at it".
The thunder and shaking continues as the bombs fall again. Munich is ablaze from the station to the river.
"Everything's burning, Ron. Why do they do that? Bomb us,
first then set fire to everything with firebombs. It's not fair,
they're just killing people for nothing".
The black smoke clouds from fires hangs so low they cover the street, preventing the boys from seeing across to the other side of the road. Billowing rolls of brown dust from falling walls spread a blanket of

darkness. The air is filled with sounds of crushing wood and crashing masonry mixed with the constant screams of people they cannot see. Heavy moans vent from the gigantic grinding walls of apartments, toppling and falling into clouds of flame and dust-filled smoke. The whole front of a building with windows ablaze falls like the cover of a large book, crashing in to the street and breaking up into a cloud of flaming dust choking the boys.

The bombing stops, then the guns stop, but the fires of the inferno are just getting started Ron yells,

"Ken, we have to run, let's go, don't let go of my hand".

The boys start to run to the wider part of the street and are just missed by a puff of smoke and brick dust that is billowing out from their doorway, its ceiling seemed to wait until the twins were clear before collapsing and crushing the very spot where they were standing.

Everything is on fire all around them. They fight for each breath; their eyes are watering, their pulses pounding in their ears, the scarves that cover their mouths have dark patches where they have blocked some of the dust from entering their lungs. Suddenly the street becomes a river of flames.

Long tongues of fire lick out through a row of blasted-out windows, turning them back. More house-fronts fall. Whipped up by a strong wind, the fires, with their huge roaring sound, seemed to be trying to suck them into its flaming center. The wind is now like a hurricane. People are running and screaming in all directions. Ron yells,

"We must keep moving; look, my boots are melting".

"Ron, your hair! It's all burnt, it's all frizzy".

"Ken, my soles are sticking to the road, wow… let's go, come on Ken, come on we must keep going. Let's stay in the middle of the street".

The flames are eating all the air. Whirlwinds of smoke and ash cause the flames to spin like tops dancing down the street, charring everything in their path. The boys just run and run, always to the darker sides of the street.

Dead people lay on the sidewalk. They had jumped out of the windows fleeing from the flaming apartments.

An old man with his back on fire staggers into an open flaming shop doorway and disappears in a cloud of sparks.

Some dead people are still burning, lying in the gutter. Ron grabs Ken and shoves him behind and shouts,

"Hang on to my belt… Hold on tight and don't let go…

Let's stay on the tram lines".

The twins run in each other's footprints stepping only on the steel rail so as not to stick to the melting tar and asphalt road.

12 The Oath

A policeman looking like a nun with a big wet blanket over his head races to them and throws his blanket over the boy's heads.

Sharing it between the three of them, he shouts,

"Come on, this way: there is a shelter down here".

Sitting in the deep cellar that has been reinforced as an air-raid shelter, office people and families are getting yellow ointment dabbed on their burns by a policeman with a big can. He smears it all over the boys' heads and hands. Ken and Ron look at each other and laugh, Ron says.

"You've got no eyebrows and your hair's all gone, Ha".

"Look at you. Your eyebrows are brown and crispy.

Ron, my feet are burned, shit was it bloody hot out there".

Ron sees that the shelter is not that full. The thick wooden beams and the bomb pressure-resistant steel doors, with an emergency exit encased in massive concrete, look solid enough. Better than being outside, they both agree. Ron asks the policeman,

"Where are all the people from this street and the apartments?

Is there another shelter around here?"

The policeman shakes his head as he dabs Ken's arms and feet,

"Not a deep one like this. The folks in the shallow basements
of those apartment blocks will all be dead. They all have
wooden ceilings. Their buildings will just burn right through
and the people will suffocate".

The boys watch him in silence as he comforts the burned people with his can of yellow ointment. Ken looks down and starts to laugh.

"Look Ron, look, ha".

Where they were sitting a small river of water starts to run away from them. Ken laughs,

"It's not me… It's you… You pissed your knickers".

"Yes… Shh, shit, you better not tell anyone…

Promise, Ken, you promise me you won't tell anyone?"

Ken smiles and Ron curses,

"This is bloody madness, this stupid war, we might
just get one of us killed… The next stupid thing,
our platoon will get drafted in the stupid army".

Ken, his voice still shaking says,

"We're only fourteen, they can't do that… Can they?"

Ron takes a deep breath.

"The bombers seem to have passed".

He smiles as he watches the river of pee run. Ken smiles,

"Pissy knickers, it's all right. I won't tell, honest ha".

Ron smiles, looks down at the pee, closes his eyes in relief and lets the rest go and says quietly.

"Listen Ken, most of our platoon are fifteen. There is a bloody
Hitler Youth regiment fighting the Bolsheviks on the eastern
front. They are only sixteen and seventeen".
Ken asks, still trembling.
"Ron, do you think they will make another
bombing run on their way home?"
"Hope not"
"So if we get drafted, we won't split up, right?
Together like glue, you and me, right?"
Ron gives Ken a squeeze,
"No one's getting drafted. Dieter told me.
If we skip school and they bring us back,
we would just be runaways. We would
only get a thrashing as regular school boys".
Ron looks up at the roof as the 'All Clear' sirens sound. Ken says,
"Ron, if we wait and get drafted and then run away we would
be deserters. You know, soldiers deserting. They will stand us
up against a wall and shoot us, dead".
Ron has a little shiver,
"Shit, yes, really!"
"We have to run now Ron, before the army call-up gets us"
The twins go back, pick up their bikes with burned flat tires and start
walking down the smoldering deserted street. The swirling dust sticks to
the ointment smeared all over them. They don't care what they look like,
they're just glad to be alive.
Ken grins and points down to Ron's pants. They're all wet. Ron
stops, looks both ways and as quick as a flash unbuckles his belt, drops
his shorts and whips off his soiled underwear, then hangs them over the
bike handlebars. Ken laughs out loud, so does Ron. Ken yells out at the
top of his voice,
"Who's got the smelly knickers and a bare bum then, Ha".
"Ho Ken, why don't you just tell everyone asshole?"
Ken runs on ahead yelling,
"My brother's got no shorts on! Look at his pink bum?"
There are fire hoses running down the street. Ron stops and rinses
his underpants out in a large puddle of water in the gutter. The boys twist
the pants between them, wringing out most of the water. Ken laughs,
"Are they the shorts with a hole in the
right-hand pocket for an easy feel? Ha".
Ron nods his head,
"Pocket snooker for you this afternoon ha".
They push their bikes through the smoking streets of Munich,
dodging the rubble on the roads and Ron swinging his damp underpants
over his head to try to dry them.

Ken points to the skeleton of a burned-out house. They can see all the wires that were once in the walls. The radiators and heavy water plumbing are still in their place holding up the toilet that is just standing there with nothing but pipes holding it up, like a toilet on a stick.

The rest of the building is burned away. The boy's laughter is choked when they see a huge pile of bodies. All black and charred, the hands and feet are all burned away to sharp points. Police and men with clipboards are trying to establish identities. The boys want to push on, but have to pause to look. Ron waves his underpants in circles over his head yelling,

"Fucking RAF, Fucking stupid war, stupid fucking Hitler".

They turn the corner. The center of the street has been set up as a morgue. Bodies are laid out in rows, some with white labels tied to them, their heads black without any recognizable facial features. On the sidewalk is a pile of small bodies of children. One little girl still clutching her doll, its tiny clothes all burned off but the china face still smiling unharmed by the heat of the fires.

When they get back to the school, their burns are dressed and the nurse gently cuts their frizzed hair off and shaves their eyebrows.

Ron smiles and says,

"Ken, you look like a like a woman that's
been shaved for sleeping with a Jew".

The platoon gathers around to hear about the raid and fires,
Dieter says,

"We watched Munich glow from the roof of the school.

Karl had us all up there with hoses wetting it down in case sparks should reach here.

"Was it very bad? It looked terrible,
it looked as if the whole city was on fire"
"Mm... It was, almost".

After a few weeks the boy's hair grows back and their burns heal. They quickly rejoin their platoon and are soon back at their civic duties. One bright Saturday morning Dieter's platoon are all dressed in their summer HJ uniforms; each boy is wearing a second white armband "Ordungs-Dienst" (Control Service). A group of tables have been set up in a Munich street. Ration coupons in boxes are being distributed. Government officials are seated at the tables, signing and issuing the new ration cards. A very long line of civilians, mostly old men and women with small children stand in line waiting.

Dieter's assignment is to keep some sort of order in the line of people, to sort them out into single file as they approach the tables and to watch the table for theft. There have been some problems with people applying for ration cards who had already received them.

Disturbing incidents of screaming women pushing and shoving and trying to grab cards had surprised one set of officials.

It had been reported that at another distribution center a group of teenage boys had rushed in and snatched fistfuls of cards and run off. So today Dieter is wearing a black pistol holster on his belt. It makes him look a lot more official, but all he has in the holster is an apple and some pencils.

When a sixteen-year-old boy in a uniform with short pants is trying to keep order in a very tense situation, a pistol on his belt has a calming influence on the crowd.

Dieter walks up to Ron at the end of the tables and slides a fat brown envelope under the box in front of him. Ron quickly adjusts the box to cover the envelope completely. Winking Dieter whispers.

"I'm going to the end of this line. When I blow my whistle and get everyone's attention, stuff that envelope up your jacket. I will see you in the station toilet, right?"

Ron nods. Dieter wanders slowly to the far end of the line. The people are all facing the tables and away from him. He waits to choose his moment, watching for the policeman to be in a favorable position. Ron moves the box closer to the edge of the table and stares at the corner of the brown envelope that he has to snatch. His heart starts pounding. Waiting to grab the envelope, he mutters to himself,

"Lift the box, grab it, stuff it up my sweater, stand still and hope they're all looking the other way".

Dieter's moment arrives. He blows his whistle, four short blasts. The whole queue of people and the policeman turn their heads to see what the commotion is all about. Whilst everyone is looking in Dieter's direction, Ron takes his chance. He grabs the envelope and stuffs it up inside his jacket and stands still… Ron slowly and nervously looks both ways; he is amazed that no one has seen him. It worked.

Dieter is shouting,

"Just keep your places please, no pushing, there, no pushing".

When no one is looking, Ron slides away into a side street and disappears. He waits for Dieter in a toilet cubicle at the station, not daring to open the fat brown envelope. The wait seems forever, he is sure a cleaner or some guard would know he has been in there too long. At last Dieter shows up and locks them both up inside the cubicle He grabs the envelope from Ron.

"Did you see what was in here?"

Ron shakes his head. Dieter tears open the large brown envelope and shows Ron a thick wad of ration cards. Ron gasps and says,

"Oh shit, look at that wad, Dieter, we could all be shot for this. Won't they know they're missing?"

"No, they came off the truck, after our consignment
had been counted out... Our unit is in the clear".
"Ron it's our runaway money".

It's dark when Dieter, the twins and Hans wander into the school
boiler room. The place smells different now the central heating is off in
the school. Dieter starts to look about him with his flashlight. Gerhard
steps out from behind the boiler.

"So, what are you lot looking for?"

Dieter moves close to him and pokes him in the chest with his finger,
"You"

Dieter continues to look around searching the whole cellar with his
light. Satisfied that no one except Gerhard and the twins are there, he
pulls Gerhard into his little bedroom at the back of the boiler house,
leaving Hans outside as a lookout, and closes the door.

Ron speaks first,

"We may be able to get our hands on some ration cards,
and clothing cards too".

Gerhard snaps back like a recording,

"What colors, signed or unsigned, with names or blank,
stamped or unstamped how many have you got?
We could get shot for just having this conversation,
do you lot know that?"

Dieter puts his arm around Gerhard's shoulders, and says,

"Slow down, we may be able to get all colors,
signed, stamped but not yet issued.
No names and addresses. The best. We know their value...
We have some very special requirements...
Can you handle it on your own?"

Gerhard thinks for a while,

"I have a partner".

Dieter shakes his head,

"No partners, we don't want to deal with middlemen.
The fewer know about this the better".

Gerhard whispers,

"My father is my city contact, we go through him or no deal".

The boys look at each other and nod. Ron hands Gerhard a sheet of
paper,

"Here is a list of the ration cards we have to sell.
We know their value. Look at the price,
we are asking twenty percent under market price.
On the back is a list of what we want for them.
Cash plus everything on this list".

Gerhard stares at the paper reading every item slowly, and looks up
at the boys,

"There is a lot of tinned food here, fish hooks, 22 gage piano
wire, blankets, a new big tent and a small tent.... You lot going
on some sort of travel safari?"
He strikes a match and burns the list. Dieter looks at the flames and
whispers,
"Do you remember all the stuff on that list?
When can we get an answer?"
Gerhard smiles mysteriously,
"I could give you an answer as soon as I see the goods".
Dieter pulls up his shirt and takes out a large brown envelope and
pulls out a wad of ration cards, one for each color. Ron starts to lay one
of each card on the bed and explains,
"These are a samples in good faith, one of each: blue for meat,
yellow for fat and dairy, they are worth twice as much as these
white, green, orange, pink or purple. As you see not folded yet,
prime stuff".
Dieter gets very stern,
"You fuck us about and we will put you
in your own furnace head first and light it!"
Ron adds grinning,
"And you won't come out".
Gerhard smiles showing a row of bad teeth. He opens a wooden
box next to his bed and takes out a bottle of brandy. Each boy takes a
swig. Dieter turns to the brothers and gives them the envelope of ration
cards,
"You two get this stuff back and stash it.
I have something to talk to Gerhard about".
Ken and Ron stand still defiantly. Dieter waves them off smiling
mischievously, making a sexual gesture.
"Go on, I want to rent his bedroom, I will tell you about it later".
They shake hands with Gerhard and slip away into the night.

13. THE PLAN

In the station message office on a quiet afternoon, Ken and Ron are plotting to gain access into the locked storeroom. Ken remarks,
"That storeroom's really in a mess. If anybody ever
wanted something in a hurry he'd be in dead trouble".
The sergeant overhears what he was meant to and picks up on the complaint very quickly. He grabs Ron's collar and Ken by his ear,
"Hey, you two, so you think our storeroom is
a big mess? Well I have a nice job for you both".
He orders the brothers to clean out the store and organize all the forms on the shelves. The sergeant grins and throws them a bunch of keys. The twins wade into their task with glee, pocketing a spare key.

Hans and the brothers start stealing the things they need for their escape: Pouches, stationary, on-duty armbands, envelopes and date stamps, all from the station office. Their hiding place is an old boathouse that's situated on the school grounds. The cavity under a balcony on the front of the hut is well away from any of the other buildings.

Teachers and visitors used to sit up on the balcony and watch the boat races. The hiding space is big enough to put a small car, but because of the slightly sloping soft damp ground it has been deemed useless as storage and a wooden wall fills in between the posts, beams and rafters that support the elaborate decorative balcony above. By carefully prying off the planks, the boys make a removable door, a secret door that you had to know about to be able to open. This is their meeting place and where they store all the things they will need to run away and survive all summer in the mountains.

Hans helps Dieter steal tent quarters, ground sheets, cooking pots, blankets, tent pegs, a sharp axe, a saw, good cord and a lot of strong climbing rope, a steel grill and a folding field stove, an iron stew pot and a water kettle.

Dieter swaps their thin worn socks for thick newer ones out of the other boys' lockers while the dormitory is empty. All the supplies get stashed in their secret space under the balcony. The boys nickname it 'The Stash Box'.

The largest object Dieter steals is a four-boy handcart with big wheels. A cart used by most of the Hitler Youth units.

It is designed strong and light with long shafts that slide through to the front or rear. Two boys in the front and two boys at the rear. With its fat tires, four boys can easily manage it across the roughest country. It has an aluminum lid that's watertight secured with two big padlocks; just the thing to stash small precious objects you want kept safe from the sharp teeth of small furry creatures that scurry about the edge of the lake.

Up in the school loft, Dieter and the twins are sitting on a pile of old drapes. The sun streams through a small dormer window. Hans is keeping watch at the door to make sure they don't get overheard,
Dieter says,
"We should have everything from Gerhard by now,
except the tinned food".
Ron nods his head,
"It's all first-rate stuff, I have hidden the whole lot in the
Stash Box. Here is the rest of what we need from the list".
Ron reads from a sheet of folded paper,
"A small strong magnifying glass and flint sticks to start fires.
Fish hooks, fishing line and reels, floats and lead weights, lots
of piano wire for making traps, small pliers and wire cutters,
four good compasses and a big army first aid kit. Seeds, lettuce,
potatoes, carrots and stuff we can eat that grows fast".
Dieter looks pleased,
"They want to meet us at the school's old farm stable".
"I said that will be fine for us. They don't need to know about
our cart and our Stash Box, do they? We will take another cart
for the pick-up. Ha! I will organize an aluminum salvage drive
for cover".
Hans says,
"We have got six big airtight tins from the kitchen, all boiled
out and steam cleaned for the flour; oh, and rubber sticky tape
for sealing them. Also a sealed un-opened 50-kilo can of rice".
Dieter takes the list from Hans, folds it and gives it back to Ken,
Ron looks at Dieter with a sideways suspicious glance,
"So, what are you and Gerhard cooking up?"
Dieter gets slightly flustered, then blurts it all out,
"He's going to rent me his bedroom for the night.
I'm sleeping with Hanna. She wants a baby for Hitler.
She says I'm stupid but she wants my body, because
I'm blond and have blue eyes. You know, they are asking girls,
married or not, to have babies for Germany".
Ken grins and nudges Ron,
"Do you know what to do?"
Dieter breaks into a broad smile and lies back on the drapes,
"No, but she says she does. Well I'm almost seventeen
and still a virgin. I have to get it out of my system
and Hanna wants to do it… Look".
Dieter unclasps his belt and unbuttons his shorts.
I have to get it out of my system, don't I?"
Ken laughs,
"I'm going, if you're going to start wanking yourself stupid".

180

Dieter grins, then laughs,
    "No, I'm saving all this for tonight".
Dieter stands up and reaches up to a rafter beam and starts to do
pull-ups. His shorts fall down round his boots.
Ron gets up, picks up Dieter's hat and hangs it on his erection. The
boys all laugh as Dieter makes the hat jump up and down. Ron says,
    "Dieter, are you really going to do Hanna, you know,
    go up in her all the way, right up inside her?"
Dieter pulls himself up to the rafters again,
    "That's what she wants to do;
    all seventeen centimeters of it, right up there".
    "That's right, you measure yours, don't you…
    does she know you've got a big fat one?"
    "No, ha, but she soon will".
    "Can we watch…?"
Dieter lets go of the rafter, jumps lightly down and pulls up his pants.
He leans close to Ron and whispers into his ear,   "No".
    "Well I just thought I would ask".
Ken getting very curious,
    "Dieter, has Hanna done it with anyone else,
    you know, will you be the first?"
Dieter gets all concerned and flops down on a pile of old drapes,
    "You know, I don't know about that; I never asked her… It's
    not the sort of thing you say to a girl on your first meeting,
    "Excuse me, but are you a virgin?"
    I would get a smack around the ears. Ha, it would be
    worth it to know. I know one thing for sure, she knows more
    about it than I do; she might have done it with someone.
    She must get lots of offers. I think she is so beautiful.
    Did you notice her arms, how brown they are?
    With such very fine blond hairs in her armpits"
Ken and Ron look at each other and grin, Ken says,
    "She has been saving herself and waiting for Dieter's dong to
    grow big enough. You mind she doesn't suck you in and blow
    you out in bubbles Dieter, Ha".

*On the 12th of December 1935, the Riechführer-SS Heinrich Himmler
ordered the SS Race and Resettlement Office to set up a program known as the
'Lebensborn' or (Fountain of Life).*
    *It was dedicated to producing a 'Master Race' and increasing Germany's
population. The goal was to man six hundred extra regiments in twenty years.
With blond young men, all sired from the right genetic Nordic types.*
    *In 1942, blond male babies who were judged to be 'racially valuable' by the
SS Brown Sisters, were being kidnapped or stolen from their mothers' arms in the*

New German territories of Holland, Yugoslavia, Belgium, Finland, Latvia, Poland and France. They were then put in to school-camps or adopted out to racially preferred German families. Young children of the occupied regions quickly learned to flee the squads of the specially trained SS women who roamed around the cities in large cars offering sweets or toffees to bait and grab them.

At home in Germany, the male population was seriously depleted as a result of the two world wars. So the young blond Nordic girls of childbearing age were encouraged and taught that is was their 'sacred duty to the Führer' to 'have babies for Hitler',

Providing the father's pedigree had been ascertained as pure 'Aryan' with no Jewish, Slavic, or Gipsy blood back for three generations. In the periodical 'Rasse' (Race) of March 1937 and other magazines read by young people this statement appeared:

> *"Every healthy child means one more battle won in the fight for existence of the German people. So, Have Baby's for Hitler and Germany. There are plenty of willing and qualified youths ready to unite with the girls and young women on hand. Fortunately, one boy between the age of fourteen and eighteen of good pure race suffices for twenty girls. The girls over fourteen for their part should gladly fulfill this demand. Marriage at this age is not important. The single purpose of this national union of young teenagers is to produce babies. When a young single girl becomes a mother she will be entitled to be called 'Mrs.' and given the full ration cards of a married woman for her and her expected child. So you young German teenage Women. "Have babies for Hitler".*

Young girls would set their sights on fair-haired blue-eyed young men. When single girls became pregnant they could move into a congenial Lebensborn maternity hostel, where they received the very best of everything, eating good nourishing food with fresh milk for the babies. All this at times when food was scarce and when the German people and their soldiers went hungry.

Dieter spends a long time in the shower washing every bit of his body twice or three times. Thinking of Hanna, he fights hard and disciplines himself not to play with his erection,

"Must save it for Hanna tonight," he thinks.

Then he turns the water cold, but it doesn't work. It won't go away; it's still there as big as ever.

"Clean clothes will do it", he thinks.

He dresses, tries to comb his curly blond mop of hair, then messes it up again,

"I never comb my hair, it looks better dried off natural".

He looks at his pocket watch: three quarters of an hour to go.

He inspects his face in the polished steel mirror. He sees a healthy good-looking fresh-faced boy with a little blond shadow suggesting a moustache; his first facial hair. Pale blue eyes that are smiling and kind. He says to himself.

"Well I hope she doesn't want me for my manly looks, ha.
Tonight's the night. Tonight Dieter you will become a man.
I wonder if I will really do it? Ho yes, do I ever want to…
I hope she knows what to do".

When Dieter arrives at the boiler room. Gerhard's bedroom door is open and a red light is glowing over the bed.

Hanna, to his total surprise, is already there, twenty minutes early. She has clean sheets and is pulling Gerhard's grubby sheets off the bed. She looks up and sees Dieter,

"Come on, help me, I'm not lying on his sweaty sheets".
"Did you bring your own?"

She nods and smoothes the sheets as if she is making the boys' beds; changing the sheets in the boys' dormitories is one of her weekly duties. Dieter looks at her as she fusses about with the bed. She is beautiful in a wholesome fresh country way. He can smell the lavender water she had doused herself with. She stops; realizing Dieter is watching her, spins around pointing her finger to the door and orders,

"Go and put the bolt on that door, we don't want any
of your little monsters sneaking in for free looks, do we?"

Dieter goes out of the bedroom, crosses the boiler room and bolts the heavy doors. He gets back and locks the bedroom door.

Hanna is in the bed with the sheets pulled up to her nose.

Dieter stands looking at her clothes piled neatly on the chair. The dark brown service regulation nickers are on top of the pile. With a stupid grin on his face he says,

"My, you got in bed quick, I wanted to see you"…
"No, not yet, we do this my way, or not at all,
You had better get undressed, put your clothes
on the other chair over there".

Dieter whispers,

"Do you have anything on in there?"
"No"
"Nothing at all?"
"No… Get undressed".
"Alright, I will, but don't be so bossy".

Dieter takes off his jacket and puts it over the back of the chair. Then his shirt, boots, and socks; then he pulls down his shorts and underpants that come off with one quick movement and he stands at the side of the bed naked. Hanna looks at his body all over, exploring every part, and pats the bed for Dieter to lie down.

He reaches to grasp the bedclothes to get under the covers but Hanna shakes her head and says quietly,

"Dieter, can you just lie on top for a moment.

I want to see something".

He nods and sits on top of the bed and puts his feet up and stretches out. Hanna sits up on one elbow,

"Close your eyes and don't move,

whatever I do to you, don't move, alright?"

Dieter nods and shuts his eyes.

He feels her cool hand exploring every part of his body, lifting up his arms feeling the light fair hairs just starting to grow in his armpit. Lifting his leg and running her hands up and around his bottom. He was bursting to open his eyes and look at her and see her body... He thinks,

"Oh she touched it, I can't stop it now from going hard".

He opens his legs to allow her access, to get into his most private places. She moves around and he feels her soft head gently lying on his stomach.

"I can hear your tummy rumbling and your heart beating".

Dieter opens his eyes. He can see the back of her blond hair, her braids running down his waist and see down her back to her bottom. It is white in contrast to her tanned back and arms. Her cool fingers play with his testicles, she whispers,

"This is where the babies are made?"

"Mm".

Dieter takes her head gently in his hands and pushes her down until her lips and nose touch his throbbing erection. He feels wet lips running up and down the base, then in to the light fuzz of his blond hair.

She suddenly sits up and for the first time he sees her face and her small round breasts. They are so white... something he hadn't thought about. They stare at each other for a long time, she whispers,

"Can you shoot sperm at any time, you know, like peeing?"

"No... No, I have to be worked up... Or wanked off".

"If I put it in my mouth you won't pee will you?"

"No that wouldn't be very nice".

"Alright".

She jumps out of bed and stands looking at him. Dieter looks at her youthful body with just a thin line of blond maidenhair. She gets back on the bed, turns around and puts her head on his upper leg. Then she thrusts one arm under his waist and pulls herself into him close moving and shuffling and he feels her kissing the top end of his member,

"You have to do me, you know, kiss me down there too".

Dieter rolls over on his side and puts both of his arms around her slim waist and burrows his face into her little wisp of maidenhair.

A thrill passes through his whole body as he feels warm wet lips and tongue exploring the top of his penis. Hanna thrusts herself into Dieter's face and at the same time opens her legs wide forcing Dieter to explore deeper with his tongue. The gentle aroma he has never smelled before excites him, his tongue exploring deeper and deeper. He sits up, thinking to himself looking at the small and closed spot,

"Where does it go, how can it go in the tiny little place?"

He licks his finger and put it where his tongue had been. He explores all around and tries to put a thumb up inside her. The place is too small and Hanna jumps,

"Ow, what are you doing? That hurt".

Dieter grabs her and kisses her as gently as he can, seconds later she throws her arm around Dieter in a long and tight embrace.

"Oh Dieter let's do it. Do it to me Dieter".

She grabs the pillows and puts them under her bottom, arching her back up, then raises her knees and opens her legs as wide as she can. The girls had told her about that, they saw it in a book. Dieter gets on top, his knees between her legs taking his full weight on his elbows,

"You have to put it in the right place,

I can't see what to do down there".

After a lot of positioning and pushing, then replacing and pushing,

"Dieter no, it's too low...

Ow, you're trying to go up into my bottom".

Hanna rolls Dieter on his back and sits over the top of him.

With very careful positioning she nods to Dieter,

"That's it, we have to push"...

Hanna lets out a scream that makes Dieter almost jump out of his skin.

"Oh, what did I do?"

"Nothing, it hurts so much when you try to go inside.

We need some lubricant, here try again....

Ow, ho no. So, try to push it inside".

Again a scream,

"Ho Dieter, why won't it go? It hurts so much".

Dieter looks at her in tears,

"What about the other times, did you get it in then?"

"Other times, what other times, yours is the first one

I have ever had in my hand. You are the first Dieter".

Dieter takes command. He lays her back and puts his face into her maidenhair. She opens her legs and he seeks and explores with his tongue. She takes his head and between them they find their ecstasy. She grabs him around his waist and sucks as hard as she can. They roll clutching and embracing. They thrash and roll about the bed in ecstasy.

"It's coming," he whispers, "it's coming".

She grasps him tighter and holds still, Dieter feels himself shooting. He knows he has shot more than he ever has in his life.

The young lovers lay locked in each other's arms.

Dieter's erection softens but Hanna still holds him next to her cheek.

"We both came together, didn't we?"

"Yes, but we didn't do it yet did we?"

"No"

They fall asleep in each other's arms.

After a while Dieter wakes up. Hanna is playing with his foreskin.

"What's the time?"

Hanna looks at the old alarm clock.

"About eleven thirty. Look what I have found".

She holds up a jar of Vaseline.

"I found it in his bathroom cabinet. C'mon, let's try again".

Dieter lying on his back feels Hanna smearing the lubricant all over him pulling back his foreskin. This produces a fast erection.

Hanna hands Dieter the tube.

"You do me now, put plenty there".

Again they try. Hanna guides him to the right spot. There is more positioning and wiggling, and then Hanna lets out a little cry and pulls Dieter to her. He feels himself sink slowly up inside her; it is the strangest feeling he has ever experienced.

He watches the pain in her face.

"How far do I go?"

"Shh... Just do it Dieter".

Very slowly with shallow thrusts he starts to move. Each time Dieter goes a little deeper. She grabs him by his bottom and pulls hard. Dieter senses the rhythm and starts to push each time deeper and deeper. They lock themselves and their pace gets so regular their breathing becomes synchronized.

Now he is going in as far as he can, pushing and thrusting. Hanna starts to cry out,

"Do it Dieter, do it Dieter, Oh Dieter oh yes, do it".

"Oh, Oh, Hanna, it's coming Hanna,

here comes all the babies Oh, Oh, Ha, Oh"...

"Oh, did you feel me shoot inside you, I came so much.

Oh Hanna, we did it Hanna, we made wonderful love".

They lay back in each other's arms, she whispers dreamily,

"That was the most love I ever felt in my whole life".

Dieter lies drifting in a semi-conscious release, realizing he had never experienced any sexual climax like the one he has just had. They fall asleep. The alarm wakes them up at five and they do it again. This time it's light and Dieter sees her body for the first time and whispers,

"Hanna you are so beautiful, so fresh, I could eat you".

Hanna smiles wistfully she has this wonderful feeling, a glow all over her body, every touch of Dieters tingles, she whispers,

"Dieter you are beautiful too we will make fine babies".

The twins and Hans are in the 'Box' hideaway stacking all the new supplies in the cart and coiling up ropes into tight coils and folding the big bell tent in to a small lump, Hans says,

"It's three nights now that Dieter has been out all night.
He's breeding himself stupid. I pulled myself off twice last night getting all worked up inside just thinking about him with Hanna and her beautiful body, doing it together, all naked".

Ken smiles,

"Him with his big thing right up inside her, oh look".

Dieter strides into the box looking radiant and pleased with himself. He slaps Ken on the shoulder, hugs Ron.

"All taken care of, we got everything on our list and more".

Ron points to Dieter's crotch,

"How did your three nights of sex go?
It hasn't fallen off yet then?"

Dieter grins sheepishly,

"Well I needed to do that. I no longer feel like a
virgin. I feel like a man and not a young wanker".

Hans curious,

"What's it like? Did you go in all the way, as far as it'd go?"

Dieter nods,

"Oh yes, oh it's the most fantastic thing I have ever done
in my whole life. Better even than seeing Italy beat the SS at soccer six nil last year. But I was scared. I thought I'd hurt her".
"But she said it was how it was supposed to be".

Ron, changing the subject,

"So let's not gloat. When and where do we get our stuff?"

Dieter becomes the sergeant again,

"We will need to borrow a big hand truck. We have to meet
them at the old farm. We get the money and everything on our list. We need to take the cart and get it over to the farm before they get there, then re-stash it here. It's a risk we have to take. We can't let them know where we keep our stash.
I don't trust anyone. We will do the exchange
the night Karl is on his anti-aircraft gun duty".

Ken, inquisitive,
    "What about the cash?"
Dieter prods Ken and smiles,
    "Did you think I was going to rob us? We get that too.
    I'm not sure how much yet. Come on; it's a great day;
    let's go for a swim. We can talk freely out there,
    these walls just may have ears".
The four boys amble out of the Box, turn the corner and run head
on into Karl he grins and paces around them,
    "Well, see how fortunes change, now I have the rank,
    I'm going to be pleased to make your lives a living hell".
The four boys just stand in silence, stunned. Karl goes on,
    "I know you lot are cooking up something, or plotting some
    lark. But I will find out. I'm making it my life's work to find out
    what you lot are up to".
He pokes Dieter's shirt and flicks his fly buttons that are undone,
pulls his shirt out,
    "Look at you, you're supposed to be setting an example
    to these boys. No wonder they're all in shit order.
    You're a dirty shit, what are you?"
Dieter looks him in the eye smiles and whispers,
    "I'm a dirty shit, sir".
    "What, louder sergeant I can't hear you. Speak up".
Dieter almost shouts, "I'm a dirty little shit, sir".
Ken smiles,
    "Well congratulations on your promotion Karl.
    I thought we were friends".
    "No we're not friends, not you four.
    What are you all doing now? I have a job for you".
Dieter shakes his head.
    "Sorry we are working for Captain Mitter, all four of us, sir".
Karl sneers,
    "I have a duty with the anti-aircraft battery this afternoon. I'm
    being trained on 88s you know. When I'm put in charge of my
    own battery, I'm going to pick out a crew to train from this
    school and it won't be any of you grubby slackers.
    When I come back I'm going to watch you very carefully".
When Karl is out of earshot Dieter whispers saying,
    "I bet that shit Karl's red blood cells are shaped like little
    swastikas, that asshole is a pure Nazi".

At the diving stage in the lake, Ken and Ron are sunning themselves
after a swim. Dieter and Hans are just coming out of the water up the
ladder, Hans proudly yells,

"I just swam from the point; all the way.

Dieter made me do it; it's a long way out there".

Dieter laughing says,

"Well I bet you're glad I did now, ha.

It's alright if I push you then, now you can swim, Ha"...

Dieter lumbers towards Hans as if to push him off the pontoon,

But Hans ducks down, steps lightly to one side and using Dieter's own momentum, pushes him into the lake. They all laugh. Dieter is out of the water in a flash and shakes the water all over everyone. Dieter says laughing,

"If it was like this all the time I wouldn't mind staying here".

Ron wipes his face with a towel,

"Well it's not and we have to make a plan. I have a good one".

The three boys gather around Ron and flop out on the deck.

Ron sits up on his elbows,

"The beauty of this plan is that it is so simple...

Fact number one... If a group of four boys run away,

the school won't report it to Munich... Reason:

It would be a black mark on their unblemished record".

Ken points out,

"And, the food rations would be cut by four boy units.

They didn't report when the girls took off with the soldier".

Dieter smirking,

"He must have had a good time, three girls".

Hans looks at Dieter stretched out all wet,

"Dieter, can't you think of anything else but sex?"

Dieter grins,

"No".

Ken pokes Dieter in his crotch,

"I thought you got it all out of your system

by doing Hanna for three nights?"

Dieter looks up into the clear blue sky,

"Well its back in my system again...

Wouldn't it be wonderful to make love in the sun here?

And go in for a swim naked, locked in each other's arms;

our love would keep us floating forever".

Ron getting irritated,

"Do you want to hear this plan or not?"

Hans looks at Dieter's erection trying to burst through his trunks,

"Look Dieter's getting a hard-on... Hey Dieter,

does the water go up inside them when they swim?"

Ron jumps to his feet in disgust and goes towards the water.

Dieter grabs his ankles, gives him a friendly bear hug and walks him back to the others. Dieter says warmly,

"Come on Ron, let's hear your plan,
we have to get out of this place".
Ron sits down. Dieter puts a towel over his waist. Ron says angrily,
"No more stupid sex talk?"
The boys all nod in agreement. Dieter nods, Ron explains,
"Well, if no one is looking for us, we don't have to go very far
away, just hide in the woods... For the summer. We leave all
the warm winter clothes hidden in the hideaway box. There's
no need for us to cart them all up there in the woods. If the war
lasts through to the winter, we come back at night, pick up our
winter stuff and just move to the city and live in bombed out
basements. There must be lots of basements you should see the
places that have been bombed".
Dieter is enthusiastic, he rubs his hands together, Ron
continues,
"I stole the big maps out of the geography class, I have a place
picked out, for a summer camp, it is in a valley and has water,
fish and woods; a good place to hide. It is almost south facing,
so it will be warm and the best part is, it's a dead end valley. No
one will want to come in to this valley because it is a dead end,
blocked by a big mountain".
Dieter asks,
"When do we go?"
Ron stands up, stretches his arms out and casually says,
"How about Saturday morning?"
The boys all jump with joy, Dieter holds up his hand concerned,
"Saturday morning, wait, people will see us".
All the boys' heads turn to Ron. He smiles, waits to milk the moment
and then smiles and nods,
"I hope so, sergeant. You're taking us all out on a hike. As soon
as we are clear of the school you open your phony sealed orders
that Ken and I will make for you, promote one boy as a new
leader, send everybody except us four, on some mission north-
west. Then we go due east with our flags flying and a two-day
head-start... So what do you think?"
The boys look at each other and smile, Dieter nods his approval. He
grabs Ron's shoulders,
"You, my lad, are a bloody genius,
it sounds like a good plan to me...
We have to keep clear of Karl till then".
Dieter picks up Hans, puts him on his shoulders, grabs Ken under
one arm and Ron under the other, and carrying the three boys he runs off
the end of the dock into the water. The sergeant is a boy again splashing
in the water like an overgrown child.

The boys pack their rucksacks. Ken grabs his old teddy bear. Ron stuffs the money tin their father gave them into the bear's body and pulls up the hidden zipper. Then he rolls the teddy into a warm shirt and stuffs it into Ken's bag. When everything is all packed, their traveling gear is locked into Dieter's room. The four boys take their last shower in the school. Dieter lifts a towel on a bench in the corner of the shower room and hands the boys their PT shorts, vests and running shoes, saying,

"Because we are all good and best friends,
I have a wonderful gift for all three of you".
Ken laughing,
"What is it, our last drill duty?"
Dieter whispers,

"Please just put them on. It's very important, we have to be in running kit so we can stay out as long as we like. If we are challenged we can say we were out on a cross country run and have just got back".

The boys reluctantly dress in their gym gear and trot outside following Dieter into the cool night air, Hans jogs up to Dieter and asks,
"So where are we going?"

Dieter turns and puts his finger up to his mouth,
"Shh, don't spoil the surprise, no questions, please".
The joggers all arrive at the boiler room. The door is open so they jog right in. Dieter taps on the bedroom door.
It opens and Gerhard looks out grinning.
"Three or four?"
Dieter says,
"These three first, then me, that's what we agreed".
Gerhard smiles, puts one finger up for them to wait then closes the door. Ken whispering,
"What's going on?"
Dieter says softly,

"It's my treat. I have paid for the room again. You boys are going to lose your virginity. They are both Frau Claria's girls, only sixteen and fifteen, good strong sexy maids. One of them is a virgin, well almost they say, the other is Hanna".
Ron grabs Ken's hand and yanks him towards the door. Dieter yells,

"Come on, it's my treat, do you want to do it with a girl? Or do you want to stay young wankers all your lives? The girls want to have babies for Hitler. If we don't give it to them someone else will, they are nice and they want to do it too".
The door opens, Gerhard asks,
"Who's first?"

Dieter nods to Hans, then grabs him by the shoulder and pushes him in. As he closes the door, Gerhard winks at Dieter and leaves. Ron and Ken stare blankly at each other, Ken says,
 "I hope these girls know how to do it".
Dieter grinning,
 "They know... I know they know".
Ken tries to peep through the crack in the door.
Dieter pulls him away. After a while Hans comes out, as naked as the day he was born, his shorts and vest in one hand and his gym shoes in the other. He has a glazed expression on his face. Dieter says softly,
 "Come on, you two, you're going to make babies for Hitler".
The brothers are pushed into the room and the door is closed.
The small bedroom is sparsely furnished; a shaded red light still glows. Sittings on the edge of the bed are two girls, totally naked their underwear on the floor. Both in their early teens, one slightly underdeveloped, she is looking very uncomfortable.
 The other girl the two boys recognize as Hanna, Dieter's girl; the one Dieter *did it with*. Both girls, as if in a dream, slowly rise from the bed and pull off the boys' gym shirts, then their PT shorts and underpants. Naked, Ron looks at his nude brother with a stupid grin. Hanna whispers as she fondles them both, one in each hand,
  "Two very beautiful young men, look Greta, see how they
  stand... same size... they feel the same too".
Hanna pushes both boys back on to the bed and pulls them together at their waists, Hanna excited,
  "Oh I must kiss them both at the same time, Mm,"
 "Come on Greta you take Ken".
Greta lowers her face down to Ken's throbbing erection.
Ken takes a deep breath, looks at Ron, both boys look down to the two bobbing blond heads. Ron lets out a quiet cry,
 "Ow, you have sharp teeth".
The two boys let themselves be taken, swaying and breathing heavily. With great gasps, it is all over very quickly. They get their live male juices sucked out of them.
Hanna kisses each boy,
  "Was that nice? That was a French kiss. You two were very
  quick. Now sit on the couch over there; it's time to learn. In a
  little while, you will both be ready to make love with us. You
  will take longer to come to your climaxes the second time. We
  will show you how, it will be your turn later".
Ron starts to stand up,
  "Can I see yours, we want to see where it goes inside you?"
 "You will, just you watch Dieter, he's good at it".

Hanna taps on the thin wall. The door opens immediately. Dieter enters dragging in a reluctant Hans. Hanna and Dieter kiss, she starts to take off his clothes. Then passion gets the better of them, without breaking off their kiss Dieter's shorts get kicked off and they go at it. Greta and Hans get on to the bed too.

Dieter makes love to Hanna, trying different positions. Hans, coaxed by Greta, produces a surprising erection, finds his mark and works at his sex, fast and furious like a young rabbit. Dieter, sensing the brothers are curious to see where everything goes, beckons the boys to come over to the bed and they take turns to have a good look...

Ron looks at his brother with a slight frown, grabs his clothing and bids Ken to follow him. They leave the bedroom and quietly close the door. They both dress to the sounds of lovemaking that can be heard through the thin walls as four people bounce about on the bed with,

"Ohs, mms" and grunts.

Ron asks Ken softly,

"Ken, did you want to do it with one of those girls?"

Ken, tucking his shirt in, nods sadly,

"Yes I want to. I want to feel what it is like...

Ron, don't you ever feel like doing it?

I have a feeling down here, all the time... So why"...

When they get outside into the fresh air, Ron blurts out,

"I wanted to too... with both girls, but... well, Dieter with his big thing, he will shoot lots of stuff up inside her and Hans... You know, all their stuff will be right up inside the girls"... "

"So?"

"Well, they shoot all their stuff in them first and then we are expected to go up inside them and slosh on their stuff.

It would make me feel sick, wouldn't you?"

Ken gasps,

"Oh yuck, I never thought about that. Their sperms will still be inside them, yuck... Let's take a shower,

I'm all sweaty... Ron, did you let it go in her mouth?"

Ron nods with a grin; Ken puts his arm round his brother,

"Yes, so did I. It felt wonderful.

Let's go, we need to have a good wank off

in the shower with soap. I think mine's grown bigger today".

Ron laughing,

"Not as big as mine.

Come on, let's get it out of our systems, ha".

Ken shows Ron his right hand pocket turned inside out. There is a hole big enough for him to get his hand through. He thrusts his hand deep into his pocket. Laughing and jumping about grinning stupidly, Ken says,

"Look Ron, pocket billiards, Ha".
Ron laughs, "No pocket snooker, Ha".

It's Friday afternoon. Ken is alone in their hideout 'Box', lying back against a pile of blankets that are rolled ready to be stashed in their cart.

We are a tight group of chums, just us four. Dieter and Hans will be good friends together, Dieter will look after him like a big brother, Hans needs a lot of looking after and Dieter needs someone to look after, so that's nice.

Ron and I... Well, we are really one person, but we let Ron be the leader because he is a lot better at it than me. I will always support him because we have sworn our own brothers' oath".

Dieter Ron and Hans arrive and close themselves in the hideaway. Dieter leans over Ken and reads Ken's writings,

"What you writing in that book lad? I hope it won't get us all
shot if someone finds it, I can't read English but I see my
name's in there, you should use a code for names and places.
That wouldn't be the first diary that has got its owner sent to a
concentration camp".

Ken shrugs it off and whispers.

"All right! I will cut out all the names
and your code name will be "Poo" as in Poo Bear".

Ken closes the book and rolls it up and zips it in his Teddy Bear.

The boys load the cart stashing all the heavy things at the bottom and balancing the rest of the tinned food and tents evenly so the cart rides well and is not lopsided. They don't want it too heavy at one end or the other. Most of the supplies are for their permanent summer camp.

They have some tinned food for the journey there and return, but not enough to last four hungry teenagers all the summer; so, they are going to have to live off the land, running trap lines and hunting. Dieter looks serious and says,

"That's it then. Now, we have a problem. Karl knows about the
weekend march that I'm leading tomorrow and he is on the
warpath. He's got a strong hate on for you lot for some reason.
He told me to leave you three behind because he has a job for
you at three thirty in the afternoon, so stay out of his way.
Don't get into any fights with him. Remember we leave at six in
the morning that will give us a seven hour start, If you bump
into Karl be nice to him, call him sir all the time, he likes that".

Ron looks at Dieter with a big grin and says,

"I don't think Karl will be awake at six tomorrow morning
unless he has to. He is on night duty at his beloved anti-aircraft
battery tonight".

Dieter laughs.

"Oh yes, he will be up, he wants to catch you lot going out
against his orders with me, then he can set an example with his
cane again. Just keep out of his way".

Ron looks at Dieter and smiles

"So what was all that going on in Captain Mitter's office
behind closed doors? I saw you all leaving;
that must have been some meeting".

Dieter has a very guilty look on his face and blusters out,

"I can't tell you anything yet, it's no big thing,
but I promise I will tell you all about the meeting soon,
it has nothing to do with us leaving, honest"

Ron looks at him hard and relaxes and says.

"Well it's of no matter we won't be here will we".

Dieter carefully wraps his camera with its telephoto lens and rolls of
film in a soft towel and puts them into an airtight screw-top can,

"I have eight rolls of Agfa film, that's over two hundred and
eighty photos I can take of you bunch of uglys. I got some nice
shots of the girls yesterday, but there is no time to get them
developed before we go."

Dieter locks the lid of the cart with his two padlocks stolen from the
school office

14. THE TREK

The morning of their escape is misty, damp and quite dark. The rain has stopped but it is still very wet underfoot. Dieter's platoon of boys are all lined up outside the school dormitory in three ranks; each boy's pack and overnight kits are laid in front of him ready for inspection. Dieter looks at his clipboard and announces,

"First we have some sad news.... Frans Thorwald was killed last night; he died heroically, at his post on an 88mm anti-aircraft gun during an air raid in Gerlinden... Shit he was only fifteen. Did anyone know his parents?
It would be nice if someone sent a short letter to them...
No one knew him that well... I hope Karl writes something, he was one of his boys; someone should write something".

The boys' faces are sad as they put on their kit.
Ken gets in a huddle with Ron and Hans and says,

"He never knew what it's like to go with a girl you know".

Ron adds,

"I know he never kissed one, he told me".

Dieter comes up and drags the twins and Hans out of the line, pulls them to one side and says,

"Listen, if you two leave the school now, you will have a nine-hour start on Karl. Go east across country, stay off the roads and we will see you all at the fountain in Jachenau later.
It's about twelve kilometers so travel light just take your water bottles, I will put your packs in our cart... go!"

Ron protests,

"What, and miss breakfast?"
"Yes - go. I will bring you something to eat, just go".

Ron glances at Ken,

"Got your Teddy?"

Ken stuffs the teddy bear into his bread-bag, smiles and nods.
The three boys sling their bags over their shoulders, throw their backpacks on the truck and march off down to the lake.
Ron says sadly,

"I didn't think Frans Thorwald was fifteen, he only looked thirteen to me I saw him in the showers after gym last week, he didn't even have any hairs on his dinky yet and now he's dead"...

Hans says quietly,

"Hairs don't stop you getting killed if your number comes up, I think we are getting out of this place at the right time, before we get killed too".

Just as the three boys turn the corner under one of the few lights in the school grounds they run into Karl. He grins,
"So, where are you three little shits going so early?"
Ron quickly replies,
"We are going to get some breakfast, before it's all gone.
Dieter said you didn't want to see us until three thirty".
"Right, you three be at the office at three sharp,
wear overalls I have some painting for you to do".
The boys stand waiting for his next words. He pokes Ron's bag,
"What are the bread bags for?"
Ron thinks, then, quick as a flash, says,
"Oh, we are going to scrub them out at the back of the kitchen
with boiling water and steam, Dieter said they smell sour".
Karl believes them,
"Good, get on with it then, remember three".
They click to attention, throw a smart salute and say.
"Yes sir".
The boys run off in the direction of the great hall. But they turn a sharp left as soon as they get out of Karl's sight to circumnavigate the main gates, keeping an eye on Karl's movements, watching him until he closes his door.
 Climbing over the stone and wooden wall at the edge of the school grounds, they strike off to the village. They feel better when there is a kilometer between them and the school. Ron stops,
"We forgot to look back to have a last look at the school".
Hans says,
"I did, not much to see, it is all dark over there".
Ken yells,
"Well that's it then… It's official; we have run away…
Definitely".
Ron grins and whispers,
"Let's not get caught by making too much noise"
When they put another half a kilometer between themselves and the school walls they start to go wild, flailing their arms, running through the soft wet grass meadow jumping high in the air with the exuberance of free youth yelling and singing,
"Oh, Any old iron, any old iron.
Any any-any-any old iron
Oh Auntie Nelly's got a fat belly
with a red pimple on her bum.
WHITH A RED PIMPLE ON HER BUM.
Ha, Ha, Ha, Ha, He, He,
little brown jug and buns for tea".

The boys' shrill voices echo in the woods, they each grab one of Hans's arms and run him almost off his feet; he jumps higher than he ever has.

The rest of the platoon have just had breakfast and are all lined up outside the hut with their packs on the ground in front of them. Dieter walks up and down, tapping the boys' water bottles to check that they are full. He turns and faces his platoon and holds his hand up for quiet,

"This weekend is going to be nice, for all of us

and for a few of us, extra nice... No wet fields".

The boy's cheer,

"No forced marches this weekend".

More cheering. The two handcarts stand waiting with their flags fluttering. The newer of the two carts has Dieter's two strong padlocks securing its lid. Dieter says quietly,

"The Lambert twins and Hans Kardorff have jobs to do and may catch up with us later. Keep the banners up so the dozy truck drivers can see us, and make sure the boys in the rear wear the red reflectors on their backs.

We don't want to be run down. I will open my sealed orders when we get to the town. If anyone needs to take a pee, do it now: we leave in three minutes".

It is still dark when the platoon marches out of the school gates, banners flying, and the boys singing.

The two handcarts with their own flags are at the rear of the column. Karl, who has now moved into the teacher's quarters with his own room, stands at his front door and watches them leave. Dieter yells to Karl,

"The twins and Kardorff are over in the Great Hall...

Getting some breakfast. Heil Hitler".

Karl nods, he's checking just to see if the Lambert's and Hans had doubled back and were going with the platoon against his orders. Thinking he would have some fun dealing with them later, decides to go back to bed for a few hours and think up some interesting painting jobs that need attention this weekend.

Dieter and his platoon of tanned healthy lads march through the small town of Jachenau. They arrive in the center market square for a rest and a drink and find Hans with the Lambert twins sitting at the fountain. Hans laughs,

"Good morning you lot, anyone seen Karl?"

The platoon all giggle. They know that Karl will be looking for the trio at 3pm. Hans nudges Ron to watch Dieter open his official secret-looking envelope. He takes a long time to read the papers and look at the maps and the two padlock keys. Ron and Ken have done a good job preparing them. They had all decided it would be a good idea for Dieter not to see the papers before today.

He calls the platoon to gather around him and then fixes the papers and a map to his clipboard. He sits on the edge of the fountain and waves the clipboard at the boys.

"These are the sealed orders. It seems we are to split the
platoon here. We will meet again on Monday afternoon in the
school. I have to promote a second leader".

All the boys look to Ken and Ron.

Dieter steps forward and pulls a very surprised lanky youth out of the line and promotes him to acting patrol leader on the spot.

Dieter gives him a map, compass and his written orders. The new patrol leader reads his orders and studies the map with a puzzled look on his face.

He orders the platoon to march off in a northwesterly direction with the older of the carts.

When the platoon disappears from view, Dieter loads his backpack into the new cart and takes out three big chunks of bread, some fat sausages and six hard-boiled eggs for the boys' breakfast. They munch hungrily into their meal. Ken finishes his breakfast and proposes hopefully,

"We shouldn't hang about in the town here too long;
we should get off the road as soon as possible".

Hans gets into the front shafts with Dieter, Ken and Ron in the rear shafts. They take off in an easterly direction, their faces full of excitement. Ron yells,

"That's it, we are gone and we're free... No more sodding
leaders, no more lights out, or short hair inspections".

Ken yells,

"We're free... no more washing behind our ears,
no more washing our bums after each poo,
no more parades, PT or war games, we're free now".

Hans's hisses,

"No more Oberscharführer shit-bag Karl and his stick".

"Yes... come on... Let's go!" Dieter yells.

Across open country and over lush green meadows, the four pull the cart that moves easily on its big wheels through the tall grassland. Always up-hill gaining altitude through bright new vistas.

The boys wander high into the alpine mountain foothills with the fresh smell of spring in their faces. The winter snows still cap the peaks of the Alps that seem to be crowding in on them at every step they take, their zig-zag route takes them further in to Alpine wilderness pulling their cart breathing in the pure fresh pure air.

They keep a wary eye behind them to check they are not followed and stay away from the few roads.

After walking for three days, sleeping in empty hillside cattle sheds, dodging the farmers and not daring to light fires, the four boys arrive at the last road they have to cross before they turn deep into the mountain wilderness. A small white map is spread out on the cart. Ron sets his compass and looks up and down the deserted road,

"North that way is Lake Tegernsee and the village
of Rottach-Egern, south is a small hamlet of Kreuth.
We don't want to be seen crossing here.
It's the last road we have to get over.
It will be open country and forest from now on".

Ron folds his map and puts it away. He stands up on top of the cart and listens for sounds of trucks or cars coming, watching both ways, north and south, up and down the road,

"When I say go, we dash across this road".

Ron whispers and has a look up and down the empty road...

"Now!" he whispers.

The four boys whisk the cart across the road and disappear unseen into the thick brush and woods on the other side.

The way is a little easier now; the higher ground is not so wet under foot. Dieter and Ron take compass bearings. Ron points to a spot on the hill. After a drink of water, they all continue their walk. The big wheels cope easily with the soft grass. Boys' boots squelch in the mud, working legs shine wet from the long damp grasses, their faces working too, pulling, as the going gets steeper.

A boot kicks a giant toadstool to bits, the other boots trample it to a pulp; on and on through the long grass.

Their way is now northeast around the base of the great Wallberg mountain then south to the small hamlet of Enterrottach. The boys spread out until they find the little river Rottach.

Ron grins, picks up a stick and scratches a map in the mud bank.

"We follow this river south now,
until we get to another river that runs from the west
into this one. It's called the Siebligraben at a place
called Hufnagel Stube, it's not a village or anything
it's just a place where two rivers meet,
but it should have a marker".

Arriving at a small clearing under big shady tree, Hans says,

"So when are we going to stop for lunch? This looks like a
good place".

Dieter stops the cart and looks around,

"Look at this place, look at the beautiful snow
on the peaks over there. You would never think
there was a war on. We could stay here tonight".

Ron calmly,
  "No... We have to get into the woods over there.
  We are too exposed here... We can see right to the
  Crossroads down in the valley, from here,
  so they can see us".
Hans puts his hands up to his eyes,
  "Ha, if they had binoculars".
Ron and Ken say together,
  "They have binoculars".
Dieter says firmly,
  "Well, I'm the sergeant, and I say we stop here
  for lunch and a cool wash, and that's the end of it".
Ron looks at Dieter and says firmly,
  "You're not a sergeant, not up here you're not.
  It's my route and we all agreed to keep to it...
  Our night's camp is in the trees way over there.
  They won't see us, and there is a stream in the woods too".
Dieter nods reluctantly, unlocks the shafts on the cart and pushes
them through so four boys can all pull from the front.

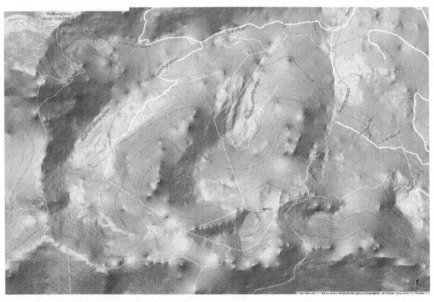

Detail of map. Lake at bottom center, Blankenstein rocks at
center left.

They arrive at their fourth night camp spot, covering the cart with brush to hide it. They eat bread, sausage and apples for dinner. No fire, because it is too close to civilization. The boys put down a big ground sheet and curl up in their own blankets to sleep for the night.

The next morning there is a hard ground frost, the boys are all sitting wrapped in their blankets, eating sausage and bread again for breakfast, Dieter shivers,

"My, it was bloody cold out here last night.
You forget how cold it gets up here".

Ron shakes his water bottle,

"We are going higher today and it will be colder, my water had a little ice on the top. But tonight we should sleep in our tent".

Ken complains,

"I was breaking my neck for a piss early this morning, but I was too cold to get out".

Hans laughs,

"Cold enough to freeze the balls off a brass monkey".

Ken asks,

"How many blankets do we get?
I was really cold last night too".

Dieter reassures them,

"You won't be cold tonight we'll get all the other blankets out, I will make sleeping bags with the giant safety pins".

The boys follow the river Rottach upstream. It runs fast and cold from the melting spring snows. They pass through wooded slopes, across wide-open meadows and into a higher forest where the trees grow upright on steep sloping ground.

The trees are now well spaced apart making the going easier for the cart. Ron steers them on to rougher ground tight to the river. Dieter complains to Ron, pointing to a low valley,

"Why are we staying so close to the river? The way looks so much easier over there".

Ron points to the river,

We have to get across this river. I'm looking for a good place to cross".

Dieter and the boys look at the river in dismay. Ken points out,

"Look at it, there is no way we can get across that, it's a torrent. See how fast it's running? It's deep too".

Ron looks at his map,

"We have to be on the other side of the bloody big Wallberg.
Our base camp is on the south side of this chunk of mountain.
If we follow the river, it must get wider. It'll be shallow there".

Dieter gets a little angry,

"A river gets narrower as we go uphill, not wider".
"Well this one gets wider and we can wade across".
Dieter raises his voice getting irritated,
    "So you have been there have you?
    You crossed this river once or twice?"
"No, but I know from the big map in school... Dieter,
you couldn't navigate shit out of your own bum.
Look, five kilometers upstream the river widens
because the ground flattens out. We cross there, up there".
Dieter snatches the map and sits down. Hans senses the tension
building and tries to change the subject,
    "Wow, look at all the scratches on my legs....
    I was freezing cold all night".
Dieter calms down and looks at Hans' legs,
    "We'll make up two beds when we make camp.
    We can keep each other warm. I froze last night too;
    it gets so bloody cold up here, but not for long,
    it's spring time now it's warming up,
    and each day it should get warmer".

The little platoon, pushing their cart, plod upstream on the east side of the river in silence, saving their wind. As it gets steeper they find that small fallen trees block their way.

The shafts of the cart have to be re-set back so two boys in front and two boys at the rear can lift the cart over dead trees.

After what seems to be a lifetime, Ken lets out a yell and points,
    "Look, there's the top of the hill. The ground is leveling out;
    it will be easier up there, come on".

Their boots sink deep into the soft brush. The shafts of the cart are still in the center position, two boys in front and a pair in the rear. The wheels of the cart have to be heaved over rocks as they follow the river upstream through heavy woods.

The ground is flat now and the river is getting much wider.

They come to a clearing in the woods. The river is about sixty meters wide now. Ron strips off his clothes. Naked except for a rope tied around his waist, he wades into the shallow water.

At first the water only comes up to his knees, but then very suddenly he disappears and the boys pull the rope taught. He comes up hanging onto the rope and stands waist deep. Dieter starts to wade in, pulling on the rope. Ron yells, pointing upstream,
    "Don't get your clothes wet Dieter. We can cross there".

About two hundred meters upstream the river bubbles over a wide sand and shingle bed, the deepest part only coming up to the boys knees. The cart makes it across the river to a small sand beach.

Dieter yells,
"Time for a rest and change our wet socks".
Ron says quietly.
"Dieter stop giving orders; but you're right,
let's change in to dry socks"
As the group works its way around to the south of the great Wallberg Mountain, the countryside looks prettier and warmer.

Spring is much more advanced here: Green shrubs are sprouting through last year's grass. When the sun comes out, hot and clear, from behind a cloud, the abrupt heat causes the buds on the trees to suddenly burst, sounding just like the pitter patter of rain falling all around them.

Wisps of steam curl up from the south of the young tree trunks.

Now trudging uphill, always gaining altitude they can see back into the deep valleys and mountains they have left behind them. Ron calls a halt and asks to borrow Dieters little brass telescope, he looks slowly around and down into the valley, searching as far as he can see.

He whispers,
"No sign of man anywhere, can anyone see anything,
a hut or farm, smoke from a fire?"
The others take turns looking hard through the telescope searching the horizon for signs of life. Hans says laughing,
"Now we are on our own, no one can see us up here.
Can we camp here tonight and light a fire to keep us warm".
"Yes, we can stay here tonight, but we should make a fire now
to cook our meal, but then put it out before it gets too dark".
Dieter shrugs his shoulders, opens the lid of the cart singing,
"Let's make camp, and eat,
Until our bellies go bang ho, ho,
Till our bellies go bang ho, ho".

They all bustle about making a camp, putting up the small tent, covering the tent floor with a stack of bracken under the ground sheet. Dieter makes up two warm beds with the twelve blankets they had carted up the mountain, each bed with three blankets under and three blankets over. He pins them up like giant sleeping bags with very large oversized safety pins. He calls out from the tent,
"We won't be cold tonight lads.
We're going to keep each other warm".
Soon they are eating supper from two large tins of stew that simmer in the ashes of a small fire. They toast chunks of the hard dried bread in the low embers. Ken, gazing in the flames of the fire muses,
"Wouldn't it be wonderful if the river here was big and wide?
We could make a raft and rig our large tent on it for sleeping.
We could drift on the current all the way to Paris or London".

Hans says,
  "And we could see all the castles on the way".
Ron laughs,
  "Sounds a bit like Mark Twain's Tom and Huck to me.
  You know what is so stupid? They banned all his books.
  What a bunch of assholes".
When the meal is finished, Ken buries the empty cans and points to
the sun disappearing behind the high mountains to the west,
  "It's going to get dark very quickly; we'd better put the fire out.
  We don't want to get any curious bodies wandering up here to
  warm themselves by our fire".
They douse the embers by all standing around the fire and peeing on
it. Then they make ready for the night.
  Dieter runs a fishing line around the perimeter of the camp, tying
one end to the handle of a tin mug full of small rocks, so any night
intruder will trip the fishing line and wake them.
  The boys sit quietly watching the snow on the mountains get
tipped with the last of the daytime sun, changing slowly from a warm
rosy gold to a deep red. The mountain to the west slowly spreads its
shadows down the valley, bringing black velvet darkness and a night
chill. Dieter and Hans nod their goodnights, not wanting to break the
moment or to shatter the mountains' silence. They go into the tent.
Ken whispers,
  "What are we waiting for? It's so dark".
  "I'm waiting to see if there is a light from a farm or
  woodcutter's hut".
  "I want to know if there is any life down there".
  "Ron, there's no one around here.
  We are truly alone, just us, don't you find that odd?
  No moon, it's as black as ink out there".
  "Not a breath of breeze, not a sound; listen"…
Ron's eyes shine in the dark night. The twins sit looking, and then
when it is so dark they have to almost feel their way, they get inside the
tent and into the warm bed that Dieter has made up for them. They
snuggle down, drawing on each other's warmth.
  They can hear the deep regular breathing of Hans and Dieter curled
up in their own deep sleep on the other side of the tent pole. Ken
whispers very quietly in Ron's ear,
  "Good lark this Ron?"
  "Shh, go to sleep… Take your cold feet off me".
Ken whispers very quietly, almost under his breath,
  "Good night Mum, Good night Dad… Good night Ron".
The Alpine mountain dew falls gently coating everything with its
microscopic glass beads all ready to turn to frost by morning.

Dieter is the first to wake. He sits up and opens the tent flap,
    "Shit it's raining out there".
Ron, still tired says,
    "It started about an hour ago.
    It's dry over here. Are you two dry?"
    "Yes" says Dieter,
    "You know what, we should lay in bed here and
    wait to see if the rain stops. No point in trudging
    through the rain when it's nice and warm in here".
Hans's voice from under the blankets says,
    "What if it rains all day? We have all the time in the world
    don't we? No one's chasing us up here are they?
    We could stay in bed all day or until the rain stops".
Ken's voice muffled from under the blankets says,
    "I'm for staying in bed. How long will it take
    to get to our final camp Ron?"
    "A day maybe two, slow pace, but it's going to be
    heavy going in the wet. Maybe we should stay here today".
Dieter yells,
    "Done, well, that's it. I'm going to have
    a quick piss and it's back to bed for a bit".
The boys laze their day away sleeping and waiting for the rain to
stop. Telling their 'What if' stories about Karl.

Ron comes back into the tent in the afternoon and says,
    "You can only see a half a kilometer down the valley.
    It's all misty. I think the clouds are below us, at least it has
    stopped raining, looks as if it might just clear up soon too".
Ken gets up and sits on the foot of Dieter's bed; he looks hard at
Dieter lying flat out in his underpants, after a while he asks,
    "Dieter, do you think the girls will have your baby?"
Dieter opens his eyes,
    "Don't know we shot into them plenty of times".
Ron smiles and says,
    "Both of you in each girl. Wow, they must have been
    full up to their ears with your slosh, ha".
Ken asks,
    "So if there are babies how will you know
    who is the father? Could a baby have some of
    Dieter's looks and some of Hans's brains?"
Dieter laughs,
    My, good looks and Hans's brain, now that would be
    some baby boy, big, good-looking and very brainy...
    You know you two should have stayed on that night.

The girls really wanted to get done by you twins.
Hanna got little Hans here going with her hand
and just when he was about to come she put it up
inside of herself so his sperms wouldn't be wasted.
She wants to have a baby for Hitler, very much.
I bet she will be grabbing hold of every little blond boy
with blue eyes she can get her hands on; she loves it".
Ron looks interested,
"So how many times do you think you two shot into her?"
Hans sounding bored,
"I don't know. Each of us about four times in each girl
all through the night... and in the morning".
Dieter ads,
"When I felt myself coming I pushed in as hard as I could".
"So did I," Hans adds.
"It would be good to have them up here now.
They could cook for us... I don't know why you two
didn't do them".
Ron looks at Ken and smiles,
"We didn't want to slosh on top of yours
and Dieter's stuff, yuck".
Dieter looks at Hans and grins,
"Slosh, slosh, oh how I wish the girls were up here now,
I would shove a load of my sperms in to them, wow I'd
push it right hard inside and shoot a fat load right up there".
The boys giggle and Ron murmurs,
"Go to sleep Dieter, save your strength
for tomorrow's march, you'll need it".

The weather clears and the boys are able to get a start at first light
the next morning. They continue to make their way around the base of
the Risserkogel Mountain to the south and keep the mighty Wallberg to
their north. Going southwest over very rough ground. They cross deep
gullies and fallen trees, sometimes having to zigzag two or three
kilometers out of their way. Ken and Ron are in the front shafts of the
cart when Ken suddenly holds his hand up, a sign the boys know. They
all stop and freeze looking around. After a moment Dieter says.
"So what did you stop for?"
Ken turns around looking over the valley below them, he whispers,
"Can you feel it? Can't you feel it"?
"What" his brother asks quietly. Ken whispers
"We are all alone up here, there's no one here but us,

14 The Trek

All the boys slowly look around. Dieter breaks the silence.
"Good, that's what we came up here for,
to get away from the fucking war".

They are now looking for the last river they have to cross to get up
to the hidden valley that Ron has chosen for their summer camp.

The ground starts to rise steeply, so steep in some places that the
boys need a pair of strong hands on each of the wheels. They stop for
rest every ten minutes. Ron is all dejected; he is scrutinizing his map. The
other boys sense that he is surprised that the going is a lot rougher than
he thought it would be.

Ken chirps up, looking hard at Ron,
"Well at least it's not raining… Ron are we lost?"
Ron spins around and snaps,
"No, we are not fucking lost asshole, yes it would have been a
lot easier to have come round the west side of this mountain
but we would have been exposed to a road for at least ten
kilometers. We just have to take it slowly the Siebligraben River
will lead us to our final campsite at a little lake called the
Riederecksee I think two of us should go on ahead, climb up a
bit and scout out a better route and two should stay here and
guard the cart. Who wants to come?"
Dieter says,
"I'll come, I'm the best climber here. We had better take some
ropes so we can climb up there a bit to see where we are and
what we are up against".

They find a nice flat spot to rest the cart and Dieter and Ron take
off with ropes over their shoulders. Ron turns to Ken and Hans and
orders,
"Whatever happens, don't move from here. If we are not back
by dark, light a fire so we can spot you and get some supper
going".
Dieter and Ron take off with a coil of climbing rope each over their
shoulders. Hans watches them go and says to Ken,
"How long do you think they will be gone Ken?"
Ken shrugs and says,
"Ron is the best navigator I know.
Come on and I will show you where we are".
Ken produces a map from his rucksack and spreads it out on the lid
of the cart. Hans gasps,
"Didn't they take the map with them?"
"No, this is a copy; we have one each. Ron actually made three;
there is another one in his sack. Look; see this valley here and
the big mountain, the Risserkogel.

209

We are here somewhere on the north east of it, but see that
little valley due south of the peak there where the little lake
is? Well that's where we are going to spend our summer.
We have to cross this river and find the little Siebligraben it
could be a stream or a river. We follow that and it will take
us to the little lake. It should be easy going once we cross
this river. Ron and Dieter are going to find a way around,
see?"
Hans brightens up and folds the map very carefully,
"Ken, what will we do when all this food runs out,
what will we eat then? I haven't seen any deer or rabbits,
few birds even. There is not much up here to eat at all".
Ken laughs and puts his arm around Hans's neck and gives him a
hug. The sudden show of warmth trips Hans into tears. All the things he
has been worrying about ever since the start of this venture are all coming
into focus and are very real. He sobs saying,
"Here we are, up here far from anywhere, with some food
but that won't last very long. We are never going to get
this cart up this mountain, then what?
We will all die for sure up here in a snow storm".
Ken smiles and shakes his head saying,
"Come on Hans, cheer up, it's not that bad,
it's better than fighting the Russians, isn't it?"
Hans brightens up slightly and sniffs,
"Ken, do you think we will be all right, really,
will we have enough to eat for the whole summer here?
Dieter said he has no idea what wild stuff
you can eat or how to trap rabbits".
Ken smiles and tries Ron's 'I know more than you do' voice,
"Hans, we know all that stuff. Ron and I can survive anywhere.
We will show you how to run trap lines and
what's good up here to eat. There is lots of food
All around us, if you know what to look for.
Remember Ron and I did all those survival courses when you
and the rest of the platoon were working on the farms?
Well we didn't take notes, we stole the book.
It's in the cart; you will be able to read it later.
It's one of the things this stupid school did for us, taught us
how to survive. We are going to be all right, don't worry".
Hans takes a deep sigh and blows his nose, and says between sobs,
"Oh… I feel better now…
Do you think they will find a way through for us?"
"Don't worry about it Hans, you will make yourself
sick, we will be all right, really we will".

Hans smiles and nods,
"We should find some wood in case we have to build a fire".
Ken and Hans gather a big pile of dry wood, then undo their shirts and lie back on the soft leaves and soak up some midday sun. Hans takes his glasses off and carefully puts them in their hard case.
He looks at Ken,
"Ken... Can I ask you something?"
Ken sits up on his elbows,
"Yes, I might not answer, ha".
Hans sits up and looks at Ken face to face,
"Al right, you know the other night, when we were in with the girls. We called you two in for your turn and we found you had both left. Did we upset you doing it on the bed together in front of you like that, why did you both go away?"
Ken thinks a bit,
"Well, we talked about it and"...
Hans nods, Ken looks at the sky,
"Hans you went all the way with both of the girls, well, you know, you said you shot up inside them?"
Hans's nods,
"Dieter he shot inside both of the girls too right?"
Hans nods again,
"Well that's it then. We didn't want to go into the girls on top of all of yours and Dieter's sperms. That's what turned us off, just that. You know, sloshing on two lots of sperms, ha. So we went to the showers and had a good wank-off with soap; that made us feel better".
Hans looks a little perplexed,
"Mm, I never thought about that; it did feel a bit wet.
But it was so wonderful; it was the most exhausting thing I have ever done. It's a pity you missed out doing it".

Ken leans over and holds Hans' shoulder,
"So you and Dieter just might be dads soon.
Ron and I want our first girls to be someone we find and not someone who has been fixed up for us".
Hans smiles,
"It would be very nice to have girls up here with us, do it any time we wanted, sleep with them every night...
Ken, how often to you and Ron pull yourselves off?"
Ken falls back laughing,
"What a question to ask someone".
"Well someone once told me if you do it too much you could go blind".

"Once a day, sometimes twice.
And you won't go blind, that's stupid".
Hans leans back and lets the sun warm his face,
"It must be nice to have a brother
to look out for you all the time".
"Well Hans, you have got three brothers now,
all looking out for you all the time. So don't be
such a baby; it's going to be all right, really it is".
Hans takes another big sigh and dozes off. Ken lies back and falls
asleep wondering if his penis will ever grow as big as Dieter's. After a
while they are awakened by a prod from Dieter's boot,
"Wake up you two; sleeping on the job.
We found a much easier route. It was
so plain to see when we climbed up there".
Ron arrives looking very pleased. He spreads his map out on the cart,
"Look, we just have to go back a little way to the river
and go around the mountain further south at its base.
We are too high up here, the other river we are looking
for is south of us here".
They turn the cart around and start to allow it to pull them back down
the hill. The handbarrow starts to gather speed but Dieter slows it down
with the brake. The boys still have to dig their heels deep into the soft
grass to slow it down. Dieter grabs the hand-brake again and holds it on
as hard as he can, controlling the slide back down to the bottom of the
little valley. They work their way south and around the bottom northeast
side of the Risserkogel on to much easier ground.

After about two hours at a good pace they come to the second river
that flows from the west. The boys jump about and cheer. The country
looks so much more inviting on the other side; wide open meadows,
gentle sloping woods, a warmer place where the spring season has
advanced to make the valley look greener and very lush.

The river is wide, looks shallow and is moving fast. They work their
way up the river looking for a good crossing place. A little way up the
bank Dieter whistles and waves for the rest to join him.
"This is the best place, I think. I will go first to see how deep it is".
Dieter strips off his clothes, ties a rope round his waist and starts to
wade into the fast running water.
"Wow! Oh wow! Is this water ever bloody cold? Oh shit it's
cold… Oh this is the coldest bloody water I've ever been in….
Hey! You lot get out the other ropes. Tie one on Hans;
we will have to pull him across with me.
We will need to work this out fast.
Is it ever cold, wow, shit its cold!"

Dieter gets to the other side, the deepest water coming up to his chest. All the boys strip off and put their clothes and boots into the cart with Dieter's. Ken smears the tight-fitting lid with mud to get a good seal and locks it fast. The twins fasten the center of the rope around Hans's skinny waist Dieter pulls him across, while Ron and Ken hold onto his rope from the other side.

They see him disappear under the fast running water, Dieter runs with his end of the rope and Hans pops to the surface, takes a gasp of air and almost surfs across to the other side.

The two ropes get tied securely on to the cart. The twins start to push it into the fast running water. Ron yells to the two on the other bank,

"Pull, you buggers; pull...

You must keep the ropes taught or we will turn over!"

Dieter and Hans start to pull and the cart moves easily across the river. Hans shouts at everyone and laughs,

"If this stupid cart sinks in a deep hole and gets lost,

we will be all stuck out here totally naked, totally bum naked.

Did you think about that Dieter? Ha".

Dieter takes charge yelling and shivering,

"Shut up Hans and bloody pull".

He yells to the twins,

"Listen, you two, all you have to do is to keep the thing

the right way up. We will pull you across".

Hans and Dieter tug on the ropes. With the ropes tied securely to the handles of the cart, the twins steady the cart into the river, stopping it from toppling over. Hans and Dieter pull from across the other side.

The cart rolls easily into the water up to its hubs.

To the boys' surprise, the cart starts to float and drift quickly downstream, Ron yells,

"Pull you, buggers, pull! Look it's floating...

Pull harder! Look we are going downstream!"

Dieter and Hans start pulling back. Ken and Ron hang on, treading and thrashing in the water, trying to stop the cart from turning over. Dieter and Hans are pulling as hard as they can, their heels digging into the muddy bank, trying to hold the cart and the twins from being washed downstream with the runoff from the melting snows. Slowly, with much heaving and grunting, the cart gets to shallow water and stands on its wheels again. The boys rest and then pull it out onto the bank.

Shivering, they all flop out exhausted and lie panting on the bank. Ron spots water running out of a seam in the cart.

They open the lid to find just a little water in the bottom but the towels and blankets seem dry. They dry off and get dressed, empty the cart out and pour out the small amount of water. Dieter watches Ken wash the mud off the rim of the lid.

"Your mud saved us Ken".

They wash off the cart and repack it, hanging their wet towels over the long cart handles to dry in the breeze.

Ron cuts a fat sausage into four chunks and hands them around. The boys' spirits are high as they strike off with a new spring in their pace. Dieter yells,

"Well I think I organized that little crossing very well".

Hans says quietly,

"Oh, I thought we were going to lose the cart...

What would we have done then? We were all naked you know".

Ron laughs,

"Ha, you're not going to need clothes where we are going.

There won't be anyone to see us".

Ken smiles,

"We could call ourselves 'The bare bum platoon' Ha".

They follow the Siebligraben River west upstream for about six kilometers, wandering into a beautiful valley that gets narrower as they climb. With gentle woods and soft meadows, it is a warm and inviting place that traps the sun.

The boys enter the woods and after a while they stop at a small clearing. There is a bend in the river and it widens to a small lake about half a kilometer round circled on three sides by high rocks. A steep Risserkogel mountain rises to the south west of them.

There are woods with pleasant open trees to hide them from above. Ron unfolds his map, looks around, then back at his map.

"This is it... this is where we spend our summer;

in the shade from nosey aircraft. There is water to drink;

we can swim and have plenty of good game to trap.

We can try fishing in that big river back there".

The boys all look around very pleased. Ron spreads the map out on the lid of the cart to show them all where they are. Dieter gives Ron one of his *I am very pleased looks*.

"Good planning Ron, good campsite".

Hans looks worried,

"What about army patrols or border patrols.

Isn't this place very close to the Austrian border here?"

Ron turns around his map and lines it up with his compass.

"Not that close. If you were a tank commander with tanks

going north, southeast or west, you would not want to send

your tanks or infantry up this valley past our camp...

Why? I hear you all ask at once".

Ron checks the map with his compass again. Dieter stares at the map and looks very bewildered...

Then his face lights up, he smiles at Ron, puts his arm around his shoulder and nods.

"You crafty little shit Ron; I know why there is no point
in coming up this valley, it doesn't bloody go anywhere,
it's a dead end. You can see on the map that it's a dead end.
The surrounding peaks and ridges are too steep for tanks.

It's easier to go past this valley and go around to the next one. Some of them have passes through them".

Ron spins around to Dieter and points 'yes' and says,

"See those big rock faces to the north-west of us here,
they are called the 'Blankenstein Range' and they
will keep us warm in this little valley".

The boys look to where Ron is pointing and see a massive rock face rising behind them towering straight up 1500ft like a massive wall.

Dieter jumps about flinging off his clothes, yelling he runs and jumps into the little lake. The rest of the boys join him splashing about like children.

Hans yells,

"No pissing in the water, we have to drink it. Right Ron ha".

Dieter looks at the long shadows and the setting sun,

"We should just sleep under a ground sheet tonight and
put our big tent up tomorrow. It's getting very late. Fire, food,
I will get the beds and shelter ready, you lot get the supper".

Ron snaps back defiantly,

"All right, but this is the last day you give orders
as a sergeant. Tomorrow we all have a vote".

The rest of the boys all yell,

"Yes!"
"No roll calls".
"No lights out".
"No short haircuts".
"No laws... Rule number one... No rules".
"No washing your bums after a poo, and
no washing behind your sodding ears".
"No parades, no route marches"
"No PT, no Nazi Karl's and his bum, dick and armpit
inspections".

Dieter laughs and yells,

"No sergeants; and we can wank off any time we like,
and with either hand, ten times a day if we want.
Ha, wank, wank, wank, ha, ha, ha".

The four boys are savoring their new freedom.

The relief of actually finding Ron's hideaway has raised their spirits. They all work at bedding down for the night. Hans says,

"Ho Ron, this place is better than I ever dreamed of.
How did you know it was so nice here?"
"It's all on the big twenty five thousand scale map
at the school if you look properly. If it hadn't been
mounted on plywood I would have stolen it for sure".

Dieter busily gathers dry bracken for soft padding under the ground sheet, then takes their twelve blankets and makes his two big double sleeping bags. He sets up a lean-to cover between two bushes and hides their handcart in thick brush.

Meanwhile, the other boys are making a ring of rocks for the campfire. The matches they had brought with them were ruined when they crossed the river so they used one of the ten army flint sticks to make their fire. If they look after them and don't lose them they will last for years. Each boy carried one around his neck on a leather bootlace. The four-centimeter stick of pure flint with a hole at one end for the lace will produce a shower of sparks when scraped with the back of a knife blade. But sparks don't make a fire on damp days.

15. THE VALLEY

The boys collect tinder made from dried moss and the light fluffy linings of some bird's nests, but it has to be very dry and very finely shredded. One of the two-kilo tins with an airtight top is used to keep their tinder dry. Starting fires without matches or a lighter is one of the useful things the boys learned from the Hitler Youth survival classes.

Ken takes a wad of their dry tinder about the size of a man's fist and rubs it in a tight ball then carefully pulls it apart so it is nice and fluffy. Ron stands by with a pile of small dry twigs that had been shredded and split. Ken scrapes the flint stick with the back of his camp knife using fast strokes that produce a mass of sparks which he directs into the wad of tinder.

After a few attempts a wisp of blue smoke curls up and Ken blows very gently. Suddenly the moss bursts into flames and they have their fire.

They settle down to a hot supper of thick tinned stew and the last of their bread that is now hard as rock, but it's good dipped in the gravy of the stew.

The boys sit warming themselves around the fire.

Ron looks over to his brother,

"Some good lark this, Ken make sure you get this
place down in your diary, you may need to locate
it again some day. I will show you on this map".

Ken nods,

"I wonder where the nearest human being is;
some army outpost somewhere I should think.
We should start our daily meal very early so we
don't have to have big fires in the dark".

Ron says,

"Yes, we should get up with the light
and go to bed when it gets dark".

Hans laughs nervously,

"What are we going to do when
all this food runs out; what will we eat?"

Ken bangs his camp knife on his belt,

"That's one reason we have to be thankful
to the shitty Hitler Youth. At least they taught us
how to live off the land and survive out here".

Dieter looks dismayed,

"Not me, I didn't take any of that outdoors stuff".

Hans shakes his head,

"Me neither".

Ken looks up at Hans,

"Ha, we did... So we will all be all right then, won't we Ron?"

Ken wants to change the subject so he shoves Hans in his ribs,
>"Hans, where's your Mum and Dad? You never talk about them".

Hans pokes the fire and puts more wood on,
>"My father is in Munich. He is a Colonel in the SS.
>My Mother died when I was six".

Ken says quietly,
>"Do you miss them?"
>
>"No, I hate him. He used to burn me with his cigarettes.
>I will show the scars one day. I was sent to the school
>paid for by the SS".

Dieter asks,
>"What about Christmas and holidays?"
>
>"I went to youth camps or hostels; wasn't that bad…
>Better than being with him and his boozy pals".

Ron looks up at the firelight in the trees. Hans has a sad look on his face. Each boy is thinking about someone or somewhere; the fire is going down; it's getting chilly. A fine mist starts to roll in, making everything damp. Dieter gets up,
>"Well it's a good job I made the beds up when it was dry.
>We will get used to bedding down before the damp comes in
>with the dusk… Everyone clean his own canteen,
>I'm going to run my trip line".

Dieter ties his fishing line to a tree and runs it around the camp perimeter, then to the pot and pan rack hung in the tree, tying his last knot he says,
>"If we get visitors, we will know about it.
>What we need is a gun or a pistol. The best weapon
>we have is the spear point on the end of the flagpole…
>Burr, it's cold; I think it might snow".

Hans is about to pee on the fire to put it out but Ron shakes his head and kicks soil on the fire and makes sure it is out, and says,
>"We have to cook our own food on this…
>It's going to be much colder up here. It may be springtime
>in the valley, but it's not quite springtime at this altitude.
>It will freeze tonight. We should stuff extra bracken
>under the groundsheet when we put up our big tent ".

Dieter has spread the two big thick beds out, one each side of the center tent pole of the smaller of their two tents and has rolled up shirts to act as pillows.

The boys undress down to their underwear and light a small night light candle. Ken and Ron get in one bed, Hans and Dieter in the other. Dieter hangs the flashlight on the tent pole.
>"If anyone has to get out in the night, don't use this flashlight.
>It's for emergencies only; we have to save the batteries".

Hans is bright and awake,
    "I'm not very tired; it's only about seven P.M...
    Dieter what's the time by your pocket watch?"
Dieter reaches in to his pocket and fishes out his watch, shakes it and
holds it to his ear,
    "I forgot to wind it two days ago...
    We won't need to know time up here anyway".
Ken whispers,
    "What time did you two leave the girls the other night?"
Dieter laughs,
    "Oh it was late. We swapped over, I did Greta...
    Ho, was she ever tight; I made her go wild".
Ron asks,
    "Hans?"
    "Yes"
    "Well?"
    "Well what".
Ken pleads,
    "Well, tell us what is was like Hans, don't keep it
    to yourself, two girls in one night; your first time too".
Hans says very philosophically,
    "Well, I liked doing it with Greta best; she was very tight. There
    was a lot of feel, but when I went in and out of Hanna, she was
    slack and had no grip. She dug her fingernails into my bottom
    too".
Dieter laughs,
    "Ha, that's because you have a long skinny one.
    Ha, your's goes in and out without touching the sides.
    Ha, but once you got going with Hanna you lasted longer".
Ken exasperated,
    "So what was it like?"
    "I don't know; how can I tell you how it felt?"
Ron pushes Hans in the back,
    "Well was it like wanking off in bed with a dry hand
    or in the shower with soap, or what?"
Hans says all dreamy,
    "Oh, it was wonderful; like wanking off
    in bed with a handful of warm butter".

The wind outside blows the little tent; there is an icy chill in the cold
mountain air. The boys snuggle down close for warmth. The gentle sway of
the tent brings deep sleep to the tired happy youngsters.
    In the morning, birds and small animals scurry about the boys' camp.
All the new strange scents make the creatures of the forest curious. The

smell of the pine is fresh; the woods are cool and dim with the damp twinkling laurel undergrowth. The sun peeps through the trees casting long beautiful sun streaks on a big blue jay... He squawks at the intruders. The noisy squawk of the jay wakes Dieter. He sits bolt upright in his bed and pushes the tent door open. The sun floods in and Dieter announces loudly.

"Oh, I need to have a long piss".

He jumps out of bed, and folds back the tent flaps. The boys are now lying with the sun dazzling them. Ron says sleepily,

"The sergeant needs to take a nice long piss. What a lovely
way to wake up, hey Dieter get away from the camp!"

Ken joins in,

"Look out all you insects; here comes the sergeant.
He's going to pee all over you".

"I'm going back to sleep, wake us when breakfast is ready".

Dieter strips down and runs into the shallow part of the lake, splashing about and dunking his head under the ice-cold water, running out after only a few seconds. Gasping for air, he runs to the boys who are still under the covers in their beds, pulls the blankets off them and shakes his wet hair like a dog, splashing water all over them. They wake up and take a swipe at Dieter; he runs off back into the water.

The boys chase him into the pool and try to splash him. Hans stops before he enters the water realizing that it must be very cold. The rest of the boys see that Hans is the only one who's not wet yet. They make getting Hans wet, their most urgent task and he allows himself to be thrown in; then everyone runs to grab their towels and rub themselves vigorously. Ken nods to Ron to look at Hans' backside. His wet underpants are drooped low around his skinny waist, showing small round burns scars on his bottom. Ron shivers,

"Burr, its bloody cold....
It could freeze the balls off a brass monkey, ha".

Ken says to Hans quietly,

"Is that where your father burned you with his cigarettes?"

Hans pulls down the back of his pants showing more scars and two larger ones,

"Yes the big ones are cigars; they really hurt the most.
He took his time with those. The small ones are cigarettes;
they hurt too but they were quick".

Ron and Dieter walk over to look. Ron says,

"What a shit-bag. Was he drunk?"

Dieter leans over to get a closer look. He pulls the boys pants lower revealing even more scars. He spins around shaking his head in dismay and says angrily,

"Why would an SS Officer do this to his own
son's backside? It's all madness just sheer madness".

Hans still shivering,
>"He did it because I did not salute him
>in front of his young Officers and other things".

Dieter looks up into the trees:
>"What is it with these Nazi shits?
>They are just a pack of fanatics, afraid of being loved....
>So why do they have to be so fucking mean and hateful?
>How could he do this to his own son?"

The boys spend most of the day making camp. They put up the big tent with lots of dry bracken ferns as a soft mattress, piling soil and dry stones around the bottom to keep out the drafts. They roll the ground sheet tight to the tent inner walls and tightening the laces make a good seal to keep out ants and creepers.

They build a rock and mud firewall, so that the fire cannot be seen by anyone coming up the valley. A table is fashioned from local cut saplings and a sheet of thin plywood that they lugged up the hill in the cart. The cooking stove is another smaller fireplace with iron racks and a flat steel plate; it too got dragged up from the school.

Wood racks are made for the pots and pans. The boys take turns digging the hole for their toilet, downstream. They then cut a single pole to sit on as a toilet seat. A shovel is handy to fill in after.

Gathering dead wood is a big task; sawing and cutting it to size is a half-day's work. Then they store the wood in the second small tent so as to have dry kindling in wet weather.

By the late afternoon their camp is in good shape. Their good saws, axes, and tinned food are all stored in the cart with its lid locked. Ron says,
>"Tomorrow we all have to dig out a garden;
>we want to get the seeds and potatoes
>in the soil as soon as possible".

The following afternoon, Hans and Ken mark out the ground that has to be turned over by the boys for their garden.

It forms a long narrow strip that winds close to the bank of the river so water can be splashed in by hand for irrigation; a fun job when the water is warm, but the melting snows makes the water very cold. A winding strip of garden is far less noticeable from the air than a square or oblong patch. Carrots, onions, cabbage seeds are carefully run in curved lines. Ken counts out the seed potatoes they stole from the school's garden shed and lays them out with their heads up.

>"Look Hans we have fifty seed potatoes. Now I'll show you how
>we can get two hundred plants that will grow quicker".

Ken carefully cuts each seed potato into four pieces, showing Hans how to avoid cutting through the eyes. Then he plants each piece of potato in its own hole. They cover the potatoes with wet dead leaves,
"See Hans the leaves will keep them
warm and moist until they start growing.
Then we keep covering them with more leaves.
The onions will give us flavor for our stews.
The carrots will be the first up".
The meal on their second day in the camp is a lot more civilized.
They eat with knives and forks off tin plates at their table with two bench seats. And they drink their hot chocolate out of tin mugs. Their hideaway feels safe, with the fresh water close by. They feel comfortable and at home in their camp. Being under the big shady trees brings a good feeling to their table. After dinner Ken asks,
"Who wants to come with me and set snares for rabbits
tomorrow? We have to start living off the land now".
Hans nods to Ken and Ron says,
"Dieter should come with me;
I know what plants and roots we have to look for".
Dieter nods but gets all serious,
"If a plane passes low, let's all hide; let's not show ourselves.
We don't want to be spotted from the air.
It's best no one knows we are here".
"Let's not get caught until this war is all over".

The boys settle down to their first night in the big bell tent. The inner walls have been stretched tight and are well fitted; the low tent wall has a high front door threshold that they have to step over to enter. Boots are left outside to keep from treading in mud and leaves. It's their little bit of civilization to be able step into a clean and soil-free space.
Ken lies next to his brother staring at the tent walls and the ventilator flaps being gently opened and closed by the outside breeze. He falls asleep feeling safe and secure.
Ken and Hans leave early the next day to lay their trap lines. They make their way through beautiful alpine scenery of soft woods and wide grassy slopes. The early morning mist and dew is still beaded on the tops of the grass. Ken shows Hans how to get down low to the ground to see the rabbit or hare tracks left in the damp dew; then to rig snares, sprung by bending over young saplings for small game. He teaches Hans the importance of rubbing the thin trap piano wire with dandelion leaves to hide the human scent. Ken whistles, mimicking the birds, so his shrills cover the crunch of the boys' footsteps in the dry grass.

He tells Hans, a rabbit will turn at the sound of a footstep but not if it
is covered by a bird sound. Ken points to the large brown grasshopper that's
drying itself in the early morning sun,
> "Look, see the grasshoppers; they like to climb to the tops of
> reeds in the night. See, they're easy to catch when they're wet".

Hans looks horrified,
> "We can't eat them, can we?"

Ken nods and scoops up the grasshopper and puts it in his tin.
Then explains to Hans,
> "We can eat most insects, but you must cook them well.
> They carry parasites that will die when heated.
> You know a boy can live for a day on a handful of crickets
> or grasshoppers; they're full of nutrition.
> They taste good in a stew too".

Ken starts to turn rocks over and grabs the fleeing grubs and bugs.
They all go in his tin. Soon Hans is grabbing grasshoppers and grubs. Hans
picks up a very hairy caterpillar; Ken grabs it and shakes his head,
> "No, those with hair or fuzz on them may be poisonous.
> Ants are good, bake them and grind them up for the stew....
> Hans listen to me; we can eat anything with fur, feathers or scales.
> Most little birds are too small to bother with. We will spend
> as much energy catching them, as we will get from eating them.
> But crows, ducks, pheasants, partridge and good old pigeons
> will all go in the pot. The best foods up here are rabbits, hares,
> hedgehogs, fish and greens with wild roots".

Hans asks,
> "How do you catch crows without a gun?"
> "Ha, they're easy; crows are stupid.
> First, we find a high tree were they roost and watch them;
> they always fly off in one direction and come back from
> another direction. When they come back, they are not hungry.
> They just want to roost and go to sleep, but by the morning
> they are hungry and looking for food. We will lay the bait
> in their morning path so they see it out in the open".
> "What sort of bait?"
> "Oh, smelly stuff, rabbit guts, or some rotting fish".
> "They come down to eat and wham, you have them in your trap.
> I will show you how to set bird traps, its easy".

After four hours their tins are full of crickets and grubs. Ken says,
> "It's time to start to backtrack and go home
> to see what we have caught in the traps we laid.
> Look, the river is that way".

Hans grabs a large grasshopper, puts it in his tin, looks up at Ken,
"Ken, how do you know the river is that way, without looking at
the compass?"
Ken stops, points to a big tree,
"See the dark side of that trunk?
That's the north side; we need to go north, that way".
Ken points to a big shady tree, Hans says,
"Ken, let's say we were a long way from a river;
how would we find water to drink?"
The two boys sit down under the tree and Ken puts on his brother's 'I
know more than you do voice',
"Well every afternoon about this time the swallows and swifts
like to drink before they go to roost. So, you look at the swallows;
and see what way they are flying".
Hans looks into the tree and thinks for a moment,
"Yes but how do you know if they have had their drink,
or are just going to find a drink?"
"Ha, a very good question, if they are going for a drink,
their little beaks are shiny clean. If they have had their drink
and are going home to bed for the night, then my friend,
their little beaks will have mud on them from the edge of the
river. They don't clean their mouths off until they get home in the
nest".
"Yes but how can you see their little beaks
when they're flying so fast?"
"You don't. Just lie under a tree and look up, watch them fly.
Look through your fingers; make a little hole about the diameter
of a matchstick…
Beaks that shine are clean; dull beaks are muddy".
Hans looks dejected and screws his nose up, trying to peer through a
small hole he made in his fist. He looks at Ken to ask a question, but he's a
little afraid what the answer will be.
"So that means we are going to live on
grubs, weeds, and creepy things?"
Ken bends down and rips up a handful of young fresh grass.
"See this, grass, we chew it until all the taste has gone,
and then spit it out, our tummies can't digest grass like a cow
does, but the juice is rich in protein. We only need to chew grass if
the food gets scarce; there is all you can eat all around us here".
Hans picks a few blades of grass and starts to chew,
"Mm… Not bad, tastes a bit like cabbage stalks".
He spits it out. Ken runs over to a young pine tree, picks a fist-full of
the young needles and shows them to Hans,

"See these pine needles, we brew these in fresh boiling water for about five minutes and it makes a nice tea that tastes good and it contains more vitamin C than two freshly squeezed oranges... If you put the cones near the fire they slowly open and the seeds are good eating, see, lots of stuff to eat".

Hans looks up the tree for cones that haven't grown yet and moans,

"Well it seems like a lot of work for little food".

"We will spend most of our time looking for food".

Ken picks a thick bunch of early spring Cat-tails, he turns them upside down and shows Hans the white young shoots and starts to peel them down, he offers some to Hans,

"See we can eat these raw or boil them, try it, its good".

Both boys munch on the shoots as they make their way back to their valley.

Two large rabbits have been caught in Ken's traps; Ken picks the first rabbit up and screws its head around like a doorknob then quickly dispatches the other. Hans looks on with horror.

Ron and Dieter have returned to the camp and are sorting out all the roots and wild vegetables they have gathered. Dieter washes them clean in the river. Wet and fresh looking, they cover most of the table: dandelions, stinging nettles, arrow leaf and burdock. They all get cut-up into small bits and go into the pot for scalding. Biscuit-roots, bulrush roots and lots of thistle roots are also being chopped up for the pot. Ron boils water in the biggest pot they have and fills it to the brim, pushing them down until the lid is tight shut. The wild watercress is to eat raw. Dieter and Ron turn out the bottom of their bread bags and tip out a pile of Acorns. Ron scopes the Acorns in to a tin can and shows them to Dieter,

"Dieter look... This can full of acorns will give us
as much nutrition as half a kilo of ground beef, but we have
to boil out the bitter taste before we put them in the stew.
We keep the acorn water because it's a powerful antiseptic.
Good to gargle for a sore throat too.
Don't eat the acorns raw; because they might have
tiny parasites in them, they will die when they are boiled,
then shove them in the stew pot".

Ken and Hans arrive holding three big rabbits. They hold them up, Ken yells,

"Roast bunnies tonight folks; good weight too.
Wow, look at all the greens you two got".

Hans holds up Ken's can and shakes it saying,

"Look, this is full of creepies".

Ron says,

"Good; put the tin on the fire for a bit. They need roasting".

Hans looks totally horrified,

"Roasting alive; but that's cruel".

"They're only insects and they'll keep us alive, shove them on".

Ron pokes a series of small holes in the lid of the tins and pushes them into the ashes of the fire. Hans puts his hands over his ears so as not to hear the insects fry and says,

"Tell me they feel no pain Ken, do they, do they?"

Ken shakes his head and grabs Hans' arm,

"Come on Hans you have to watch this".

Ken walks him over to hole that's been dug as a trash disposal, then hangs the three rabbits up by their front feet on an overhead branch. The rest of the boys gather around.

With the point of his sharp knife he makes a slit down the center of the rabbit's stomach. The guts fall out and into the hole with a plop.

Ken says,

"Watch this; it is important you remove the bladder

without letting the pee spill on the meat. Look.

Ken carefully cuts out the bladder without a spilling a drop.

Then he starts to skin them. Dieter thinks they look a lot smaller skinned.

Hans moans and quietly passes out at the sight of all the intestines. Dieter catches him before he falls into the hole with the guts. Ron says,

"Dieter, when he wakes up, get him to cover the guts with soil.

Make sure he looks at them hard; he has to get used to this".

Ron takes the two cans full of the hot baked insects, chops them up so fine that not one part, wing or leg is recognizable and drops the powdered insects into the stew pot. The rabbits, get cut up, and also go into the stew. Ron stirs the stew, sniffs it and adds some brown spices and salt they brought from the school,

"If we didn't have the rabbits, we would need about

three times more insects than this to make this

a very nutritious meal for four people".

Hans and Dieter sniff the pot, Dieter says,

"Mm, smells good; how long before it is ready?"

Ron prods the meat with his knife,

"A good stew should cook for as long as possible,

but this will be ready in about an hour".

Late that afternoon the boys sit down to their first meal found totally in the wild; a vegetable and rabbit stew with a salad of watercress and thin strips of bulrush roots.

Hans looks at the big helping of stew in front of him, picks gingerly at first looking for the unmentionable insects, but he can't see them, he pushes his tin plate away with a sour look on his face and says,

"Can't I have some tinned stew? There's a lot in the cart"
Dieter and the twins tuck in to the meal with Os and mms, Dieter says.
"You can't see or taste any of the insects...
I will eat yours if you don't want it".
Ken smiles,
"If you bake them, they taste like roast chestnuts....
Hans we have to eat this, it's good and our tinned food won't last two weeks. It's for an emergency. We may have to move or run away from here and then we will need it to stay alive.
Ron smiles and pushes the plate to Hans, he turns his nose up and pushes it away,
"He will eat anything when he gets hungry; I chewed
on grass when I was on my survival training solo".
Hans chews on his watercress and bulrush looking sorry for himself. He spoons out a mouthful of his stew and sniffs it, then gingerly tastes it.
"Mm it smells good... Mm, not too bad".
He is soon eating and finishing his plate. Ron tries to change the subject and perk everyone up.
"We have to lay more snares, bird traps too; remember,
we will only eat one meal a day from now on, we must all work
at finding at least as many greens and roots as we had today,
plus at least a pair of rabbits or six birds".
Dieter glances at Ron and Ken and sadly says,
"That's the best rabbit stew I have ever eaten".
The boys finish their meal and they all nod their approval. Ron prods Ken and nods at him to look at Dieter who is looking gloomy and on the verge of tears. Ken says softly,
"What's up Dieter, old chum?
You look so upset; our cooking is not that bad, is it?"
Dieter's voice breaks into a sob; he turns to Ron and Ken.
"You two don't really know where your parents are, do you?
They put numbers on your feet, for what?
The Gestapo took my dad away; and now I don't know
where he is, or if I will ever see him again...
Hans gets his bum almost burned off
for not saluting some bunch of shitheads".
Dieter sniffing,
"No one's going to hurt us up here. Not while I live".
Ken grins and tries to cheer Dieter up,
"It would be good to have Hanna up here as a cook;
we could take turns sleeping with her".
Ken looks at Dieter, but there is no reaction; he is preoccupied and far away. Hans leans forward and pokes Dieter in the crotch trying to make a joke and says,

"Then he wouldn't have to wank himself off so much, ha.
Dieter, you still doing it three times a day then?"
Still no reaction. Ron catches Dieter's dark mood and is concerned so he asks him,
"Dieter, what's the matter old chum?"
Dieter sniffs,
"Let's get in the tent. I will tell you when we are all in bed".
The table is cleared and the tin plates and stew pot are all washed in silence. Ken looks at Ron, who shrugs his shoulders as if to say 'I don't know'. The damp mist starts to roll down the hill and through their camp bringing a chill with it. Inside the tent it's cozy. Ron lights the candle; the boys sit on their beds.
Ken asks Dieter,
"So what's all the mystery?"
Dieter doesn't answer; he is still in his dark mood. He sits up and composes himself and takes a deep breath.
"Our whole platoon was drafted to active service today,
all of them, the thirteen and fourteen year old boys too;
everyone... All of them drafted into the army...
Don't you see we would have all gone to fight the Russians in
the east? They're taking everyone who's had the slightest
military training".
Hans says,
"Me too? I'm only just fifteen".
Dieter continues.
"Yes, even the thirteen year old boys, if they are tall enough;
we would have all been in the army, all gone, shipped out.
Karl and I made up the list days ago... Us four...
We were all going off to the east to fight the Russians.
We got out just in time".
Dieter starts to rummage through his rucksack.
He draws out a long brown envelope, moves over to the brothers' bed and sits down and says very seriously,
"I know I should have given you two this
before we left the school... But"...
Ron interrupts,
"What's in the letter Dieter?"

Ron goes to grab the letter. Dieter stuffs it back in his rucksack. Tears are just starting to well up in his eyes as he says firmly,
"I have to tell you something first".
Ken says softly,
"So tell us Dieter".
"I couldn't risk giving you two this...

You both may never have come up here at all".
Ron says very earnestly,
"Dieter, give us the envelope... please".
Dieter's big tears roll down his cheeks, he sobs,
"It's from your mother... Sniff... She's in Vienna".
The twins look at each other.
"Vienna"!
Dieter draws the brown envelope out of his rucksack and hands it to Ron. Ken moves closer to Ron; Hans turns on the flashlight. The twins just stare at the envelope. It has no address or stamps; just the name 'Lamberts' printed in blue school crayon. Ron hands the letter to Ken who sees it has already been slit open.
He draws out three single sheets of paper. Dieter is now sobbing almost uncontrollably,
"They are the only three letters that
ever came to the school for you both".
Ken reading says,
"Mum's in Vienna... Our mother is in Vienna".
They read the letters in silence, tears coming from both boys,
"Father... He never did go to England".
To remove the sensitive names and addresses the censor has cut little oblong holes in the pages. Ken asks,
"Dieter, where's the addresses;
who cut out the addresses from these?"
Ron sobbing,
"Dieter, who would know? We can't answer
if we don't have the address in Vienna".
Ken sniffing,
"Come on Dieter, where did you get them from?"
Hans has sat up and is crying too, Dieter holds up his hands sobbing,
"I had to hold on to the letters; or you two would have never
left the school and come up here with Hans and me.
If you had seen the letters, you would have both gone off to
find your Mother...
You would both have been picked up on the road as deserters.
Then Hans and I would all be off to the front by now getting
shot by the Bolsheviks like the rest of the platoon".
Ron asks quietly,
"Where Dieter... Where did you get them, where are the
original envelopes with the stamps and return addresses?"
Dieter sobbing,
"It was a matter of life or death".

Ron leans over and gently puts his hand on Dieter's arm. This slight touch of warmth brings out deeper sobs from him, his big shoulders shaking uncontrollably, Ron gently asks,

"Just tell us Dieter; we're all one family here now.
Just tell us... please?"

Dieter composing himself with deep breaths,

"Gerhard Knoll found them in the Headmaster's office.
He swears they're the only ones that arrived at the school".

His sobs get stronger.

"He used to search that office, sob... every week
when he cleaned it. He is a stinking informer for the Gestapo.
That's when he wants to be one,
and when he's not dealing in the black market.
The letters came to the school already censored...
he says without any envelopes. It's his job,
he picks up the mail; it's what he does".

Ron sits with his arm around his brother; both boys re-read the three letters in silence. Ken says sadly to the others,

"Do you want to hear about Vienna?"

Dieter and Hans both nod; Ron reads,

"Our mother was taken with our Aunt Inga to Vienna
the day the war started. She said they went to a camp first.
Then after six months, they were let go and they went to
Aunt Inga's place. We know that she used to live in Vienna.
She said she knows our father didn't go to England. Mother
thinks he is in a camp near Munich at a town called Dachau,
but she is not too sure. In this other letter, there are no dates...
It says our Aunt Inga was killed in an air raid...
It is not possible to travel in or out of Vienna".

Ken looks at Dieter sadly,

"Dieter was our group called up, are they really
in the Wehrmacht? They're all just school boys".

Dieter turns out the flashlight and hangs it on the tent pole,

"Yes, three platoons went. I knew about it a week
before we ran away. Karl has gone with them.
So you see I couldn't risk telling you about the letters
when we were back at the school.
I thought you two would have tried to get to Vienna.
They would have gotten you both, for sure.
All the roads to Austria are jammed with army".

The boys undress and get into bed. The letters are carefully placed into Ron's bag. He blows out the candle. The breeze is very cold coming off the mountain. They get down under their blankets.

It's dark but for the strips of moonlight coming through the vents. Ken says cheerfully,

"So Dieter, how about getting young Hanna and Greta up here?
To get it out of your system, ha?"

Ron laughs,

"And Dieter has so much of it in his system".

Hans yells,

"Hey, you two, shut up; I have to sleep
with him in here. It's too cold out there".

Dieter whispers in English,

"Balls bugger lugs; arm holes"

Ken laughs,

"Arm holes? Don't you mean assholes?"

Dieter whispers,

"Assholes then… just go to sleep, goodnight".

Ken says,

"Dieter, thank you for giving us our letters".

"Goodnight"

It's a beautiful morning, with the sun bursting through rain clouds that are hanging about on the tops of the mountains. The twins walk along the riverbank looking for tracks and little piles of rabbit stools. They come to a soft grassy bank and sit down. Ken asks,

"So how far is it to Vienna, Ron?"

"Over four hundred kilometers; too bloody far to walk".

"How do we get across the Austrian boarder?"

"Let's say we do get there, with no papers,
no Austrian ration cards, no address to look for.
You remember Vienna, it's a bigger city than Munich".

"We would get picked up so easily.
So we can't go to Vienna can we Ken?"

"So we are better off to stay here, for the summer…?"

"Good. We like it here don't we?"

Soft warm rain starts to fall. Ron holds his head up to feel it on his face. The rain is fresh in the hills, not sulfurous like the air in the city.

As Ron is walking slowly along with his eyes closed, feeling the rain on his face. Ken jumps around in front of him, grabs the branch of a young beech tree and shakes it hard. Water showers off it onto Ron, soaking him. He just smiles and quickly strips off all his clothes, runs to the next young tree and shakes it; bringing a shower of warm water over his body. Soon both boys run from one young sapling to the next giving themselves wonderful warm showers.

The Riederecksee Lake seen from the south-east, spring morning.

The Riederecksee as seen from above, facing the north.

Ron   Ken and Hans

Ron and Ken

Ken

Dieter

Just a little deeper into the woods, Ken points slowly to a grassy clearing. A baby deer is quietly grazing, totally unaware of the boys. Slowly, the boys lower themselves on all fours. Ken being the closest runs and dives over a bush, heading off the young deer... Ron arrives to see Ken sitting on the ground holding the deer. It is not afraid of him, his Bamby-like face close to Ken's.

"Look Ron, he likes me, look at his big eyes".

Ron slowly draws his camp knife, and tosses it close to Ken's elbow.

"Here, take the knife, cut his throat quick. It's good eating".

"What! That's murder. Look, there's its mother".

Ken lets go his grip on the calf; it stumbles to its feet and just stands there. Ron gives it a pat on its head and it runs off to join its mother.

"Well some hunters we are, that would have fed us all for a week".

Ken asks

"So, would you have cut its throat?"

Ron shakes his head and smiles,

"It's about midday and we have nothing to eat for tonight".

Ken says cheerfully,

"Well, we've got nine traps out; we had better backtrack
and see what we have caught".

The boys just put on their boots and trudge off; their skins wet and shiny in the rain, swinging their shorts and shirts in the air.

A young baby hare is caught in one of the traps. Ken gently frees it. He holds it in his arms close to him, stroking its ears down. Ron comes over; he has three rabbits hanging from his belt. Ron smiles,

"Wring its neck. It's a bit skinny
but it will all go into the pot".

"What? Oh no, it's only a baby yet;
let's give it time to grow up.
In a few months we may be hungry
and he will make a nice dinner".

Ron shakes his head and picks a bunch of dandelion leaves out of his pocket. He rubs them on the wire trap and all over the young Hare and then resets the trap.

"Here, this will hide our scent. If the mother
smells too much of you on her baby, she will kill it.
And then only the ants will have it for dinner".

Hans and Dieter are somewhere in the woods near a riverbank on the other side of the mountain. Their bread bags and sacks are stuffed with edible greens and roots. They have had a good haul, lots of young fern fiddleheads, thistle roots, young burdock leaves and watercress with wild asparagus and arrow-leaf from the soft banks of the river. They break out into a small clearing.

Dieter says,

"Oh, it's so hot now but tonight we will freeze our bums off…
Hans, do you think the Lambert boys will go to Vienna?"
"I hope not… we wouldn't survive without them".

Dieter looks at the river bend. A shale beach makes a small bay and the clear pebble-bottomed water is still and looks warm,

"Want to go for a swim?"

Dieter pulls off his shirt, his shorts, boots and thick socks, walks to the edge of the water, drops his underpants and throws them back on top of his clothes,

"Come on; the water's nice".

Hans strips down too. They look like a man and a boy as they splash about to cool themselves.

Then they run out and lay on their backs on the hot shale beach to dry in the sun. After a while Hans sits up and studies Dieter's stretched out naked body. Dieter becomes aware that Hans is looking at him,

"What are you staring at lad?"
"Not much…Dieter, you're growing into a man.
You have a few hairs under your arms,
a man's body but you still have a little boy's face".
"You don't have to shave yet do you?"

Dieter smiles, shakes his head and closes his eyes. Hans says,

"Look at me; I'm still a little boy. Hairless armpits;
The girls thought I had shaved the short hairs
from around my dong. See, there are so few growing yet…
Now if I had a chance to swap my body, I would want one
like yours, but with my hair. I like my own hair".

Dieter looks at Hans. He sees a sprout of a boy whose feet seem too big; his legs too long, knobby knees, shoulders too narrow, and a body bursting with raging hormones. He says quietly,

"Hans, you're a good looking boy,
you just haven't grown fully yet. It will happen soon.
You will fill out, grow taller and your hairs will get bushy…
Tell you what boy… You got Hanna all worked up and going;
that's more than I did. You were at it like a young rabbit;
you brought her to a climax. Wow, did you ever, ha.
When I was inside her, I came before she did,
she wanted more and I couldn't keep it hard.
But you brought her to her climax my lad, hair or no hair…"

Ron walks into the camp with Ken and holds up three rabbits. Dieter and Hans cheer and greet them warmly. They show them their roots and greens. Hans watches Ken draw his knife and start to sharpen the edge with a long flat stone. Hans says.

"I have to go for a pee"

He runs off into the woods, Dieter runs after him and drags him back to where Ken is hanging the rabbits over the hole for cleaning. Dieter smiles and says

"Hans you have to watch this because you
and I will have to do this soon"

Hans shudders and whispers,

"Never, not this puppy"

Ken parts the fur on the rabbit's stomach and gently makes the first cut so as not to burst the bladder.

As the guts falls into the pit with a plop, Hans closes his eyes, sways a bit but controls himself. He finally makes himself watch Ken clean and skin the three rabbits.

A spit is rigged and the three rabbit carcasses get stretched out on a green sapling. They look delicious roasting over low embers. Dinner is served: roast rabbit, wild vegetable stew containing a large tin of roasted ground up grasshoppers, fresh picked asparagus and watercress with hot chocolate. Ron dishes up the meal on the tin plates; a big helping for each boy.

Hans is now very hungry. He lifts up his plate and smells it; a slow smile comes over his face as he tucks in and enjoys every spoonful.

Dieter sits back and licks his tin plate clean, then wipes his greasy face with his shirt sleeve and says,

"This is the life, good food, good friends, a good place to sleep,
safe and secure, so, are you two going off to Vienna then or not?"

Ron and Ken get very serious, look at each other, milking the moment, and then look at Dieter… Dieter and Hans look very expectantly at the brothers…

Ron breaks into a smile so does Ken and they both shake their heads. Hans and Dieter yell out with joy and exuberance. Dieter jumps up, and runs over to the brothers, gives them a big bear hug. Dieter laughs,

"Good, good, good stuff, Hans and I…
we would be totally helpless up here without you two…
I don't even know where we are, up here".

Ken smiling,

"Yes, ha that's why we are staying;
we can't go and leave you two helpless babies".

One afternoon the boys are playing cards, sitting around their table and Ron walks into the camp carrying a baby fox cub in his arms,

"Look, he must have wandered away from his mother…
I'm going to call him Rufus".

15 The Valley

Ken yells,
"Hey Dieter get your camera and take a photo of this little Fox".
"We can keep him as a pet; he will act as a guard dog".
The boys all gather around to inspect the new arrival. Dieter looks hard at Ron and says.
"So who's share of the food is he going to eat?"
Hans taps Ron's arm and points over his shoulder. They all turn to see.
"Look".
Standing on the edge of the camp with her three other cubs is the mother fox... She has followed Ron to see what he is going to do with one of her cubs. The boys just stand very still. Ken is the first to move he grabs a fist-full of dandelion leaves and rubs them into the cub's fur and all over its back. Ron walks slowly to the fox and puts the young cub down and gives it a push toward its mother. The fox turns and walks off followed by her litter of babies. Ron's little cub turns to have a last look at the boys and then trots off with its brothers and sisters. Dieter whispers.
"Well, have you ever seen anything like that"?
Ron looks annoyed saying.
"We should have killed the mother and the babies.
We have to share our rabbits and hares on this mountain
with them, I bet they will kill at least one a day I recon".
Ron and Ken have a sad smile on their faces and shake their heads.
Dieter's camera is still warm and dry in its tin box.

16. ONSET OF WINTER

The weeks pass and the little garden gets regular watering by the boys standing knee deep in the lake and splashing the water with their hands. The seeds the boys planted start to grow, carrots, onions, shallots, garlic, potatoes and all kinds of salad leaves sprout up. Fishing lines with bits of white birch bark flutter over the young shoots to keep the birds from stealing them.

Very early one morning the twins were out in the lower valley to check on a deer trap they had set the day before. The trap they set will only arrest and hold the deer but not kill it. So Ken has brought along the flagpole off the cart. It has a spear point on the top end that Dieter has ground razor sharp. They have no guns, so the sharpened spear is the only weapon they have to kill a deer, should they find one alive in their snare. Ken hands the spear to Ron and whispers sadly.

"Here Ron you take it, if we have caught one...
I don't know if I could kill such a large creature
without hurting it".

Ron grabs the spear and says.

"Listen, we will have to get the thing lying down,
you grab its neck and wrestle it to the ground.
When it's down I will run it through with this".

Ken nods and puts his fingers to his lips. "Shh, we're close".

The twins silently approach the site where the trap is set. Ken carefully coils his length of rope ready to throw it.

They turn a corner around an outcrop of rock and see a male deer just lying down nibbling the soft grass. It has been caught by its antlers in the rope of Ken's trap and has given up the struggle. It is just lying down quite contented. Ken looks at Ron and they nod together and rush the creature. Ken grabs its horns and throws all his weight on its neck to keep it down on the ground.

To the boys surprise the deer puts up no struggle.

Ron finds his mark and thrusts the spear deep in to the creatures heart. It kicks once or twice without a sound, and lies very still.

"Oh wow! Oh my! Just look at it Ken, a whole deer, it will
feed us all for a week! How are we ever going to cook it?"

Ken scratches his head and says.

"Ron, I know! I know! I read about it
in that survival book we stole".

Ron pulls out his spear and says.

"Good you have the job of cooking it then".

The animal is hoisted up by its feet into a tree. Ken guts it and removes the head and trusses it up by its feet on the stout pole of the spear so they can carry it between them.

The twins march triumphantly in to their camp, Dieter and Hans look totally amazed. The story of the kill gets told and retold whilst the carcass is carried to the river and washed.

Ken lays it out on the table and fills its stomach cavity with cut up onions potatoes and carrots, some garlic and a little salt with some spices. He removes the legs, skins them and presses them flat into the stomach cavity on top of the vegetables then sews the whole thing up tight with wire. It looks like an overgrown-trussed furry banana. A large fire is lit from dried pinewood and a hole is dug close to the fire about one meter deep.

Ken gets the boys to bring soft mud from the riverbank and they all join-in and plaster a thick coating of the gooey mud all over the fur of the carcass. He leaves two holes in the top with two green reeds as chimneys to let out the steam. The final touch, a wire handle on a pole, long enough for two boys to lower the deer into the hole.

When the fire burns down to glowing embers Ken shovels a thick layer of hot ash and glowing wood into the bottom of the hole. Chopped up dried wood chips get mixed in with the glowing embers. He then lays a layer of fresh long grass on top of the hot embers. They gently lower the mud-caked deer into the hole; then quickly cover the deer with a lot more grass and hot glowing wood embers. More long green grass and then fresh large dock leaves and soil packed tight, filling the hole to a smoldering pile.

All that is visible now is the lifting pole and its wires.

Some small wisps of steam and smoke rise through the packed soil.

Hans asks,

"So Ken, how long will it take to cook?"

Ken grins and holds up his hand showing five fingers.

"Five hours, so we won't eat this until tonight then?"

Dieter looks at the steam wistfully saying.

"Ken have you cooked a deer like this before?

How do you know it will cook right?"

Ken smiles,

"It will cook alright, but we must leave it untouched until tonight".

That evening, as it was getting dark, the steam could still be seen coming from their cooking hole.

"So how do we know it's done under all that soil?" says Dieter.

Hans looks up at the sky and says,

"I should think it's been in there at least nine hours, it must be done by now it was very early this morning when it went in".

The boys gather around as Ken and Ron shovel out the topsoil. To everyone's surprise the wood embers are still glowing on top and underneath the deer. The thick-caked mud has set like concrete.

Hans and Dieter lift out the steaming carcass with the wire handles and Ken brushes off the ashes. They lay it on their table.

Ron takes his knife and prods the top but it is solid. Ken brushes Ron's hand away saying.

"No we have to cut a big hole in the top like a lid,
because all the good stuff will be at the bottom".

So with a knife and a small rock Ken chisels open a large lid about half the diameter of the deer. The boys all gather around close to the table to watch the lid get pried off.

"Wow! Oh! Mm! Oh my!

The boys all cry out together as they see the huge dish of well-cooked meat and vegetables swimming in their own juices. A delicious aroma arises with the steam. Ken says,

"Let's eat it right out of here, we don't need plates".

The boys eat their fill with "Oos" and "Mmms", dipping their forks and spoons; the largest one-pot-meal they had ever eaten.

The legs are hung in the tent to be cut in to strips to smoke over the cooking fires. This will feed them for weeks.

Other strips of meat were banged out flat and strung up to dry.

At the end of seven days there isn't enough meat left to go bad. Then they cut up bones that will go into the boy's nightly stews.

Deer was only an occasional treat for the lads. Most of the older deer were too clever to be fooled by traps Ken made from rope.

On a sunny morning, all four boys are naked and knee-deep in the river. They are supposed to be splashing water on the young plants that are sprouting all over their garden.

But the event has turned into a splashing fight. Hans runs out of the water laughing, chased by Dieter and the two brothers.

A wrestling match starts on the beach, all three boys onto Dieter.

Dieter stands up with Hans clinging to him on his back, Ron and Ken under each arm like sacks of potatoes. He starts to spin the three boys around and around... Then he suddenly stops and freezes on the spot; staring open mouthed. He drops the boys from under his arms.

They all see the young man who has just walked out of the trees, standing and watching them. His uniform seems strange: High brown fur-lined boots, a gun belt with a brown canvas holster hanging heavy and drooping from his waist. He takes off his big rucksack, puts it down, waves and says in English,

"I don't suppose any of you young chaps
speak English or French, do you?"

The boys look blankly at each other. Dieter points to Ron and Ken. The young man steps into their camp and walks towards Ron.

"Do you boys speak any English?
Oh bugger, I wish I had taken German at school".

The boys grab their shorts; the young man picks up a tin mug off the table and dips it into the lake for a drink.

"That's a pity, because I'm totally lost. I have been coming
up this hill smelling your dinner for the last two miles...
You're not the White Rose people or the partisans are you?"

The boys start to dry themselves. Ron steps forward walks up close to the young man and speaks to him quietly in English.

"How's Hammersmith doing? Who's their center forward?"
"Oh thank goodness someone who speaks English.
I'm afraid I don't follow soccer. Ask me about cricket.
I used to go to the Test Match every year".

Ken comes up next to his brother,

"Cricket is a stupid game, you must be British".

The boys look at his strange boots, the RAF uniform with the pilot's wings over his left pocket, concealed under a farmer's rain cape, his mop of bright ginger hair and a matching handlebar moustache

"He is air crew all right, Ken whispers, no German
would grow a stupid looking moustache like that,
look at those boots and that funny pistol case. Bombers?"

The pilot puts his rucksack on the table,

"I was shot down three days ago".

Ken steps forward smiling and shakes the pilot's hand very vigorously and introduces him to Ron and the other boys, then he asks him in aristocratic English.

"I say old chap, you will stay to dinner, I hope".

Dieter says warmly,

"Ask him if he is hungry".
"I just asked him if he could stay for dinner".

The young pilot tucks into thick slices of deer leg and tinned biscuits from their reserve store in the locked cart. After dinner he sips coco and asks,

"How on earth did two English boys get all the way out here?
What are you all doing in the middle of nowhere?
On some sort of field exercise?"

Ron replies with a quick lie,

"Yes, we are on a survival training course...
Well not really, we are also trying to sit out the war".

The pilot tells the boys about the war and how badly it is going for Germany. Ken and Ron translate,

"We are bombing the hell out of Germany. Terrible bombing
of Cologne, most industrial cities bombed day and night.
I was a part of raid we called the Big Week. One hundred and
fifty bombers raided the Messerschmitt works at Regensburg

and Augsberg… Five days ago two hundred British Lancaster's
dropped Flying Meteors, (methane petrol incendiary bombs)
over Munich between the central station and the river Isar.
Most of it was burned flat. I saw it from the air, looked terrible".
Ron translates and the boys look aghast,
    "We know all about your bombing, we have been
    on the receiving end of your raids. Why do you have to
    bomb us, then set fire to everything and kill so many people?"
The young pilot looks down and into the fire:
    "Orders".
Hans asks,
    "Where were our ME 109 fighters?"
Ron translates as the Pilot sips his coco,
    "Very few, some allied planes were shot down by your
    antiaircraft fire. That's how I pranged, bailed out, landed
    in the woods two days walk north of here and here I am".
Ron and Ken tell the Englishman their story, translating for Dieter and
Hans, Dieter asks.
    "What's he mean, he pranged?"
Ken grins,
    "He means he had to leave his aircraft,
    because he was hit with anti-aircraft fire".
The pilot suggests,
    "You two should come with me, try to get to
    Switzerland; you look as if you two could live off the land".
Ken smiles warmly,
    "No thanks, our folks are still here in Germany,
    we have to try and find them when this war is over".
Dieter whispers something in German to Ron, he translates,
    "He said you're not to tell anyone our position up here.
    We will all be shot if we are caught aiding a British airman,
    shot immediately".
The young pilot nods that he understands.
    "I didn't really smell your dinner.
    I got lost or I wouldn't have ever come up this valley".
Ron smiles and says,
    "I know the wind blows up the valley not down".

Ken arrives with a hand-drawn map and some food. They plot a route
for him. He shows them his own compass and Ron is impressed with just
how compact it is. The pilot puts his backpack on and is ready to leave. They
all shake hands. He strides off through the woods, the boys all wave as he
disappears.

Ron nods and says,
>"Funny, he didn't really trust us. I wonder where he got
>that backpack; it's German. That rain cape is very Bavarian,
>I bet he stole it from a local farmer. It's not part of his flight gear".

Ken agrees,
>"Well you can't really blame him for being careful;
>It's his life too".

Dieter asks,
>"I wonder where the White Rose people are…
>I wonder who they are".

Hans gets up and stretches,
>"We don't know his name; you notice, he didn't ask ours".

About three days later Hans runs in to the camp in a flat panic and pours water over the fire.

The hiss stirs Dieter who's dozing off fishing on the riverbank.
>"There's an Army patrol in the valley! Where are the twins?"

Dieter sits up,
>"What sort of patrol, where?"

Hans grabs Dieter's arm and shakes it,
>"Come on Dieter we have to find the Lamberts.
>There are some soldiers; they must be looking for that English
>pilot out there".

Dieter stands up looking out of the camp. He's awake now,
>"Where is my little telescope?"

Hans has already found it, and hands it to Dieter, who says,
>"Wait, we have to leave them a note, on the table".

Dieter writes on the back of Ron's map,
>"Army patrols in the valley hide".

Dieter sticks a fork through the note into the table.
A signal all the boys know, they will notice the note for sure.
Hans and Dieter creep out to the bend in the valley and slowly make their way down the east side, under cover of the woods. Dieter stops, slowly ducks down pointing, he pulls out his telescope and peers down the open country.
>"Alpine patrols. It's the army, look".

Hans looks through the little military telescope counting,
>"There are ten of them, they are closer now and they must be
>traversing the valley back and forth working their way up here.
>Where the hell are the Lamberts, you don't think they're down
>there do you Dieter?"

Dieter takes command, grabs Hans's shoulder,
>"Hans, you go back to camp. Keep hidden in the trees,
>stay out of sight. I will stay here and keep an eye on them.

No fires, you hide close to the camp.
If they get too close I'll warn you. We will have time to get to
higher ground, stay near the camp. We don't want the Lamberts
lighting the fires for tonight's stew, go".

Hans makes his way back to camp and Dieter works his way around to
higher ground on the eastern side of the valley and climbs a tree to get a
better view of the foot of the Halerspitz in the northwest.

At the foot of the mountain, across the mouth of the valley, there is an
army half-track personnel carrier parked under a tree. It's not too well
hidden, Dieter thinks,

"That's how they came in here,
from the north-west, from Kreuth.
That old heap won't make it up this hill to our camp;
it's far too steep. They are looking for that airman all right".

Dieter scans the open ground above the patrols and then starts to watch
the woods on the western edge of the open valley.

His eye catches a movement in the woods on the other side of the valley.
Peering through his little telescope, he sees it's the Lamberts, their
unmistakable long blond hair bobbing through the trees.

They are on their way back to camp carrying four rabbits and they are
deep into their own conversation. Dieter knows he has no way of warning
them. If they cut across the open ground to take a shortcut back to camp
they will be spotted by the patrol.

Dieter swings his telescope from the boys to the patrol.

The twins get closer and closer to the edge of the woods, then just as
they are about to make their way across the open ground where they could
be spotted they stop at the edge and look to their right. Then slowly duck
down and back into the deep cover of the woods. Dieter breathes a deep
sigh and says to himself,

"Shit, that's great; they have seen the patrol…
Now let's see if the soldiers have seen them?"

Dieter swings his telescope back to the patrol and they haven't broken
their line. The patrol is still trudging with their heads down looking tired,
making their way back to their half-track.

He watches them until they get back to their truck and waits for them
to light a fire. Dieter thinks, well they won't be coming up here tonight, and
climbs down from his tree and makes his way back to camp. At first it looks
deserted and then the boys come out from their cover.

"I watched you two on the west ridge.
It's a good job you didn't try to cross that meadow.
They would have spotted you for sure".

Ron picks up Dieter's little telescope,

"Did you see them close enough
to tell if they were Alpine Scouts?"

"No, they were just Volkssturm (Home Guard).
They looked like a lot of old men.
They didn't seem to have much go in them;
they looked very slow and tired".
Ron says,
"We will have to keep an eye on them. We should
post a guard tonight and watch until they go".
Hans looks at the wet fireplace that is usually bright and cooking their
evening meal and whispers,
"There's no supper on, shall we eat some of the canned food,
Ron?"
"That's what it's for. I would say this is an emergency;
so we eat canned sausage tonight, no lights and cold stew".
Ken asks,
"We should watch them until they go.
We could work four three hour shifts so we have
at least one pair of eyes watching them all the time".
Dieter thinks and then stands up shaking his head,
"No, we should work it in pairs,
I don't want to sit out there on my own".
Ron laughs,
"So Dieter, a big lad like you, afraid of the dark,
scared the boogey-man is going to get you, ha".
Dieter looks hurt and pissed off,
"No, do you want to sit out there on your own?
You two are so relaxed you would probably fall asleep.
No let's work it in pairs three-hour shifts…
All right we all agree, who wants to go first?"
    The boys watch the army patrol all night and at first light the next
morning the truck takes off, and drives west to pick-up the road to the
village of Kreuth, about six kilometers north west of the Helerspitz. The
twins creep down the valley and see that there is no sign of the patrol;
they are gone. They kick the ashes of their fire and find a few empty meat
cans and some empty paper bags.

    The summer drifts by; the four boys become experts at survival. Their
hair gets longer, bodies fit, brown, lean, stealthy, quick and silent. The twins
look even more alike growing beautifully proportioned, their physique not
particularly muscular, but well-coordinated and very limber. They all
discarded their clothes as soon as the weather warmed up. They run around
in their underpants and a belt to hold their camp knives and snares.
    Dieter has long gone barefoot too, as he has grown out of his boots.
    Most of the boys have to cut a cross in the front cap of their boots to
allow room to for their big toe to grow.

Hans learns to swim better. Ken builds a fish trap from woven vines in the big river down the valley. Gathering birds' eggs, roots, vegetables, berries and trapping small game takes most of the boys' time. Their garden yields carrots and onions. The potatoes are small but tasty. All their gatherings go into the one stew pot every night. Sometimes if there has been a good catch like a large hare or four rabbits they roast them on spits.

Dieter and Hans become experts with the traps and snares too.

When they trap a deer or find they have snared too many hares or rabbits, Ron shows them how to save meat by cutting it into thin strips and banging it flat on a rock, then drying it in the sun and smoking it in their small tent. It can then be stewed on wet days when they can't trap.

They hang the meat out on a tight fishing line strung in their small storage tent. To keep the ants off, they smear the line at both ends with the sticky resin from pine saplings.

Fishing in the big river down the hill fetches them a bounty: trout, perch, pike; then as a real treat sometimes, green tench, the poor man's salmon. Bits of fish guts make wonderful bait for the bird snares. Rabbits and hares also love tasty bits of dried fish. They explore their surroundings, crossing two more deep valleys to peer down at a small hamlet called Spitzingsee on a tiny lake, set in beautiful alpine terrain.

Wandering through the rolling grasslands, snow-topped mountains and green woods, they have become a part of the quiet whispering breath of the forest. Dieter gets his camera out and takes candid shots of the boys from a distance watching them through his telephoto lens, catching them unaware.

At night, sleeping in their cozy tent they know that when the noise of the woods suddenly falls silent, it's soon followed by the drone of the allied bombers flying very high to a target somewhere.

One evening, Ron is dishing up a particularly good meal, one made with the first cut of a small deer they had caught yesterday. Large chunks of meat float in the stew made from carrots, onions and cut potatoes, the aroma is wonderful. Hans with a sullen face is watching Ron's every move and finally blurts out saying,

"So, how come, when you or Ken divide up the dinner
and share it out you both end up with larger portions
than us, how come that, Lambert R?"

Ken snaps back,

"Do you really think we set out to short-change you,
Kardoff bloody four eyes ah?"

"Well you may not do it intentionally but
we do get smaller shares don't we Dieter?"

Ron bangs the big spoon on the side of the pot.

"Oh no you bloody don't... We all get the same as each other
don't we Dieter, we all get our fair share...
All right, you bloody dish it up then,

you share it out if you think you're being
served short by the greedy Lamberts you do it".

Ken getting very angry yells,
"And you can cook it yourself too!
That's it... It's your turn to do all the cooking!
We will sit on our bums and fish all day tomorrow, you two can
do the cooking, now we will see how we all eat, bloody Kardoff".
The meal was eaten in silence, Dieter staying out of the rift. Things were
very close to boiling point when they all went into bed. Hans spots Ken's
grubby and ragged underpants on his bed. When Ken returns from washing
in the river, Hans throws them at him hitting him in the face.
"Keep your shitty pants off our bed Lambert K,
look at them; they have a gold watch in the seat,
don't you ever wipe your bum, ha".
Ken, still wet from the river, picks up his slightly soiled underpants and
rubs them into Hans's face poking them in his mouth.
"Have a taste Kardoff, taste of my smelly bum then".
Ken and Ron fall about laughing. Dieter just sits on their bed and grins.
Ken is laughing so hard he can hardly stand up, Ron yells,
"Who got shit in his face then, ha, didn't you know
Ken kept a secret gold watch in his underpants".
Hans, carefully timing a full swing, punches Ken on the side of his face.
He was not expecting the blow; it knocked him right off his feet on to his
backside. He sits up holding his face yelling,
"We can't hit him back... The little four eyed asshole is wearing
his bloody glasses, take your glasses off Hans and let Dieter hold
on to them for a bit and fight me fairly, outside".
Hans is about as angry as the boys have ever seen him, he blurts out
shouting,
"Oh yes! If I mixed it with you, Ronny bloody Lambert there
would come in on it and I would have to fight both of you, isn't
that how it always works! I would get the shit beaten out of me by
the both of you.... Right?"
Ron pulls the blanket Hans is standing on out from under his feet, he
falls on to Ken who grabs him and holds him fast so Ron can rub the grubby
underpants into his nose. Hans yells and Dieter breaks up the fight yelling,
"Come on you three; shake hands and make it up.
I will dish out dinner tomorrow".
Ron laughs,
"Oh yes, Oh yes, if you dish up, you will get the lion's share
and we will all starve. Let Ken do it, he is best at sharing the food
out, isn't he Hans?"

Hans nods. The tension is not yet broken and the boys settle down for the night.

The next day Hans and Ken go out looking for green vegetables. Hans is still sulking slightly from yesterday's fight, so they set their traps walking along the bank of the river in silence.

Ken looks hard down-river to where it turns to make its way to the lower valley. There is a wide bend, the water is shallow calm and as clear as crystal in the little bay. He stops and freezes, Hans stops instinctively too, motionless looking at Ken wondering what he had seen. Ken crouches low, his hand signaling to Hans to lie flat. Their argument now forgotten, Hans thinks: this is most likely to be food or danger.

He knows that Ken must have seen something. After a few moments Ken starts to move like a cat. He very slowly climbs a small rock outcrop and eases himself carefully to the edge so he can see down into the sheltered bank of the river. He looks slowly back at Hans who is watching his every move, puts his finger to his lips, grins then beckons Hans to creep up and join him. Both boys look down into the river; the bend beneath them has formed a little sheltered bay covered from the sun by the rock they have just climbed.

There, wallowing in the shallow shaded waters, hiding from the bright sun of the day are four big salmon. They have sought the quiet warm water to rest and bask for the afternoon, away from the cold faster-running center stream, where they would have to work hard swimming, just to stay in one place. Ken puts his finger to his lips and bids Hans to stay very still. Moving like a fox, quietly whistling bird shrills to cover what little sound he is making, Ken makes his way very slowly back down the rock and takes off his boots and pants.

Then crawling on all fours along the soft bank of the river, he smears his naked body all over with mud, takes his time and slowly slides along the muddy edge of the water and draws level with the fish. He rubs his right arm and upper body in the soft brown mud until he is the same color as the riverbank. Then lying flat on his stomach he squirms like a snake, very slowly to the edge of the water. Waving his hand like the reeds in the ever-moving waters, he gradually lets his hand sink in below the surface, the mud drifting away from his arm like a cloud of underwater smoke.

His hand never stops, moving back and forth trying to become a part of the flow of the creek, his fingers no more intimidating to the fish than the reeds or the fronds of grass. Working slowly and carefully behind the big fish, his hand feels under its belly very gently and remains very still.

Then, just at the right moment he rams his fingers up into the fish's gills and flips it silently onto the bank. The sleepy salmon doesn't wake up until it hit the grass on the bank.

Ken clamps the big fish's head between his knees to hold it quiet and re-smears his arm with mud. The other three fish move a little further away but are soon anxious to return to the warm spot that has been vacated by Ken's first catch.

Hans, watches in stunned amazement as Ken tosses three of the big fish out onto the bank the same way. Ken jumps to his feet and holds up two of the big fish, one in each hand yelling,

"Hans look, fishes for din-dins, want to go in for a swim?"

Ken clamps the last fish on its head to stop it wiggling and runs over to Hans and grabs him, smearing him with the brown goo. Both the boys laugh and roll in the soft mud of the bank ending up in the water, friends again. They slosh the mud off their bodies with a splashing fight. As the two boys lay out in the soft grass to let the sun dry them off, Hans says,

"So Ken, how did you know there were big fish in the river, right at this place too?"

"I didn't, but it is a good spot, I thought it might just be a good place, you know, where they are likely to be. If I was a fish and I wanted a rest that's where I would go".

"It was all the things together, the fast cold center of the river, the warm bay and the outcrop cover. You have to watch them; get to know their little habits and move slowly because they can see us better than we can see them. You never move any faster than the things around you".

Ken tries to put on his brother's I know more than you do voice,

"Well fish like to feed very early in the morning before the sun gets up and then again just after sunset. If there is going to be a storm and it gets dark suddenly that may just start a feeding frenzy… They think it's night; you can see them catching the flies on the surface… The rest of the day they are lazy, they don't like swimming against the current much. So they look for places like this to sleep. Well I don't think they really sleep, they just doze and bask. What I did is called fish tickling. It is against the law, but poachers do it all the time".

Hans picks up the fish,

"My, these will make a fine dinner, tickled salmon, wow!
I didn't know fish were ticklish ha".

"Come on, let's go back to camp; we will eat well tonight".

The boys cut a sapling and make a pole to carry their catch between them on their shoulders. They march off singing, the young sapling bending under the weight of the four big fish.

"Ho Auntie Nelly
had a fat belly with a red pimple
On her bum, with a red pimple on her bum".
"Ho, any old iron, any old iron".

A fine dinner of roast salmon and local camp-grown carrots,
With wild young watercress leaves all went down very well. Then for dessert, they had shredded wild parsnips with a pile of sweet blue honeysuckle berries that Ron and Dieter gathered. All washed down with water from the little spring just uphill from their camp.

The meal is devoured with lots of Mm's and Yum's.

Dieter asks,

> "Ken, do you remember where you caught these?"
> "Yes, but I don't want anyone trying to tickle the fish there.
> I don't want to spoil the waters. The fish don't know about me
> yet; they still think it's a safe place. They don't know what I smell
> like yet; let's try and keep it that way".

Ron smiles,

> "We know what you smell like don't we lads?"

Dieter taps his stomach,

> "Look Ken, you bring home fish like this...
> It's your fishing place and you can stink as much as you like".

Hans joins in,

> "It was the most amazing thing I have ever seen;
> he just stripped off nude, covered himself with mud
> and tossed them out with his hand".

Ron laughs,

> "Ha, it's the sight of Ken's naked body
> that sent the fish into a trance, that's how he does it, ha".

Dieter grins,

> No, it's his little dinky; the fish are so fascinated
> by the sight of it they think it's a worm, Ha Ha".

Ken grins,

> "If Dieter stripped to mud himself up,
> the fish would see his thing and think
> it was a big old eel and run for their lives".

Hans licks his tin plate and says,

> "I don't know why the other fish didn't escape
> after the first one got himself chucked out of the river,
> it was amazing".

One warm afternoon, after a heavy morning rain shower Ken and Hans are out looking for new rabbit and hare runs, Ken points to a rise in the hillside,

> "Look Hans, over there on that rise, see all the short grass...
> That's where they will be".

Hans bounds up the steep cliff yelling.

> "Oh yes I see it.... I'll race you to that ridge up there".

The boys scramble up the wet slippery grass, both of them in bare feet wearing only their belts, undershirt and underpants. They carefully work their way around to the edge of the ridge and spot little piles of rabbit stool, a good fresh place to run a trap line.

Keeping close to the edge of the ridge the boys set six traps working in silence.

Ken looks up when he hears Hans cry out.

"Oh Shit!"...

Ken turns and watches him lose his foothold on the wet grass and slide off the ridge. He falls four meters on to a hard rocky ledge, his fall broken slightly by a vicious sharp hawthorn bush that would feel worse than a barbed wire entanglement.

Ken scrambles down ridge to Hans; he is lying very still, wedged, deep in the thorny bramble bush. His body is badly scratched and bleeding.

"Oh shit Hans don't move, I will try to get you out".

"Hans... Hans... Say something you bugger"

Hans is still, he has a nasty cut over his eye that's bleeding, and a long cut running up the outside of his thigh. Ken thinks, if he is unconscious; now would be a good time to pull him out of that bush, while he is not feeling much pain.

Ken grabs his skinny legs and drags him out through the bush inflicting long scratches on the sides of his torso. He pulls him out on to the soft grass. The blood is pulsing freely from the cut on his head. The long cut on his outer thigh, although bleeding, is not that deep.

Ken now sees a third terrible cut on his inner upper leg, up close to his groin, that is lying open with a flap of flesh folded back exposing his muscle and the femoral artery that is throbbing but has not been cut. Ken knows from his medical training that if that large artery that supplies blood to the whole leg is cut, there is no way to save the boy's leg. Without blood flowing it will go bad and gangrene will set in and that will kill him.

Ken decides to start with the wound near the groin first; and folds the flap back to its proper position and presses it stopping the bleeding a little.

Then he applies pressure to the cut on Hans's head by placing his hands on each side of the cut and pushes the edges together.

The pulsing slowly stops. Hans is still in a semi-conscious state and groans. Ken looks around for some sort of padding to use as a dressing. Apart from their belts hung with trap wires and camp knives, underwear is their only other possession on that hillside. After keeping the hold on his head-wound for about five minutes, Ken lets off the pressure, the blood pulses and spurts out again,

"Oh shit Hans, we have to move you and get you
back to camp, only stitches will hold this cut together".

Ken draws his camp knife and cuts off Hans's undershirt and rolls it up in a wad; he finds the cleanest spot on the vest and presses it on Hans's cut.

Ken takes both their belts and secures the dressing tight, then stays and watches to see if the wad is working. The bleeding is now greatly reduced and the pulsing has stopped. Ken pulls off his own undershirt and wraps it around his upper leg.

Hans looks asleep and peaceful. Ken thinks for a bit and then starts to shout.

"Hans... Can you hear me; you mustn't go into shock.
Don't go to sleep Hans or you will go in to shock!
Hey! Hans! Wake up!"
Hans starts to moan and regain his consciousness,
"What, what you shouting at? Ow my head.
Ho shit I'm scratched all over".
Ken makes a pillow for him out of a wad of bracken saying,
"Listen Hans,
I have to get someone to help me carry you back to camp.
There is a nasty cut there; can you hold this vest on your head
and this one on your leg until we get back?"
"Mm... I think so".
"All right I'm going to get the others; you lay still and stay awake,
and keep the pressure on both of those dressings, all right.
Don't touch any of your cuts with your fingers; we must try to
prevent you from getting infected... all right?"
"Mmm".
"I won't be long, remember Hans,
just stay awake it's very important to stay awake".
Ken scrambles down the hillside and runs back to their camp.

Hans is brought back to camp on a stretcher made from the two long shafts of the cart and some blankets. They lay him out on the table. Ron gets the acorn water boiling for a strong antiseptic and Dieter boils water to sterilize the curved sewing needle the two forceps and thread from the army first aid kit. Ken takes charge saying,
"Dieter you get hold of his shoulders and Ron
you hold on to his legs... When I start to stitch him up,
he may just start kicking out, so you must both
hold on to him very tight, all right?"
Dieter looks skeptical,
"We will hold him... But do you know...?"
Ron smiles,
"Yes, he knows what he is doing,
he's the one with the Medical badge, remember".

Hans yells out when Ken puts the first stitch on the wound on his thigh. It takes Dieter and Ron to hold him still while the other four stitches are put in. It takes fourteen stitches to close the flap on his inner thigh.

When Ken has finished dressing the cut he lifts Hans's head up on a rolled blanket, takes hold of his face very firmly, looks at him closely and says in a loud voice,

"Hans can you hear me!"

Hans blinks and nods,

"Listen to me Hans!
I have to stitch up the cut on your head now, it's a bad one;
you must keep still. It's too bloody close to your eye for you to
wiggle about like a baby, you must keep as still as you can...
Don't move you must bear the pain Hans.
You got to just take the pain, all right, talk to me Hans,
do you understand what I'm saying?"

Hans winces a slight smile and says,

"Yes, yes, but why are you shouting, I'm not deaf, I'll keep still,
I can't do much else with all you apes holding on to me like this".

Hans doesn't flinch as Ken works with the thread and two forceps. He lies quite still as six small stitches are sown in to his forehead.

When it's all over, Dieter explains what has happened and Hans picks up his bloody under-vest, he smiles saying,

"Oh, wonderful;
I might just die now of my own underwear poisoning.
Oh, I've got a massive headache;
do I get a pill out of that Army box?"

Ken smiles and nods. Dieter hands him a small steel mirror and Hans stares at the cut on his head that's bristling with knots and ends of the stitches, after a few moments he smiles and whispers.

"Well this will make my baby face look a little tougher".

After about four days of bathing with the boiled acorn juice the cuts on Hans's head and his outer thigh start healing cleanly, but the deep V shape cut on his inner thigh starts to get red and his upper leg and groin become very swollen and oozes a reddish yellow puss.

Ken calls Dieter and Ron down to the river bank away from the tent so Hans cannot hear them. The three serious boys look to Ken for some explanation. He says in a quiet voice.

"Hans has got a bad infection; the acorn juice isn't a powerful
enough antiseptic to fight all that scar tissue. The wound smells
bad so I am going to have to take out the stitches and open the
wound to drain it. It's the only way we can save him. We need
some maggots, lots of them, big fat ones. If flies lay their eggs on
his wound we will get more maggots they will eat all his dead and
poisoned tissue. That is all we have to fight the infection with.

It's in a very dangerous part of his body close to that big Artery,
Hans just may die, and we don't have the time to carry him to a
hospital. He just wouldn't make it.
Dieter screws his nose up and says,
    "Flies, like the ones that buzz around the shithole?"
Ken nods,
    "Yes, they are just the ones we need, there will be lots of maggots
    in the hole from last week's rabbit intestines, catch as many as you
    can, they must be alive. The maggots will only eat rotten flesh
    they won't eat healthy tissue".

The boys collect half a jar of fat maggots in a large sterilized glass jar.
They tie Hans's hands and feet and stake him out spread-eagled, prone on
the table to prevent him from scratching his injury while the maggots do
their work.
    Dieter and Ron hold Hans down while Ken removes the stitches in his
groin then gently peels back the V shaped flap. The open wound is yellow
with puss. Ken cleans it off with boiled bandages. He carefully places the
large jar of maggots over the open wound and they all watch the maggots
start to settle on to the open flesh.
    "We have to leave the jar for at least two or three days,
    we will have to take turns holding it there".
    In three days Hans's wound is still crawling with little white maggots.
They devoured only the rotten infected flesh, leaving the healthy part of the
wound clean. As the maggots gorged themselves on the infection they
produced a pale red foam that Ken wipes away gently. Hans feels the
maggots working and pleads.
    "Oh they itch, it itches, please untie me, please…
    Ron? Why do I have to be tied up like this? Ken?
    Dieter please let me up; the itching is driving me mad!"
    After four days the wound is clean and stops producing puss. The
maggots have died because there is no more rotten flesh. Ken removes the
maggots and re-stitches the cut. This time the twenty-four stitches are much
neater and closer together. Hans swelling goes down and he starts to heal
cleanly, but the scar on his inner thigh is very jagged.
    "How did you know about maggots?" Hans asks.
    "It's all in the medical books if you read them" Ken says casually.
Hans walks with a limp for weeks.

Autumn is creeping up on the camp. The days are getting much shorter.
It is hot in the daytime and the boys still run about in their ragged underpants
as they have done all summer. When the sun sets behind their mountain
now, it brings cold and damp with the darkness, so the winter blankets are
again made into two big beds, marking the coming of the end of summer.

Hans heals clean, without infection, thanks to the army First Aid kit and the hot boiled acorn water that Ken uses to bathe his cuts every day.

They all notice that the rabbits are getting scarcer on the high ground around their camp. Now they have to walk down the valley where it is warmer to set their traps. Some birds that were easy to trap have disappeared and a lot of the wild greens that used to be so plentiful are just not growing anymore and are simply rotting. So the boys are depending more on the vegetables from their garden. Plenty of carrots, onions, and potatoes but they wished they had planted more salad, lettuce and radishes. They have been all used-up weeks ago.

One day Dieter is preoccupied and suddenly announces that he has to make a trip to the small hamlet of Spitzingsee that is two day's walk away.

Ron asks,
"Why, what do you need down there? You will blow our cover".
Dieter starts to get angry,
"We need a rifle and a bigger two-handed saw.
Winter's coming and we will need to shoot the deer for food,
and start cutting wood for a hut and fuel".
Ron laughs,
"No, Dieter, we will be in a warm cellar in Munich".
Dieter snaps back,
"Well you may be. I will be cutting wood
if I can find a good saw".
Ron getting angry,
"Listen you great stupid ox.
You can't live up here in the winter in a bloody tent.
If you wanted to start cutting trees for firewood, we should
have started last year. They take more than a year to dry out;
trees just won't burn when they are green Dieter...
Are you ever thick in the head, stupid, stupid, stupid"?

Dieter becomes red in the face with rage. He glares at Ron, the fury rising in him like a kettle about to boil over. He gets up and walks over to Ron and tries to blurt out...
"Well I thought we... Well, I could be taken as a deserter in
Munich".
Ron mocking,
"Thick, thick, thick, all muscle and
a brain smaller than your big cock"...

Ron only just gets his last word out. Dieter whacks him with a backhanded slap across his face. Ken jumps up behind Dieter and in a flash a fight starts. Hans, Ron and Ken are all on to Dieter.

Ron picks up a stout log; Dieter and Ron, all bloody, square off. Dieter is ready to receive a blow. Ron swings at his head and then with the skill of a commando Dieter ducks the blow and disarms Ron. He gives him a bash on his backside with his own weapon. All three boys attack Dieter, fighting and hammering on him like young bear cubs being set on by a swarm of wasps.

The three boys all rush Dieter again.

He falls backward and the three jump on him, Hans sitting on his legs, Ron and Ken on each arm. Ron delivers a well-aimed open-handed slap across Dieter's face.

"That's it; bash me when I'm held down, fucking cowards".

Dieter heaves his body up trying to throw off the three on top of him. But he is held fast. Ron says quietly

"Just calm down, we are making too much noise".

Dieter shouts,

"Fuck the noise, fuck you lot, and get off".

Ron tries to calm him down,

"Not until you settle down. If we let you get up,

will you be nice, no punching?"

"Fuck off, get off me".

Dieter has a last heave trying to free himself, then goes limp and stops squirming.

"All right, all right, let me up".

Ken says,

"Promise?"

"Yes"

"Yes what?"

Dieter, trying to hold a smile says.

"I promise… Yes, to be nice".

The boys release their grip. Dieter throws them off roughly. He tries to swing a punch at Hans, but he ducks out of the way.

Dieter is still very angry and red faced. He strips off his clothes, walks into the water up to his waist, turns to the boys and grins.

"So, come on you babies, the water is fine".

The three strip off and run into the water. Dieter holds out his hand in friendship. Ken takes it to shake, but Dieter grabs him, turns him over and dunks him in the water. A fun water fight starts and they all laugh and giggle like big kids again.

Dieter is very worried. He knows he looks call-up age and he will be challenged as soon as he reaches a fair-sized town and knows he wouldn't last too long in a big city without passes or papers.

He brightens up as a happy thought passes through his blond head,

"Hey, perhaps the war is over and the British are already in

Munich… Well how would we know?"

Ron nurses his sore face and says,

"Dieter, the war is not over, not yet,
we would have heard by now".
Hans stands up and yells,
"How… How… how would we have heard, all the way
up here? Do you think the rabbits would knock on our tent?
Ho, hello there Dieter, did you know the stupid war is over,
so you can stop eating us now; and bugger-off back to Munich".
Ron laughs and ads,
"Ho yes".
"The fish are really going to miss us eating them".
Ken quietly says,
"Well we will all be down there soon, we will find out
then if the war is still going on, won't we"?
Ken senses Dieter's concern and becomes all sympathetic,
"Dieter, we will bluff it out.
In clean uniforms with our hair cut our message belts and
working armbands, we will pretend to be on duty.
We have it all, stamps envelopes, everything.
We can wangle and work our way through anything".
Ron and Hans agree, Ken says,
"We won't let Dieter be caught, will we lads".
The boys all nod smiling.

On the boys' last night in their mountain camp the first snow of the season starts to fall making the place look like a twinkling Christmas card, it's very cold. They have all squashed themselves together in the tent to keep warm. The edges of the river have a thin sheet of ice that glitters against the dark almost still water. Tomorrow they start their long walk back to the railway station. They have disciplined themselves and saved some of the tinned food they carted up there in the spring for their return journey.

Local food from the land around them has been getting scarce as winter approaches; the small creatures and birds have all hibernated or flown south. They have dug up as many vegetables as they can carry from their little garden and loaded them into the cart. The cart will be a lot lighter on the return journey because they are leaving the large tent, the heavy iron grills and the camping gear behind. It is all packed away and wrapped up in the ground sheet, stashed under the trees hidden for next year. The small tent and their stew pots will now serve them for their return journey.

17. THE CELLAR

This morning they will be taking the easier route back to Munich around the west side of the mountain so they have no deep rivers to cross. As they pack the small tent and last of their camping gear into the cart, Hans pumps air into the big fat tires. The boys, now dressed in their uniforms, look like a platoon again. Their boots have been rubbed with deer. Ron looks at Ken's shoulder-long hair and says,

"We have to get our hair cut.

Dieter, you have to shave those twenty six hairs off your chin".

Dieter, feeling his chin,

"You know, I have never owned a razor.

If we walk into the city looking like this,

they will take us for Wolf kids and pick us up for sure".

Dieter looks around and takes a big sigh,

"You know I don't even know the name of this place...

Ron what's that mountain back there?"

Ron spreads his map out on top of the cart, turns it to have it facing north and says.

"Risserkogel, remember where this camp is. You're north east of the top peak of the Risserkogel Mountain here. We should call this place the Riedereckee Camp because that is the name of our little lake here. That huge south facing rock face over there to the north west of us is called Blankenstein and we are only six kilometers from the Austrian border".

The boys all stand quietly and look around them soaking in their surroundings. Hans says.

"It's been a good summer, I wish it was summer

all the time so we could stay here forever.

I felt totally safe up here".

Ken puts his arm around Hans,

"It's all right; we will be back next spring".

The boys quietly hide all the heavy things they will need for the next year. The grill irons, shovels, the big tent all get neatly stored deep under the laurel bushes out of sight. With the cart loaded, the boys look at the empty space that was once their camp.

The round patch where the big bell tent stood for the summer will soon grow over and disappear. Ron looks about him and says quietly,

"That's it then, we should go. It's been a good camp...

It's a shame we have to leave here".

Ken nods,

"The winter would kill us all. We just have to go.

But you're right, it's the best campsite we have ever had.

I will always remember this place".

Ron stands and slowly looks around and puts his hands on his hips.
Dieter smiles and says softly,
  "Ho, I think Ron's going to make one of his"…
Ken puts his finger up to his lips,
  "Shut up Dieter, leave him alone".
The boys stand looking at their bare camp, then look to Ron who
has their attention. He softly says,
      "This is a good place; it has been a Mother
      to us and has fed us and hidden us from the war.
      But the land will go to sleep now, for the winter…
      It's our secret place… Let's never tell anyone where it is,
      come on, let's go".
Dieter brightens up,
      "Well that's nice… So which way, where do we go Ron?"
Ron folds his map,
      "Downhill! Where else! Ha! The nearest town is Rottach-Egern,
      six kilometers west, then eight kilometers north. That brings us
      around the mountain to Lake Tegernsee".
Ken ads,
      "There we can get a train to Munich, if we are lucky.
      I don't know if there's even a train station there.
      We may have to lie our way on to the train".
  Dieter and Hans are in the front shafts of the cart and Ken and Ron
are pushing in the rear. They start their trip back with blankets over their
shoulders, as they have no topcoats. The mist is heavy, making the start
of their journey cold and damp. They travel downhill through lush green
countryside. As they get lower down the valley, it gets warmer. The boys
are cool in their summer uniforms. The weak autumn sun breaks through
and raises the spirits of the four. The mist burns off and they can see the
descending valleys. Dieter jovially announces,
      "I'm looking forward to finding a nice girl
      who wants to make babies for Hitler.
      Wow do I ever have the feeling for that".
Ron inquires,
      "Dieter, you have it in your system again then?"
Dieter grins,
      "Yes sir, I have it in my system and my balls and my thing;
      all my parts are ready, at any time".
Ken laughing,
      "Heavy breathing tonight folks, ha, heavy breathing tonight.
      Dieter's got it in his system, ha…
      Hans, you should sleep with your tin nickers on tonight;
      Dieter's got it in his system".

17 The Cellar

Dieter spins around and shouts at the sky.
"No, not me, Hans needs to have no fear of me.
Every time I think of little Willie, I feel like shooting
those perverted Catholic Priests, you know that Priest
was sent to a concentration camp in Poland, well Karl
told me he has been executed with ten other sex offenders".
The twins look at each other with raised eyebrows.

The boys pass through mountain passes of deep green valleys and beautiful alpine country. The shafts have been pushed through to the rear of the cart and the four boys are all together at the back to hold the thing from running away with them down the hill. Sturdy legs, boots with toes sticking out, dig into the soft wet grass, as they make their way down the mountain. Steam hisses from the cart's brake drums as Dieter controls their decent.

They make their first return camp in a quiet wood, shaded from aerial view, early enough so it is still light and the fire is not seen from down the valley. They make a stew from dried rabbit strips and cut up vegetables. Dieter makes up the beds with the blankets and the boys get their heads down just as it is getting dark. Dieter is the last to crawl into the little tent.
"I've run the trip line, if you get out in the night for a pee,
don't wander too far from the tent or you will tangle in it
and wake us all up".
Ken lies on his back and looks at the top ridge of the tent,
"It's small but very cozy in here...
I wonder if anyone will ever find all our things up there."
Hans says,
"I hope the war be all over by next spring.
When I'm older, and married with my own sons,
I will bring them up here... I'll teach them
how to live off the land like we did".
Dieter smiles,
So Hans, do you want to bring children into this rotten world?"
"It won't always be like this, the war can't last forever can it?
Ron how far is it to the first town?"
Ron sits up and takes his map out of his pocket, hands it over.
"You look, I don't know... Come on, let's get some sleep".
The next day the going is easier and by early afternoon the boys stop in their tracks when they spot a small alpine hunter's lodge, they duck back into the woods. Ron gets out his map and spreads it out on the cart. He places his compass on the map and turns it around slowly. Looks about at the surrounding peaks, then he says brightly,

"Mm, I know where we are now, yes, beyond that lodge is the
Sankt Leonhard Monastery or some sort of old religious school.
The river running through this valley is the Sagenbach.
Just beyond the Monastery down there
is the road that runs north to Kreuth.
Dieter looks at the map and says.
"We should stash the cart here and wait and just two of us
go and look the place over when it gets dark. That Monastery
might just be an Alpine Army Patrol garrison now".
Ken adds.
"Yes we don't want to walk in to a nest of wasps
or anything do we?"
The boys make themselves comfortable and wait until it gets dark.
Ken grabs a chunk of dried rabbit meat and stuffs it in to his pocket.
Hans whispers,
"What's that for, in case you get hungry?"
"No for dogs, to keep them quiet".
Dieter grabs the flagpole with the sharpened blade on its end, looks
at the boys and says.
"Let's rig for silent running, nothing
that rattles or clinks we have to be very quiet".
The boys check their belts and steel sheathed camp knives making
sure they don't rattle.

They creep out and make their way slowly down the valley staying
close to the woods. The first building they come to is the Lodge. A half-
timbered old log and stucco mountain Inn. There is a light in the large
room on the ground floor. The boys move like shadows and peer carefully
through the window.

They see a cheery fire in the stove and a boy about twelve sitting
with a woman that may be his mother; they are at a table eating soup with
large chunks of bread.

Dieter beckons them to follow him, as they pass the old front steps
to the door, they see a weathered carved sign; it's the name of the Inn.
'Schwaiger Haus'. They make their way down past the lodge and down
into the valley. The Monastery looks more like a school.

The building is totally dark, no lights or signs of life. The boys creep
around the whole building and see that the doors have been locked with
large padlocks from the outside.

They creep back up the valley to their cart and snuggle down in the
woods under their ground sheets for the night.

Ron opens a large tin of sausage meat and cuts it in four very equal
slices. The boys munch on their first meal that day and fall asleep.

The next morning the boys decide to arrive at the Lodge officially.
That is all, wearing their uniforms and with flags flying on the cart. They

feel their chances of getting a meal and a haircut may be better if they try to bluff it out with their 'We have been on an exercise story'.

Dieter is a sergeant again. His little platoon dressed in their uniforms (that look as if they have been packed up and rolled in a tight bundle for too long). They march up to the front steps. He dismisses his little platoon outside the Inn and sets their HJ banners that look new. They all go into the Inn and stand looking, soaking up the welcome feeling of the place: the warmth of the big stone fire hearth with its smell of pine logs, the knotty pine carved doors and tables and red chequered table cloths.

Frau Hoepner, a true Bavarian countrywoman, is delighted to serve clients who offer to pay in real money and not worthless military coupons from the army.

She embraces the boys and makes them welcome. A quiet young boy about twelve stands shyly at the door watching. All the boys sit down to large bowls of thick vegetable soup, homemade bread and watered-down beer.

The innkeeper's wife fusses about, delighted to be an innkeeper again. Ron says,

"Mm, we haven't tasted real bread like this all summer.
Is it possible we could stay here tonight? We could pay;
of course, and perhaps buy some of this delicious bread
to take with us? We do have money".

The innkeeper's wife's eyes light up; she runs her fingers through the boy's long hair,

"We have one large room with two big beds. It's the only one
I have left. The rest are all taken by the alpine patrols.
They won't be back until the day after tomorrow.
I could give you boys haircuts and a bath.
You will all need that before you get into my clean sheets.
Do you have your own soap"?

Ron nods and smiles.

"You have real soap"? She asks earnestly.

Ron nods again.

"I could do some washing for you if you have some".

Dieter nods the innkeeper's wife beams and ladles out second helpings of the thick soup. Another big loaf of bread is put on the table. Frau Hoepner looks hard at each boy; their long hair, tanned fit bodies, their boots too small and worn soft and round. The leather washed almost white from walking for months in soft underbrush. She smiles and nods towards the windows,

"So, you have all been up there in the mountains all summer".

The boys stop eating. She smiles and nods,

"Sure you have. I was born in this house; I know
what young boys look like when they have been in the woods

for a long time. You all smell of the mountains.
It's all right; I don't blame you for running.
If you go back up there next spring, perhaps you could
take my two boys with you; keep them out of the army".
    In the warm barn at the back of the inn Ron has just had his haircut
by Frau Hoepner. Dieter is already sporting his new haircut and is sitting
in a big wooden tub covered with soap. Frau Hoepner gets Dieter to stand
up in the tub, then stands on a stool and pours buckets of cool fresh water
over him to rinse off all the soap. Ken and Hans sit on a bench, wrapped
in big white towels. All their clothes are hanging on a line to dry.
    The innkeeper's son Ludwig pushes their cart into the barn out of
sight and shuts the doors. His mother points her finger at him to join in
the bath. He strips off and jumps into the warm soapy water of the tub.
Ron and Ken jump with him and they rub each other's backs with the big
soapy sponge. The jovial Frau Hoepner pours a wooden bucket of fresh
water over the boys' heads, then stands them up to be washed down with
the big sponge. There is lots of fun and laughter. Soap is so rare and scarce
that the whole family grabs at the chance for the real treat of a hot bath
with real soap.
    Later that evening the boys, all wrapped in big white towels sit
around a warm fire with Frau Hoepner and her son. Their damp clothes
that were washed in the soapy bath water are all drying on lines above
their heads. The new haircuts make them all look so much younger. With
their hands wrapped around big mugs of hot mulled wine they tell the
story of their summer high in the mountains and how they lived off the
land.
    Young Ludwig hangs on every word. Frau Hoepner smiles and says,
    "There are no trains at this village.
    You must go over to Schliersee. It's about twenty kilometers
    around there by road, but you would be better off
    going across country and dodging the patrols. Look".
    Frau Hoepner spreads Ron's map out on the table and the boys
gather around to see.
    "Go north staying on the east side of the road to Tegernsee
    on the lake. There is a footpath that leads west over to
    Schliersee. Ludwig has walked that a few times.
    How far is to Schliersee, Ludwig?"
    Ludwig says, pointing at the map,
    "Oh, about ten kilometers I could take you
    and show you the path, it's very hard to find".
    Ludwig looks at his mother and she nods; he leans over the map,
    "You should camp overnight before you get into Schliersee.
    It's too far to go in one day. That's rough country across there.
    Here is a good place to camp under the mountain. It's the

highest point on the path; it's all downhill from there".
Frau Hoepner says,

"You boys are very lucky you didn't run into any of their
patrols. This village has been a training center for a unit of the
Alpine Corps. We have all their officers staying here and the
men all stay in the Monastery down the hill. They take every
room and pay with this useless army paper money.
They will be back in a day or so. Your best bet is to stay clean
in those uniforms and bluff it out".

Dieter says hopefully,

"Do you really think we could get away with it in Münich,
with all the patrols and police that will be there?"

Frau Hoepner beams,

"Why not, you all look well fed enough to be a part of a
headquarters unit. I wish you could stay here, but the patrols
will be back in a few days"

Frau Hoepner tucks the four boys into the two big beds; a small
wood-burning stove throws light that flickers shadows on the ceiling.
Their faces shine clean in the white sheets, she stokes up the fire for the
night, turns and looks at the boys,

"Good night lads, you will be safe here tonight.
Sleep late in the morning. I won't wake you. You all look
as if you could do with a good long night's sleep".

She walks over to the boys, kisses each one goodnight on his
forehead, blows out the oil lamp and leaves them, closing the door gently.
The fire casts long shadows on the ceiling. Hans is quietly crying. Ron
whispers,

"Hans, what's the matter?"

Hans sniffing,

"I'm so happy… It's so nice here".

Dieter says,

"Hans, the war will be over soon.
Then we can all sleep in beds like this every night".
"Yes but whose bed?"
"Remember our oath Hans, we are all going to stick together".
"Like glue old chaps, like glue".

Ken whispers.

"It's like sleeping on a cloud of feathers, it's so fluffy".

The boys sleep late and are awakened by the wonderful smell of
fresh baked bread. They sit and eat their breakfast with young Ludwig,
who asks,

"Did you see any wolves up there, they say they get
so hungry they will try to chew on your feet while you sleep".

Ken laughs saying,
        "Ho yes a few but they were much more afraid of us
        than we were of them, we saw a few foxes too.
        They too would keep well away. They are up there, we saw
        them from a distance and often you can hear them at night
        but they are too shy to come anywhere near our camp".
    Ludwig, fascinated, asks,
        "So what did you eat all that time?"
Dieter gets up and cuts a thick slice of bread then puts his arm on
Ludwig's shoulder,
        "All the food you can eat is up there boy, fish, fir and greens;
        you just have to work at getting it all in. We ran trap lines,
        fished in the river and grew our own vegetables.
        But I wish we could have made fresh bread like this".
Ludwig helps the lads pick out boots that fit them well, four pairs
taken from a large pile of army officers hiking boots. They had been left
for Ludwig to clean.
        "I wish my brother and I had been up there with you,
        all the boys thirteen and over were taken away for the RAD".
        The R.A.D. (Reightsarbeitsdienst) is a conscripted mandatory
        agricultural unit that was originally meant to supply the farms
        with workers but was drawn on for front line fighting soldiers.
        Thousands of boy's aged 13 to 17 were slaughtered in the front
        lines, that were conscripted through the RAD.
    Ludwig continues,
        "I will get called up soon; they took my father and
        my brother; he's only fourteen, and we haven't
        heard from them in three months".
    Dieter gives the boy a hug,
        "Well… We will come back this way in the spring
        if this war is still going. We will take you up in the hills with us
        for the summer. We will teach you how to survive"
They load five large loaves of fresh baked bread into their cart and
lock it tight. Ron settles their account and counts out a wad of money
into Frau Hoepner's hand to pay the bill. She gives him a kiss and shows
the money to her son. They wave goodbye and stride off down the road.
Their shorts have been washed and pressed, shirts freshly washed, boots
cleaned, Ludwig even washed the cart. They all look clean, healthy and
well fed.

    The boys arrive at the Schliersee station with the flags on their cart
fluttering. They march their cart in and stop at the ticket window. It's
closed. The station is almost empty but for a few uniformed servicemen.
Dieter draws an official-looking envelope from his message pouch, shows

it to Ron. He reads it, then stamps and seals it to make it look genuine.
The boys had put it together at the inn.

It is addressed to....

> General Siegfried Westphal, Chief of Staff
> PRIVATE and PERSONAL
> Classification: (NOT URGENT)

Ron says quietly,

> "The stamps look very official; I hope they are still using the
> same ones, Dieter, you have to do all the talking. Remember
> that we are pretending to have the General's wife's personal
> things in here. We are a part of her staff moving to Munich
> from their place in the country... Please Dieter don't overdo it,
> be natural and slightly pissed off, headquarter people always
> look pissed off for some reason".

Dieter is a little nervous,

> "Yes, yes, all right I know. The General's staff didn't have time
> to get the rail warrants signed... Keep your fingers crossed for
> me. Do I look all right?"

Ken says,

> "Yes, we look as if we belong to a General's staff.
> Look how clean and well fed we all look".

Ken snaps the two padlocks closed on the side of the cart.

Ron whispers,

> "Dieter please be calm.
> Here's enough money. Remember we came here
> by truck or we would have return tickets...
> Go Dieter, they're looking at us".

Dieter takes a deep breath, sets his cap straight and walks to the
ticket office. He bangs on the closed window with a positive and official
rap. After a moment the window opens. A tired old man looks out. He
wears the red-capped uniform of a stationmaster.

He looks at Dieter, then at the three boys and their cart.

> "Yes sergeant?"

> "Four youth singles to Munich please".

The bored old man looks at the cash in Dieter's hand and says
With indifference,

> "No personal travel... Permits or rail warrants only".

Dieter asks assertively,

> "Sir, we are part of General Siegfried Westphal's staff.
> He has moved, but I'm not at liberty to say where...
> We have his wife's personal things to deliver to Munich".

The man closes the window... The boys' faces look a bit worried.

A small door opens and the man comes out. He looks at the boys
then at the cart; he tries to open it.

"Where's the keys?"

"We don't have them sir. Here is a letter for the General".

The man looks hard at the letter,

"Why didn't you show me this in the first place?"

"I will have to write you out warrants.

I will need all your names... I can't take the money either...

Yes, you look too well fed and healthy to be on the run.

You must be General Staff, come on... So they feed you

all very well by the look of it, you're lucky".

The boy's push their cart down the station platform looking at their rail warrants, Ken says,

"It worked, it worked. Now we have to get past the rail police".

The boys stop at the police gate. They all give the older policeman a smart salute. He looks at Dieter and smiles,

"What have we got here? Do you have any food

in the box, where are the keys?"

"Sir, you will have to ask General Westphal's

wife that question, sir".

The policeman looks at their warrant and nods,

"Well General Staff I see; my, you people look well.

Just tell me what you had for breakfast this morning...

You know what I had... Nothing... Platform two,

in forty minutes, if it's still running".

It was a three-hour wait. The boys are getting hungry but they dare not open the cart to get themselves any food, not with hungry soldiers looking at them. The train for Munich eventually arrives. It is slow and very long; so long it doesn't fit the length of the platform. The conductor yells,

"Get the flags down off the cart and

get it into the baggage car at the end of the train".

The boys run to the end of the train and find that half the wagon is taken up with wounded soldiers on stretchers. The wounded in their gurneys are secured to the walls with lengths of rope. A nurse hands Ron a length of rope to secure their cart to stop it from bumping into the stretchers and jolting the wounded. Another nurse with a motherly face says,

"Tie it against the wall tight. We don't want it

bumping the wounded, they have enough pain".

The nurse's faces show the strain and long hours they have been looking after the young wounded. The first nurse gives Hans a plasma bottle to hold steady as the train jerks forward. Soon all the boys are actively working to make the wounded comfortable: steadying gurneys, holding bottles up while the nurses make the wounded more comfortable. After a while the connecting door opens and a military policeman in a green rubber raincoat and a large metal gorget painted over with yellow luminous paint stands at the door. He sees nurses and a section of Hitler Youth coping with a truckload of wounded. The Policeman says,

"You people are doing a fine service
for the Fatherland... Heil Hitler".

He salutes and leaves.

The boys look at the soldiers lying there in pain; some are no older than they are. One young lad, not yet old enough to shave, is looking at Ken and trying to say something, Ken bends down, putting his ear close... Ken says to a nurse,

"He said his foot itches and can he have some water?"

The first nurse whispers to Ken kindly,

"No water, he has a stomach wound
and he doesn't have any feet".

The nurse un-tucks his blanket exposing the wire cage.

Ken sees that both of his legs are off at the knees. She gently strokes the bandages, replaces the blanket.

The first nurse grabs Ken's hand and looks at it,

"Do you have clean fingers?"

Ken holds out his hand. She nods, hands him a tin mug.

"Dip your fingers in this, let him suck them.
Don't let him drink from the mug or you will kill him".

Ken dips his fingers in the mug of blue liquid and holds it dripping to the boy's face. He readily sucks. It gives him relief. The boys look around at the wounded. They are all very young amputees.

The train gets into Munich after many stops, for the last hour they have been travelling very slowly through bombed-out rail sidings. The train lurches to a stop inside Munich station. The two nurses and Dieter's boys each hold onto a gurney to ease the bang as the train stops. Ken watches the railway porter set the wooden ramps against the door, but the ramps have strips of wood nailed across them as foot holds. Ken jumps out and turns the ramps upside-down so the gurneys have a smoother run.

The boys get very involved in easing the trolleys smoothly down the wooden ramps. The nurses and Dieter's platoon make a convoy down the long platform. The tall military policeman pushes the boys' handcart for them, clearing a way through the crowd of soldiers. The nurses thank the boys and are gone with their wounded to the waiting trucks.

The boys look about the station; not much has changed. But the noise and bustle seem so loud after the quiet of their camp. The policeman grins at Dieter's platoon and gives them a big smile,

"So, when did you boys eat last?"
Hans smiles as sweetly as he can, then lies,
   "The day before yesterday, Sir".
The policeman takes off his coat and throws it on the boys' cart.
   "Come on, we will eat with the SS today".
The SS canteen has survived the air raids and is undamaged.
A bowl of watery soup and a chunk of sausage with some hard black
bread are dished up to each boy and the policeman. They carry their mess
trays and sit amongst the SS Officers. After the meal the policeman sits
back and lights his pipe looking hard at Dieter.
   "So how come you're not in the army, how old are you?"
Dieter lies, as cool as a cucumber,
   "Just fifteen sir. We are all on the
   personal staff of General Westphal's home.
   I'm his grandson. Look we have a letter for him".
Ken and Ron look up and see Dieter showing the policeman the
letter out of his pouch. The policeman turns the letter over slowly,
   "General Staff, I thought you all looked a little too clean.
   So where does he live, this General Grandfather of yours?"
Dieter smiles,
   "You know we can't tell you that sir".
The policeman becomes all fatherly,
   "Stay out of the war, don't volunteer for anything,
   you boys wouldn't last three days at the front.
   Survive, that's the word today.
   It can't be too much longer now...
   Ha don't tell the General I said that, Good luck".
The policeman leaves the table and the boys breathe a deep sigh of
relief. Ron says,
   "The General's Grandson, ha, you have a nerve.
   I almost died. What if he had asked you your name?"
   "I would have said Sergeant Dieter Westphal;
   I was ready to snap it out".
   "Don't you think that was a bit risky,
   a General's Grandson, ha"?
Ron points to the wall; there is a big street map of Munich with black
spaces marking the bombed streets. The boys stand looking at the map.
Ron starts to draw black marks on his own map,
   "We have to go to our house on Leopold Strasse first.
   We might be able to live there.
   If not, we'll try the bombsites, burnouts,
   they are mostly south of here. I think we should
   go to the worst damaged areas first".

17 The Cellar

Dieter leans over to look,
   "Do you think we can find a nice warm cellar?"
Hans looking slightly worried says
   "We can have a good look, there's lots of streets and ho,
   we had better keep a sharp look out for shitty Sergeant Steiner
   and his black hat".
Ron and Ken work out a route for their first day in the bombed out districts of Munich. In the main lobby of the station, tired military personnel are lying about on their equipment. Notices on the walls warn everybody 'Beware of Wolf Children, they steal'. The big colored posters, Show pictures of half-starved boys with sick gray faces, stealing a wounded soldier's food out of his backpack.

The little platoon leaves the station with their cart and starts walking through the streets. Passing bombed out buildings and into an area where whole blocks of buildings have been destroyed by fire and bombing. The boys look clean, fit and totally out of place, but walking with their flag flying gives them an official air.

They finally arrive at Leopold Strasse and find the burned out ruins of the beautiful old house where the twins grew up. The two Linden trees that had once cast shade on the front gates have had all the small branches burned off. Ken says, all choked up,
   "Look at all this, that's it then. Nothing left to come home to".
Ron kicks away chunks of burned wood, trying to find his way down to the cellar. Dieter pulls him away,
   "Come on Ron... The building has fallen into the basement.
   This is not for us, it's all gone".
Ron turns away, his tears welling up. He blurts out:
   "Dieter, get off. You are stamping all over our home.
   Wait for us on the road".
Dieter turns and signals to Hans to leave the twins alone.
Ken spots the burned out skeleton of the family's old walnut grand piano that once stood in the living room. All that is left of it now is the blackened harp that has been propped up by vandals, held in place by a section of iron stair banister. Ken runs a stick across it; its still-taut strings emit a crisp and eerie gliss, a sound that causes Ron's head to spin around.
He slowly climbs over the rubble and joins his brother.
Both boys, with their arms over each other's shoulders, tearfully pluck the strings in a duet to the tune of the Cuckoo waltz as they had done so many times before the war as a party piece.
They used to pluck the tune on the piano's harp without touching the keys. Ken turns away before finishing the tune and wanders over and finds the smashed dining room china cabinet. He lifts up a plank from its back and sees a stack of broken crockery. He calls to Ron sobbing,

"Look Ron, at Mum's china cabinet. It's all broken.
All of her Crown Derby is smashed. You'd think
there would be one piece left. It's all smashed".
Ron sniffs,
"None of our stuff, no books, nothing, only this".
Ron holds up a twisted Hornby toy trains' line and tries to bend it
into shape but it just crumples in his hand. He flings it on the pile and
sobs,
"We must take something.
There must be something we can save".
The pile of rubble that was their home has long been picked over by
vandals and bombsite thieves.
All that is left are piles of bricks, smashed timbers and roof slates.
Ken slides down the ruins to the burned out front door that is lying crazily
at an odd angle.
He picks up the letterbox lid and shows it to Ron.
It has the name 'Lambert' deeply engraved in the metal. Ron nods.
Tears are streaming down both boys' faces; Ron puts the letterbox lid
under his jacket.
Ken puts his arm around his brother's neck and whispers,
"Come on Ron, let's get away from this place.
I'm glad we were not in here with Mum and Dad
when the bomb hit"
Ken shoots a glance at his brother,
"You don't think she was here when"…
Ron shakes his head,
"What about the letters from Vienna?"
They all turn sadly and start making their way south. A small scruffy
boy in rags scurries away over the piles of rubble. When they come to a
house that is only partially destroyed, Dieter tries to find his way to the
basement. He scrambles over bricks and smashed wood only to find it is
being lived in by two or three families.
At one storefront, where the upper floors have been burned out,
Dieter sees that the door is off its hinges. Pushing the door aside, he steps
gingerly over the threshold to be confronted by an old man pointing a
shotgun.
"What do you want now boy? We have nothing left,
nothing to give to the Fatherland, nothing to eat…
Go away, or I will shoot you! This is my shop
and it's closed for the duration of the war".
Dieter holds his hands up with an 'excuse me' gesture and hurriedly
joins the others. The old man shouts and waves his shotgun. Wandering
through the streets, the boys try to find a hole or a slit to climb through,
a cellar or store basement to sleep in.

The streets get narrow where the bomb damage has not been cleared.

The roads are not passable for large trucks; even their small handcart has problems getting through.

Dieters platoon turns in to a side street; the houses on both sides of the road are burned and empty.

A pile of wood that seems to have been put there deliberately blocks the boys' way.

Hans and Dieter start to move some of the wood aside, because the way ahead looks interesting.

A street boy about their age wearing a felt hat that's too big for him appears in a doorway just ahead of them, he aims a pistol at Dieter.

"What are you shithead Nazis doing with my wood?

And what are you doing on my street? Fuck Off!"

The boy's voice trembles and breaks showing his adolescence; he starts to walk towards Dieter, still pointing his pistol. Dieter now angry,

"Why me, why me! Why do they all point guns at me?"

A second street boy, with a younger voice, pops up from behind a high pile of rubble and yells,

"Because you're the sergeant, asshole!"

Dieter spins around to see where the second voice is coming from. It is another young dirty face on the top of the heap. He then jumps and runs over the pile of rubble to the street with the agility of a mountain goat yelling.

"Shoot him! Oskar shoot him!"

His squeaky voice echoes in the empty street. Oskar yells,

"Throw out your pistol, Hitler boy,

or I will shoot you where you stand.

Your Nazi police patrols won't come in here will-they Bo?

We shoot them for sport, don't-we Bo... Did you lot get lost?"

Dieter and his little band raise their hands. Dieter shouts,

"We don't have any guns or food...

We are runaways, we deserted".

The two street boys approach. The older one has dirty blond hair, a fair complexion with a few wispy chin hairs and a slight blond mustache. He is about fourteen or fifteen years old, dressed in rags, his grubby white long socks rolled down over his army boots. A soft felt hat has 'Wolf Boy' marked with ink across its front. He walks around the cart and tries to open it; holds his hand out for the keys but Dieter shakes his head. Dieter looks hard at the revolver,

"That's not loaded you grubby little shit, is it?"

With a broad smile, Oskar says,

"But I might have one bullet in the barrel, a live one...

You don't know that do you, asshole?

His voice softens and he grins.
    "My name is Oskar; that's my brother Bo.
    Are you lot really runaways? It looks as if
    you have been eating very well, so you must
    be HJ from Headquarters then".
The other street boy Bo comes up to Hans and stands next to him.
He is a younger version of the first boy but with no hat. It is very obvious
that they are brothers; they look so alike.
Bo sniffs Hans,
    "This one has eaten well today. How can they be runaways?
    What's in the cart, anything to eat four-eyes?"
Then Bo starts to search through Hans' pockets. Dieter moves close
to him with his hand on his knife. Bo backs off. His jacket looks two sizes
too big for him, his shorts too small with the top button undone tied up
with string. No shirt, his skinny ribs showing under the big jacket. Hans
pushes Bo away; the boy shoves him back; punches fly. Dieter and Oskar
break up the fight. Dieter says,
    "Come on, let's get away from here, these two
    little shits have nowhere to live either".
The older boy Oskar comes over to Dieter,
    "Oh yes we do, don't we Bo? Don't go...
    Are you really all runaways?"
    "Yes".
Oskar says gently,
    "All right, don't go, please".
Dieter cautiously,
    "We are looking for somewhere to sleep,
    an empty cellar or basement".
Oskar grins and says mocking,
    "Empty cellar or basement, with or without heat and power...
    Did you escape yesterday from Switzerland?"
Oskar steps back and points at Dieter's uniform.
    "Did your mother wash your shirts?
    Look at the polish on the boots.
    Your shorts have been ironed; so has your shirt.
    No one in Munich irons shirts.
    You haven't lived in Munich lately, have you?
    Did you runaway this morning?"
    "Mm... We arrived today by train".
Dieter turns to walk away; he beckons his little platoon to follow.
Oskar looks at the ground,
    "You can all stay at our place if you make us a meal".
Dieter and Ron look at each other, Ron nods saying.
    "All right let's have a look at your place first".

The two street boys start to walk and Dieter and his boys follow.
Dieter chats on,
>"We ran away from school eight months ago.
>We have been living in the mountains all summer".

Bo asks casually,
>"Much to eat up there?"

Ron replies,
>"Yes, if you know how to catch it".

Bo grabs a shaft of the cart to help but Hans pushes him away.
Hans asks trying to sound cheerful,
>"How far is your place?"
>"Just around the corner.
>Who does your laundry in the woods?"

Ken tries to get friendly,
>"Is it just the two of you?"

Oskar returns the warmth,
>"Yes, I'm a 'Wolf Boy;' my real name is Oskar Kranz.
>This is my brother Bo. I'm fifteen and he's fourteen".

Ron, pointing to Ken and Hans,
>"All three of us are fourteen; Dieter there is sixteen.
>What about your folks?"

Bo says sadly,
>"They're both dead... In the bombing".

Oskar points up the street,
>"We live in our own basement; it used to be our house.
>Next door got a direct hit and wrecked our house.
>It killed our Mum and Dad".

Bo chimes in,
>"No-one can throw us out, it's our house; what's left of it, is".

The boys walk around the corner. On one side of the street all the
houses have been burned to the ground. On the other side, the houses
are bombed wrecks but not burned. It was once a very fashionable street
where doctors and other professionals lived. The little band of six arrives
pushing the cart. They stop outside the end house of a terraced row of
four large houses. The three-story building has lost most of its two upper
floors. The remaining ground floors are filled with the wreckage of the
fallen upper floors. The whole street is deserted. Dieter, looking about,
>"Who lives here?"
>"Just us, we get the odd gang of kids or
>The HJ come snooping, but we throw rocks
>at them or point the pistol. They soon go away".

Bo says, trying to get a word in,
>"A Hitler Youth boy shot at me once but he missed.
>We pelted him with bricks; he didn't come back".

The boys push a section of the fence to one side and pull their cart through. They find themselves in a small overgrown garden.

The two kids replace the fence. High foliage hides an entrance to the basement. An Official City sign with the words 'BEWARE TYPHUS'.

It causes Dieter to hesitate. Bo laughs,

"Don't worry, it keeps most thieves out when we are not there".

They all go down the wide steps in to a large and cavernous basement with brick-built arched ceilings. There is an old iron bed, a few odd bits of clothing hanging on a line drying, a few odd but good quality chairs and a table. In one corner there is a workbench and a tool chest, a big cast iron laundry sink and a tap. Dieter tries the tap: fresh water. Dieter asks,

"Is this all right to drink?"

The brothers nod,

"We drink it".

Dieter moves around checking the place out,

"How long have you two lived in here?"

"All our lives, but we were bombed out and

our Mum and Dad were killed about six months ago".

"You two have lived here for six months?

You're not very organized are you".

"Oh no. We were put in a boys' camp.

We ran away and came back here two weeks ago;

we hated the camp".

Dieter starts to look about, opening cupboards and peering into them. He opens a small door under the stairs,

"A toilet, a real toilet, does this thing work?"

The boys nod, embarrassed by its dirtiness.

Dieter leans in and pulls the chain; the toilet flushes. He spins around with a broad smile, walks over and grabs the older brother by his skinny shoulders. Dieter says beaming,

"It's your lucky day boys, this place has possibilities.

Water; drains that work; all the wood we can burn

just outside for free. Where's the stove?

He looks around... Is there a stove? Well as soon

as we get a stove we will make a nice meal".

The six boys struggle to get their cart through the door and down the stairs... They set about searching through the bombed houses and rescue two large mattresses, chairs, a small black wood-burning stove with an oven, and some chimney piping.

They cut a hole in the ceiling to stick the stovepipe through.

Bo and Oskar chop up wood for the stove.

Ken and Ron clean the toilet. The six struggle with the stove to get it in position. Ken looks up to the roof,
"If you light that stove, it will smoke us all out of here".
Oskar looks up at the smokestack,
"What's wrong with it? It looks all right to me".
Oskar stuffs paper and small bits of wood into the round hole at the top of the stove and throws a match in and closes the lid.
After a few seconds blue smoke starts to seep out of every crack in the old stove. The smokestack starts to leak smoke out of the loose joints. Ken starts to laugh and opens the door. Dieter walks forward and pours water in the hole and the result is worse.
Steam and smoke fill the place and the boys run out laughing. Oskar throws the box of matches to Ken,
"You think you can do better? You have a go,
you light it if you think you're so bloody clever".
When the smoke clears, Ken and Ron set to tightening the chimney pipe sealing it with mud and pliers. A good fire is lit and soon the place is warm without smoke and fumes.
Dieter takes a padlock key that's on a cord around his neck and unlocks one of the cart's padlocks and Ron unlocks the other with his own key on a similar cord. Soon there is a pot of stew steaming on top of the stove and a big old kettle is filled with water from the laundry tap.
The table is set; Ken comes over with a large can of ham from the cart. Each boy gets a big chunk. Dieter serves out large portions of the thick stew with slices of Frau Hoepner's fresh baked bread and a jug-full of hot chocolate. The boys all tuck in like hungry teenagers with lots of mm's and Oh's.

After dinner while Ken and Bo are washing up the dinner dishes, Oskar spreads his map out on the table and shows Dieter where they are. Ron makes up the two beds on the newly acquired mattresses. Later, when all six boys are sitting around the table, Dieter lights a stub of candle. Ron looks at Oskar and Bo,
"So how often do you two eat like this?"
They shake their heads, Ron says,
"Not that often, well we could all eat well all the time,
but we have to make a plan".
Ken and Hans look at each other smiling and mime together...
"He has to make a plan".

18. WOLF BOYS

Dieter asks,
"Do you two have any ration cards?"
They shake their heads.
"Neither do we. So no ration cards.
Do you trade on the black market?"
They shake their heads. Dieter smiles,
"So how do you eat?"
Oskar looks at his brother,
"We beg... At the station and bus stops...
We rake over the freshly bombed out houses.
Sometimes you find stashed tinned food.
We go around the kitchens of the big restaurants.
Some of the trash has enough food for days".
Ron smiles,
"You two run the streets looking like Wolf Children".
Bo grins,
"We are Wolf Boys".
Hans teases,
"We saw posters in the station and
in the SS canteen about Wolf Children".
Bo says,
"You were in the SS canteen and got out alive?"
The boy's nod and grin. Oskar says,
"Well we have no parents, no papers no ration cards
and we have run away from a boy's camp for delinquents.
Getting our folks killed in the bombing made us delinquents,
so we are real wolf children, I'm a wolf boy and so are you four,
you're just a bit cleaner than us and in uniforms, that's all".
Bo goes over to the corner and brings out a rolled up poster that
looks as if it had been torn off a wall.
"Like this."
Bo slowly unrolls the poster. It has a picture of a pair of teenagers
in rags, with thin drawn faces and deep-set eyes, dark with the signs of
malnutrition. They are stealing from a sleeping wounded soldier. Ken
reads the message under the picture.

BEWARE OF THE ROBBER WOLF BOYS!
A new pest has arisen in our cities, lost and runaway young boys,
'Wolf Boys'; they prey on unwary soldiers, robbing them.
Some of these robbers are very young, ten to sixteen.

Attention: Robber Wolf Boys are deceptive.
They tell touching stories but offer little or no services.
They seem very pathetic and lost. But beware!
Remember the 'Wolf Boy' has winning ways, before you know it;
his teeth are at your throat. Beware of the 'Wolf Boys'! They Steal.

Ken asks,

"Oskar, so why do you have a hat with Wolf Boy on it?
Running the streets, looking like that, you must be targets.
However do you get around town without getting arrested?"

Bo laughs,

"We can run fast".

Ron explains,

"Your looks keep you here in the ruins.
If you looked like us, you could go anywhere".

Ken says,

"When you saw us you thought we were an HJ patrol, right?"

Bo nods but his brother looks suspicious,
Dieter says softly.

"We have to get you cleaned up so you can join our patrol".

Oskar is now getting angry,

"So why do we have to look like you?
We ran away from two rotten meals a day at camp
to get away from all that shitty Nazi stuff".

Ken reminding them,

"Ha, you don't have to look like this all the time.
We are as free as birds. We don't believe all that
Nazi shit either. We don't look like this all the time".

Hans says to Oskar and Bo,

"In the mountains we didn't wear very much at all".

Oskar and Bo look at each other and shrug their shoulders.
Dieter says,

"With our belts and message pouches and bicycles,
We look like active messenger boys.
"We can get in anywhere, hospitals, army barracks…"

Oskar screws up his nose and whispers,

"But why? What bicycles?"

"To get food. They feed messenger boys, no questions asked…
But you have to look as if you are messengers".

Ken says a touch boastfully.

"It works; we were all very well fed at the
SS staff canteen at the station for lunch today".

Oskar and Bo are very impressed; both nod. Bo brings out two
Hitler Youth caps. Oskar asks,

"So where are your bikes?"

278

Ron laughs,
"They are keeping them at the Message Office
in the station for us, we can pick them up any time
we want, there's about thirty good bikes there".
Bo cries out defiantly,
"Oh yes… You go in there and take them; just like that?"
"Yes, just like that", Ron teases.
"We have the belts and pouches and duty armbands,
we used to be messengers, we stole all the things we need,
with duty armbands on, we can get into anywhere.
We could walk in to the SS Barracks where
we dined today and say we were on duty".
Bo is impressed,
"And they would feed you, just like that?"
Ron grins,
"Well they did today didn't they Ken?"
Ken smiles and nods Dieter changes the subject and asks,
"So, any neighbors living in the cellars next door?"
"No, we are the only ones on this street.
Who would want to live here?"
"Have you ever looked in any of your neighbors' basements?"
The street brothers shake their heads,
"There is no way in through the wreckage".
Dieter goes over to the walls and bangs them with his fist.
"How thick are these walls?"
Bo shrugs his shoulders. Dieter points to a wooden air duct that goes
through the basement wall to the next house.
Dieter climbs up on a box, bangs the air duct,
"We could get through there, if we took this duct out".
Bo says out loud,
"I don't think our neighbor Herr Wuzen would like that".
Oskar condescendingly says,
"I don't think Her Wuzen will mind.
He's dead, so is his wife".
Ron proposes,
"We have to make an escape route out, so if we are attacked,
we could all escape by climbing through the cellars
and emerge at the end of the street".
Ken says,
"At this moment we could be trapped in here
like rats with only one door to get out".
Hans asks,
"Have you ever tried to get into
the other cellars from the outside?"

"Yes but they're all blocked up".
Dieter reminds them,
    "Good, it will keep visitors out.
    Our first job in the morning is to break through,
    see what we can find and make an escape route
    for ourselves. May save our lives one day
    we could get out and come up behind them".
Ken echoes,
    "There may be some canned food in one of the cellars,
    something they had stashed for emergencies".

The group gets settled in the three beds. Hans blows the candle out.
The next morning, Dieter's boys, wearing old clothes from Oskar and Bo, break down the wooden air duct.

The square tube comes out of the wall with a cloud of dust, making a hole big enough for a slim boy to pass through. Dieter and the boys scramble through, leaving Ken and Bo to keep watch on top of the wrecked house. In the next-door basement, the boys tumble through, they see daylight cutting through the wreckage of the cellar roof. They rummage about. Hans holds up a wooden box full of candles. Ron finds a large sledgehammer.

Dieter starts to work on the second wall to cut through to the next basement, making a hole at ground level. The boys take turns at the hammer and Dieter quickly realizes just how out of condition Oskar is. He can hardly swing the heavy hammer, so Hans takes over for him.

Ken and Bo take a break and sit on the top of the pile of rubble that used to be Bo's home. They are keeping a watchful eye out for strangers. Ken is lying back, letting the weak late autumn sun warm his face.
Bo asks,
    "How did you four live up there in the mountains?
    Weren't you worried about wolves or snakes?"
Ken smiled,
    "We lived very well…
    There are few wolves and no snakes where we were up there;
    not even the ones in black uniforms with guns…
    We have a secret camp deep in the woods, high up in the
    mountains where no one ever goes… It's by a small fresh-water
    lake on a river with plenty of fish in it".
Bo is getting very curious,
    "So, how did you all eat?"
    "We ran trap lines for rabbits, hares and some birds.
    Eggs from the birds' nests, berries and roots; we had a bit
    of a garden and grew potatoes, carrots and all sorts of
    vegetables. And it all went into the stew pot.

We ate once a day. It's a good life up there".
"So why did you all come back here to Munich?"
"Well in the winter the ground freezes solid, the small animals
hibernate... It's too cold to live in a tent. We would die of the
cold. The ground freezes so you can't get at the roots".
"Me and Oskar... We are very glad you're all staying here
to look after us. How did you learn all that survival stuff,
who taught you all that?"
"The school we were at; it's about the only thing they ever
taught us that was of any use. That and how to read a map
and navigate up there in the woods".

Ron and Oskar arrive looking all dusty, with rags around their
mouths. Ron mutters through his mask,
"Wow it's nice up here... We busted through to the second
basement. We found a box of candles and a radio, but it won't
work because we have no electricity".

Bo and Ken get up to go. Ron says,
"Hang on a bit, Hans and Dieter are going mad bashing
through the walls down there. Oskar almost passed out;
He's so weak and under-nourished... You people haven't been
eating so well lately. Dieter says that you are excused from wall
duty from now on. You have to get your strength back first".

The boys all lay back and soak up the sun. In the distance they can
hear the thump of Dieter's hammer. Oskar asks with a grin,
"Any girls up there in the woods?"

Ken shakes his head. Oskar looks at a blister on his hand and shows
it to Ken. He smiles.
"Honest labor, buds of toil".

Dieter and Hans pop up through the rafters, very excited,
"Hey, come and see what we have found".

All the boys climb back down through the debris to the cellar.

The boys all scramble through into the third cellar. It's very clean
and dry with little or no structural damage. Most of the space is taken up
with shelves. It is a storeroom with rows of preserve jars full of fruit,
potatoes, tomatoes, bottled eggs and a hanging slab of bacon. There's
three sacks of flour, tins of biscuits, large jars of jam, canned beans,
canned stews in cartons: enough food to feed them all for a long time.
The boy's light candles and with excitement peer into the shelves like a
bunch of kids let loose in a toy shop at Christmas. Ron says,
"The people who own all this must be dead
or they would have got some help and dug it all out".

Oskar says quietly,
"They are dead... They were buried
at the same time as our folks".

Dieter becomes official,
"All right... We tell no one about this, no one at all.
We could all get killed for just a small bit of this".
Bo picks up an old soccer ball, holds it up triumphantly.
"Look, this is our ball. It went over their fence, remember
Oskar? We asked for it back and they wouldn't give it to us.
They said it broke their flowers".
Dieter waves Bo to hush. The boys walk around looking at the store
of food. Ken calls and the boys go around to see the back row of shelves.
Hangings in nets are sausages, and cheeses.
Dieter murmurs,
"We tell no-one at all. The black market people
would slit our throats without the slightest hesitation,
just to get their hands on this lot".
Ron reminds them,
"We should finish our escape route, hide the exit hole
in our basement and take only what we need from here".
Ken smiles,
"We will eat well tonight".
Dieter jokes,
"Work first; let's see what's in the fourth basement".
All the boys' faces are looking at Dieter, he waves his hands in the
air and relents,
"Listen, let's open one tin of the French biscuits, a small one.
Share them and no one touches anything after... Right...
Tonight I'll cook dinner, it'll be like Christmas, what a dinner".
The boys, all excited, choose a small square tin of French assorted
sweet tea biscuits. They all stand around quietly as Dieter and Ron open
the factory sealed tin, it hisses.
Ron slowly takes off the lid, gently peels back the white crepe paper
and reveals the little square sections separated by soft white paper, each
with a different flavor. Dieter makes six little stacks, one for each boy,
snapping two biscuits in half so the total contents of the tin are equally
shared. Dieter nods to Bo.
"Youngest first".
Ken steps forward holding up his hand.
"We are fourteen too, what month was your birthday?"
Bo says,
"April".
Ken throws his hands in the air,
"We are May, so you're a month younger".
Bo takes a moment to choose then carefully picks up a pile.
The rest all grab. With lots of smiles and 'Yums'. Bo says,
"We don't have to save these till later, do we?"

Hans laughs saying,
  "No, these are to eat right now, no need to save these till later
  Mm, what a treat".

The boys start to dig with new vigor, Dieter breaking the wall into
the fourth cellar with his hammer, the rest clearing the rubble away. Ron
pokes his head in, looks back and says,
  "Nothing in here"
The cellar door gets forced open with a crack and a cloud of dust. A
cut of harsh sunlight streaks in and lights up the place. The boys look at
each other and see their own black faces covered in soot and giggle.
  Dieter and Ron stay and carefully cover up the broken cellar door
with debris and then remove all traces of their breakout.

It is a warm happy basement. Dieter has cooked up a feast.
The boys are eating, laughing, joking.
The weather grows colder. The stove with the oven has been rigged
better; a new potbelly-heating stove has also been added. A heap of
firewood is piled in one corner. Holes in the roof have been fixed. There
is now a secret panel and a large cabinet hiding the breakthrough. A small
tin bath hangs on the wall.
  One evening they are all sitting around the table with a single candle,
playing cards. The air raid sirens start their wail. The boys put down their
cards. Bo looks up to the strong steel beams that once held a three-floor
house,
  "We will be all right. I don't think they will bomb the same
  house twice, will they? We have been bombed out and fire
  bombed, so we have had our share, haven't we?"
Oskar adds
  "Twice: bombed on Monday, fire incendiaries on Tuesday".
Ken looks scared,
  "Oskar, so where's the best place to be in here during a raid?
  Is this the strongest arch? Will that steel hold?
  Ho, I have to take a piss".
A few moments later Ron goes over to the toilet and opens the door.
Ken is sitting on the seat; his pants are still on, his hands are over his ears,
  "Leave me alone".
Ron gets hold of his arm. He is terrified and shaking like a leaf.
  "Ken, come on; let's get under the bed. We will be safe there".
Ron leads Ken across the basement and all four boys grab their
blankets and hide under the iron bed frame. The bombing gets closer and
chunks of the plaster from the old ceiling start to fall. The heavy bombs
are now crashing in the next street. The shock waves make the bed frame
jump in the air and knock the breath out of the boys. Ron and Ken stare

at the big iron girders in the roof of the basement. Ken starts to sob in deep trembling breaths. He is shaking all over,

"I can't stop shaking Ron. Will they hold Ron?
If one hits us, will they hold?"

Ron wraps his arms tight around his terrified brother and tries to hide his own fear,

"Yes they will hold. They did the first time this place got hit,
didn't they, didn't they Oskar?"

The bombs keep banging all around them. Bo starts to whimper,

"I've got to get out of here. I've just got to get out
of this fucking rat trap".

He slides out from under the bed and makes for the door.

Dieter heads him off and grabs him and lifts him off his feet. His skinny frame is not much for Dieter to carry.

He slides him back to his brother's arms under the bed. His brother yells,

"Bo, it's all the same. We will all die if we get a direct hit.
We wouldn't know what hit us".

The bombing gets further away and the ground-shaking stops. Trickles of dust fall on the table.

Each boy tries to look brave, but is very scared. The anti-aircraft guns stop hammering and blasting. From under the bed, Ron starts to sing,

"Oh dear what can the matter be,
Seven old ladies got locked in the lavatory".

Ken sings along with Ron,

"They were there from Friday till Saturday,
Nobody knew they were there".

The sound of the bombs drifts away to another part of the city.

The boys crawl out from under the bed, pick up their cards, blow off the dust, and resume the game, smiling and joking with relief.

Bo is white as a sheet, mostly from powder plaster from the ceiling; he says with a trembling voice,

"On their way back they will drop
the fire incendiary bombs. They always do".

Ken looks up from his cards. His face is white with fear that's hidden by the dust,

"They're coming back, tonight?"

Before the boys finish their card game the anti-aircraft guns start thumping away again and the boys all dive for cover under their beds. They wait for the bombs, the magnesium flares start coming down with their smoky red fog. Then the widespread pitter-patter of the firebombs. Dieter looks out from under the blanket he's sharing with Hans,

"Listen... hear the pops? Magnesium incendiaries,
that's what they are... I'm glad we broke open
the cellar walls; at least we have a way of getting out...
We won't get trapped and burn if we get hit with a few".

The guns stop as abruptly as they started. The boys slowly emerge from under the bed and out to the garden. They climb up the pile of rubble that was once Bo and Oskar's house and now forms the roof of their cellar. The city of Munich skyline is on fire; the night sky is red and black with smoke from all the burning houses. The searchlights in the distance are still raking the smoky sky looking for stragglers. Ron says,

"Look at those fires. I wonder how many people died tonight."

Ken takes a deep breath, smelling the acrid city air,

"At least it wasn't us. We are all still here right?
That's what's important isn't it?"

The cellar is decorated for Christmas 1944; a small tree has bits of paper decorations and a paper star on the top. One wall is stacked to the rooftop with broken and chopped firewood.

Two stoves are burning brightly. The gaps in the walls and roof have been filled in and stuffed with rags to keep the cold weather out. The boys are all sitting around the table with the remains of their Christmas dinner. Thick candles burn brightly on the table. Dieter proposes,

"We are lucky, we have food, and good friends...
With this mug of water I want to make a toast".

He raises his mug,

"To us, may we all get through this stupid war and survive"...

The boys shout,

"Survival!"

Ron gets all serious and stands up,

"Let's make an oath... Let none of us in this room
ever betray or tell on each other. Ever... all right?
To loyalty".

The boys all shout,

"Loyalty!"

The boys jump into their beds, Ron says,

"No bombs tonight; its Christmas".

The cellar looks warm, with the glow from the two fires casting red and black shadows across the broken ceiling. Dieter packs down the fires for the night. Ken says,

"It's Christmas night, we should think about loved ones
who we miss, or a good time we once had with someone
we loved. Bo, you're the youngest; you start".

Bo thinks for a bit,

"No I'm not sure what to say... Start with the oldest, Dieter".

"Yes, I'm the oldest, I'm the ripe old age of sixteen now...
My best memory, Mm... does it have to be Christmas
or can it be any time of our life?"
"Anything you like".
Dieter starts,
"Well my best memory was when I was twelve.
I went on a camping trip with my dad one autumn.
Just the two of us, no mothers or sisters, just my dad and me.
We went to Austria in a beautiful wood by a big lake.
No tent, just fishing gear and just one sleeping bag I shared
with my dad. We caught fish and cooked them on the open fire.
I got to know my dad on that trip, we talked and talked about
everything, he knew so much about all sorts of things. When it
got cold we cuddled up to keep warm at night under the stars.
It didn't rain at all. We hiked all around the lake the next day
and went to a cafe. There were some Austrian Hitler Youth.
I let them all know he was my dad. I was so proud of him...
I loved my dad so much more after that holiday"...
Dieter's eyes blink and the tears run down his cheeks...
"Now I don't know where he is, or where they have taken him".
Dieter is all choked up and sniffs, takes a swig of his water and gets
into bed. Oskar says brightly,
"Our happy times were at the Circus Krona".
Bo nods and smiles,
"Yes that's the best time, you tell it for both of us Oskar".
"Well it was before we were bombed out.
Our Mother came home with four tickets to the circus.
She used to know the usherettes there. We got very good seats
in the front. It was the first time we had ever been to the circus
and Mother's friend had told the clowns where we were sitting
and who we were".
Bo excited,
"Tell them, Oskar. Tell them about the clowns".
"When the clowns came on, they called us by our names.
They pulled Bo and me out in to the center of the ring...
We were asked to hold the fire ring and to throw whitewash
over the clowns. Then they gave us a bucket that looked as if it
had whitewash in it and told us to throw it over the audience.
We did, but it only had cut-up paper in the bucket;
but it looked just like water and the people thought we
were chucking whitewash all over them. What a laugh".
The boys laugh, Bo smiles to himself, says,
"Our Mum and Dad laughed so hard, Dad fell off his bench".

Bo's face is streaming with tears. He looks at his brother's face who is also crying. Bo buries his face into Oskar's chest.

Oskar puts his arm around his little brother,

"Go on Bo… It's good to cry".

Ken jumps out of bed and blows out the candles to hide the Kranz brothers' tears. Now the cellar is lit only by the red light of the stoves. Hans says cheerfully,

"My turn?"

Dieter replies,

"Yes Hans, we don't know very much about you at all".

Hans quite casual,

"My best time was this summer up in the mountains
with you bunch of idiots".

Ken asks,

"What about your folks Hans?"

"I don't remember much about my mother and him, I don't want to remember…
My happiest time was learning to swim with you lot, in the mountains, when I swam across the lake with Dieter…
I wasn't scared in the water for the first time in my life".

Ron teased,

"Is that it then, don't you know anyone nicer than us?
Poor little shit, we're the nicest people he knows".

Hans nods his head.

"Who's next?"

Ron sits up,

"Us, Christmas of 1938 at home with Mum and Dad and Aunt Inga. The big Christmas tree, shopping, walks in the park…
Last summer in the mountains".

Ken agrees,

"Yes the mountains.
We have to go back next year and take these two with us".

Ken looks at Ron and laughs,

"What about the cross channel ferry from England;
when it was very bad weather and the sea was so rough.
Everyone on board was so seasick except us.
We were walking about on deck; you with big ham and cheese sandwiches and me with a big egg salad sandwich eating them in front of the most seasick looking people, making them run for the side of the ship…
Ha, what a lark".

Oskar asks,

"Ken, tell us about the mountains; they sound beautiful".

Ken yawning says,

"Ron tells it better than me".
Ron quietly,
   "No you tell it".
Ken turns over to face Oskar and Bo,
   "Well, we have a camp in a very well hidden valley,
   a place you would go to get lost. It's not on the way to
   anywhere, so people don't have to go past by us at all.
   It's deep in the woods by a stream with a little lake of shallow
   warm water to drink and swim in. We have a heavy tent with
   soft bracken under our beds. A rock-built hearth for cooking
   and a pit for sitting around and keeping warm.
   We eat well off the land, running trap lines for rabbits and
   hares. Birds' eggs in the springtime. Picking berries, roots,
   watercress, and dandelion leaves with wild spinach.
   It all goes into the pot. It's a full time job
   just to stay alive, but it's a good life.
   When we first arrived the ground was still frozen
   but when it thawed out, we planted some seed potatoes,
   carrots and turnips… It's all still up there, in the ground
   and will be ready for when we get there next spring.
   Pots, pans, a heavy tent, trap wires, all you need to survive,
   all hidden in our secret valley".
Dieter, Hans and Ron are asleep. Oskar and Bo are wide-awake; eyes
wide open hanging on to Ken's every word. Oskar says quietly,
   "Will you take us there in the summer?"
Bo asks,
   "Why can't we go now?"
Oskar whispers,
   "It's too cold, we would freeze".

Ken continues,
   "The snow covers everything. Most of the animals, go to sleep
   underground for the winter. We would all starve".
Bo laughs,
   "They are not too stupid are they?
   Sleeping through the cold winter; how do they eat?"
   "They don't; they just sleep a long sleep,
   nice and warm in their burrows under the frost…"
   "Good night".
   "I will dream of your beautiful mountains. Goodnight".
   "You will take us… Ken… Ken?"
   "Shh, he's asleep".

19. SGT. STEINER

The weather turns very cold, so the boys have been confined to the cellar for eight days, waiting for the freezing rain and winds to subside. None of them have any winter warm clothing. Today the sun has come out, it's warmed up a little and the winds have dropped. So Dieter Hans and the twins have ventured out and are on their way to the park. Bo and his brother don't look too well so they stay in the cellar.

They want to try to barter or swap some food for warm overcoats, caps, scarves and gloves for all six of them. There is a fine covering of winter snow blowing around like powder. Dieter, Hans and the twins are dressed in their thin Hitler Youth uniforms, with no overcoats, pushing their cart, using woolen socks as gloves. They approach the large army barracks. Dieter halts his little platoon and leans toward his boys,

"This is the place. Why don't we just have a look
in here; we might find something".

Ron looks very apprehensively at the guard sitting in his box.

"Dieter, don't overdo it, just tell him we have
a message for his commanding officer".

With their ski caps flaps pulled down over their ears, HJ belt pouches and armbands, pushing their cart with its flag fluttering, they approach the army barracks looking as if they belong there. The guard is in the small pillbox with its door closed, trying to keep warm.

Dieter pulls out a fat official envelope with very important-looking stamps all over it.

He shows it to the guard through his glass window. The guard waves them to open the gate themselves. They push the heavy iron gate open, walk through and the gate closes with a clang behind them on its own spring.

The twins march smartly in front and Dieter and Hans in the rear. Dieter thinks it looks as if they were on duty that way.

The barracks are almost deserted. A soldier rides by on a bicycle. Ron asks him the way to the Officers' Mess. The soldier points and the boys take off smartly. They stop outside the kitchen.

The place is deserted. It's 3pm by the big clock in the parade square. The boys look casually around.

Dieter slips through the kitchen door, emerging seconds later with two overcoats and a wad of gloves. He approaches the cart; Ron opens the lid and the warm clothes disappear into the cart. The lid shuts tight almost on Dieter's fingers.

They resume their march and stop outside a small brick building.

A sign on the door says Radio Communications, Ron peers through

the window and then ducks down. Dieter gets into a huddle with the
other boys; they make a quick plan. Dieter starts them all counting; Hans
and Ken go to the front door. Dieter and Ron go around to the rear door.
Ken and Hans wait for a moment; counting to themselves... They open
the front door wide. Dieter walks into the rear door at the same time. Ken
stands at the wide-open front door smiling. The Sergeant stands up and
the other two men glare at Ken. The sergeant yells,
>"Shut that fucking door".

Ken takes his time moving in, so Hans delays closing the door.
Sergeant now very angry,
>"Come on, shut it boy!"

The sergeant stands up as if to walk to Ken. Ken fumbles with his
papers and asks very politely,
>"Is this the Officers' Mess?"

While all the attention is focused on Ken and Hans at the front door,
Dieter has slipped through the back door, quickly looks around and picks
up all the coats, gloves, warm scarves and ski caps that are hanging on the
pegs by the back door. He leaves as quietly as he arrived.

He piles his booty into the cart and shuts the lid.

The sergeant is now livid,
>"Are you going to shut the fucking door?!"

Ken smiling says,
>"Sorry, yes, we are looking for"...

The sergeant exasperated yells,
>"Out, out, go away. I don't care who the hell
>you're looking for; just get out, and shut that door!"

Ken and Hans leave and close the door. They meet Dieter with a
broad grin on his face.

The boys march back to the gates, salute the guard who's still
warming himself in his box. Dieter puts his hand up as if to say,
>"Don't get up, we can let ourselves out".

The guard waves them through. As soon as they are around the
corner and clear of the barracks, they dive into the cart and put on the
gloves, long wool scarves and sort themselves out warm overcoats. Hans
says,
>"We look older in these army coats,
>but at least we will be warm lads".

The boys arrive back at their home cellar. Dieter stops in his tracks
as he spots that the fence has been pulled to one side.

Wide tracks have been made in the snow by a truck or a car crashing
its way through the bushes and knocking down the fence. Dieter draws
his knife and looks around. The boys creep forward cautiously... The
cellar door has been broken and swings loose. Dieter puts his finger to

his lips for silence, nods for the boys to follow. The rest of the boys draw their knives and creep down into the cellar.

The place is a shambles, beds turned over and most of the things that were on shelves are scattered all over the floor.

Oskar and Bo are missing. The boys maintain silence.

Ken points to the breakthrough, the panel hiding it has been ripped off. Ken puts his hand up to Ron's cash hiding hole and pulls out the Lamberts' money tin. It is still intact. He replaces it back deep in the hiding-hole. Ken opens the toilet door and lifts up the short floorboards. Candles, matches, flash light batteries, Oskar's gun are all still there. He takes out the small pistol, pushes off the safety catch. Dieter creeps over to the breakthrough and listens. They hear quiet whimpering. Dieter shouts boldly,

"Who's in there?"

He turns and yells to Ken who is standing close to him,

"Ken, give me the shot gun quick".

Ken looks around puzzled whispering,

"What shotgun"…

Dieter looks at Ken with a pleading look and whispers,

"Just pretend we've got a shot gun, you twit!"

A small voice from the hole in the wall bleats weakly,

"Dieter, don't shoot… It's me Bo…

Oskar is here too and he's hurt very bad,

don't shoot; it's us in the corner".

Dieter and Ron scramble through and into the storeroom. It has been stripped almost bare; the shelves are empty, everything taken. Oskar is lying in the corner unconscious with Bo sitting holding his brother's head. The Krantz brothers look as if they have put up a fight. Dieter calls Ron and Ken to give him a hand,

"Come on, let's get you two out of here... Where's he hurt?"

Bo still whimpering,

"He stuck Oskar with a bayonet, then bashed him with a rifle…

He is still breathing".

Oskar gets gently stretched out on the table. He has a nasty cut over his eye. Blood is pulsing out of a big stab wound in his shoulder. Ken arrives with the army first aid kit. He cuts the bloody shirt away with the scissors and slightly raises Oskar's arm. A spurt of fresh blood comes from the wound. Ken takes charge,

"We have to get stitches in this cut or he will bleed to death…

Keep pressure on each side of the cut. Push it together.

That will stop the bleeding a bit. Someone stoke the fire up

and get some water boiling we need to sterilize the needle

and forceps. Let's do it before he wakes up".

The boys bustle about. A pot is soon boiling on the stove.

They put the cellar door back in its frame and the fires warm up the place. Ken threads the curved needle drops, it with some strong-looking forceps into the boiling water and says.

"We have to hold him tight;

the stitches may wake him up.

Ron, you get his legs".

Ken goes to work with the needle and thread whilst Oskar is still unconscious. When it's all over, Bo bathes his head with cold water and Oskar starts to wake up and groan. All groggy, he says,

"Shit I'm cold… Oh did they take everything?"

Ron hands Oskar a drink of water, points to his shoulder and peers into Oskar's face,

"Ken sowed you all up".

"I'm dizzy".

Ken says,

"Oskar you are going to be all right now.

You're cold because you have lost a lot of blood.

I have sewn you up, you will be all right now".

Oskar looks at his wound and the eight neat stitches, with the tufts of thread bristling up, his eyes roll up and he passes out again.

The cellar gets set up and put back together. Oskar lies in his bed propped up with rolled-up blankets and all the pillows. He comes around again and groans as Ron bathes his face,

"Ow, my head hurts… Oh, we couldn't do a thing;

it was a big shit in a truck and he had a boy with him.

They knew about the food stash… Did they take everything?"

Ron nods, Oskar cries,

"Oh no, Oh no, shit… what, everything!?"

Bo says,

"I think I know who they are.

The young one is Alf, he was at my school".

"The older one is his cousin Peter.

He had the rifle with the bayonet on the end of it.

He struck Oskar and bashed him on the head".

Dieter asks Bo,

"Do you know where they live?"

Bo thinks for a while, then says,

"No, they have a bike repair shop somewhere".

Oskar remembers,

"Alf's mother used to work at the same factory as our mum.

She was very friendly with the family who had the cellar

full of food".

Dieter gets all concerned,
"We will sort these people out later".
Hans and Ron finish putting the door back together. Ken helps
Oskar with his clean shirt and makes an arm sling for him. Hans closes
up the breakthrough,
"Well they have cleaned almost everything,
but they missed all these".
Hans holds out a bunch of long fat sausages,
"Half a bag of potatoes, there are a lot more sausages
on top of the shelves they missed, so these should last
us for a week or two. What will we eat then?"
Dieter nods,
"So, then we go to work, we go to work at
getting our food back. A stockpile of food like that
will start showing up on the black market soon.
Now it's our turn to start dealing, only we will do it
properly. We have our master planner, Ron here".
Dieter goes over to Ron and puts his arm around his shoulder.
The boys are glum and quiet, sitting around the table. Oskar looks
as if he has been in a war, his arm in a sling, his face is all swollen and he
has a big plaster over his eye. Bo has a black eye, and his cheek is all
swollen up too. He is wearing one of the overcoats that Dieter stole.
Dieter divides up a Spartan dinner of potatoes and some slices of sausage
meat. It is eaten quickly. Ken says,
"Well this is it then, this won't last long?"
Dieter nods,
"Oskar and Bo, you two, stay here and rest tomorrow.
Us four will go out and see what we can buy on the black
market. How did you lot eat before we came along?
Where did you get your food from?"
Bo smiles,
"Well, we didn't eat that often. We made the rounds
of the restaurants; you should see what they throw out
of their kitchens sometimes.
If people have money they can always find a meal,
so when they cook they throw away some leftovers.
Some of the stuff is very good".
Dieter turns his nose up,
"What sort of stuff is good?"
Bo replies,
"Potato peelings, outside leaves off the cabbages.
Once we got a whole pile of bones from half eaten chops;
it made a bit of a stew".

Ron gathers up some paper bags and starts to fold them so that they fit into their pouches,
"We will all take these bags and bring everything home.
We share everything; that's how we will stay alive.
We should split up tomorrow and go out in pairs".

The next day Ron and Ken find their way to the station and wander into the crowd. Ron says,
"If I grab something to eat, we run, go our separate ways,
then meet up later at the bus station; all right?"
Ken nods. They look very official with their almost new greatcoats over their uniforms. The armbands, message pouches, and belts with cross straps give the boys a 'On duty' air. They wander through the station staying away from the message office. The vast station lobby is teeming with service people, many soldiers, walking wounded sitting on their kit, waiting. There are hardly any civilians since travel is restricted. On one side of the station lobby the big wide doors are open and a long line of soldiers are standing waiting to be served from a truck that's backed up to the doors.

They are being served chunks of black bread, a small sausage and a mug of brown coffee substitute. A big notice over the truck proclaims.

MILITARY PERSONNEL WITH TRAVEL WARRANTS ONLY

Ron leans over to Ken and whispers,
"Shall we ask them if we can give them a hand?
We might be able to whip some of the sausages".
The boys make their way around to the side of the truck. There is a fat sergeant sitting on the running board. Ron is extra polite,
"Excuse me sergeant.
We have just been dismissed from the message office early.
Our sergeant told us to come over here and give you a hand.
Well, because there's not too much activity in the radio room".
The fat sergeant looks up at the boys and starts to laugh,
"You two must think I just came out of the toilet
with my pants down... Not too much activity
in the radio room, Ha, Ha. At least that's a new one.
I have heard every scam excuse there is to get food off
this truck. So why don't you two just fuck off
to your radio room and let them feed you".
Ron smiles as sweetly as he can,
"But we are hungry sergeant, if you could see your way to"...
"Just sod off... everybody is hungry".

Ken nods towards the fat sergeant's stomach and points saying,
"I bet you're not too hungry, are you sergeant".
The sergeant makes a rude sign and waves them away.
The boys thank the sergeant and wander back into the station.
"He didn't look very hungry, Ken,
do you want to try the SS canteen?"
Ken nods as he watches a soldier eating a sausage out of his mess
tin. Ron looks up to the big clock. It's almost four pm. and they haven't
eaten since yesterday.

Ken nods to an officer sitting on his cases with his foot in a large
dressing. He nods back. They wander on through the station lobby
passing groups of military sitting on their kit. Ron says,
"Yes let's try the SS canteen".
They find there is a guard at the SS canteen door.
He laughs at their reasons for wanting to eat there and sends them
on their way. The twins wander back across the crowded station looking
at the food tins used by the service men hoping to find a half-eaten
sandwich or sausage that has been left. They look hopefully in the trash
basket, but it's empty.
"Stand still you two! Stand still!"
An acid voice they recognize sends a chill through both boys.

They freeze in their tracks, then slowly turn to see the young Nazi
Cadet Sergeant Steiner, now a SS Youth Leader, in his dark uniform,
standing with his feet apart, hands on his hips, one hand on his gun
holster. His hat is at a jaunty angle. Steiner grinning sneers and hisses,
"Oh, it's you two little shits... I have been trying
to find out what unit you both came from".
He struts around the twins yelling in his adolescent squeaky voice.
"Stand up straight! Point your fingers down! Thumbs forward.
That fool of a sergeant in the messenger office said he didn't
know what school you were from. Well my Captain wants to
see you two, I know it was you two who let the stinking Jews
escape by cutting away the door lock with your HJ knives...
We are missing a date stamp too; you are a pair of shitty little
thieves... What are you? You two will be shot or shoved into
a concentration camp before this day is over"
As the young officer goes on ranting and shouting Ron stares at the
long black Führerdolch (Leader's Dagger) that dangles on a pair of black
polished leather straps from his belt. Ken catches his brother's stare and
waits for his moment. Ron taps Ken's finger lightly, a signal for a routine
the brothers know well. Ron, very sarcastically smirks,
"Steiner, do you ever look stupid
with your hat on the side like that, ha, ha"...

Steiner is not going to take this from two little shit Jew-lovers; he is convinced it was them who let his Jews out. He starts to grab the flap of his pistol holster.

Ken like a flash kicks him in the groin, with a well-aimed, well-thought-out, boot in his balls, putting all his weight behind it. Steiner bends over grasping his crotch with both hands and falls to his knees in agony.

Ron nips around the back of him, draws Steiner's black dress Dagger and as quick as a flash thrusts the long thin blade in to the soft kidney area of his lower back. Then rams a second and third stab in as far as they will go, hard in, right to the hilt.

Steiner reels back, his mouth wide open, drawing in gasps of air from the shock. Ron grabs Steiner's face from behind him, muffling his screams, pulling his head back and sideways, tugs out the knife from his back and thrusts three quick downward stabs into the soft part of his neck, over the collarbone.

At the same time Ken rams his own camp knife deep up under his ribs. Ken is sure he will have to leave the knife sticking in him because it is so hard to pull out, he can feel the boys stomach muscles gripping the blade, but he twists it, and it comes out with a hot spurt of blood. Ken rams in his knife again upward deep under his ribs with all his strength. Steiner grasps Ken's forearm in his agony, Ken in his terror has put so much upward force into his knife thrust that it stands Steiner back up on his own feet.

A squirt of blood spurts and bubbles out of the boy's mouth and between Ron's fingers. Steiner falls dead with his own dress dagger still stuck in his neck up to its hilt. Ken is forced to use his foot to pull his own knife out of the boy's ribs and wrench his hand away from the death grip he has on his forearm.

Steiner's blood oozes up his knife handle as Ron bends down and remaining icy cool, unclips the pistol holster off his belt, turns and runs yelling to Ken,

"Run boy! Run!"

A tired wounded soldier sitting on the ground eating his lunch looks on totally disinterested, but an SS guard sitting on his case spotted the attack and leaps to his feet to give chase. Ken turns and runs off in one direction, Ron runs the other way, turns the corner, stops to look back and sees the SS man running toward him. Ron spins around and runs into the thickest part of the crowd but the SS guard using his height spots him and keeps up. Ron is now running as fast as his legs will carry him, gasping for air; his mind races.

"I must get out of this place… then I can
double back in here again and try to lose him".

Ron twists out of the crowd and starts to run down the empty platform to where the trains enter the station. He can hear running boots and shouting behind him. A shot whizzes past his ear. He sees the bullet strike the white tiles on the wall in front of him.

"Oh shit".

He gasps,

"I must weave about, don't let them get
a good aim on me. Zigzag. I have to zigzag".

He dodges to the left and right, still running for his life. More shots whiz by his head. At the end of the station platform the tracks run out into the bright day.

An army troop train is just starting to pull slowly out of the station from the next platform. Ron runs straight to it. Bored looking faces stare at him from the windows. Trotting alongside the train, he times his move allowing a set of train wheels to pass him and then he dives under the moving train. Lays still for a moment in the center of the track with the train passing over him, times his move and rolls out the other side of the track. He then runs back into the station with the moving train between him and his pursuer.

When he gets back to the ticket office area, Ron starts to walk trying to look as casual as possible. He spots a door into an office slightly open and walks through and closes it after him. Turns and slams the bolt locked. He takes a moment to compose himself. Then he walks calmly down the corridor past offices and the sound of clicking typewriters, into a toilet, shuts the door and locks himself in.

He stands looking at himself in the mirror and slowly takes control of his breathing. He talks to himself, looking hard into his own eyes,

"We did it… We did him in… Him or us".

Yes it was him or us. We would have been totally dead
for sure and that black pig was going to shoot us.
Or we would have ended up in front of a firing squad
for helping the Jews".

He notices that his upper leg and chest are soaked wet with Steiner's blood. Suddenly he feels nauseous and turns to the toilet, gets on his knees and tries to throw up.

But he hasn't eaten for so long he just puts his head in the toilet bowl and unproductively tries to find something to vomit.

He washes the blood off his hands and holds the front of his overcoat under the running water. The cold water on his face makes him feel better. Ron looks at the hand basin it's red with blood everywhere. He washes away blood, being very careful to get rid of every spot. He stands on the toilet and slowly pushes the small window open and looks out. There's a yard with postal carts and station trolleys.

Two oldish railway workers with their backs to his window are talking over some papers. Ron quietly climbs out of the window, jumps lightly down and ducks down behind a cart and watches the two old men argue.

When the time seems right he just strolls out and walks casually past the two rail workers. He nods to them, they nod back.

He goes through the gate and is gone. As he hurries through the streets he talks to himself in whispers,

"We killed him dead... We will never get into Heaven now.

Him or us, it was him or us now he is dead, all right?"

Ron is the last to arrive back at the cellar. Ken breathes a sigh of relief at seeing his brother safe, he has not yet told his side of the story, except that they had seen Steiner. Dieter says,

"We can't go to the station, not while Steiner is about,

he knows what we all look like".

Ron quietly says,

"He won't be around anymore, because he's dead".

Ken is waiting to hear what he was thinking, confirmed,

"We did him in, totally?"

Ron nods and points to his own neck. Dieter grabs Ron's arm,

"How do you know he's dead?"

Ron coolly says,

"He's dead all right; I know he's dead... I did him twice in his back and twice in his neck with his own knife.

Ken did him a few times in his chest and twice in his guts with his knife. It was him or us Dieter.

He was going for his pistol... This one".

Ron lays the black polished pistol holster on the table and says cheerfully,

"So what's to eat? Did anybody get anything at all?

The boys all shake their heads.

"Nothing to eat at all, I haven't eaten a thing today".

Dieter takes the small Walther 7.65mm automatic pistol out of its black leather holster. It has a full magazine and a second spare loaded magazine. Dieter turns the pistol over saying,

"Oskar, what caliber is your pistol?"

"7.65mm".

"Do you know how to use it?"

Oskar nods, and retrieves his pistol from the floorboard in the toilet. Dieter runs the six rounds out of the spare magazine,

"Here's some ammunition. It's for life or death only;

no target shooting".

Dieter asks the twins quietly,
  "Who saw your faces, was Steiner with anyone?"
Ron shakes his head saying,
  "The only one who got a good look at us was a black pig
  who chased me and shot at me but he was a rotten shot
  and missed. That's a few of my nine lives a-goner for sure.
  No one, other than him saw us. A wounded one saw us
  but he wasn't that interested anyway".
Hans stands up and is curious. He looks at Ron and asks quietly,
  "Ron, what did it feel like to kill Steiner?"
Ron all upset yells,
  "You shut up about that, I don't want to hear about Steiner
  from anybody... All-right, all of you, understand this...
  He's dead and that's good because we are all still alive...
  We are fucking alive! He was a killer and now he's dead.
  He was going to kill us or turn us in for saving the Jews
  and that's the same thing isn't it"
Ron is now shouting,
  "All right?"
The faces around the table get his message. Ron goes into the toilet
and slams the door. They hear him trying to throw up. Ken waits for him
with his towel.

When the toilet door opens, Ron comes out. He is very shaken and
goes over and throws himself on their bed. Ken dampens the towel and
wipes Ron's face. Ron looks up at his brother, grabs the towel to cover
his deep sobs,
  "Ken, what are we going to eat...
  Shit Ken we did him in, we had to do it didn't we?
  We would have been up for a firing squad for certain...
  Think about it, he had us for sure, two capital offenses:
  aiding Jews to escape and stealing the date stamp.
  We were dead meat, they would take his word
  against ours anytime".
Ken puts his arm around his brother, gives him a big hug.
  "It's good Ron, it's good that he's dead and we are alive.
  It's all right, Ron, it's all right".
The six boys go to bed hungry again, they lay on their backs because
it eases the hunger pangs.

Dressed in old street clothes, on a busy corner Ken and Ron meet
Dieter and Hans. They all look at each other and shake their heads. The
boys go through trash bins behind restaurants, beg from passers-by; a
woman shrinks from their pleading.

They walk past the Lebensmittel shop that is only selling bottles of vinegar and other non-edibles until the rations come in. The six all meet at the bus station. Hans arrives with a large bag full of potato peelings. They share them by making six little equal piles on a cement table. They all stroll out munching on their find.

A woman with two children in a stroller points at the little gang.

"Look, Wolf Boys, someone should call the police".

The boys run off to check a recently burned house, to see if they can find anything to eat. Ken points to a pile of charred bodies laid in a row outside,

"Look Ron, they have no eyes".

Ken says quietly,

"Crows, the birds pick out the eyes, they're hungry too.

We have to split up; we are too exposed in a bunch like this".

Ron sighs,

"I'm so hungry I could eat a whole steak and kidney pie

with mashed potatoes to myself".

Hans dreams,

"What about a plate of brown toast, with real butter".

Dieter's little rag-tag platoon has been scrounging the streets for two weeks now, looking like Wolf Boys. They are starving. They look for new or fresh bombed out houses to rake through, hoping to find a can of food or a bag of flour, looking for valuables such as matches, candles, soap, paraffin.

Peering into burnings for scrap food they can eat, anything they can sell or swap for food, with always at least two of them watching out for patrols. They could be shot on the spot for looting or even looking through bomb-damaged houses.

One afternoon they are meandering through a quiet residential area. They turn the corner and come upon a small corner grocery store.

A group of women are standing in a line cheerfully chatting. Dieter speaks to a woman with a kind face, he asks,

"What will they have in today?"

"Bread, Sausage, Jam... Lots of it"

She looks hard at Dieter's collection of rag-tag little boys.

"If you have your ration cards".

Dieter beckons his lads around the corner. They get into a tight bunch to plot their next move. They wait until the line of women start to move and some come out clutching their bags as if they were full of gold. Dieter blows his whistle and the boys all run into the shop yelling and pushing people. Chaos, the boys all shouting, grabbing loaves of bread, tins of jam, and armfuls of sausages, filling their bread bags. Dieter blows his whistle again and the boys run out of the shop as fast as they went in, barging past the women as they run off in all directions… The twins are chasing after Dieter.

They are suddenly aware that a fat teenage grocery boy is chasing them on his delivery bike with its front container full of groceries. Ken, with two four-kilo cans of jam in his bread bag, stops, turns and faces the oncoming boy.

He swings his bag at the fat kid, hitting him square in the chest, sending him reeling back off his bike. Then he picks up the spilled grocery packages, tries to mount the bike and ride off but the grocery boy grabs Ken around his neck in a chokehold. Ron runs up behind him, draws his camp knife and with an upward thrust stabs the fat boy in the backside. He yells and lets go of Ken. Ron and Ken grab the square basket out of the front of the bike, pile their stolen food in it on top of the boy's groceries and run off holding the basket between them.

The fat grocer arrives out of breath and looks at the blood running down his son's leg. The grocer's son crying,

"They stabbed me in the bum Papa, the Wolf Kids stabbed me… They stole all the groceries… Will I get blood poisoning now Papa?"

Back in the cellar, the boys are all sitting at the table swapping getaway stories. They have eaten their fill of bread, sausage and jam. Hans says,

"I wish we had got some of the chocolate there, did you see all the food in the back room, stacks of it?"

Dieter looks worried,

"I can't run like I used to. Look at us; we are all so thin.
One day we won't be able to run away at all".

Ken shakes his head,

"We can't keep getting food like this.
But it's fun, what larks Ron"?

The boys try to venture out two days later, but the streets are crawling with patrols, picking up people for looting or dealing on the black market. Some are being shot on the spot by black-uniformed SS.

That night, the sirens sound, the anti-aircraft 88mm guns start to bang away. The boys lay in their beds looking at the ceiling.

Dieter says,

"I'm so hungry I could eat little Hans here".

Ron adds,

"Yes, we could eat his legs as a roast,
the rest we could put in the stew pot".

Hans asks,

"Would you eat my eyes?"
Ken laughs,
   "Yuck, ho no, only smelly Arabs eat eyeballs".
Dieter says,
   "I could eat a smelly Arab, eyeballs and all".
   "Yuck".
Ken moans,
   "I hate going to sleep hungry. If you lie
   on your back, it seems to stop the hunger pangs".
Ron laughs,
   "Ken, what about some fish and chips
   from the English seaside?"
The boys fall asleep dreaming of their own feasts.

One afternoon, after an air raid, Bo runs in to the cellar all excited
waving a fist full of money, Ron's eyes widen and he says,
   "Wow, where did you get all that! How much is there?"

Bo spreads the notes out on the table with a blood soaked wallet.
The circle of amazed faces just stare at the money then at Bo waiting for
his story,
   "He was dead, he won't need it now, will he?"
Dieter smiles and puts his arms around his skinny shoulders saying,
   "Bo, if you rob the dead you won't go to heaven...
   Unless it is for a good cause... Feeding us all here
   is a very good cause, so you will get in all right".
Dieter picks over the wallet and pulls out a Gestapo pass and a small
book of names and addresses.
   "Look he was a Gestapo agent, did anyone see you Bo?"
Bo shakes his head and says,
   "During the air raid I watched him jump out of a window...
   The building was all on fire, I went over to him to see if
   I could help him get out of the way of the falling bricks
   and stuff... but he was dead, his head was broken open
   and his brains were on the pavement"
Bo went very quiet,
   "I didn't know brains were gray...
   Did you know that our brains are gray?...
   Then there was all this money just lying there.
   So I pulled him into the gutter, grabbed the wallet,
   and ran away, no one saw me"
Dieter sorts out the money, scoops up the wallet and the rest of the
dead man's papers and pops them in the stove slamming the door.
   "We are going shopping in the park to get some food, Ron

stash the rest of this money in your tin for safe keeping later".
Ken asks,
   "How much money is there?"
Dieter folds the notes neatly,
   "Enough to feed us lot for a bit, come on lets dress warm
   and all go, Bo and Oskar can watch our backs".
The boys buy sausages, a small bag of potatoes and skinny loaves of
bread from a black market man in the park. Ron bargains with another
man selling sausages and vegetables. He hands over the money for six fat
sausages and a big bag of carrots.
   All the time Bo and Oskar watch from a safe distance ready to raise
the alert if there is any danger. The months tick by, the boys find that
buying food on the black market is very expensive and the money soon
runs out, they are hungry again.
   That night the boys are lying in their beds. There's a glow from the
stove. Hans says cheerfully,
   "Wouldn't it be wonderful if the Americans blew-up
   a sausage factory and they all came tumbling down
   from the sky all cooked and ready to eat".
Ken asks,
   "Did we eat yesterday? No we ate two days ago, am I
   ever hungry... Do we have any of our money left Ron?"
In the distance the sirens wail the start of another air raid.
Ron barks back,
   "No, go to sleep, it's raining 88s shit outside".
Oskar tries a joke,
   "I think I will eat Bo".
   "Yuck, I'm not very tasty, no meat on me".
Ken moans,
   "Don't start that all over again we did it yesterday".
Bo suddenly sits up in his bed and says,
   "I know, we could use your cart to get some coal,
   we could swap the coal for food".
Dieter looks interested,
   "Good idea Bo, but where are we going to get coal?"
Oskar looks up and says,
   "Bo knows where the coal is and how to get it don't you,
   tell them Bo, tell them about the railway sidings".
Bo spreads the map out on the table and points to the railway
sidings.
   Clad in their newly acquired topcoats, gloves, with their stolen
woolen scarves Dieter's boys set out for the rail-yards close to the power
generating station.

Coal loaded trains without guards shunt in and out at all times of the day. They can see the smoke stacks of the powerhouse and pass people hurrying by carrying sacks and pushing baby carriages loaded with huge lumps of coal. They stop on an iron footbridge that crosses the lines and look down to see groups of boys and some women waiting at the edge of the tracks, Bo says,

"They are doing it the hard way. They will jump on the train
when it slows down and throw the coal off to their friends".
Bo points up the track,

"See the shed way up there with the tall chimney? If we take
the cart round the back of that shed, there's piles of coal".
Ken says,

"What about the guards? How do we get inside the yard,
worse still, how do we get out of the yard with the cart?"
Bo, smiles,

"Come on I will show you I've never seen a guard inside
the yards, they all hang around the trains. They patrol
the power house, but that's a kilometer up the track".

Just then a long coal train passes underneath them and the people waiting at the side of the track go into action. They scramble up on to the wagons and throw lumps of coal off to their friends trotting alongside.

A dangerous and not very productive way of keeping warm.

Bo leads them down a long narrow lane flanked by a rusting corrugated steel fence. At a bend in the path he stops and points to a section of the fence marked with a small letter 'C' in chalk. He pushes hard on the bottom of the panel and it swings inward pivoting on its top beam leaving a gap wide enough to push the cart through. Dieter holds the panel and they all slip through, he lets the section drop gently. They are now in the coal yard where the engines re-fill their tenders and see huge piles of coal just laying around unattended.

Dieter sends Bo to keep watch and the rest of the boys quickly fill the cart as quietly as they can. Soon the cart is so full they can only just shut the lid. Ken digs Dieter in the ribs to look at the flat tires, the cart will hardly move with its big white rubber tires flattened with all the extra weight.

Ron yells quietly and points to the underside of the cart.

"The pump, the pump is under there".

Dieter un-clips the pump and the boys take turns working it as fast as they can, Bo whistles as a truck drives into the yard. The six lads crouch behind their cart keeping as still as they can.

The truck makes its delivery and drives off. The boys quickly resume their frantic pumping. When the tires are hard enough to roll the cart they move. With two boys in the front shafts and two in the rear they speed their way out of the yard to a large house where Bo and Oskar had sold little sacks of coal bits before. Standing outside the tall iron gates Ron says,

> "Oskar, tell them we want potatoes, sausage food,
> lots of it all this coal must be worth a fortune,
> what did you get for the little sacks you could carry?"

Oskar shrugs his shoulders,

> "Just a meal each and a fat baloney sausage to take away".

Ron takes charge,

> "I will go in there with you and drive a harder barging".

Ron and Bo were gone for what seemed a long time, Ken says,

> "I wonder what they are doing in there.
> I hope they come out with something to eat".

When Ron does come out he is beaming and carrying six lumps of sausages, each fifteen-centimeter long. He gives one to every boy and they quickly get devoured, Dieter pauses his chewing,

> "Is this it?... Is this all we get Ron?"

Ron grins, shakes his head as Dieter checks the empty cart.

> "We have to come back the day after tomorrow to get the
> potatoes and lots more of these".

Ron holds up his sausage. They make their way back to the cellar, that night they fall asleep less hungry than usual.

20. STARVATION

The next day Dieter is deep in his own thoughts, looking into a broken chunk of mirror, pulling out a single whisker from his chin. Dieter says quietly,

"I know one place we could get a meal…
We could get fed at the SS barracks,
but we would all have to be in uniforms".
Ken gets all enthusiastic,
"We could dress these two up in what we have got here".
"If we all looked the same, we could march right in".
Hans asks,
"So what's our cover; why are we going to the barracks?
I don't want to get shot yet".
Dieter reassuring,
"To eat, we could be a medical aid team.
Just like in the train when we came here,
walk in and tell them our commanding officer sent us".

The cart is washed and empty, ready with the flag fluttering. Dieter's little band of six is looking like a platoon of Hitler Youth, Oskar and Bo are sporting new haircuts. Bo has his arm in a sling. Each boy has a matching scarf. Dieter makes them all wear them the same way.

Ron and Ken are in the front shafts, with Bo and Hans in the rear. Dieter and Oskar march in front. As they make their way north on Garmischer Strasse toward Bahnhof Platz and the central station, a pack of about four large abandoned starving dogs suddenly dash out of the West Park, barking and snarling.

Mad with hunger and ready to tear the boys to bits. Dieter grabs the flagpole and yelling at the top of his voice puts himself between the dogs and the boys. Swinging the stout flagpole, he gives the first dog, the obvious leader a whack across his head with the pole's brass end. Stunned, it just stands there. The second dog grabs the flag, snarling and ripping at it. Dieter prods him in the shoulder with the spear pointed tip of the shaft. The dog lets go with a yelp and runs off. Seeing the two leaders defeated the rest of the pack run off.

Ron and Ken have pulled out one of the shafts of the cart and are standing ready to fend off the attackers with it. Ron yells,

"Shit, they could kill you, what if we were some old lady
or a child… They would bloody eat you, for sure".
"That's why they roam in packs". Dieter says.
Bo, white with fear is sitting on top of the cart. He jumps down and says,

"We heard about a woman and her baby who was set on by a

pack of starved, crazed dogs. She was killed and they never
found the baby, I bet I know what happened to it, I bet the
dogs took it off into the bushes in the park and devoured the
poor little shit. Wow were they ever vicious, it must be the
hunger that drives them crazy".
Ken shrugs his shoulders,
  "Oh, let's just add a few crazed, man-eating dogs
  to the list of those who want to grab us and kill us".
Oskar says,
  "You know they come out of the parks when
  the bombs fall and chew on the burned dead people".
Dieter looks at the point of their flag pole and says,
  "I'm going to put a sharper point on this,
  we need to find some metal pipes or heavy sticks.
  We must to be able to defend ourselves...
  Come on, let's get going".
Two boys in front and four at the rear, they march off on this cold
crisp sunny day making their way through the streets of Munich. The
snow is hard and crunches under their clean boots.
  The armbands with Einsatz-Gefolgsch (Special Employment)
printed in the white stripe on top of their Hitler Youth armbands gives
them the finishing touch of credibility. They now look like a unit going
about its duty.
  As they turn a corner, they approach a platoon of Hitler Youth
coming from the other direction. A rag-tag bunch of all ages, led by a
fourteen-year-old that is just full of his own importance. Strutting out in
front, he is wearing the armband of the Strafendienst, the Hitler Youth's
own police force. He halts his platoon, and strides over to Dieter, salutes
and says,
  "What's in the cart?"
Dieter who is a head taller smiles,
  "Classified".
The boy reels back, thinks a bit and reasserts himself.
  "Papers... I have to see your orders".
The patrol leader tries to open the lid of the cart and asks Hans,
  "Come on open up, open up".
Hans shakes his head and says,
  "Stand back fart face".
Dieter, with bored authority says
  "We are on special assignment for Gestapo Officer
  Odilo Globozuik. Out of our way you dirty pig's shit".
The patrol leader thinks about the situation and about the size of
Dieter and the fact he has only got some bread and cheese in his pistol
holster. Dieter smiles, puts his finger to his lips and walks over to the cart,

unlocks and lifts the lid and brings out Steiner's pistol in its black holster.
He expertly opens the gun and loads it, snaps it closed.

Applies the safety, slips the pistol into its holster and clips it to his own belt. Suddenly he looks very grown up. The young leader plucks up his courage and says,

"You know boys over fifteen have to register for war work...
Do you have your registration papers yet?"

The boys watch in silence. Dieter gives the boy a smart salute saying,

"Yes, we are doing ours, what are you doing?
Where are your orders? Just fuck off, before
I arrest you and all your little fleabags".

The patrol leader salutes and marches his little band away.
Ron quietly says to Dieter,

"Flea bags? Ha, where did you get that one from?
Do you think it's a good idea to wave
that gun around? It might get us all shot".

Dieter smiles,

"It goes with the armband.
That little shit was only just fourteen, fifteen at the most.
He was wearing an empty pistol holster;
I saw it bend on his belt when he came over to the cart.
Come on; let's get some food. I'm hungry.
The dinner bell will go and we will miss it".

They all march off.

Dieter feels like a real patrol leader with the pistol on his belt. They approach the Barracks' main gate. Dieter strides forward and shows the envelope to the guard; he waves them through and shouts.

"Hey, you boys, what have you got in the box?"
"Girls for the Officer's Mess; want one?
They are one hundred marks each".

The guard smiles and waves them on. The other ranks' Mess Hall is quite busy. There's a line of soldiers waiting to go past the kitchen serving tables. Three plump kitchen cooks in white uniforms and white hats are serving a thick vegetable soup, one fat sausage and a chunk of bread with a mug of ersatz coffee (made from roasted barley seeds and acorns). The boys stand in line. Ron is the first to be served. The server pauses with his big spoon in the air; he looks at the boys and says,

"Where did you come from lad?"
"No one told me about the boy's army.
What unit are you supposed to be?"

Dieter steps forward and faces the man, his hand on his pistol.
The server says,

"So sergeant, what can we do for you?"

Dieter casually,
>"They are with me… We are the last six…
>all that is left of our company"

Dieter lies with conviction
>"We have been fighting the Russians at the eastern front.
>We are all here to receive our Iron crosses from General
>Siegfried Westphal, your chief of Staff here".

The Server pulls a face,
>"Well, we have to feed the heroes
>of the Third Reich, don't we".

The boys get served with big helpings of food. The server asks,
>"Will you all be here tomorrow? Come back any time,
>we will try to find you a steak or a bit of salmon, ha".

Dieter says seriously,
>"It may take two or three days for the General
>to find time to see us, we may be here every day".
>"Well you better come back with some paperwork.
>I can't keep feeding you without paperwork".
>"Thank you sergeant"

The boys are all seated at a table, tucking into their meal. The cook arrives with a clipboard with a paper for Dieter to sign. He looks at Oskar's arm in a sling.
>"What happened to him?"

Ron as quick as a flash says,
>"He got run through by a Russian bayonet, but
>he killed the Ivan with his bare hands; throttled him".

The cook gets genuinely sympathetic,
>"He should go over to the medical room,
>get a clean dressing on that arm".

Dieter signs the paper. The boys continue to enjoy their food.

Dieter's little platoon marches towards the central station feeling good after their big meal. Oskar is sporting a new dressing with a real Army Medical Wound label and sling. They pass bombsites in a street where less than half of the houses are left standing.

It's not too cold, and the boys march along with a new spring in their step. As they turn a corner they come face to face with a huge gray Zundapp motorcycle sidecar unit. It stops in front of them. An SS Officer in a long rubberized coat with a Schmeisser machine gun slung across his chest wearing long leggings holds his hand up in a halt sign. Dieter stands to attention and salutes.

The SS Officer returns his salute with a slight wave.
>"You lot, all of you, you're now a part of an
>SS special duty unit for the next hour or so".

The Officer looks at Oskar's wounded arm label and puts his hands on his good shoulder,

"You, you're walking wounded are you?
Good, so you guard my motorcycle and shout
if someone tries to steal it".

He turns and looks at the other boys and calls Dieter over and hands him a clipboard,

"Sergeant, how many names on that list?"

Dieter stares at the paper on the clipboard.

"Nine names sir, nine".

The SS Officer gives Dieter a pencil,

"Print the names of your boys, sergeant,
and the name of your unit on the bottom there...
You're all witnesses. You sign your name and number
and put the date under your signature".

A few moments later an escort squad of SS Guards in black uniforms arrives. They are force-marching a group of nine people to the edge of the road in front of a burned out house: a desperate scene.

The nine prisoners, all with their hands tied behind their backs with wire are being pushed and shoved into a line at the edge of the road. Some are quite young, a boy of about fifteen, two pretty young women, three men in suits, an army mechanic and an older couple who are trying to maintain their dignity. The two young women are getting hysterical and are being pushed back by the guards with rifles.

The Officer orders them back against the wall. The squad of guards is now turning brutal, thumping people into position with the butts of their Schmeissers. The two young women are just staring at each other and screaming frantically. The Officer strides forward and grabs one of the rifles from a guard and with a quick thrust, butts one of the screaming woman in her stomach. She sinks to her knees whimpering.

"My babies are at home. What's going to happen to them?"

The Officer draws back the rifle to strike the other woman. She shuts up. The teenage boy tries to attract the Officer's attention, yelling and pleading. The boy prisoner yells over to the Officer.

"Sir, I'm under age. I'm only just fifteen".

The SS Officer snatches the clipboard from Dieter,

"It says here age unknown; it's not my decision,
it was the court that decided your sentence.
You had your chance...
You, Sergeant, read out their names".

The Officer ignores the boy's cries. Dieter starts to shout out the names and ages of the people on the list. A small crowd, mostly women have gathered to watch the scene at a safe distance. The Officer waves a fist full of papers at the prisoners and shouts:

"You prisoners whose names have been called
have been found guilty by the courts
of the crimes stated in these reports...
Under wartime emergency laws you have all
been sentenced to be shot by a firing squad...
effective immediately, Heil Hitler".

The one pretty woman who is left standing starts to scream and howl.
The Officer strides over to her. He draws his pistol and puts the pistol to
her head; she screams louder. He pulls the trigger. The crack of the shot
seems to sound like a toy, but the woman drops like a stone. A hush
settles over the street.

As the Officer starts to walk away, the teenage boy, tears streaming
down his face, has managed to get his hands free of the wire bindings. He
bends down and picks up a half brick. His wrists are all bloody from the
wire bindings. With all his strength he throws the brick at the Officer. It
crashes on the man's shoulder, spinning him around and knocking him
down.

The boy takes his chance and starts to run for his life, taking off
across the rubble, stumbling in his frantic bid to escape. One of the black
uniformed SS guards steps forward and taking careful aim, fires a single
shot. The boy falls, screaming and writhing on the ground in agony,
clutching a gaping wound in his stomach, blood spurting out from
between his fingers. The Officer gets up rubbing his shoulder, looks at
the boy and waves his pistol barking at Dieter,

"Sergeant, take two of your men and bring
back that prisoner... Move now move boy!"

Dieter and the twins run over to the boy who is still screaming and
clutching his middle. The boys hesitate, not knowing quite how to pick
him up without hurting him. Gently, they take an arm and a leg each to
carry him back. As they move him he screams with agony, then loses all
consciousness. His head flops forward.

They set him gently down, sitting him up against the wall between
the other condemned people. He topples over on his side. Blood is
running and pulsing out of his shorts and down his legs he looks very
young.

The boys feel the fear and terror from the people by the wall.

Ken looks at the faces of the two men in suits; they both have an
ashen look. The older folk have resigned themselves to their fate and are
calm. The old lady looks hard into Ken's eyes and says,

"My, you're only a boy,
why are you doing this evil man's work?"

Ken and Ron turn to pick up the boy but the SS Officer shouts.

"Get out of there, move... Squad take aim".

The Officer waits until Dieter and his boys have scrambled out of the area, then yells at Dieter and his little platoon,

"Turn around and look at the prisoners.

You're supposed to be witnesses,

so be witnesses, look at them!"

The Officer waits to make sure all the boys are watching, and then he yells,

"Fire!"

A volley of machine gun fire spits up clouds of dust and snow. After a few seconds, the firing stops. The teenage boy has not been hit by the firing squad; he slowly starts to regain consciousness. The other eight prisoners are all dead.

The Officer walks over to the boy and draws his pistol. The boy sees him coming and raises his hand to shield himself. The Officer stands over him, pointing his pistol at the boy's head.

Dieter's platoon and the crowd can all hear the boy pleading. The Officer changes his mind and slowly shifts his aim to the pit of the boy's stomach and fires. His forlorn adolescent screams and cries of agony echo around the bombed out buildings. After what seemed a long time the Officer re-aims his pistol at the boy's head. The screams continue whilst he coolly fires a shot.

Everyone breathes a sigh of relief for the peace the last shot must have brought to the young boy.

Dieter's little platoon stare, their faces as white as the snow at their feet. The Officer waves Oskar off his sidecar.

He climbs on, and looks at the crowd.

"Is anyone claiming any of these bodies?"

There is no response from the crowd.

The SS Officer points at Dieter,

"You sergeant, what's your name?"

"Dieter Wolff sir".

The Officer hands Dieter his fist-full of papers,

"Well, Sergeant Dieter Wolff, your Platoon

can bury these bodies… Just cover them up with rubble,

and then post these over the top of them.

They will be dug up later for proper disposal".

The Officer throws a packet of thumbtacks out of the sidecar.

He drives off and the black SS Guards march off.

Dieter turns and looks at the crowd,

"Anyone know these people, are there any relatives here?"

No one moves, they all just stand there. Dieter walks over to them and puts his hand on his pistol and says softly,

"It's all over now; just move along, please".

IV The Fight

The crowd disperses and drifts away. The boys slowly walk over to the wall. The snow is bright red from all the fresh blood. Most of the dead bodies look at peace. Hans and Ken start to pull the victims together so they lie side by side. One of the pretty girls has a look of total disbelief on her face. They pull the coats over the heads of the dead to hide their faces. Ron beckons the boys over. The young boy, who had died in such agony stares up, his mouth open. His face is contorted; his are eyes wide open and terrified.

In his pain he pulled his shirt out showing a bare juvenile lower torso. The fingers of his right hand are thrust deep into the bullet holes in his stomach.

The fingers of his left hand are bent wrong. A black welt with a hole through the middle of his hand shows where he tried to shield himself from the bullet that passed through his hand then his forehead.

The boys work in silence with as much reverence as they can. After stacking the bodies, they cover them with bricks and rubble.

Dieter makes a crude cross from broken wood, rolls the original death warrants up in oilcloth, fastening the warrants on to the cross with the wire from one of the victim's hands.

He puts the nine death warrant copies in his pocket.

Back in the cellar the boys sit around the table looking at the copies of the death warrants. There is a heavy sadness in the cellar. The death certificates are spread all over the table. Dieter reads,

"The old folks were executed for hiding two young deserters.
I wonder what happened to the two deserters."

Hans holds up the paper,

"Look at this, the two young women were trying
to buy stolen ration cards to feed their children.
It's the fucking government's fault
they were hungry in the first place".

Ron reads over Ken's shoulder,

"The army mechanic was shot for stealing and selling petrol…
The three men in suits trying to buy food on the black market.
Poor old shits, they must have walked into a trap set by the Gestapo".

Ken looks at the boy's sheet,

"The boy lost his life for a tin of jam…
He stole a half-kilo of jam from a grocery store…
Well at least we know where we stand".

Bo asks,

"Where's that then?"

Ken says,

"Nowhere, that's where we stand.

314

They give no quarter, no second chances...
If Ron had been nice to the little shit Steiner
at the Station and we had not killed him,
we would be very dead. He would have put us up
in front of a firing squad and enjoyed it".
Dieter points to the paper,
"Whatever your age. Look, he was fifteen
just eighteen days ago, just fifteen.
We have done ten times more crimes
against the State than this poor little sod".
Oskar says,
"Why did the black shit say his age was unknown?"
Dieter explains,
"Because he had no paperwork to prove his age.
He was a runaway too. We just cannot get caught,
or we are all dead... We can't go along with their courts.
They make up the laws to suit themselves".
Oskar says,
"We could all be shot for something or other, Bo and me
for running away and stealing stuff from our school".
Dieter shrugs,
"Me for deserting, stealing, eating and breathing.
I could get shot for anything, ha".
Ken laughs,
"I'm giving up breathing, it's too risky.
We could all be stood against the walls and shot,
just for what we have to do to stay alive".
Dieter says,
"If we turned ourselves in to the police,
they would cook up some phony evidence.
We would get shot like the poor shits today...
We are an embarrassment to this city; that's what we are.
They just want us all out of the way".
Ron holds his hand up to get everyone's attention,
"To survive, we must stay alert, trust
no one outside this room and be strong.
Bo, you haven't said much, what do you think?"
"We may have to kill like Ron and Ken did
to stay alive. We have to get more pistols".
Ken looks at Bo,
"It's nature's own way, them or us.
The survival of the strongest, kill or be killed".
Oskar asks,
"Why did the asshole Peter get away with robbing us?

Because they had a K98 carbine with a bayonet on its end,
  they said they would shoot us if we moved or shouted".
Hans looks upset,
  "They could come back tomorrow and
  take what they like. What could we do?"
Dieter shakes his head and puts his finger up to Ron,
  "Ron, you must make one of your crafty plans
  for us. We need food, guns and girls".

The food they got from the house where they left the coal was nice but it didn't last very long. The weather outside was terrible, a real blizzard, snow and a high wind. It rained heavily, non-stop, washing all the snow into slosh. No one wanted to go out looking for food. It was decided it was better to save their strength, wait out the rain and go out when the weather cleared up. The boys hadn't eaten for almost twenty-four hours and Dieter says,
  "If we go out in the ice cold, we would burn up too much
  of our strength, just keeping warm and walking".
Ron looks at the very hungry faces around him and the pots scrubbed clean on the stove. He sits up from his bed and says,
  "You know there is food out there wandering about
  on four legs, all you have to do is catch it and cook it".
Dieter who is catching rainwater that is leaking through the roof looks up and says,
  "What food, horses?"
Ken looks up, smiles and says, bursting with enthusiasm,
  "No, the dogs, we can eat the dogs.
  They will make a fine stew...
  We need wire to make a neck loop".
Oskar and Bo pull faces, Oskar glares at Ken,
  "Well I'm not eating any dogs... Yuck.
  What if they have eaten some people?...
  We would be cannibals".
Dieter says
  "No we wouldn't, we would be eating dogs.
  We don't know that all the dogs in Munich have eaten people...
  So how do we go about catching them Ken?"

The twins come in from the rain soaked through to their skins, carrying a small coil of barbed wire and two lengths of steel gas piping. They sit around the stove and slowly un-twist the barbed wire to make a long single strand, then double it in two and thread it through the pipe making a noose loop that can be pulled tight by pulling the wire through the end of the pipe. They twist the ends around a short stick for a grip.

Ron creeps up behind Dieter who is reading and quietly slips the loop over his head and pulls on the grip at the other end of the pipe tightening the noose about his neck. Dieter's instant reaction is to grab the noose, but Ron had him fast.

"All right! All right! Ow, you have me, shit
where did you learn to make such a thing as this?"
"We saw it in the zoo, the keepers had a big cat
held fast with something like this".
Ken says,
"Come on, we will tell you the plan;
how we can get some meat for our stew pot".

The rain stops the next day, but it is still cold and wet underfoot. The boys set out for the park, each armed with a length of steel gas pipe. Ron has his pipe with the wire noose at the ready, Dieter with the flagpole; its point now sharpened like a razor and the flag replaced with a knot of old rag. They have all wrapped and bound their legs and forearms with old newspapers tied up with sacking and string to provide some sort of protection against bites.

The few people hurrying through the park are using it as a shortcut to somewhere. They barely glance at the strange looking squad trying to hide their steel poles down their sides. No one gives a second thought to the fact that their arms and legs are bound with paper and wire; it was common practice, to keep out the cold and damp. They arrive at the center of the park, having seen no dogs. Ron says,

"We should go deeper into the bushes.
It's too open out here. Let's try over by the pond".

As the boys push deeper into the park, the bushes that haven't been trimmed back for years, thicken and become dense.

They hear a deep growl from behind and spin around to see two big dogs. The closest one, a big wolf-like German shepherd, just stands baring its teeth. Ron quickly slips his wire loop over Dieter's spear. The two of them start to walk closer to the growling animal. Dieter thrusts his rag-covered spear at the dog's face; it charges biting on to the rag at the end of the spear.

As the dog shakes the rag, Ron slides the loop down the spear and over its neck and pulls the grip, tightening the noose. The big dog bucks and shakes its head trying to free itself. It's too strong for Ron to keep hold, so Dieter grabs onto the pipe with him. Ron yells to Ken,

"Bash it Ken, bash its head".

Ken runs forward to whack the dog's head. At the same time the smaller of the dogs charges at Ken but Oskar heads it off, catching it a swipe on its shoulder with his steel pipe. It runs off squealing. Ken then takes a whack at the big dog's head but he misses and hits Ron's pipe, almost knocking it out of his hand. Dieter yells,

"Bash it one Lambert.

We can't hold this thing much longer, just bash it hard!"

Ken brings his steel pipe down on the dog's head with all the strength
he can muster, catching the dog between the ears with a crack. With a
sneeze the dog drops like a stone; its big tongue hanging out of its mouth.
Ron yells,

"Ken, bash it again… It may not be dead".

Ken takes a second swipe at the dog's head but it was already dead.
The three boys stand around looking at the big dog.

Its ears have the scars of many fights; its teeth are well worn.

"It's dead all right now". Ken says, then thinks a bit,

"So how do you gut a dog? The same way as a rabbit

or a deer I suppose?"

Dieter looks about,

"Where's Oskar and Bo, did they run off?"

After a few moments Oskar and Bo walk out of the bushes carrying
the smaller dog; it too is dead. Oskar yells,

"Bo just whistled to it and it came up,

all very friendly to be fed or petted and I bashed it".

The boys hoist the two dogs, front feet first; up on to a low branch
of a tree with the coil of wire Dieter has around his waist. Ken guts the
two animals just like rabbits. Oskar and Bo keep their distance while the
heads, tails and paws are cut off. Trussed up by their legs on two iron
fence poles, the boys carry the headless and tailless carcasses out of the
park.

The dogs looked like two young butchered veal as they turned back
onto Garmishcher Strasse. A man with a bicycle and a box-trailer stops
them and asks what sort of meat it is and how much they want for it.

"Young veal, what have you got?" Dieter asks,

"Potatoes, carrots and onions,

three kilos of each, for the big one".

Ron steps in and says,

"No we have plenty of vegetables,

but we will give you the smaller one for them".

The man nods and takes out a small sack, puts it down on the
pavement. Ron and Ken look in the bag and turn the contents over to see
if it was all edible. They nod. Oskar and Bo lower the small dog into the
man's box cart. Ken watches the man bicycle away and grins,

"Do you really think he believes the dog is veal, ha"?

That evening the aroma of the cooking meat fills the cellar.

The boys are all munching on raw carrots whilst they wait,

watching Ken and Ron cut up the last ingredient, the onions,

and put them in the two big pots of simmering stew.

Six tin plates are set out on the table and the stew is served.

The smell of the cooking had been driving them all crazy for the last two and half-hours.

When the plates are piled up all very equally, there is a pause; all the boys look at Dieter who slowly scoops up a spoonful being careful to include a chunk of meat on his spoon. The boys watch him as he sniffs the meat, sips the food at first then with a big smile eats the whole spoonful... Mm, Mm. Oh it's wonderful, yum, yum. The boys fall on the meal with gasps of Oh's and lots of Mm's. Bo says,

"Mm, this is very good.

Let's not tell anyone about us eating dogs".

Bo's brother Oskar says,

"Why not?"

"Because everybody would be out there

grabbing the dogs if they knew how good they tasted...

There won't be any left for us".

The boys all laugh and munch into their wonderful meal. After dinner Ken says,

"Munich Veal, we shouldn't call it dog,

we should call it Munich Veal".

"It tastes more like strong English Lamb" Ken says.

Dieter yells out,

"Well, here's to Munich Veal. So we're hunters again.

What about cats? There are thousands of pussycats about.

Cut the heads and tails off, sell them, Bavarian Rabbits, ha".

Ron looks into the stew pot and says,

"There is enough food here for a meal tomorrow".

Bo asks,

"Won't it go bad?"

"Not if it is brought up to the boil every day

and we keep the lid on tight". Ken says.

Ron smiles at Ken saying,

"Save some bits of meat for bait.

We can set some traps in the bushes in the park.

Let's catch a few Bavarian pussy rabbits".

IV The Fight

21. THE APARTMENT

Oskar and Bo run hard through the streets, taking all the shortcuts they know to get home as fast as possible. They burst into the cellar out of breath, all excited, and empty out their cloth bags on the table: a chunk of ham, some sausage, a loaf of bread, two tins of fruit, three kilos of potatoes. Bo yells all excited,

"We got them from Alf... Alf, you know, the youngest
one of those two shits who stole all our stuff".

Oskar, all out of breath says.

"We spotted him in the park, he just gave
the food to us, for nothing. He was so scared,
he thought I might knife him".

Bo grinning,

"After he gave us this stuff we left the park,
but we doubled back. Alf hung around and waited
for a long time, so we hid and waited. Then we followed him
when he left the park, he didn't see us, we kept well back
out of sight; and listen, this is the best bit... We found out
where the little shit lives, they are still in the bike shop!"

Dieter stands and holds his hands up to calm the boys,

"Calm down, calm down.
Are you sure he didn't know you were following him?"

Oskar said,

"Yes, we stayed a long way back. He didn't see us.
It's about an hour's walk. Look, here on the map".

Ron says firmly,

"Did he see you at all?"

"No he didn't, did he Bo? We left the park first and doubled
back and waited for him to leave. I know he didn't see us".

"All right all right, we will go there tomorrow, all of us.
This time we will have our guns too".

The next day Dieter and his five lads are all in uniform, just around the corner from where Alf lives. It's cold; they are all warming themselves by a blazing fire in an oil drum that has holes bashed in it. A bunch of street kids and some old men are sitting on boxes warming themselves. Dieter throws in a chunk of wood and looks at the map with Oskar and says,

"The bike shop; it's just around the corner here?"

Oskar nods getting all excited. Dieter makes his plan,

"We four will go in first. They don't know us yet.
Oskar and Bo, you two stay here out of sight.

Keep warm; don't say anything to anyone.
Any trouble, three blasts on your whistle, all right?
Just don't walk in, wait until we come for you.
They know your faces, but they don't know us yet.
Just sit tight, all right?"

Oskar and Bo nod and smile. Dieter, Hans and the twins stroll down the street very casually to the bike shop. It's really a pair of garages with a large overhanging wooden awning.

Old rusty bike wheels are hanging in bunches. There are piles of bike tires. The boys start to look around; there's no sign of trade or repairs going on. A cord with a sign 'Service' hangs over the empty desk. Dieter gives it a tug. Somewhere in the back a bell rings.

A boy about fourteen sporting a new tweed suit that's slightly too big for him appears from the back eating a cheese sandwich.

"Sorry, we are closed. No new parts for bikes".
Dieter smiles and asks,

"Are you Peter?"

"No, I'm Alf. Peter is away today; what can I do for you?"
Dieter winks at him and smiles craftily,

"We came here for some trade".

"Peter takes care of all that side of the business.
If you want scrap metal, take all you like.
Another Hitler Youth patrol came last week and picked up
all the aluminum, but there's still plenty of scrap steel left.
Take what you want".

Ron has moved around behind Alf. He glances around and is very conscious that he is out-numbered. Dieter grabs one of Alf's hands, turns it over, looks at it and shows it to him and says,

"They don't look like a bike mechanic's hands to me.
They haven't seen real work for a long time".

Alf is now getting scared. The twins have closed in on him. Alf stammers,

"Look, I'm fourteen and I have a medical military
exemption certificate. Wait here and I'll get it".

Dieter draws his pistol and cocks the action with a snap. The color drains from Alf's face. Dieter pushes him back through the piles of bike frames to a grubby kitchen that is used as an office.

He hands the pistol to Ken and pushes Alf into an old chair. Dieter now sounds very vicious,

"You, sit there... Ken, if he moves shoot him in the balls.
I'm going to have a look around; this place smells of food.
There must be some Black Marketing going on".

Dieter grabs the remaining half of the boy's sandwich and eats it. Hans starts to go through Alf's pockets and brings out a small pocketknife and some money. Alf is now in tears and is very scared. Dieter points to an old inner door and tries it; it's locked.

"What's in here Alf, where's the key?"

"Peter has the key". He sobs. "I don't know what's in there. I'm only looking after the place for him…

I don't have anything to do with his business, honest".

Dieter takes a step back and gives the old door a kick.

It flies open revealing what was once a living room. It still has family pictures on the walls.

The only window in the room is boarded up. Stacked on shelves are piles of tinned foods, sacks of rice, crates of French wine, boxes of whisky and a lot of the food that was stolen from the boys' neighbors' cellar. Hans finds a heavy wooden box with a big padlock just behind the door.

Dieter looks around and finds a big screwdriver. With some difficulty, he pries off the lock and opens the box. The boys gaze at its contents: a service 9mm pistol with ammunition and an extra magazine. In a small cardboard box there are four egg grenades. Dieter loads the new pistol, walks back to the kitchen and sticks the long barrel of the pistol into Alf's belly. Alf is now trembling and shaking with fear. He thinks this is an official raid looking for black market dealers. He hasn't yet made the connection with Oskar and Bo. Alf is getting hysterical,

"I don't know anything, honest. Please, please,

I have nothing to do with his deals.

I'm just looking after the place for him".

The twins have a tight grip on Alf's wrists. Dieter un-clips the boy's belt, undoes his fly buttons pulls out his shirt, and pulls his underpants open, lowers the pistol pushing the muzzle deep into his crotch then slowly lets off the safety catch. Dieter whispers close to his face."

"Shall we blow a few little bits off down here for a start?"

Alf starts to sob uncontrollably.

"All right, all right, don't shoot me please.

I'll tell you. Peter's taken the truck to Augsburg".

"When did he leave?"

Alf with deep sobs,

"8am this morning. He said he would be back before dark".

Dieter digs him with the pistol,

"What's he carrying? How does he get through

the roadblocks? Is he alone? Come on, answer boy?"

Alf still very scared,

"He is picking up a load of Dutch cigars and some cigarettes…

He works for a real pharmaceutical company… he has all the

proper papers to get through roadblocks. He delivers to the

hospitals… He has petrol ration cards too".

Dieter pokes the pistol barrel hard into the base of the boy's penis.

Alf feels the cold metal and almost passes out.

"Listen, Alf, for black market dealing, you can die…

For arms dealing, you can die…

How many times can you die, Alf?…

We will have to do you in a little bit at a time.

We will start by blowing this little thing right off".

Ken becomes all sympathetic,

"Dieter come on. We don't have to torture him.

Let's get it over quick. Let's take him outside and

shoot him through the head; he won't feel a thing".

Alf spins around and looks at Ken with total disbelief.

Dieter takes the pistol out of the boy's pants and resets the safety catch, picks up Alf's pocket knife, opens the blade and starts to cut off the buttons of Alf's new tweed shorts,

"We could start by shredding a few bits off down here".

Ron says,

"Hold on Dieter, he just might want to

do something for us to save his own skin".

Dieter and Ron walk over to the corner of the room whispering.

Alf trembling, strains to hear what they are saying.

Dieter then comes back to Alf, puts his arm around him and starts to talk to him very confidentially. Alf nods eagerly and says,

"Yes, oh yes, it's not my racket. I just keep watch for Peter.

He gives me food. I'll do anything you want".

It is getting dark, a small truck rumbles up the narrow street. Its lights are shrouded to small slits.

The lights are off in the garage next to the bike shop. Hans, Dieter and the twins are well hidden as Peter's truck lumbers up to the big doors. Alf runs over and pushes them open, as he would normally do. The truck drives in. Alf closes the doors and in as much of a normal voice as he can muster says,

"Everything all right, did you get them?"

Peter says,

"Yes… Any orders?"

"No".

Peter gets out of the cab and stretches his arms up to ease the cramps from the long journey. He is a coarse working type, heavyset, balding and in his late fifties. When Alf has closed the doors, Peter clicks on the light; it was an unexpected move taking everyone by surprise. Peter spots Ron hiding in the corner through the mirror of the truck and yells,

"Who the hell is that!?"

He draws a pistol from his belt and fumbles with the safety catch, trying to push past Alf to get a clear shot at Ron.

Dieter, moving like a shadow from behind the man, pushes his pistol into the back of Peter's head and before he has a chance to turn around or get a really good aim at Ron, Dieter pulls his trigger.

Both pistols fire almost simultaneously. Peter's blood splatters all over the whitewashed wall and he crashes to the garage floor, dead, bleeding from his eyes and an ugly hole in his cheek.

Ron spits and splutters out the white paint dust that shattered out of the wall when Peter's bullet hit it. It was too close to his head.

The sound of the shots brings Oskar and Bo running in with their knives drawn. Oskar stops and looks at Peter on the ground and says,

"Yes, that's him. That's the shit-bag who struck me".

He kicks the dead man in the face, Bo looks dumfounded,

"Is he dead?"

Alf has recognized Oskar and Bo and what color was left in his face drains away. Hans says,

"I think I want to be sick".

Hans runs out into the street, Ken follow him.

Dieter grabs Alf by the scruff of his neck and says,

"What about this one? We shouldn't leave him alive".

Alf is now close to collapse,

"Oh please, I won't be any trouble... I know his
black market. I know all his contacts and clients".

Dieter puts his gun back into its holster,

"Well, as I see it, you have two choices.
You can go free and chance getting shot in the back
before you reach the door... or join us".

Alf is very relieved. He breathes a deep sigh,

"Oh, join you; I'll join your platoon and be
a part of your gang... We could all live here".

Dieter looks around,

"We are not a gang... We are not the Hitler Youth either,
but if you want to join us, well, we will have to put it
to the vote. Don't forget that business with Oskar and Bo".
"I didn't hit or cut anyone. I just got dragged along to carry
stuff".

Oskar gets a little friendlier,

"Yes, it was just Peter".

Dieter asks everyone,

"So, do we want him in?"

Dieter looks at the boys; they all nod one by one. Dieter grins,

"That's it; it looks as if you're in then".

Alf is so relieved he just sits down heavily on a chair and takes a deep breath fumbling with his fly buttons.

Hans, looking very pale and shaken, asks,
    "So, anybody else live here?"
    "Just Peter and me".
Ron, looking around with his nose turned up
    "Well he doesn't live here now, so where do you sleep?"
Alf looks up at the ceiling,
    "In the apartment upstairs".
Ron and Ken look at each other and say together,
    "The apartment upstairs!"
Dieter and Hans mime 'Apartment'. Oskar goes through the dead
man's pockets: keys, wallet, passbook, petrol coupons and some money.
He piles them all on the table. Alf tells them,
    "There is a big safe key around his neck".
Oskar opens the dead man's bloody shirt, pulls out the key on a
string, rips it off and shows it to Alf. Alf nods. Dieter asks,
    "How do we get up to this apartment, where's the stairs?"
Alf says,
    "There is a door on the street".
Dieter looks at Ron and Ken,
    "Would you two get rid of that bag of shit?
    There is a bike trailer over there. Roll him up in this old rug.
    There's a bombed out cellar in the shop on the corner; we
    passed it on the way. It's flooded with water, put something
    heavy in with him to weigh him down so he sinks".
Ken looks at Dieter,
    "So why us, why do we get to do the shitty job?"
Dieter smiles and nods to Alf who is white as a sheet and shaking all
over,
    "I can't leave this one, and Hans here is all upset.
    He's useless to anyone at the moment, and I know
    it will be done properly if you two do it… See".
Ken and Ron start to pick up the man's feet and drag him to the
center of the garage, Dieter says,
    "We will wait for you both here. When you get back,
    we will all go upstairs together. Two and a half knocks
    on the door when you come back".
Ron and Ken start to roll Peter's body. Ken points to the man's head,
    "Look Ron, his are have gone. The bullet came out
    there in his cheek, and blew his eyes out".
Ron looks around,
    "They will be on the floor somewhere, I hope someone
    doesn't tread on them. Come on let's get him out of here".
    They roll him up in the dirty old rug with a bunch of bike front forks
to add weight. They tie the rolled carpet up with wire from the workshop.

Ron moans,
"We always get to do the shitty jobs?"
Ken strains heaving the rolled carpet into the bike trailer,
"Let's just do it. I don't like being around dead bodies".
They walk out without speaking. It's snowing; the fresh snow makes their movements silent. Ken grips Peter's pistol tight in his right hand clicking the safety off so he won't get caught like Peter, and pushes it deep into his overcoat pocket.
They walk about six blocks and come to the bombed out store with its basement full of water. The boys look left and right and stand still listening for signs of movement. With another glance over their shoulders, they roll the cart as close as they can to the window and tip the body out; then they have to lift it over the burned out windowsill and drop it into the hole. They heave and strain and bit-by-bit they get it up onto the sill, topple the body over and through the window.
It falls breaking the ice and it slides gently into the black water. They watch it float.
Ken whispers,
"Ron... It's not going to sink".
Ron digs Ken in the ribs,
"We said when we were on major larks like this
we wouldn't use our real names. So, you just did, you know,
you called me by my real name... Look he's going down now".
The body starts to sink slowly under the broken ice.
On the way back Ken says,
"You know, this is killing... Murder...
Well shooting Peter like that, what do you think Ron?"
"So? He would have shot all of us if he had the chance.
Dieter just got in first; he was aiming his gun at me you know,
in that second I looked right down the barrel of his pistol.
You can see when a gun is aimed right at you, I froze. He was
trying to take the safety off but his thumb missed the catch.
I thought I was dead when Dieter's pistol went off.
I would be dead now if Dieter hadn't shot him first.
It's the war, if you want to stay alive... Well people
have to do that stuff in wartime sometimes".
Ken gets very thoughtful,
"What about Alf? Will we have to kill him? He's only
fourteen, he's trying to survive like us. It isn't his fault".
Ron grabs Ken around his shoulders and whispers,
"I bet he is already dead Ken,
Dieter may have done him in by now".
Ken looks at his brother in horror,
"Why Ron, what has he done?"

"Come on, we don't know if he's dead, do we, he just may be?"
The twins walk in silences for a bit. Ken whispers,
"What about Peter? I wonder where his mother is.
Perhaps he didn't have a mother or father".
Ron smiles and says,
"He looks too old to have a mother or father. I bet he was
issued as a baby to a black market family during the 1914 war".

Ron taps his two and a half knocks on the garage door and they are
let in. The twins are relieved to see Alf still alive and tell Dieter about their
trip in the snow. Dieter gives Alf a friendly shove. They all follow him
out to the street and into a door next to the bike shop, up a flight of
gloomy stairs to a very strong looking steel door with two locks. Alf
fumbles with more keys and he opens the door to another world: A very
large apartment, beautifully furnished with good leather armchairs, heavy
plate glass tables and tasteful art on the walls. There are three bedrooms,
each with huge double beds, a living room and a well-stocked kitchen
with two big refrigerators. Dieter opens the fridges one by one; they are
stacked with food. Dieter asks,
"Just you two live here?"
"Yes, I clean house, guard the place,
do as I am told, sometimes I go out on his deals".
"What about his women?"
"Yes he has them, but never in this apartment".
Oskar and Bo walk in and look around. Bo says,
"Just look at this place,
the black market racket must be doing very well".
Oskar opens the fridge,
"Why would he want to steal our stuff when he has all this?"
Dieter scoffs,
"Greed".
Ken and Ron come in; they too look about in amazement.
They walk through the place, taking it all in. Dieter asks,
"Who owns the building?"
"He did".
"What about the neighbors next door on either side?"
"Empty, they were Jews. Peter reported them.
They got taken away a long time ago.
A lot of this furniture used to belong to them".

Bo looks under rugs and behind the pictures,
"Where's the safe?"
Alf points to a bookcase on the wall. Ron grabs it and tries to swing
it open like a door. Alf pushes past him and touches a hidden catch. The

whole bookcase swings open, revealing a large strong-looking safe. Dieter takes the key on the string and opens the huge steel door.

There is a lot of cash: Swiss Francs, US Dollars and a long thin notebook. Dieter flips through the money, puts it all back and locks the safe, then pulls the cord off the key and presses it into the soil of a dead potted plant.

Alf cooks a nice meal for all seven of them. Ron taps Alf on his shoulder,

"So what is stopping all of us moving in here?"

Alf laughs,

"It's a bit crowded; there's only three bedrooms".

The boys all laugh. Hans is now all brightened up, he says,

"Ha, you should have seen how we have been living
for the last few weeks. This is wonderful".

Ken leans into Alf and is concerned,

"Alf, is there anyone who may arrive we don't know about?
What about a girl or wife. Did Peter have anyone
around here as guests at all?"

Alf, very sure,

"He had women, but he used to rent rooms for them.
No one knows where he lives and he said he would kill me
if I ever told anyone about this place. I have been here
about a year and there has never been a visitor".

Bo quietly,

"You don't seem too upset about him dying"…

"No I hated him; he used to beat me with a cane, look".

Alf stands up, opens up his shirt and shows the scars on his back. The lower scars look fresh.

Alf says,

"These were for not washing up,
the others for not cleaning the toilet properly".

Ron says kindly.

"So Alf, would you mind if we all just moved in?
You could cook and we could keep this place clean.
Whatever we make we will split seven ways.
We could all live together like a family, share all the work.
No needless risks, we will all try to survive this stupid war?"

Alf has tears streaming down his face, like a small boy. It's the first time someone has said a kind word to him for a long time.

He nods and goes to his bedroom. Ron follows him. Alf flops face down on his bed sobbing deep sobs. Ron sits on the edge of his bed. Ron softly,

"It's all right. We are not going to hurt you.
We want to be your friends. If you don't want us here,

329

just say so, we won't push ourselves on to you.
We will just take our food back and go away".
Alf turns over and wipes his eyes, sits up and looks at Ron.
"I do want you to stay here. I'm crying because I'm so happy.
Peter was a real cruel bastard you know".
Alf gets up and closes the heavy drapes tight,
"The blackout drapes are very good in this place.
You can't see any light from the street.
You wouldn't know anyone was living here at all".
Dieter walks into the bedroom,
"Alf, how did Peter make his contacts?"
"I used to go to the park or the church and some cafes.
People know me. I take the orders.
Peter would deliver the stuff".
"What is the safest? Isn't it risky working out of the park?"
"Cafes and restaurants are best, and we sell to people we know.
So Alf, do you think we can take over his racket?"
Alf nods, Dieter walks over and grabs his hand and shakes it,
"Well Alf you will be all right now. We will all
be working for ourselves, in a very small way at first".
The twins appear at the door wrapped in big white towels,
"We just took a bath, with real hot water; do you remember
that stuff lads? That bath is big enough for all four of us.
We were floating up and down it's so big, you should see
all the soaps and stuff in the bathroom and an endless supply
of hot water and it keeps coming too".
"You lot should take a nice hot bath before you sleep
in the clean beds here".

At midnight Dieter takes the cartons of cigars and cigarettes out of the truck, stashes them in the backroom and drives it back to the factory depot and dumps it at the front gates leaving the key in the ignition. He slips away unseen, he does not want to be found in a stolen truck.

The boys quickly settle into apartment living.

Dieter and Hans take the master bedroom, Oskar and Bo take the small room and the twins share with Alf in his room. There is plenty of room for three skinny boys in Alf's enormous bed.

The boys had never seen such large beds.

As the weeks go by the weather turns bitterly cold and the food starts to run low. So Ron goes through the books with Alf pulling out the easy and safe clients. They start making little deals in cafes and on street corners. Buying food from farmers and selling it to a list of trusted clients, they are always very careful to keep a lookouts posted, to watch for the Gestapo or SS.

One night it is raining and cold, good weather for dealing. Bo and Oskar push a little wooded cart outside the back door of a small beer hall. Looking left and right to see that no one is about, they open the lid of the cart and take out a sack of potatoes and a cardboard box of tinned food that they are selling to the beer hall chef. They move quietly carrying their contraband into the yard.

A Gestapo Agent in a long black rubber overcoat and two SS guards that have been waiting in the shadows, suddenly step out in front of them. Oskar is the first to react; he flings his box at the Agent and yells,

"Run Bo run!"

At the same time Bo swings his sack at the other guard then the two boys take off running down the alley. There is a short burst of machine gun fire and Oskar falls sliding on the wet stone.

Bo stops, turns around and runs back to help his brother. He is lying very still. Bo tries to pick him up but he is limp.

His head falls back, his eyes are staring open and there are three large bullet wounds oozing blood from the center of his chest. Bo cries,

"Oskar, Oh Oskar, wake up, Oskar, Oskar".

Bo lifts up his limp brother and hugs him sobbing. The rain washes the boys' blood down his shirt.

A black boot prods him. Bo looks up to see a guard pointing a machine gun at him and saying to the agent,

"Look what you shot sir, it's just a pair of children, you were supposed to shoot over their heads?"

A third SS guard arrives and pulls Bo to his feet by the scruff of his neck. Bo yells,

"I'm dead, that's it; I'm totally dead aren't I?"

"You scum will kill me next won't you?"

A Gestapo agent grabs Bo by his long wet hair.

"Don't hurt this one. I want to find out where his supply comes from… You and I will have a little talk later, in my office boy".

Tears running down his face, Bo looks with terror at the men who are holding onto his jacket. The officer yells,

"So don't worry, we will get your little friends too".

Bo smiles and holds out his hand to give the Gestapo agent something. The man looks to see what he is offering.

Bo turns over his hand and opens his palm. An egg grenade with its pin pulled on a three second fuse sits in the boy's hand, smoking. He yells,

"This is for you scum! Wait for me Oskar!"

The guards and Gestapo agent react with looks of white panic, one of them tries to grab the grenade but Bo is too quick, they only have time to turn and take one pace before the grenade explodes.

It kills Bo, the two SS patrolmen and the Gestapo agent.

They all lay in the back alley dead, the rain-washing their blood all together down the center of the cobblestone ditch... The light from the open kitchen door catches five rain drenched blood-soaked bodies.

The boys are all sitting around the table in the apartment looking sad. Hans says,
> "Well, they took three of the black SS shits with them alright".

Dieter is not too sure,
> "Hans, how do you know all this?"

Hans says quite sadly,
> "The nice waiter who we dealt with said so".
> "It was the cook who squealed.
> He did it to win favor with a pair of Gestapo agents.
> One of those agents got himself killed by Bo's grenade".

Dieter sits at the table and carves names and dates on two bits of wood to make crosses, one slightly smaller than the other. Hans adds sadly,
> "They stood the owner of the beer hall and his wife
> against their own back wall and shot them dead.
> Their fourteen-year-old daughter ran away. Some justice".

Ken shrugs his shoulders,
> "No justices, more like it... What about their bodies, where."

Hans interrupts,
> "Gone, the black pigs, they picked them all up ".

Dieter says quietly,
> "If Bo hadn't pulled that grenade he would
> have been suffering terrible torture now.
> Then they would have killed him whatever he told them...
> I think I would have done the same thing".

The boys solemnly and slowly nod in agreement, one by one. Ron says with his very sensible voice,
> "We should stop dealing for a while".

Alf agrees,
> "We have enough food for a bit.
> There are lots of books here and a radio,
> if you can get it going".

Ken looks up from his gloom,
> "A radio, what's wrong with it then?"

Dieter gets up and looks out of the window,
> "Hans, do you know the name of the cook
> who betrayed us to the Gestapo?"

Hans nods sadly,
> "It was Heinrich Brest, nasty piece of work.

He is the new owner now, he was running the place
with that other Gestapo agent who Bo killed".
Dieter writes the name with his finger in the dust on the window,
    "I will remember this name for as long as I live".
Ken fixes the radio. The boys pass the evenings reading and sitting
around the fire listening to scratchy records on an old electric
gramophone.

One evening the twins are in each end of the bath, Ken has an egg
whisk and is beating up lots of bubbles.
Alf is stripped down to his underpants cleaning his teeth at the sink,
Ken and Ron are singing. Dieter creeps along the hall with a large bucket
of cold water in his hand. Hans is getting ready to open the bathroom
door. Dieter counts quietly, one, two, and three.
Hans opens the door and Dieter rushes into the bathroom and
douses all three boys with the cold water from the bucket. Lots of fun,
lots of splashing, and Dieter ends up in the bath with Ken, Ron and Alf
sitting on top of him. For a little while the boys are being boys again.

A week later Dieter appears in the living room dressed in his uniform
with the big topcoat, the cross strap belt and gun holster. I'm going out
for a while... I have a bit of unfinished business. I'm taking one of the
bikes. It's all right, I have Steiner's pistol here. It's loaded and the safety
is off. I shall be back in time for supper".
Ron gets up to protest, but Dieter holds up his hand,
    "This has to be done and I have to do it".
It's raining lightly and the streets are deserted. Dieter cycles off into
the darkness. In the wet alley behind the beer hall, Dieter quietly leans his
bike against the stone wall, just a few meters from where Oskar and Bo
were killed.
Sounds of boisterous singing with accordion accompaniment drifts
out of the dirty windows of the beer hall.
Dieter takes the two small crosses he had carved from his pocket;
each with two screws already drilled through them, pulls a screwdriver
from his pocket and screws them both to the thick telegraph pole.
The gate to the yard behind the Hall is open. Dieter slips through and
stands in the shadows and lets his eyes slowly get used to darkness.
Looking at the trash bins, he notes that one bin has a lock on it to
keep out the hungry scavengers. After a while the back door bursts open
flooding the yard with a streak of white light.
A kitchen boy yells goodnight to someone inside and steps into the
yard squinting to see in the darkness. Dieter waits for the kitchen door to
close, steps up behind him, and grabs the boy in a neck lock from the rear
muffling his mouth,

"Answer this truthfully or you die…
Is the cook Heinrich Brest in there?
Don't look around at me".
Dieter lets his hand off the boy's mouth so he can speak.
"He's sitting at the kitchen table…
With his Gestapo friend… Please don't"…
"Shh, just go home and come to work in the morning as usual.
If you look back at me I will have to kill you, go".
Dieter lets the boy go and listens to him run down the alley. He waits for the boy's footsteps to fade and makes sure that he hasn't gone around to the front door. Dieter ignoring the rain moves quietly around to a small window and peers through.

There's a crack in the blackout curtain and by moving his head left and right, he is able to scan most of the room.

Sitting at a small table on the far side of the kitchen under a similar window is the cook, a lumpish balding ruddy-faced man in a grubby white apron. He is talking to a thin man in a suit with a party badge in his lapel.

They have a pile of papers spread out on the table and are arguing about something. Dieter quietly moves around to the other small window and peers through. He just see their hands and the top of the table. He can hear their voices and see that they are both seated at the small table.

Quickly, he takes an egg grenade out of his pocket pulls the pin, and crashes it through the glass window then falls flat on the ground. With a three-second fuse, the cook and the Gestapo agent have no chance.

There is a bright flash and a tremendous explosion. The windows blow out over Dieter's head into the yard. He feels the stone wall at his side bump with the shock.

He gets up. The plaster dust falling off him like snowflakes. He walks calmly across the broken glass in the yard to his bike and rides around to the front of the beer hall.

People are running out of the smoky building. He waits until he can get in, then makes his way across the restaurant.

The kitchen doors are off their hinges; one waiter is sitting on the floor with a dazed look on his face. Three people at a table near the kitchen doors are just staring at each other, small trickles of blood running from their ears; they too are in total shock. Dieter moves into the smoked-filled kitchen to see if his two targets are actually dead.

The blood over the white tiles and the cook sitting up against the wall with his chest cavity open confirms his first kill. Dieter wonders if the Gestapo man has got away but then he sees his decapitated body across the other side of the kitchen under a sink. He doesn't wait to look for the man's head, but just turns and picks his way back through the beer hall giving a stunned waiter a helping hand to stagger out towards the street.

Dieter stands around for a while, watching the confusion. Then he pushes his bike a few blocks up the street, thinking about the awesome power in that little egg grenade. Almost at the end of the street he steps back into a deep dark doorway to see if the police or SS arrive.

He almost steps on what looked like a pile of coats on the doorstep. A muffled cry comes out of the pile of old rags. He bends down to see a frightened girl about fourteen or fifteen all bundled up trying to keep warm. Her drawn half-starved face looks up and says,

"What happened down there?"

"Oh someone let a bomb off".

"I think it killed the cook".

"Whoever did that, well I'd like to give him a kiss"

"Why?"

The girl stands up and looks at Dieter and sees his uniform.

She turns her back and starts to gather up her things, rolling her three great coats up in a bundle. Dieter gently touches her arm and says,

"It's all right I'm not in the Hitler Youth.

I'm a runaway... Like you".

She strikes a match and looks hard at Dieter's face.

Dieter quickly blows it out,

"No lights, they might see us".

"You look too healthy and well fed to be on the run".

"We've been eating better in the last few months".

Dieter pulls his hand out of his pocket and hands her a bread roll.

The girl grabs the roll and munches into it and doesn't stop until she has devoured half of it. She then offers the remaining half to Dieter. He pushes her hand back, gently saying,

"No, you eat it all. I have plenty in the apartment.

What's your name?"

The girl looks up at Dieter, shrugs her shoulders,

"Heidi Steer... My parents were the owners of that restaurant you just blew up. One of the waiters over there sometimes brings me food".

"What do you mean, I blew it up?"

"Yes I know who you are. You're Dieter, the leader of the black market boys who supplied my father".

Dieter puts his arm around her shoulders, gives her a hug,

"Is the Gestapo, looking for you?"

Heidi nods.

"If you like, you can come back and stay with us.

We have food and an apartment".

"Thank you, I have been living in the boiler shed, but I don't dare go back there now".

Dieter and Heidi slowly make their way through the rain with the sounds of police patrols arriving behind them.

She opens up and tells Dieter how the cook Heinrich Brest used to boast that they would all be working for him one day, and how thick he was with his Gestapo agent friend. On the night of the shootings, the cook Brest and his Gestapo friend left the restaurant just before the SS raid and re-appeared just after. Dieter says quietly,

"Well they're both dead now".

Heidi looks up to Dieter and nods without smiling.

There's a warm fire in the hearth and the apartment looks cozy; the boys are relaxed, reading. The door opens. Dieter looks around behind him and beckons Heidi to come in. She looks shy, cold and hungry. Spotting the fire, she runs over and warms herself, opening one coat after another. She looks skinny and half-starved. As she puts her hands out to warm them, she shows her thin wrists almost all bone. After a few moments she starts to look around at the opulence of the apartment. Dieter says quietly,

"This is Heidi Steer. It was her parents who were shot
at the back of their own restaurant last month...
You know, where Oskar and Bo were killed...
She's been on the run ever since".

Alf steps forward and takes her hand; they recognize each other.

"You're safe here... Would you like something to eat?"
"Hello Alf".
"Sorry to hear about your Mum and Dad".

She turns her head from the fire, nods to Alf and smiles. Alf goes out to the kitchen. Ron gets up and gives her his chair by the fire. Dieter says with sympathy,

"They confiscated their house too".

A hush falls over the room as Heidi looks about at all the luxury. She peels off an old army topcoat, under that she is wearing what looks like her mother's fur coat. Three pairs of socks, boots with the toes wrapped in sacking to keep out the cold, a pair of her father's long baggy pants. Ron asks,

"Would you like to have a nice hot bath?"

Heidi looks at Ron in almost disbelief she nods. Dieter stokes up the fire and opens the front grate to let out more heat; he looks at Ken,

"Why don't you go and light the water heater
in the bathroom and run her a hot bath?"

Ken nods cheerfully and slips out. Hans says,

"When you have had a warm bath
we will find you some nice clean clothes".

Heidi in tears nods to Hans. Dieter puts his arm around her.

21 The Apartment

They just sit there gazing into the fire. Alf walks in with a big bowl of hot thick stew, some cheese, and a half loaf of bread. Dieter helps her up to the table. She starts to eat slowly, savoring each spoonful, allowing the aroma to be breathed in.

A mug of hot Swiss chocolate arrives. Heidi asks,
"Where are we?"
Ken arrives with a big white bath-towel and introduces everyone.
"Hello, I'm Ken and this is my brother Ron.
Dieter and Hans; and you know Alf".
Heidi smiles,
"Hello, sure I haven't died and this is what it's like
waiting to go up and see Saint Peter in Heaven?"
Alf gets up and goes over and kisses her on the cheek. She returns Alf's affection with a big hug, much to Dieter's concern,
Dieter asks quietly,
"Do, err; you two know one another then?"
Heidi smiling sweetly,
"Yes, we used to sit next to each other at school.
Our folks were close friends".
Alf takes her hand,
"Sorry about your Mother and Father".
Heidi says sadly,
"Thank you. I'm very sorry...
You know, about your two little friends".
Alf hands her a napkin,
"When you have finished, you get yourself into a nice
hot bath and we will make a room ready for you".
Ron leads her out to the bathroom. When she has gone, Dieter looks hard at Alf and whispers,
"I thought she could sleep with me,
then Hans could bunk in with you?"
Alf stands up and starts to clear away the plates and mug,
"Come on Dieter, she's not like that.
Our families have known each other since we were children...
She should have Bo and Oskar's room, you and Hans
stay where you are and I'm all right sleeping with the twins...
Don't you think that's best?"
Dieter very disgruntled,
"Well, you know, I was led to understand that... she and I,
well I thought she would like to sleep with me".
Alf points out,
"Dieter, she's only the same age as me,
fourteen, and not feeling very well".
Ron sides with Alf,

"Dieter, she is just off the streets.
Give her a week or so to grow back to a human being again…
See what she wants to do then".
Dieter looks like a little boy who has just been scolded by his mother, and then he smiles.
"Yes all right".
The boys get the room ready for their new guest: clean sheets, the room heater turned on.
Heidi comes in wrapped in the large white towel. She kisses each boy equally goodnight, thanks each one warmly and goes into her room and closes the door.

Heidi slowly gets well with nourishing food and a warm dry place to sleep. She starts to cook for the boys; a big improvement on Alf's cooking, but the food eventually runs low. So the boys venture out to do some safe deals with the money they have saved and Peter's money out of the safe.
Heidi brightens up and turns out to be a bubbly, happy, fun-loving young lady. She takes a younger sister position in the family, with lots of fun and games. Dieter occasionally tries to jump into bed with Heidi but she fends him off. She is very careful not to favor one boy over the others and maintains that little sister position. The boys try to shock her by occasionally running out of the bathroom stark naked.
She laughs and pokes fun at the swinging parts as they flash by.

After a good dinner one evening, Dieter tells everyone that the food is getting low and they will have to start dealing a little to feed six teenagers every day.

22. THE RAIL SHEDS

Dealing in the black market in Munich is now very dangerous for the boys, so they only deal when they are compelled to, then only with the people they know, and just to put food on their own table. It keeps their exposure to the police and Gestapo to a minimum. Any boy who is call-up age or close is a target.

One bright cold afternoon Dieter, Hans and the twins are unloading the last sacks of potatoes and turnips from their four-man cart. They are all dressed in winter HJ uniforms. Dieter talks to the Chef of the restaurant in quiet tones. The deal is done so they make their way through the narrow back ally, all four boys pulling their cart and keeping up a good pace.

They turn a corner and come face to face with an SS truck that's blocking their way. They hear a motorcycle pull up behind them.

They turn around to see an SS Officer jump out of the motorcycle sidecar and stride over to them. He taps on their cart with his clipboard; Dieter opens the lid and shows it's empty. The SS motorcycle driver with a machine gun stands blocking their escape. The Officer looks at Dieter's shoulder patch and says,

"Ha, schoolboys, I see. What's your unit?"

Dieter tries to explain but he is cut off by a wave of the officer's hand.

"Well you're all mine now. You boys have been enlisted as volunteers for guard duty with me; I want you in that building. Two of you on each of the side doors. Don't let anyone out. Is that pistol loaded sergeant?"

Dieter nods,

"Right listen, we have four truck-loads of prisoners arriving. They are all condemned runaway Juvenile boys coming in here soon and I need all the manpower I can get. If a prisoner makes a run for it, shoot him. Do you understand boy? They have all been sentenced by the courts to be hanged anyway.
If one boy makes a run for it and gets away, they will all try it and we don't have the men to guard them. Get in there and warm yourselves by the fires until they arrive".

The boys stand their cart on its end and chain-lock it to a steel pole.

The big empty shed is the size of an aircraft hangar. In the center is a ring of steel drums that are glowing a dull red with the fires blazing away. Rows of long tables are piled high with army greatcoats and steel helmets. A handful of old men from the civilian Volkssturm (the Home Guard) are stoking the fires and sorting out army greatcoats in sizes.

Dieter and his lads stand warming themselves, Dieter says,

"Let's just stay calm. I don't like the look of the pair
of black SS shits at that door, just do as we are told".
Ron looks about and says,
"I hope we don't get asked to shoot anyone...
We should try to get away when everyone is asleep".
The boys all nod in agreement.

After an hour the big doors start to rumble open and four canvas-covered trucks with their awnings caked with dirty gray snow, back into the warehouse and form-up in line. The big warehouse doors are slammed closed and locked, then the back flaps of the trucks are flung open by the guards and the tailgates are crashed down. Crammed in tight with little room to move and huddled together for warmth is a crush of young boys. Most of them in rags but all in civilian clothes or what's left of them.

The boys range in ages from twelve to seventeen. Polish, Russian, Czechoslovakian and some Germans; slowly they all climb out and run over to the warmth of the fires. Three very young lads lay still on the floor of the first truck. They are not asleep. An SS guard pulls the nearest boy out by his bare feet; he drops lifeless to the ground his head cracking on the cement floor with a sickening bump. All three dead boys have been stripped down to their underwear and one is wearing a jersey that is too small for him. Dieter whispers,
"The other boys have taken his boots and warm clothes
after he died to keep themselves from freezing".
Two other bodies are dragged out of the other trucks; they too had been stripped of their warm clothing. A guard signals to Dieter to get his boys by the doors. The SS officer stands on a table with a tin megaphone, his voice echoes and booms in the cavernous shed. He yells, first in German:
"You condemned prisoners have all been sentenced by the
Courts to be executed because you are traitors, thieves,
criminals, or Wolf Boys...
I am acting under the special powers authorized by the Reich
Führer of the SS and signed by the public prosecutor. I have
orders to hang or shoot you all as enemies of the Third Reich.
However since you have all volunteered for a special unit in the
Army, your sentences are temporally suspended.
If you break any rules, question any orders, try to desert or run
away, your sentence will be immediate and you will be shot on
the spot. Your performance in the next few weeks may earn
you an acquittal. Work hard to earn your freedom and live!
Steel helmets and greatcoats will be drawn now. We leave for
your assignments as soon as the trucks have been refueled.
You are in the Army now, so get used to it, Heil Hitler".

A teenage boy takes the bullhorn and says the same thing in Polish. The prisoners are issued great coats and helmets. A few of the boys look as if they have been dragged out of their beds, others are dressed in summer uniforms of a boys' reformatory, in the lightest of summer shorts and jackets. Ken leans into Ron,

"I hope they don't take us with them as guards,

we could end up at the front fighting the Russians".

Then Ken says quietly,

"We stick together, right Ron?"

The old men are keeping the fires going and the young prisoners are all trying to keep warm and get some sleep.

They all bed down around the steel drum fires and have grabbed the overcoats that have not yet been issued to make some sort of warm covers. Some of the smaller boys are crying and most of them look ill and undernourished. As the night drags on the SS Guard sitting on a box by the big doors starts to nod off, dozing.

Ron tries the door they are guarding; it opens… Ken waves Dieter and Hans to come over. Keeping an eye on the old men at the fires and the guard in their view, watching them very carefully, with their boots in their hands they calmly walk over to Ron and Ken's door. When the time is right they all slip through the door and quietly close it. They find themselves in a long dimly lit corridor. The door to their right is obviously the door to the street, so they carefully try it. It is locked.

They backtrack down the long corridor to the only other door. Dieter stands listening at the door for some while, and then slowly tries the door handle. It opens into a totally dark room. Ron holds the door open against its spring to let as much light in as possible. Ken carefully makes his way across to the other door and trips on a mess can with a crash. A second later, the light is switched on,

"Stand still!" a voice yells. "Where do you think you're going?"

When the boy's eyes get used to the bright light, they see the SS Officer with a pistol in his hand sitting up in his army cot.

Ron tries the outer door; it's locked and another sleepy guard blocks the door they have just come through. Ron grins,

"Just came out to find a toilet sir".

"Toilet! What a lot of crap, with your boots in your hands, ha, you lot were all running away. Papers and let me have that pistol for now. Don't open the holster; just unclip it as it is and give it to my sergeant there".

The sergeant takes the holster off Dieter's belt, Dieter blusters,

"Our papers are in the message office in the station,

I can vouch for these boys: they are in my platoon, sir".

"But who can vouch for you sergeant?"

He waves to the guard at the door,
   "Take the four of them outside and shoot them"
Dieter yells.
   "I am a high ranking SS Officer's son,
   you are making a big mistake sir".
   "Well I could shoot you, or put you to work…
   Take them out there with the rest and put two of our people
   on the doors… Next time, if just one of you tries to run,
   I will shoot you. Do you understand?"
The burley sergeant pushes Dieter through the door back into the big shed. The old men of the Volkssturm have stoked up the fires and the barrels in the center are glowing cherry-hot again. Dieter and his boys make their way back to the warmth.

   In the morning two tables are set near the stove, each with a round disk marked 'A' and 'B' on a pole. At five A.M. the orderly shouts,
   "Wake up, stand up and shut up… Now listen…
   We want to delouse you, then get you fitted out in uniforms…
   The boys with HJ winter gear stay in your own uniforms.
   The rest get undressed; table 'A' first for delousing;
   'B' for Army medical and documentation…
   When I blow my whistle the first ten boys move, strip now".
A shrill whistle blows and echoes in the large hall.
   The production line starts. Boys get undressed and deloused. Old men with powder disinfectant puff into the boy's hair, under their armpits, up their backsides and all over their lower parts. Looking like little skinny white ghosts, the boys shuffle shivering to the next table for the paper documentation and to get their names taken and ticked off a list. At table 'B' they get the briefest of medical inspections. The sick are sent back to warm themselves by the fire but not allowed to dress. An SS sergeant marches over to the group who are sick and yells over to two guards with machine guns.
   "Take all these sick ones outside and
   stand them against a thick wall and shoot them".
All the boys in the sick group stand up grab their clothes and run over to join the fit ones. The SS guards laugh. The fit that are not in warm HJ winter gear are given new or used uniforms. Dieter and his three go back to the fire in their own warm clothes. They are the warmest-dressed boys, with their HJ winter uniforms, ski caps, two pairs of thick socks, well-fitting boots, heavy wool overcoats and fur lined gloves.
   An elderly distinguished-looking gentleman with a kind face wearing a Bavarian hunting suit, a good quality brown leather fur-lined overcoat with a white armband marked 'Volkssturm', walks over to the boys and says politely,

"I'm Captain Weislogel; I hold this rank in the Volkssturm…
Has everyone got warm clothes? Good.
You Ninety boys are my company 'B'…
Are there any HJ Youth Leaders here?"
Dieter and two other boys put up their hands. Dieter is obviously the oldest. All three step forward. Weislogel addresses the platoon and points over to two black SS guards,
"We have two armed guards coming with us,
one for each truck. There will be forty five boys
in each truck so do for the best".
The Captain looks at Dieter,
"Pick out thirty boys, you're the first platoon".
Dieter just like picking a sports team, picks Ron, Ken, Hans and twenty-seven other boys. The next two Youth Leaders pick the rest between them. Weislogel orders quietly,
"1st, 2nd, and 3rd platoons: look at your leaders,
remember them, now we eat".
There's a cheer from the boys as they all march off. The two armed SS men stay at the tail of the little army. Captain Weislogel gets very friendly and says,
"Let's all see this war through alive".
The company all clap as they march out into the cold night air.
Ron leans in to Ken and whispers,
"We have to get away from this lot, and soon".

They spend the next six days in an empty railway shed eating Spartan bad army food. Training with, but not firing, the 'Panzerfaust' (a one-shot anti-tank rocket weapon). Ron points out a label on the rocket launcher to a small boy 'Actung Feuerstrall' (Beware of flame) Ron jokes,
"Don't get behind anyone firing this…
or you will get your face burned off".
Dieter and his little platoon of boys look like cut-down men in the loose fitting steel helmets that seem much too large for them. They sit down and stuff them with newspaper to get a better fit.
The shed is like a prison; no way in or out; it is so cold the boys sleep with all their clothes on. They get fed some watery soup and a chunk of black bread every other day. Dieter says to his lads,
"I think we must be about thirty kilometers north-east of
Munich. They say they are going to move us tomorrow.
What are we going to fight with those?"
Dieter points to a huge pile of picks and shovels. Ron says quietly,
"We are not fighting anyone, with nothing, we are not getting
blown up for Fucking Hitler, Germany or anybody".

Hans says,
    "I hear that if you don't fight the officers
    shoot you in the back".
Ron smiles slyly,
    "Not if we get them first".
Dieter looks both ways apprehensively to see who's listening.

Captain Weislogel has taken over the small office at the far end of the shed. The boys get a chance to hear the radio in the office. They listen to the ravings of Joseph Goebbels at the Propaganda Ministry telling the German people about the miracle weapons that will dramatically change the outcome of the war.

But it is early February 1945 and the Red Army in the southeast has crossed the Austrian border. In the North they are about to close the noose around Berlin and make their drive for Hitler's bunker. The Allies are racing with the French, south through the Ruhr towards Munich.

At night a few boys gather around the radio to listen to the BBC broadcasting from London and learn that the great Thousand-Year Reich is on the verge of absolute collapse. The Allies having left the Rhine battle zone are now passing through towns untouched by war, except empty shelves in the stores and white flags hanging from the windows of the houses, as though it were wash day. Ron and Ken's enthusiasm for the Allies is infectious as the boys wait for Ron to translate the BBC radio to German.

Captain Weislogel's company of sentenced condemned boys march for a day to a rail junction in a suburb of Munich. The SS guard follows the line of skinny emaciated boys and he is ready to shoot any runaways.

They have been formed into a ninety boy patch-up crew. When the Allied bombers make holes with their bombs in the railways, the boys get called, descend on the craters with their shovels and bare hands fill in the holes.

A backbreaking task for boys who have been half starved over the past year. Stick wielding railway repair engineers drive them on to fill in the huge bomb holes. Then the engineers lay new rails over the filled-up craters. They spend the nights huddled around fire barrels, trying to sleep.

It's drizzling rain. Captain Weislogel's company is huddled up waiting to be relocated to a new debris-clearing job. The American bombers haven't raided yet today. It's three PM; the boys are cold and damp as they stand shivering around pair of steel fire barrels. Steam is coming from the boys standing closest to the fire. They haven't been fed today, again. Ron whispers,
    "Now we are near Munich.
    We should make a run for it, all of us".
Ken nodding towards the guard,

"What about him? He would love to shoot you, he's an SS".
A single SS guard in a black uniform stands overlooking the shed. He is guarding about ninety hungry boys. Some of them haven't the strength to stand, let alone work with a pick or shovel.

Hans moans,
> "Dieter, did you say you have a bit of a map,
> we have to know where we are. I hope we get
> something to eat today. Shit, am I ever hungry".

Ken warms his hands on the fire drum,
> "This is the second day, we didn't eat yesterday either".

Ron says,
> "How can they expect us to work
> moving great lumps of concrete and not feed us?"

Ken looks up to the roof of the railway shed,
> "I bet Heidi and Alf are eating well.
> All that food in that nice warm flat".

Captain Weislogel arrives looking very cheerful. He beckons his boys to gather around. Weislogel says,
> "Well the news is good. We stay here until tomorrow
> then we get transported to the mountains south of Munich.
> At least we don't have to face the Russians".

Ron says boldly,
> "Is that it then sir? What about our food,
> we haven't eaten for three days.

There is a murmur that rumbles through the boys who dare to agree. Hans too, being very bold says,
> "Sir, did you eat today or yesterday?"

Dieter steps forward and gives the Captain a smart salute,
> "Sir, where shall I take the boys to get them fed, Sir?"

Weislogel is now exasperated,
> "I'm trying to get food brought here".

Weislogel turns and walks away, stopping to have a word with the SS guard. All the boys of the company start to shout,
> "Food, Food, Food, Food".

The SS guard pulls the bolt back on the Schmeisser machine gun and fires a burst in the air over the boys' heads. The boys duck for cover. There is silence as Weislogel marches away.

Warming fires get started again; there is plenty of scrap and broken wood. The air raid sirens sound and the anti-aircraft guns start banging away. Some of the boys run scared for cover under the steel benches. Two small boys dressed in country farm clothes panic and make a dash for the big doors, the only exit.

The SS guard takes careful aim and fires a burst in front of them.

They stop in their tracks, turn around and run back in the shed for cover. The wide open doors are big enough for two whole trains to pass through at the same time. The boys can see the view down the tracks. The Allies are targeting the rail system again, and bombs are bursting down the lines, each one getting a little closer.

The boys scatter for whatever cover they can find. Ron grabs Ken and they dive under a big steel bench. Some boys just stand there staring at the explosions, as they get closer.

Dieter grabs his moment and tries to get closer to the SS guard who has lain down between the lines covering his head. Dieter, ignoring the shell splinters falling like red-hot rain, runs and dodges getting ever closer to the prone SS guard. He gets closer and closer, still unobserved. Looking around for a weapon, he picks up a length of thin steel pipe that has been broken sharp at one end. Stealthily he gets to almost striking distance of the man. Two small boys panic and run for the doors. The guard spots them and fires two short bursts; the boys drop dead like a stone.

Dieter is now behind the guard. He gets up and charges. The guard hears him coming, turns and at point blank range, fires his last two rounds in Dieter's direction. The guard fumbles for his new magazine. Dieter keeps charging with his pipe, spearing the guard through the soft part of his stomach.

His charge has all his weight behind it and the pipe runs right through his body and out the other side. The man screams, grasping the pipe and falls down to his knees.

Dieter sits down with a look of total disbelief on his face.

He feels his bloody chest and sees Ron and Ken running over towards him. Dieter cries,

"Oh look Ron, look, I can't feel a thing. It doesn't hurt…

Getting shot doesn't hurt at all Ron".

Dieter slumps sideways into Ken's arms. Ron undoes Dieter's coat. Blood is pumping out of two big holes in the center of his chest. He smiles,

"I got him, Ron, I got him… We can all get away now".

Dieter coughs and a trickle of blood runs from his mouth. After a few moments he chokes his last breath and dies in Ken's arms.

A groan and moans come from the speared SS guard who is now lying on his side with the broken end of the sharp pipe sticking out of his back.

He is clutching tight on to the pipe that has been run through his stomach. His eyes are wide with pain. Ron jumps up in a white rage and kicks the end of the pipe. The guard screams out.

Ron cries out and shouts,
"Why! Why? Why you stupid shit, why?
The war is almost over".
Ron loses all control, in his rage he grabs the pipe and swings it left and right. The guard holds on and screams out in agony.
Ron shouts,
"The fucking war is almost over; it will be all finished
in a few weeks; finished for you in a few minutes".
Ron changes the torture by pumping the pipe in and out causing the blood to spurt up the pipe. Ron yells with rage,
"Die, you fucking black pig, here's some of what you gave us…
Want some more? Want some more? Die, you bastard, die".
Ron stops pumping when the man's hand drops off the pipe.
He has passed out or died. Ron kicks the black helmet off the man's head, picks up a heavy clump of broken cement and brings it down on the guard's head as hard as his strength will allow. He stands just looking at the dead SS man.
He falls to his knees, his arms around Dieter his friend, crying in deep heavy sobs,
"Dieter, I've killed him for you… Dieter he's dead…
Dieter the black shit is dead now, we can go home,
and we will carry you".
Ken, sobbing deep sobs,
"Dieter's dead Ron… He's gone".
"What, he can't be, you sure?
Oh Dieter, I killed him for you…
Ken, do you think Dieter knows what I did…
I killed the black pig for Dieter.
Oh shit what a fucking mess… Ken try to find his pulse,
can you feel his heart?
Oh let's find Hans and get out of here".
Ken says quietly,
"Ron, Ron, we have to bury Dieter,
come on give me a hand to lift him".
"No… No… Ken, how do we know he's dead?
Why are you so sure he's dead Ken?
He just looks as if he is asleep to me".
Ken crying,
"He's dead Ron, when I first held him I felt his heart…
It was pounding like a hammer… I… felt it slow down
and stop… He has gone, he's dead Ron… he's dead".
The bombing and anti-aircraft fire has stopped. The boy prisoners are coming out of their hiding places. Ron and Ken carry Dieter, slowly

picking their way to the fire tubs. What's left of the platoon is wandering off in all directions, boys making their getaway in twos and threes. Some pulling the big warm great coats off the dead boys that lay on the rails. Ken recognizes Hans.

A small boy is trying to pull his coat off him, he is lying face down in the dust, his glasses broken beside him.

"Hey you, get away from him".

They lay Dieter down gently and run over to Hans. Ken's tearful face fixes his stare on Hans' glasses, he picks them up.

"Ron, look, not him too, Ron… Oh shit Ron, look".

Ron runs over to Ken. Hans's body is covered with dust, it is quite still. There is a large shrapnel hole in his left shoulder; it's not bleeding.

Ron gently turns him over. His bright blue eyes are staring; one of them has brick dust in it. Ken brushes his fingers over his eyelids, closing his eyes, puts his glasses back on his face and brushes the dust off his cheeks.

"Look Ron, he was growing a little mustache, I never noticed".

Ron brushes the dust off Dieter's coat, then they lay their two friends out side by side. Ken kneels, puts his arm around his brother; they sob and cry out loud, together.

They take the SS guard's pistol with its spare magazine.

His machine gun is now out of ammunition so they smash it on the rail lines. Ron takes the small pack that has his food ration.

On a soft grassy spot, out of sight of the sheds and rail sidings there is one new grave and two new crosses with Hans and Dieter's names and dates burned into them. The brothers are sitting close by. Ron's head is buried in Ken's chest. Ken is holding onto his brother with his arm around his shoulders. Ken sniffs,

"They were the best friends we ever had Ron.
At least they are together now. You know how Dieter
used to look out for Hans like he was his big brother".
Ron on his knees tearfully talks to the two crosses.
"Dieter you saved our lives and we are not going
to waste them by getting ourselves caught again.
Hans we will never forget you either…
Oh Ken say something, say something for Hans too".
Ken stands up and takes off his ski-cap; he grabs Ron's hand and pulls him to his feet. Ron takes off his cap, Ken takes a deep breath, puts his arm around his brother, looks up and says,
"Please God, take these two boys in
because they are good and have only tried to help people.
Oh please keep them together because they are like brothers…"

"Dieter and Hans, if you two can hear us,
your lives won't be wasted. We will see this war through.
We will always think about you two
and never forget you forever, Amen".
Ron wipes the tears from his eyes and whispers. "Amen".

Ken grabs a rock and hammers the wooden crosses in deep to the ground. Ron puts the two steel helmets side by side on top of the grave.

The brothers turn to each other and hug, standing by the grave with its two crosses stuck into the green embankment, all around them the ground is spotted with white snow. They begin their long hike north back to Munich and find it hard to swallow the sausage and black bread from the guard's bag and cry, but they are so hungry, they choke it down.

They have not walked too far down the line when they come to a small maintenance shed. As they get closer they can hear sounds of boys' voices shouting. The front door is open. Ron stands just outside the open door and beckons Ken to go around the back to peer through the window. Ken checks the pistol he took from the SS guard and lets off the safety catch. He picks his way through the pile of empty boxes and cautiously looks through the dirty windows.

About eight boys are being held at gunpoint by the other SS guard. Captain Weislogel is trying to reason with them, trying to get them to share a box of food. The guard is less than a meter from the window. Ken takes aim at the center of the man's back. A small-frightened boy sees Ken pointing his pistol through the window and instinctively ducks out of the line of fire.

The guard senses the boy's movement and turns around and spots Ken through the window. He starts to bring his machine gun to aim in Ken's direction, but Ken fires two fast shots into the man's head. The force of two 9mm bullets throws the SS man hard against the wall. He slides down the wall, dead. His machine gun falls to the floor. The captain reaches for the weapon. Ken re-aims at the captain and he freezes.

Ron steps inside the hut and grabs the machine gun. He yells at the Captain,

"You! Stand still! Or I will shoot you dead".

Two of the condemned boys feeling the captain is now under control dive into a pile of biscuit boxes and start to rip them open.

The rest of the boys start to scramble and rip into the boxes.

Ken appears at the door and fires a shot in the air.

"Stand back. Stand back, we will share
whatever there is to eat, no grabbing".

Ron orders one boy to open the boxes and share out the biscuits, while Ken holds the captain at pistol point. Ron tells the boys to scatter and stay out of sight until the Americans arrive. One boy has taken the guard's pistol off his body and gives it to Ron.

Ken takes the machine gun, removes the magazine and crashes the weapon on the concrete floor bending the gun and rendering it useless.

Ron hands a packet of biscuits to the captain and says.

"I think the war is over for all of us, don't you?"

The captain smiles, draws a deep sigh of relief, removes his armband and throws it on the table.

Ken and Ron run through the railway yards, over fences, staying off the main roads through side streets. Their hunger pangs drive the boys to rake through trashcans at the backs of cafés for scraps of food. They rush into a baker's shop brandishing the pistols they had taken from the SS guards, past a line of women, grabbing two large loaves of bread and dash out. They sneak into working kitchens, grabbing the odd scrap of food. Always ready to point their pistol and shoot at whoever challenges them.

They eat hurriedly in doorways. Ron is getting weaker as they make their way back to Alf's apartment. Walking, running stealing, anything to stay alive. On the third day of their escape, the boys turn into the narrow street and stand in a doorway watching the front door of Peter and Alf's apartment. There are no signs of life but they wait for it to get dark, shivering Ron says,

"If there was someone at home there,
they would have pulled the black-out drapes by now…
Come on let's try, take the safety off your pistol
and don't shoot me in the back".

The front door is closed but not locked. They enter very cautiously. As they climb the stairs they stop to listen. They try the steel door; it's locked. Ron goes back down three stairs and feels under the stair carpet. The key is there. Quietly he inserts the key and slowly unlocks the door; he pushes it open. The place looks as it did the day they left it. Ron closes the blackout drapes then turns on the lights. They make a quick search of the apartment. Ken opens the fridge in the kitchen.

"There's lots of good food in here".

He comes out with a sausage in each hand, gives one to Ron.

They munch on their first real food in three days.

Ron calls from the bathroom, there is a note stuck to the mirror, no address. Ron reads it when Ken arrives at the door.

"It's from Alf, it says, 'stuff in the thing', what does
that mean? They have gone to stay with her uncle…
Food is in the store room?"
"What do they mean, stuff is in the thing?"
"Money in the safe".

Ron runs over to the window, lifts a dead plant out of its pot and fishes out the safe key. They swing out the bookcase and open up the safe. There is Ron's original flat Prince Albert tin box and the key to the storeroom downstairs. Ken opens the tin box and takes out a wad of money.

"Good old Alf. Let's see what's in the store room".

The big new padlock that Dieter fitted is still in place. Ken unlocks the door. Most of the black market goods are gone. The boys survey what's left.

A small sack of potatoes, a carton of Dutch cigarettes, Dutch cigars, a box of tinned coffee and a wooden box full of canned soup. Ron says,

"We are in business brother... At least we won't starve".

The brothers sit around a warm stove holding mugs of hot soup. Ken gazes into the fire.

"Dieter, Hans, Oskar, and Bo, all dead, not one of them over sixteen... If we make it to sixteen it will be a bloody miracle".

"We will; you'll see. Let's try that radio.

Let's see who is winning this war".

Ken tries it but the batteries are dead. Ron jumps up and runs to the bathroom.

Ken can hear him throwing up. Ken says to himself:

"Too much food too quickly, we are not used to it,

(Shouting to Ron)... Feel better after that?"

Ron comes back into the room; he looks ill.

"We have plenty of chopped wood,

so I'm going to run a hot bath for us.

We will sleep well tonight".

Ron, wrapped in a big white towel, gets into the large bed. There is a fire in the bedroom stove. Ken puts the pistols under the pillows and then walks around the apartment locking doors and turning lights out. He opens a crack in the large heavy curtains and looks out over the empty street. Munich is dark, not a light to be seen. Ken's tearful face is warmed by the red glow of their fireplace.

He sees himself reflected off the glass window, he whispers.

"Oh Dieter, Hans... I hope it's nice where you are...

We are going to miss you both... We will get through this war".

Ken turns and gets in the bed with his brother. Ron is half asleep he pushes back to Ken for warmth.

Ron wakes up first; it's daylight and the sun is cutting through the heavy blackout curtains. He shakes Ken.

"Do you know what time it is?"

Ken says, half awake,

"No, but I bet you're going to tell me".

"It's 12.30, midday... Look".

Ron points to a clock on the bedside table.
  "It's still going, did you wind it?"
Ken sits up and grabs the clock, turns it over and peers at its back.
  "No, it's still going and it is an eight-day wind,
  so they must have been here seven or eight days ago".
  "So what, they're gone".
  "Don't you think it's weird?
  Alf hated clocks. He used to hide this one".
Ken grabs the clock and winds it saying,
  "It was half wound; someone wound it four days ago".
Ron fixes breakfast of powdered egg omelet, hot chocolate and a slice
of cheese. The boys search the apartment, looking through the closets.
Ron yells from one of the bedrooms,
  "Ken, look at this".
Ken comes to see a closet full of clothes, women's and men's suits,
expensive shoes, furs. Ken asks,
  "Whose are these? Someone's been living in this place.
  Ron, let's get out of here. Let's see if our bikes
  are still in the garage".
Ron nods.
  "We could go back to Oskar and Bo's cellar".
  "Yes, Ron, come on, let's get going.
  It's very odd having all that clothing, not knowing;
  well, someone may just turn up".

The boys pump air into their bicycle tires. Ken spots the back seat of
a car leaning against the wall. He nudges Ron and points to the seat.
  "That wasn't there before; someone's been in here with a car".
Ken wheels a light bicycle trailer in from the shop. Ron tapes up his
money tin and screws it to the bottom of the trailer. The boys load all the
food and the black market contraband, then cram clothing, blankets and
their cigar box with the official rubber stamps and the big first aid kit into
the trailer box and lock the lid. They mount the trailer to Ken's bike. They
empty the safe and have a last look around. Lock the door and put the
key under the third stair.
  They check the magazines of their pistols and slide them into their
greatcoat pockets. Ken peers out of the door to see if it's clear, they slip
into the street and just stand for a while to be sure they are not seen.

23. BATTLE OF MUNICH

Ken and Ron run through the railway yards, over fences, staying off the main roads through side streets. Their hunger pangs drive the boys to rake through trashcans at the backs of cafés for scraps of food. They rush into a baker's shop brandishing the pistols they had taken from the SS guards, past a line of women, grabbing two large loaves of bread and dash out. They sneak into working kitchens, grabbing the odd scrap of food. Always ready to point their pistol and shoot at whoever challenges them.

They eat hurriedly in doorways. Ron is getting weaker as they make their way back to Alf's apartment. Walking, running stealing, anything to stay alive. On the third day of their escape, the boys turn into the narrow street and stand in a doorway watching the front door of Peter and Alf's apartment. There are no signs of life but they wait for it to get dark, shivering Ron says,

"If there was someone at home there they would have pulled the black-out drapes by now... Come on let's try, take the safety off your pistol and don't shoot me in the back".

The front door is closed but not locked. They enter very cautiously, as they climb the stairs they stop to listen. They try the steel door; it's locked. Ron goes back down three stairs and feels under the stair carpet. The key is there. Quietly he inserts the key and slowly unlocks the door, pushes it open. The place looks as it did the day they left it. Ron closes the blackout drapes then turns on the lights. They make a quick search of the apartment. Ken opens the fridge in the kitchen.

"There's lots of good food in here".

He comes out with a sausage in each hand, gives one to Ron.

They munch on their first real food in three days.

Ron calls from the bathroom, there is a note stuck to the mirror, no address. Ron reads it when Ken arrives at the door.

"It's from Alf, it says, "Stuff in the thing", what does that mean? They have gone to stay with her uncle... Food is in the store room?"

"What do they mean, stuff in the thing?"

"Money in the safe".

Ron runs over to the window, lifts a dead plant out of its pot and fishes out the safe key. They swing out the bookcase and open up the safe. There is Ron's original flat Prince Albert tin box and the key to the storeroom downstairs. Ken opens the tin box and takes out a wad of money.

"Good old Alf. Let's see what's in the store room".

The big new padlock that Dieter fitted is still in place. Ken unlocks the door. Most of the black market goods are gone. The boys survey what's left.

A small sack of potatoes, a carton of Dutch cigarettes, Dutch cigars, a box of tinned coffee and a wooden box full of canned soup. Ron says,

"We are in business brother... At least we won't starve".

The brothers sit around a warm stove holding mugs of hot soup. Ken gazes into the fire.

"Dieter, Hans, Oskar, and Bo, all dead, not one of them over sixteen... If we make it to sixteen it will be a bloody miracle".
"We will; you'll see. Let's try that radio.
Let's see who is winning this war".

Ken tries it but the batteries are dead. Ron jumps up and runs to the bathroom.

Ken can hear him throwing up. Ken says to himself:
"Too much food too quickly, we are not used to it,
(Shouting to Ron)... "Feel better after that?"

Ron comes back into the room; he looks ill.
"We have plenty of chopped wood,
so I'm going to run a hot bath for us.
We will sleep well tonight".

Ron, wrapped in a big white towel, gets into the large bed. There is a fire in the bedroom stove. Ken puts the pistols under the pillows and then walks around the apartment locking doors and turning lights out. He opens a crack in the large heavy curtains and looks out over the empty street. Munich is dark, not a light to be seen. Ken's tearful face is warmed by the red glow of their fireplace.

He sees himself reflected off the glass window, he whispers.
"Oh Dieter Hans... I hope it's nice where you are...
We are going to miss you both... We will get through this war".

Ken turns and gets in the bed with his brother. Ron is half asleep he pushes back to Ken for warmth.

Ron wakes first, it's daylight and the sun is cutting through the heavy blackout curtains. He shakes Ken.
"Do you know what time it is?"

Ken says, half awake,
"No, but I bet your going to tell me".
"It's 12.30, midday... Look".

Ron points to a clock on the bedside table.
"It's still going, did you wind it?"

Ken sits up and grabs the clock, turns it over and peers at its back.
"No, it's still going and it is an eight-day wind,
so they must have been here seven or eight days ago".
"So what, they're gone".
"Don't you think it's weird?
Alf hated clocks. He used to hide this one".
Ken grabs the clock and winds it saying,
"It was half wound; someone wound it four days ago".
Ron fixes breakfast of powered egg omelet, hot chocolate and a slice
of cheese. The boys search the apartment, looking through the closets.
Ron yells from one of the bedrooms,
"Ken, look at this".
Ken comes to see a closet full of clothes, women's and men's suits,
expensive shoes, furs. Ken asks,
"Whose are these? Someone's been living in this place. Ron,
let's get out of here. Let's see if our bikes are still in the garage".
Ron nods.
"We could go back to Oskar and Bo's cellar".
"Yes, Ron, come on, let's get going.
It's very odd having all that clothing, not knowing;
well, someone may just turn up".
The boys pump air into their bicycle tires. Ken spots the back seat of
a car leaning against the wall. He nudges Ron and points to the seat.
"That wasn't there before; someone's been in here with a car".
Ken wheels a light bicycle trailer in from the shop. Ron tapes up his
money tin and screws it to the bottom of the trailer. The boys load all the
food and the black market contraband, then cram clothing, blankets and
their cigar box with the official rubber stamps and the big first aid kit into
the trailer box and lock the lid. They mount the trailer to Ken's bike. They
empty the safe and have a last look around. Lock the door and put the
key under the third stair.

They check the magazines of their pistols and slide them into their
greatcoat pockets. Ken peers out of the door to see if it is clear, they slip
into the street and just stand for a while to be sure they are not seen.

It's a cold sunny day. The boys look like active Hitler Youths again,
clean uniforms, bright red armbands. They zig-zag through the streets to
make sure they are not being followed. Sometimes they stop and
backtrack to be quite sure. It's late afternoon by the time they reach Bo
and Oscar's basement.

The street is still deserted. They clear away the junk that hides the
cellar doors. The cellar is the same as they left it. Ron picks up one of
Dieter's socks. They light the stove, check the other cellars, and stash the
money tin under the floorboards of the toilet.

Ron sorts out the ammunition for the two pistols, they have twelve 9mm rounds each and two magazines for each weapon. He picks up one pistol and gives it to Ken, slips the other one into his belt.

"We carry these at all times, even in the loo, all right?
Try not to shoot me".

The brothers are finishing their evening meal, Ron says,

"That's twice we have eaten today, I could get used to this life".
"So what do we have?
Two pistols with two magazines each, our camp knives, some
food, lots of potatoes and our stash of cigars and cigarettes…
We can trade them for something to eat when we get hungry".
"Don't forget the stamps and the messenger stuff".

Ken looks around; the cellar feels warm and secure.

"I feel better in here don't you? That flat was very nice
but I was always waiting for someone to pop in for tea.
You know anyone could have burst right in,
we had no escape route worked out".

Ron stokes the fire while Ken makes up their old bed with fresh sheets and blankets. They get into bed and blow out the candle.

It's dark with just a dull glow from the fire. Ron whispers,

"Ken, do you believe Dieter and Hans have gone
up to heaven? Do you think they are up there or
cold in the ground where we put them?"
"I don't believe there is a God or that we all go
up to the gates to meet Saint Peter. I would think it will
be so crowded by now with all the killing in this war".
"I don't think so either".
"I just feel we have to keep thinking about them
and not ever forget what they did for us".
"It's stupid, all this senseless killing".

In the distance the air raid sirens start wailing and the thump of the guns begins banging away. Ken sits up and stares at the roof of the cellar and the iron beams that have withstood that one bomb blast when there was a direct hit on the house next door and says,

"Ron, you don't think God will bring bombs on top
of us because I said I didn't believe he existed, do you?"

Ron turns over,

"No don't be silly… Let's stay here in bed…"
"There's nowhere to go". Ken says.
"Ron, what's the chance of a bomb hitting the same
house twice in one war? Not much I would think".
"So we are in the safest place in Munich, goodnight".
"Ha, goodnight".

The air raids stop. Soon the food runs out, so the brothers are back on the streets dealing their little bits of contraband in the park. The war is now in its sixth year; things are going badly for Germany. Black marketing is now a way of life despite the ruthless efforts of the local police and Gestapo.

The great German armies have now retreated on all fronts, bringing with them truckloads of spoils stolen from the countries they once occupied. French and Dutch chees, Brie from Luxembourg, cigars from Holland. The horse-mounted regiments of the SS drive great herds of cattle deep into Germany to feed the starving population. The food the boys had eaten over the past five years was never that nourishing. Most of the German meat was prepared into different types of sausages because it could include all parts of the animal and be processed with chaff and other non-foods. Also it did not need freezing.

U.S army bully beef, Spam, rice, chewing gum, aspirins, and for the price of a car, penicillin. There are British Compo rations; one box would feed one man for ten days or ten men for one day. These goods were showing up for sale where quiet deals were struck in churches and parks.

The twins' stash of contraband is valuable and can be traded for food. Farmers are the safest clients. A real farmer is easy to spot; they are usually plump and ruddy and can be easily distinguished from the pasty faced Gestapo plain-clothes police who would try to trick them.

The boys would pick up bits of news learning just how close the Allies are to Munich. Buying on the black market now is getting more open. People gather in-groups in the parks and make their little deals. Sometimes the twins put on their belts, pouches and white armbands and bluff their way as messenger boys and eat in the army barracks or in the officers' mess kitchens, but it's getting harder now as the troops evacuate and the last heavy units of the German Army move away.

One afternoon the boys are standing with a group of people around a radio at the window of a ground floor apartment. They hear the first broadcast of a BBC news program in short wave in German. It is reporting just how close the US forces are to the suburbs of Munich.

The boys decide to wait and hide out in their cellar until the battle for the city is over. Four days later the battle still hasn't started and their food has run out.

They are getting very hungry. Since the Americans are getting so close now, the stores are starting to sell off their reserve stocks of merchandise, shoes, sweaters, milk powder and potatoes all without ration coupons. But the boys have little money left, so they stick to their own deals.

Ron knows a fat man who he thinks is a farmer, a contact who is in the park every day looking for cigarettes or cigars for potatoes. They decide to go together and meet the man. Ken is to keep his distance and watch Ron's back. The twins put on their uniforms and bike out to meet the black market man in the park. They hide their bikes in the bushes. Ken keeps well hidden. A big fat man (rare these days) strolls down the path. Ron steps out of the bushes to meet him, and shows him his box of cigars. They have words. The man shakes his head, yells for his friends behind him and tries to grab Ron's box. Ron pulls away and starts to run towards Ken.

The fat man draws a pistol and fires twice at Ron. One of the bullets hits Ron in the arm, spinning him around. He falls and drops his box. The fat man runs forward and picks up the box.

Ken steps out of the bushes, draws the heavy Luger and at twenty paces and with ice-cold steadiness aims with two hands and fires. The fat man's leg shoots out from under him and he crashes to the ground screaming. Ken runs up to him and kicks the man's pistol out of reach. He points his pistol at the man's other leg and pulls the trigger. The second shot makes a small round hole in the fat man's good kneecap. His face all red with pain and rage, he yells out to people behind him.

"Shoot the bastards, shoot them".

Ron yells,

"Come on Ken, let's get in the bushes".

"I got him, I got the fat shit".

Shots are being fired; some hit the road quite close to them.

Ken picks up Ron's box. Both boys run off into the bushes, crash through the shrubbery, grab their bikes and take off fast. When they get to the edge of the park they stop and Ken looks at Ron's arm.

His forearm is bleeding fast and his chest is covered in blood.

Ken pulls his shirt open and feels his chest.

Ron is close to passing out, Ken shouts at him,

"Hang on Ron. You stay awake.

Did he get you anywhere on your body?"

Ron shakes his head and his legs give way he pushes his bike away and sits down heavily on a grassy mound. Ken takes Ron's cross strap off him and makes a tourniquet to slow the bleeding.

"Can you walk Ron? You have to walk, it's not far".

Ron lays back and winces as Ken tightens the strap on his biceps. Ken picks up Ron's bike and hides it in the bushes. He stands Ron up on his feet.

"I'm going to give you a ride on the bike's crossbar,

hang on with your good arm; you must stay awake Ron,

until we get to the cellar, all right?"

Ron puts his good arm over his brother's shoulder and they make it to the road. Ron sits on the crossbar and Ken cycles back home.

In the cellar, Ron has his arm over a bowl of hot water. The small caliber bullet entered Ron's forearm, and came out at the other side, just under the skin, not too deep. But there's a lot of bleeding and Ron is holding a tourniquet around his upper arm.

Ken says,
    "You're lucky, it missed all the bones,
    so none of them are broken"
    "I'm glad you think I'm the lucky one".
    "I'm going to have to put some stitches
    in both sides of your arm. It has to be done
    or it won't ever stop bleeding.
    Do you want to get drunk? We have some brandy".
Ron shakes his head.

The water is boiling in the saucepan. The big military First Aid Kit is open on the table. Ken threads a length of surgical thread through the needle, puts it with the forceps and tweezers in the steel wire cage, and drops them into the boiling water for sterilizing. Ron takes a big swig of the brandy and says.
    "I bet the fat man feels worse than I do.
    Right through his kneecap you say, Wow,
    he will always have a limp you know that".
    "He fired first; he could have killed us both".
    "He was trying to trick me, saying he would bring
    the food later. But I said no food no cigars.
    Then he got very pissed off...
    I'm so pleased you got him... Ow!"
Ken holds on to Ron's arm
    "Ron, just shut up, every time you talk,
    you move. Just keep still".

Ken places a dressing on Ron's wound and untwists the tourniquet on his skinny upper arm. The blood runs for a moment, then stops when it's tightened again. Ken puts a rolled up towel in Ron's mouth.
    "Bite on this; it's going to hurt very badly".
Ron says through the towel,
    "Don't touch any part of me with your dirty fingers;
    I don't want to get infected".
    "I'm not. I'm using the forceps.
    Look, they're being sterilized in the boiling water".
    "Fuck, fuck, fuck"
    "Ron It's going to hurt you a lot, very bad".
    "I know you just said that...
    Well fuck this war and sod you too!"
    "Nice, that's nice; me trying to patch you up as well".

Using the suture needle and forceps, Ken starts to stitch up the jagged holes where the bullet went in and came out. Ron pulls all the faces of pain and yells through the rolled up towel. Ken then uses scissors to trim up the little bits of skin that stick out. A douse of the strong disinfectant over the wounds makes Ron yell. Ken sits back and admires his work,

"It's all over; three stitches on one side and six on the other, untouched by human hands. Take these".

Ken puts four pain pills in Ron's mouth and hands him some water in a tin cup. Ron looks pale; he takes a swig of brandy and looks at Ken's work.

"Pretty good lad, very neat".

Ken applies the ointment dressing and makes an arm sling. He makes Ron comfortable.

Ken is reading the First Aid book that fits into the lid of the case. He breaks the seal on a syringe, sticks the needle through the lid and draws out some of the liquid. He holds the needle in the air and squirts it out until he gets the right amount. Ken smiles,

"Ron drop your pants and show me your pink bum, this is anti-tetanus".

Ron with his one good hand undoes his belt and Ken tugs down his pants and inserts the needle quick and deep injecting the serum slowly in to the cheek of his brothers backside.

"Ow… that hurt more than the fucking stitches".

Ken helps his brother get into bed, puts a tin mug of water next to the bed and pokes a pistol under his pillow.

"I'm going to get us some food".

"Where, tonight?"

"Don't you worry about it, you sleep.

I will give our knock before I come in, so don't shoot me.

Remember our knock… Bang, diddy, bang, bang, bang, bang".

Ron smiles,

"You be careful".

Ken leaves carrying a box of cigars and some money from the tin box. It's dark; the flicker of the stove flames is the only light in the cellar. Ron falls asleep feeling how lucky he is to have Ken to patch him up and look after him.

A rap on the door, tap, diddy, tap, tap… tap, tap.

Ron smiles to himself and grabs his pistol anyway. The door opens,

Ken comes in and lights the candle his face is beaming. He holds up a sack bulging.

"Potatoes, carrots, onions, turnips, and look: three cans of Spam, whatever that is. It's American… How are you?"

Ron sits up and looks at all the food on the table.
Ken is excited as he unpacks the vegetables,
> "Everyone's out there in the park.
> They are openly selling and buying.
> The farmers have the food and they want cigars…
> We are rich; I got all this for just five cigars.
> We have boxes of them here".

Ron quietly,
> "I haven't got a fever yet".

Ken takes a bottle out of his case and shakes it,
> "Ron, drink some of this.
> It's for people who have been shot.
> It stops infection and your fever won't be so bad
> when it comes, it's an iron tonic".

> "But I haven't got a fever".

> "You will have in a few days.
> I talked to a doctor at the aid station.
> He said you should take it, come on,
> I stood in line for two hours for this bottle.
> I got your bike back here too".

Ron sits up and allows Ken to feed him a spoonful of the medicine.
> "You are better off here. You should see the poor sods
> at the hospital and the aid station. There they are lying all over
> the floors, some of them without legs and arms.
> There is not enough of anything there
> and they are not getting very much food either.
> There are so many injured Ron.
> Most of the SS have moved out and taken
> all the medical supplies. You're much better off here".

> "How long did I sleep?"

> "About six hours".

> "It didn't seem as long as that".

Ken makes a thick vegetable stew with chunks of Spam and sits Ron up in bed and feeds him with a spoon, he gets a big bowl full down.

Ron's condition gets worse over the next day or so. He can just about get out of bed to go to the toilet; then just flops down again in the chair, exhausted. His arm is not healing.

Ken changes the dressing every day, boiling the old ones sterile. The doctor at the Aid Station told Ken that Ron would get a form of blood poisoning and the Americans had something called Penicillin.

A few shots of that would put him right very quickly. The next day Ken tries to get Ron to sit up but he is too weak. So he makes a strong stew and strains the broth through a sock. Ken gets Ron to take the nourishment by dipping his fingers into the broth and putting them into his mouth. He gets a whole mug full down into him like that. Ron falls back into a deep sleep, exhausted from just sitting up and swallowing the soup.

Ken has bought an old portable radio and some new batteries. He sits at the table trying to tune in to AFN (American Forces Network) on the radio. Ron wakes up and says weekly,

"Ken. I'm so cold".

"It's all right it's the fever, it will go soon,

then you'll be too hot".

"So how do you know all about that?"

He starts to shiver and shake. Ken piles the extra blankets and coats on the bed. He strips off his own clothes down to his underwear and gets into bed with him to keep him warm.

When Ron starts to shake and shiver with the cold, ken curls up behind him tight to keep him warm. An hour later Ron is sweating and is too hot. Ken dabs him down with wet towels trying to cool him.

After four hours of hot and cold spells, Ron falls back to sleep.

After a while Ken falls asleep in the chair and is suddenly awakened by Ron's week voice.

"Ken… I need to take a piss".

Ken smiles and takes the top off a large empty pickle jar, walks over to his bed and pulls back the bedcovers. Ron smiles as he relieves himself into the bottle.

"Oh, I needed that… thank you".

"Don't think I'm going to do that for you

very often. And don't you ever tell anyone".

"Is there any more of that soup? That last lot

reminded me of Dieter's feet. Isn't that weird?"

"Ha! It got strained through one of his socks".

Ron laughs out loud for the first time since the shooting. Each day he seems to get a little better but it's a slow process. They cheer when he is able to walk about shakily and get to the toilet on his own. Ken plays the black market, getting whatever he can. They are living on vegetable soups and slices of Spam.

A young Captain, Ruppert Gerngross the Commander of the Army Translator Unit at 2am. on April 28th, 1945 went into action, with a hundred or so FAB (Freedom Action Bavaria) fellow officers. They stormed the barracks and arrested the old General Franz Ritter von Epp who had been running the Munich area for the Nazi government.

Then the FAB captured one of the City's two radio stations.

Captain Gerngross himself went on the air to appeal for support urging the public not to fight the Americans and to place white sheets at their windows. At the first light the next day most of the citizens of Munich thought the war was over and some were even replacing the Nazi swastika with the beautiful blue and white diamond checkered flag of the old Kingdom of Bavaria.

Captain Gerngross sent two men to General Patch's US Seventh Army headquarters to explain their plan to make Munich an open city once the FAB had taken over. But the FAB and Captain Gerngross had failed to grab and capture the two most important men in Bavaria, Gauleiter for Munich Paul Giesler, the top Nazi, and Lieutenant General Siegfried Westphal, who was the chief of staff of Field Marshal Albert Von Kesselring's command. That morning Giesler marched into the other radio station that had not been taken by the rebels and went on the air denouncing the 'contemptible scoundrels' who had started the uprising.

Ken bursts into the cellar with a sack full of food, and, all excited, puts new batteries in the radio and turns it on.

The voice from the radio crackles.

Gauleiter Paul Giesler the Nazi party leader and General Siegfried Westphal are on the air denouncing the traitors who call themselves the FAB. They have been captured after taking over the radio station. Most of the insurgents are prisoners now and have been hanged or shot. (Captain Gerngross and his three friends actually escaped in a stolen staff Officer's car). General Patch and the US Sixth Army are going to have to fight for Munich.

The announcement starts to repeat itself.

Ken turns off the radio to save the batteries. Ron says sadly,

"They are going to put up a fight for the city".

"Yes, the Americans will blow us off the map, if we do survive this battle, then we have made it Ron".

Ken says brightly.

"It's a nice day out there".

Ron calls Ken,

"Ken come over here".

Ken walks slowly over to the bed.

Ron puts out his hand and grabs Ken's hand.

"Don't go out there, not today. When the Americans come, there will fighting in the streets. I don't want us to be last ditch fighters for Munich or shot to bits".

Ken gets into the bed and snuggles down under the blankets. Ron asks,

"How much food do we have?"

"I will make a big stew today. It should last us for at least six days, if we bring it to the boil every day and stop it going off".

That night and all the next day, sounds of heavy artillery fire shakes the cellar. The gunfire slows to the odd salvo by the end of the following day. After eating their stew ration for that day, the boys tighten their barricaded cellar-door and go to bed.

The next day, the 30th of April, it is very quiet. No more automatic or small arms fire. The brothers sit around their table trying to tune in to the BBC, but the batteries need recharging.

Ron asks Ken with a smile,
    "So, do you want to go out and see what's going on?"
    "Can you ride your bike?"
    "I can do eight push-ups with one hand; yes.
    I can ride my bike".
The boys take the badges and arm bands off their uniforms; take off their cross straps and pistol holsters.

Ken tucks his pistol in his belt under his shirt out of sight, rips a square from a white sheet and ties it to a long stick for a surrender flag. They emerge very carefully from the cellar.

The area is deserted. Ron rides slowly with his arm in a sling, holding onto the handlebars with his good hand. Ken's white flag is fluttering on a stick over his head. The city is very quiet. Acrid dust fills the air like a fog.

The streets are devoid of any sort of traffic; people are wandering about slowly as if they have nowhere to go.

A woman holding the hand of a small boy comes up to them and tearfully says sobbing,
    "It's all over you know, the Americans are here
    in the city somewhere, my husband died for nothing,
    we have lost the war, you boys had better hide; quick".

24. THE YANKS

As the twins ride their bicycles through the streets of Munich it looks like wash-day. White flags are hanging out of most of the windows. Some people have hung out the old Kingdom of Bavarian blue and white diamond flag. People stand about in small groups talking quietly. They turn a corner, and Ken points to a line of American tanks. Some of their top lids are open and a handful of local people are waving little bits of white rag or handkerchiefs. Ken unwraps his white flag and fixes it to his handlebars. They walk their bicycles up to the US soldiers and along the long line of tanks. The American tank crews look young and healthy in their clean, tight-fitting uniforms. In English, the boys ask where the U.S. First Aid station is. The friendly tank crews just shrug their shoulders or shake their heads.

After a while they come to an open truck. An MP Sergeant with a white helmet is studying a big map of the city spread out on the front of the truck. Ken runs up to him and says in his best English,
"Good morning sir, may we be of any assistance?
We know most of Munich".
The sergeant says to his driver,
"This one speaks good English, Bob".
Bob says,
"Ask him where the Prinzregenten Street is surge".
Ken smiles a big boyish smile,
"Sir, we will swap information.
If you tell us where the U.S. First Aid Station is,
we will guide you to the Prinzregenten Street... Sir".
The sergeant looks at the driver and laughs, and then looks at Ron.
"Show me where we are now".
Ken draws back and hesitates.
"Come on, we won't hurt you".
Ken steps up and looks at the man, then points to a spot on the map.
"Sir, we are English; we would like to speak
to someone about finding our father and mother".
The sergeant nods and smiles,
"You are trying to kid me boy?
English with that accent and in that uniform?"
"Oh yes sir. We got trapped
in Germany at the outbreak of the war".
Ron says,
"Sir, we really are British".
The two men look at Ron's arm, then each other and smile,
"Put your bikes on the back and get in.

We will drop you off at the civilian hospital.
And keep your heads down; we are not supposed
to pick up locals".
The truck drives off through the ruined streets. It slows down when it comes towards to a local hospital. There is a large crowd of German civilians trying to get medical attention. As soon as the people waiting at the front doors spot the U.S. truck they start to run towards it.

The truck stops and the sergeant pokes the driver and tells him to move on quick. They turn and drive off through the town past people waving at them. They arrive at the gate of the U.S. MASH Aid Station. A guard says,

"We can't let those two in here…
Allies or U.S. serviceman only.
They should go over to the civilian hospital".
Ken says in his best English,
"We are allies, sir, we are English…
We have been stuck here all through the war; honest".
The sergeant nods and the guard waves them through. The boys stay seated in the back of the truck as the sergeant talks to the young medical captain outside the door marked O.R.

Another officer joins them; he looks at the twins and shakes his head.

"They will have to go to the civilian hospital".
Ken nudges Ron and whispers in German.

"Ron, pass out; faint. Pretend to be unconscious
or they won't let you in here… Do it, now faint!"
Ron closes his eyes and flops over the driver falling on his good arm. The driver catches him and yells over to the sergeant,

"Hey Sarge, look: this one's in a bad way, he's passed out".
Ron is soon on a gurney and being is wheeled through the rubber doors by an orderly.

Ken sits waiting on the floor in the corridor when the doctor and the sergeant come through the rubber doors looking over each other's clipboards. The doctor points to the sergeant's board,

"Streptococcus infection with septicemia".
The doctor holds out his hand and gently pulls Ken to his feet,

"Did your brother have a fever?
First too hot then too cold and shivery?"
Ken nods,

"Did you nurse him through all that?"
Ken nods again,

"You saved his life, did you know that?
But now we have to open up that arm and drain it…
Did you put the stitches in?"

"Yes, my brother was shot about two weeks ago.
We had a first aid kit and some iron tonic".
"Well he has blood poisoning now. We will clean him up.
Food and Penicillin will put him right".
The doctor looks into Ken's eyes and places his fingers under his ears,
"My, you boys speak good English. Are you really a Brit?
You don't look very good. We will get some food into you".
"Thank you doctor, we are English you know".
The Captain says quietly,
"I know someone at headquarters who'll want to talk to you.
We could use some good interpreters around here and you
would eat well too. They are operating on your brother now
so he will be in Post-Op recovering for a while. He will be OK.
So don't worry, he's in our hands now".

The doctor shakes Ken's hand and goes through the rubber
doors.
The Captain smiles,
"Come on, you can come back and see him tonight.
Feeling hungry boy? Mm. We will have to get that
livestock off you first".
They turn to leave and the Captain stops a medical sergeant.
"Sergeant, can you get this lad cleaned up.
I think he has lice like his brother I shouldn't wonder".
Todd the Sergeant with a very kind face looks at his clipboard, looks
at Ken and puts his arm around his skinny shoulders,
"Your brother will be in recovery for about four days.
Now then whom do we have here? Oh, I thought I'd just
cleaned you up! Ha, you are Ronny's twin all right.
My, you do look identical. Hey, my name's Todd...
Oh, do you ever smell bad, come on
we will get you all fixed up".
Sergeant Todd leads Ken to the toilet and shower stall,
"Take all those dirty things off and put them in one
of those bags. I'll get them washed and de-loused for you.
Get in the shower there. Soap is on the shelf.
You probably have lice in your hair too just like
your brother. I'll get rid of them for you with this".
The sergeant holds up a bottle of blue liquid and a safety razor. He
starts to lather up his head with the strong-smelling soap and then gently
shaves him bald. He scrubs his back with a big sponge.
"My, are you ever dirty... when did you last have a bath?
You will feel much better after this.

The warmth of the water and the sponging of the flea soap feel wonderful to Ken, who had never had a massage like this before. He feels himself slowly dozing off.

Wearing a fresh white hospital smock with his hair all shaved and looking five years younger, Ken sits down to a meal of Spam fritters, mashed potatoes and sweet corn, served on a tin tray with segment dents in it. The Captain is talking to a Major at another table. They both walk over to Ken as he finishes his last mouthful. The Captain introduces Ken. The Major is robust and jolly. They all shake hands. The Major asks,
"They tell me you're English, boy.
How in the world did you get the uniform
you were wearing when they found you?"
Ken just stares at him,
"Talk to me boy. I want to hear your English".
Ken answers in his best English,
"Well sir, it's a very long story".
"Well, I want you to tell me all about it one day".
The Major leads him to the kitchens, his arm over his shoulder.
"Boy, you are all skin and bones,
have you had any ice cream lately?"
Ken looks at the Major...
"Ice Cream?"
"Well, have we got a treat for you".

Ken stands by Ron's hospital bed in tears. His brother is fast asleep with a new white dressing on his arm. A bottle of liquid is running into his body and a tube with dark red stuff is dripping into a clear bottle under his bed on the floor.
His long hair has also been shaved off. He looks clean and about twelve years old. Ken tries to hold back his tears. He looks at the doctor and says,
"Is he going to die Doctor?"
"He might have. He's very sick, but he will be OK
with rest and the right treatment".
Todd the sergeant comes in sniffing their HJ uniforms that are washed and dried, he says,
"Mm, these smell a little better now.
Ken you can get dressed, I have a prescription
we should pick up for young Ronny down there".
Ken follows the sergeant to the pharmacy and watches him go to a white steel refrigerated cupboard, unlock the door and take out a packet of penicillin. The sergeant hears a question from someone in the corridor outside the room. He turns his back on Ken and goes through the door.

While the mans is out of the room Ken takes a quick look around, opens the white fridge door and sees a stack of the precious penicillin in cartons lined up in neat rows. He snatches four cartons and shoves them under his shirt. He takes his time getting changed and fills his uniform pockets with dressings and a bottle of strong disinfectant. He walks through the rubber doors and they go back to Ron's bed.

The sergeant says.

"Now Kenny you watch me carefully because
you will have to do this for him every day".

Todd shows Ken how to locate the artery and put the needle into him and to draw a little blood back in to the syringe to be sure it's really in the artery.

He explains how to pump the dose in slowly because the penicillin has to go directly into the blood stream. Ken gives his brother his injection. Todd nods and smiles. He hands Ken the packet of penicillin, puts his arm over Ken's shoulder, gives him a hug and says.

"You will be able to do this for your brother alright?"

Ken smiles and nods "Thank you"

"Once a day for a week, the dose is written on the side.
Here is a new syringe too, don't forget to boil it
before each injection, it needs to be sterile".

Eight days later Ron is walking without any tubes going in or out of his body. Ken helps him on with his topcoat.

His injured arm does not pass through the sleeve but is tucked comfortably under the heavy warm mantle.

Ken ties the front of it together with string and pins the large U.S. wounded label to him. The twins say their good-byes and thank the doctor. Todd the medical orderly sergeant has given the boys some food in two boxes with cartons of U.S. cigarettes that they strap to the backs of their bikes. Very slowly they cycle off back to the cellar, with Ron stopping to rest at crossroads.

The main body of General Patch's U.S. Seventh Army has moved south, crossing the Austrian border and capturing the Salzburg area. General Patton on the East Side is bogged down by foul weather. Hitler is dead and Munich is left to the civilian police, very closely supervised by the U.S. and Allied occupation forces.

The boys try to deal a living on the black market. The food supply in Munich has dropped to an all-time low.

Germany has no more stolen supplies coming from the farms of France and Holland. The only work to be had is clearing the rubble of bombed out buildings. A mere forty marks a week and a bowl of thick U.S. meat stew a day; half of Munich is living like this.

It is all handwork with hand-pulled carts, but the twins have a very useful talent: they speak good English and can chat with the U.S. solders that are not allowed to fraternize with the German adults over eighteen.

So twins strike up deals between the GI's and the local girls.

The boys admire everything about the Americans; their clean uniforms, the jeeps, their easy way of talking, the smell of their honey fragrant cigarettes, Nescafe, Hershey Bars, the wonderful white bread with brown paste that tastes like peanuts.

The administration unit uses Ken as a translator and quickly adopts him as though he were a sort of puppy dog or a mascot.

Sometimes he gets sent over to a transport company of black soldiers to translate for their white officers who are employing local civilian labor.

The black soldiers are larger than life, big and noisy. They paint the inside of their barracks in very bright flashy colors and are always singing and drumming on their boxes.

They call their very young white officers by their first names and are very generous to Ken. They love to trade in the black market for girls. A pair of nylon stockings for a contact with a girl. Three packs of Lucky Strikes if she will do a blow job, a carton for a lay.

Ken has a list of girls who are happy to go with the black Americans and his commission is fifty percent. He gets his commission, contacts the girls, and the girls get paid after their service.

One afternoon Ken is sitting on a box in the brightly painted barrack room listening to four big black soldiers singing a wonderful spiritual folk song. A very tall coal-black man walks in from the showers naked except for a white towel around his waist.

Ken watches him, fascinated. It's the first total black body he has ever seen. He thinks to himself: My, they are really black all over, except the soles of their feet and the palms of their hands; I wonder if his thing is black too.

After a few moments the man stands up and stretches, flexing his arms he notices Ken looking at him. He smiles and takes off his towel, grabs his black penis and waves it to Ken,

"Hey pimp boy... can you find me a nice
blond German girl to take this one?"

Ken nods, thinking, gosh, it's bigger than Dieter's. It's got to be thicker than my arm. How could a girl take that, it's not even hard yet. Ken smiles and says,

"It will cost you plenty for that big one".

The black man laughs,

"Hey boy, would you like it up your ass for a dollar?"

Ken taken back by the thought of being grabbed and raped replies,

"No thanks; I wouldn't be able to shit for a month;
it would probably come out of my mouth".

The whole room laughs, and the naked man gets dressed, bunches up a dollar bill and tosses it at Ken saying,
"Hey boy, take it anyway, I don't like fucking small boys"

Ken is always on the lookout for something he can trade. The twins are unchallenged around the U.S. service barracks, the Translator Passes that hang around their necks allow the twins to come go as they please.

Everything has value for barter or trade. One Hitler Youth camp knife for three cartons of Camels. A pound of Coco, a can of Corned Beef or Spam for a good pair of German Army binoculars. Everything the Americans want can be found for a price. The American servicemen do well too. In 1946 a US dollar was worth 200 Reich marks. Twenty-five cartons of US cigarettes costing twenty US dollars in their PX could buy a Leica camera in Munich that would sell in the US for six hundred US dollars.

Forty cigarettes for a bottle of good wine and a bottle of schnapps. The Americans are always looking for Swiss watches, gold, any outlawed Nazi regalia. Luger pistols or Zeiss sunglasses all have great value.

Ken goes to the park every day to sell or barter.

The farmers come to the park to sell their food for cigarettes, wine, schnapps or coffee. Ken works the trade between the Americans and people he meets in the park. At the high end of the market, way out of the twin's price-range, a Persian rug would go for fifty kilos of good potatoes.

A bicycle for a piano. A very high quality one-carat diamond for two kilos of real US coffee and fifty cigarettes. White-wash certificates or de-Nazi papers issued by the US Government can be obtained for thos ewho can afford the price. They are a passport to Switzerland or Spain for SS members who are fleeing, but the Catholic Church and other big time black market racketeers usually organize this high-end business.

The Catholic Nuns are the big time dealers, arranging safe passage to South America for high-ranking Nazis who are wanted for war crimes. It is a costly organized route through the Vatican in Rome, usually paid for in stolen or confiscated gold.

The Catholic Priests and Nuns are not too particular from whose mouth or ears the gold was originally pried; or what concentration camp the jewels and diamonds came from.

It is their payment for aiding escaping war criminals and their families. Escaping Nazis sell their hoards of booty stolen from Jews in the countries they occupied. The local saying in the parks and on the streets is.

"Good percentages run the bloody roads to Rome
and the Vatican, via the Holy Purple Way".

V Armageddon

As history has proven the Pope and the Vatican at this time are up to their ears in the Nazi plunder. If an escaping high-ranking Nazi had enough stolen Jewish gold or diamonds to pay the Vatican, he could buy Vatican passports and sea passage for himself and his family. Getting his loot into the Swiss Banks was no problem either; it too passed through the Vatican in Rome and was worked on a simple percentage basis. The plunder made it all the way to South America, through 'Holy Purple Accounts' from the bodies of millions of Jews.

Back in the cellar Ron falls ill again and takes to his bed. Ken looks in his bread bag. He has six packs of Lucky Strikes, he says,
"I'm going out to trade the Lucky Strikes for a bit,
we can eat for a month with all these".
He clicks the action of the small pistol and pushes it under Ron's pillow, then makes him comfortable.
"Don't forget our knock, all right... Ron, you alright?"
Ron smiles weakly and nods. He reaches for the pistol.
"I have taken the safety off. All you have to do is pull the
trigger. Don't shoot me when I come back, all right?"
Ron nods again and closes his eyes. Ken waits until Ron is asleep and pushes the pistol deeper under his pillow. Then he quietly picks up his satchel and leaves.

Later that afternoon, Ken bursts into the cellar waving a fistful of notes and a bulging brown paper bag.
"Ron, wake up, we're rich... look I got all this
food and money just for three packs of Lucky's.
American cigarettes are better than cash, look".
Ron wakes up and tries to sit up but can't. He says he's in pain,
"Ken, it's time. It's time to give me some more injections,
like the doctor said... I feel really bad, Ken. I can't move".
Ken boils the water, sterilizes the needle and syringe. He takes very careful measure, holding the syringe and flicking the air bubbles up before he squirts out the precious excess penicillin back into the bottle to the exact dose. Ron doesn't flinch when Ken sticks the needle into his arm. Ken reads the bottle.
"Once a day for six days. You get some sleep.
I will wake you for dinner".
"I hope there's enough".
Ken smiles, then goes to the floorboards of the toilet and shows Ron a carton of six more bottles of penicillin,
"I filched these from the Yanks.
It's all right; they are the same batch as the first bottle.
I pinched them for you Ron, for your rotten arm".

A week passes and Ron gets better but not strong enough to ride a bike or walk too far. Ken now has a fulltime job finding wood for the stove. Their axe and saw are now worth their weight in gold. Everyone is looking for fuel. Ken's trade with the Yanks gets better and more profitable. They are staying alive by his small-time dealings in the park. Cigarettes and cigars for food.

A loud banging on their front door awakens the twin's early one morning. A gang of hungry kids are trying to break into their cellar. Ken uses the breakthrough escape to get out and comes up from the cellars three houses down the street behind them with his pistol in his pocket. The group of about eight boys aged ten or twelve years yell and start running at him brandishing sticks.

Ken draws his pistol and fires a shot over their heads. They stop in their tracks. Ken aims his pistol at the biggest boy. There is a moment while the lad thinks about his next move.

Ken takes a few paces towards the boy and aims at his head. Looking down the wrong end of the gun he has just seen fired causes his voice to flutter and waver.

"You wouldn't shoot us, would you?"

Ken smiles and nods and says quietly.

"Right between the eyes, you won't feel much".

The boy, who's about fourteen and in rags, tries his last ploy.

"We are going through all the bombed out basements
on this street, sometimes we find bits to eat.

Ken puts on the safety catch with a flourish and a loud click.

"Not this block, we live down there and
there are people in the basement with Typhus".

The lad yells,

"Ho Typhus, shit let's go!"

The boys scatter and run away.

One chilly damp evening the twins are sitting around their stove. Ron has a blanket around his shoulders, sipping hot cocoa. Ken is quite excited,

"Ron there's a big set of notice boards
in the Bahnhof Platz, outside the station.
People who want to find someone
can leave cards pinned on the boards.
What do you think about putting our own card up there…?
We just might find Mum and Dad".

"I could go by it every day.
Wouldn't it be marvelous if we found them?"

"How does it work?"

Ron opens the door to the stove and says,
    "I don't suppose it matters about us being runaways
    now Hitler's bunch don't count anymore, does it?"
Ken says,
    "Well I got these cards from the Yank Policeman.
    He said he would put it on the board. It's all-alphabetical.
    If you're nearest and dearest see it, they mark the card
    and you arrange to meet".
Ken writes a note, with the name Lambert on the top.
The two boys try many different messages, but finally settle on one
that reads:

/////////////////////

Ronald and Kenneth Lambert
Twin boys age 15 seek
Joseph and Louise Lambert
Mother and Father.
Here almost every day.

/////////////////////

Outside the Station a U.S. Military Policeman stands guard and hands
out thumbtacks. He has a pile of cut cards and short pencils. Ken waits
his turn to get close enough to the board to pin up his card. He stands
back to see how well it will be noticed.

Sometimes you would hear a cry of joy as someone finds a card from
a loved one. Ken wanders up and down the lines of faces looking to see
whoever they were. He is looking for his mother and father, but he has
forgotten what they look like, it has been almost six years.

Clearing the table after the meal early, Ken wants to settle down to
read the copy of Tom Sawyer he bought in the park for a cigarette. He
and Ron take turns reading a chapter to each other. They have dragged
the big old armchairs close to the stove and are making themselves
comfortable. Ken says,
    "Ron... I don't remember what Mum and Dad look like".
    "You will when we see them, I hope". Ron assures him.
    "Do you think they are still alive somewhere, looking for us?"
    "Mmm, absolutely. If they're alive, they will find us all right".
    "What about writing to the school?
    They may be trying to find us there".
Ron gazes into the fire and shakes his head,
    "We don't have an address here; how would they find us?"
    "We could tell them to leave a note on the big board
    outside the station. What do you think?"

Ron pokes at the fire with his good arm,
"No, writing to the school will give us away.
We might get picked up and charged with something.
Let's wait a bit and see what happens to our card.
No one knows where we live do they? It's been there
a week now. I'm coming with you tomorrow anyway;
I want to see this board for myself".
Ken starts to read from the book and Ron falls asleep from the
warmth of the fire.

The next day, outside the station, Ken locks their bikes to a lamppost
with a heavy chain and padlock. Ron has his arm in a sling and Ken stays
on his bad arm side to stop the crowd from jostling him. He points out
their card to Ron.
To their surprise there is a U.S. blue star with a number in ink in its
center stuck on to the edge of their card. Ken gets all excited and starts
to ask the crowd what the star means. A woman tells them,
"Oh, you're lucky. You have to see the U.S. guard,
tell him that number. He may have something for you.
I hope it's good news for you both".
Ken thanks the woman and they push their way through to the U.S.
guard post. Ken asks the guard,
"Sir, we have a number on our card look, 8186".
The guard writes the number down, 8186. You will have to wait here;
they will bring your message when the guard changes".
Ken asks anxiously,
"A message, from whom?"
"I don't know. Just wait over there".
The boys wait with a small group of people who are also waiting for
messages. Ron whispers,
"Do you think it's Mum from Vienna?"
"I hope so… where will we all go?"
"Don't know… England?"
It's getting dark and a jeep arrives to change the guard.
The little crowd walks over to the jeep and the sergeant starts to call
out numbers and pass out notes. There are cries of joy as the people read
their good news.
Ken and Ron watch as the little stack of cards gets smaller and the
last one is read out. The two boys are the only ones left and there are no
more cards to call out. The driver calls them over.
"Are you two the 8186 message?"
Ron answers,
"Yes sir".
"Get in, we have someone who wants to talk to you both".

Ken asks,
 "Who?"
 "I have no way of knowing that.
 Do you want to come or not? Get in".
Ken asks,
 "What about our bikes over there?"
 "Shove them on the back".
Ken piles the bikes on the back of the truck and helps Ron up in to
the passenger seat.

At the U.S. Military Police station. Ken and Ron are given a hot cup
of tea each and some donuts. A burly sergeant says,
 "Would you like a cigarette?"
Ken and Ron shake their heads. Ken says,
 "Thank you, we don't smoke
 but we will take them for trade later".
The sergeant tosses him the pack as he leaves. The boys pick up some
American comics and start to read. The MP guard behind them leans over
to read the comic. The Major that Ken had worked for bursts into the
office all smiles. Looks at Ron,
 "Hi, you two. My, you don't look too good;
 we will get you fixed up. Look at what a thick file
 we have on you two... We have heard from you mother.
 She is OK; she is in Vienna and will be here soon.
 It's not easy to move civilians out of the Russian Zone.
 It may take a few days. You can both stay in one of our cells.
 We won't lock you up".
The boys look at each other and grin.
 "Now, there's something important we need to talk about...
 But first I want to tell you that we have no interest in holding
 on to you boys. Whatever you did before we came here is of no
 interest to us, it's OK... You will both be free to go any time".
The boys nod, looking a little puzzled. The Major lights his pipe and
makes himself comfortable. He opens a big folder,
 "We are holding a Polish black market dealer by the name of
 Alvin Voss. He shot and wounded one of our patrol MPs.
 He is charging that our patrol shot him first.
 Now we know that is not true.
 We have stories from two very reliable witnesses
 at the scene that two young teenage boys,
 dressed in Hitler youth uniforms, shot him
 in a skirmish shoot-out, and that the two boys
 shouted at each other in English.
 The one called Ron was shot in the arm.

So... When your names came up on the board,
we put two and two together. Now...
All we need to do is clear our own patrolmen.
What happened before we arrived is none of our concern".
Ron asks,
"What about the Police?"
The Major smiles,
"We are not going to tell them; are you?"
Ken and Ron whisper to each other. Ken looks at the Major and says
very quietly,
"I shot the fat man Voss, after he shot my brother here".
Ron adds,
"The fat man Voss shot me first".
Ken continues,
"I shot him, because he was trying to kill us...
I could have shot him through the head,
but I'm not a murderer, so, I winged him".
The Major, looking at his notes, says:
"Just a few more questions...
Where did you hit him? Where on his body?"
Ken leans over to see the papers but the Major closes the folder,
"The first one through his upper left leg;
the other through his right knee cap".
The Major closes his folder and says,
"We need to write this up.
If you sign it, you have our gratitude and thanks
and you will be out of our hair and free.
Oh, one more thing; we need you to identify him,
he's in a ward not too far from here"

At the US army prison hospital ward they all wander down a row of
beds. A fat man is chained to his bed, sitting up reading.
Ron nods towards him,
"That's the big fat slob who shot me. That's him all right".
The fat man with a cage over his lower body takes a moment to
recognize Ron, then in a rage he grabs the only thing in his reach, an
empty bed pan, and flings it at Ron. Ron ducks and it sails harmlessly by.
The Major says,
"Sergeant I want you to witness this".

Ken points his finger close to the fat man's nose,
"That's the man I shot twice sir, that's him".
The fat man yells in German,
"Pigs, English Pigs, you're both dead".

Ron has picked up the steel bed pan that was thrown at him and wanders slowly over to the bed as if he were going to replace it quietly on the side table, but at the last second turns and crashes it down on the cage over the mans injured knees.

The fat man screams out in pain,
    "Ha, that's for my pain, you fat pig".
Ron cries defiantly,
    "Have another one".
He bangs it down again hard on his other leg. The sergeant grabs the pan out of Ron's hand,
    "Hey that's enough boy, with all his fat he is going to
    hurt a lot when he starts to walk on those legs".

Late that evening the twins are sitting on bunks in their cell eating a packet of American biscuits and bowls of rich thick meat stew. Ron has a fresh dressing on his arm. A black American soldier, who has been mopping the floors, stops by their cells and closes their door. He calls through the bars and says,
    "Hey, are you the two Limey kids from the Hitler Youth?"
The boys look through the small barred window of the door and nod. The soldier bolts the door from the outside and says with a sneer,
    "They are going to shoot you two
    in front of a firing squad at 0,700 hours tomorrow...
    It's your last night on this earth, so have a good rest.
    Sweet dreams you little Nazi assholes".
The man kicks their cell door and disappears down the corridor and slams the door. The two boys just look at each other, staring, their thoughts racing. The tears start welling up in their eyes at the same time, running down their cheeks as if a single tap turned them on.

Ken is the first to snap out of the state of shock. He grabs Ron by the collar shaking his head. Ken yells after the U.S. soldier...
    "Hey, wait, just a moment sir... Hey... Sir... Sir...
    Just a moment please hello, sir, sir".
The twins look at each other with horror and sink down to sit on the bunks. Ken says,
    "How can they do that?
    The doors here haven't been locked all this time.
    We were never locked in before...
    I don't believe it; it's not the way it works.
    They have to give us a trial first, don't they?"
Ron yells,
    "The buggers, they tricked us into confessing".
    "Wait a moment. We haven't killed anyone,
    do you think fat Voss died?"

378

Ken and Ron start to bang the cell door with their tin mugs and shout as loud as they can. Their cries are not answered.

Ken throws himself on the bed and starts to cry.

In the morning they hear movement and a door closes upstairs.

The boys start shouting again and bang their mugs on the bars of the small window in the door. No one comes; Ken starts to bang his tin mug on a steel drainpipe that goes up through the ceiling, a much louder sound booming through the building. They hear sounds of running boots and the door being unlocked. A face appears at their cell window. The guard asks,

"What the hell is all the noise about?"

It's 6am. Both boys are sitting on a couch sipping on mugs of hot co-co. The Captain is standing in his pajamas and an army great coat. Ken says,

"Some joke; if that's the American
sense of humor, I don't think much of it".

The Major explains,

"I'm sorry, but the Hitler Youth are
very much hated by some of our troops.
They just don't know all your details.
It was a sick joke. You're not being shot.
We don't do things like that without trials...
We will leave your cell door unlocked.
You can walk out at any time; so just sit tight and relax.
Your mother will be here in the next twenty-four hours,
I'll make sure you are not molested again".

The Captain hands the boys a packet of American cookies.

"Try these: they are new, with cream in the centers".

25. FAMILY

Later Ron and Ken are playing checkers in the mess tent. Ken says,
    "Ron, where do you think we will go"?
    "We will know when Mother gets here?"
    "Could be England or Vienna.
Ken gets checked, and loses interest in the game and says,
    "I wonder where Dad is right now.
    I have a feeling he is here and he's still alive too..."
    "The brown witches told us that both Mum and Dad
    had been sent back to England... We know that was a lie,
    don't we? So, well, he could be right here in Munich,
    for all we know, couldn't he?"
Ron tries to hold back his tears,
    "What about Cook, Max and Emmy? Do you think
    they were killed when the house got bombed?
    If they are alive, where are they?"
Ken catches Ron's mood,
    "They may be all under that pile of rubble at home".
Taking a big sniff, Ron forces a smile,
    "Well at least we made it didn't we, you and me?
    Everyone has gone. Dieter, Hans, Oskar and Bo, all gone...
    So we have to stick together. So don't let me die either,
    or you will all be on your own, totally".
Ken wipes his tears,
    "So what about all our stuff in the cellar?
    We have money and the big first aid kit
    with all that penicillin, we've got to get it".

Ron looks at their clothes. Their uniforms are in rags, climbing over rubble and working on the bombed railway lines has taken its toll. Ron looks at Ken's feet and knees and says,
    "Ken, look at us, we look terrible. Mother won't know us".
    "Well we can't do anything about it now".
    "Do you think they will send us back to that school?"
    "I hope they don't".
A sergeant calls to them,
    "You Lambert boys are wanted in the office".
The two boys look at the sergeant, then at each other and both say together,
    "She's here, I can feel it".
They try to make themselves look as presentable as possible, doing up their buttons and tucking in their shirts. Ron looks at Ken and grins, Ken shrugs his shoulders.

V Armageddon

The twins are seated on two chairs by the wall sharing their packet of biscuits. The door opens and a Red Cross worker with a kind face wearing a gray suit that looks too big for him comes in. His jacket has a large round Red Cross badge on the lapel. He has a wad of papers in his hand that he plonks down on the desk. He says in Swiss German,

"Are you the Lambert brothers?"

The boys nod and the man in the suit sits down,

"Your mother is here in the building. She is coming up here in a moment. Just sit quiet; I need answers to some questions first. Do you have any papers or passes?"

The boys shake their heads. The man looks at his papers and says,

"The American medical people told me about the tattoos on your feet. Will you please show me the numbers?"

The twins kick off their left boots and show the man their feet. He looks at them and writes the numbers down.

"Thank you, they will serve as the identification needed for this paperwork".

The boys sit down and put their boots back on. After what seems a long while to the boys, the door opens and their mother, Mrs. Lambert, walks in. Mother is very surprised; she stares at the twins, then leans on the desk and says to the Red Cross man very quietly,

"No... That's not them!"

"Are you sure"?

For moments all three stand looking at each other. Ken looks at his mother thinking she looks well-fed, notices her good quality clothes: a fur-lined coat, matching gloves, a thick pair of warm boots, a heavy tweed suit and a clean white cotton blouse. Such a contrast to the rags of the uniforms the boys are wearing. Mother looks at the boys. Ron with his arm in an army sling, Ken, his boots cut open to allow for his swollen feet.

They are a sorry sight, two skinny half-starved waifs with awful sores on their legs, how could they be her sons? What is she going to do with these boys; they are almost men. She doesn't know these people. Where are they going to live?

Mrs. Lambert has had a very comfortable war in Vienna as an accomplished zither player. She had played in the best restaurants where good food was served as a part of her fees. She has lived her war years in a very cozy apartment in the better part of Vienna.

There is not a glimmer of recognition from either side. Mother removes her heavy fur hat and undoes the big coat. The Red Cross man senses it's time to leave for a bit and goes quietly through the door. Mother looks hard at Ken and asks,

"Which one are you supposed to be?

My, how you have both grown".
Ken says suspiciously,
"It's been six years".
"What happened to your beautiful blond hair?"
"The Americans cut it all off, we had lice
and things you don't want to know about".
Mother recoils slightly, looks at Ken. His bare ankles are puffed up.
His eyes show the dark rings of malnutrition. The tattered uniform he has
worn for so long is far too small; he has grown out of it. She goes to hug
Ken but he steps back. She holds onto his hand and says, all choked up,
"It's me... your Mother. It's me".
She drops his hand and takes a pace towards Ron. Ken says very
flatly,
"Be very careful. Ron's sick and his arm is all shot up.
We have been stuck in a cell here for four days.
They said you were here two days ago.
Where have you been?"
Mother looks hurt at such harsh words, she chokes out the answer,
"I have been standing in line at
a Red Cross displaced person camp office...
For three days, looking for your father".
Ken changes his tone, his voice softens,
"Did you find him?"
Mother nods and walks over to Ron; he has recognized her and is all
tearful and sobbing. The twins look at each other, tears welling in Ken's
eyes now, he says softly,
"Where is he? Is he alright?"
"He is very sick; he is in a Military Hospital
here in Munich. We will go there today".
Mother looks at Ron's arm and reads the U.S. Army wound label.
"Did the Americans look after your arm all right?
It says here 'gunshot wound' how did you get that?"
Ron ignores her question; and stares at his mother thinking:
"Well she has had a good war, look at her healthy complexion.
That means only one thing, she has been eating good food...
Why didn't she contact us at school? All those years".
Ron asks quietly,
"So where have you both been for six years?"
"I was sent to Vienna, and your father has been
in the concentration camp in Dachau for most of the war".
Ken says softly,
"We thought he was in England.
That's what the Gestapo told us in 1939".

Mother puts her arms around her two tearful boys and walks them out of the office. They have to go slowly, so Ron can keep up.

Mother says,
  "Oh, you boys need some new clothes...
  Look, you're both so big. What happened?"

Ken says sobbing,
  "We grew up. We're men now; we are fifteen years old.
  We have to go home to the cellar to get Ron's penicillin.
  He needs it for his blood poisoning".

  "And all our things, we can't just leave them". Ron says quietly.

They all walk outside and say goodbye and thank the two U.S. Officers. Mother opens the doors of an old Mercedes car.

Before she starts the engine, Mother turns and looks at her boys,
  "You both look as if you have had a harsh time here.
  Did you get any of my letters? I wrote every week at first.
  I had one letter from your school in 1939.
  They said you had been sent back to England.
  I didn't believe that, so I kept on writing".

Ken is now sobbing quite uncontrollably,
  "We only got two letters... Sniff... We couldn't answer them
  because they were all cut up and all the addresses and dates
  were cut out. Dieter stole them from the school office...
  We weren't supposed to see them.
  The SS Brown Sisters told us that
  you had been sent to England too with Dad".

Mother now in tears, shakes her head and says,
  "They tell me your father will be all right now.
  He is very weak, and has been starved. When he is well,
  we will all go back to England... We will be a family again".

Mother starts the car and puts it in gear. Ken yells through his tears,
  "Where are we going? We have to get Ron's penicillin".

Mother stops the car and turns on the boys abruptly,
  "Yes, but we are going home first,
  I have to see what's left...
  I must see it to tell your father".

Ron sniffing says,
  "It's all gone; it's all bombed and burned out...
  We have been there... There is nothing left,
  it's a pile of rubble".

Mother drives them through the bombed ruins of Munich. The boys just stare out of the windows.

Mrs. Lambert is already missing her life in Vienna and is thinking about how she is going to be able to cope with these two sullen little bags of bones. She doesn't know them. The wartime occupation of Vienna, first by the Germans and then the Russians, has always needed top line places of entertainment. Places where for a price, the high ranking officer class could relax with their ladies, drink wine, eat good food and enjoy entertainment in the form of cabaret and a resident Zither player. Music is a part of Vienna's lifeblood. Mrs. Lambert would play Strauss, Frans Leher and old Viennese folk songs on the Zither.

She has been gainfully employed by two of Vienna's best restaurants and has had a good war. Living as she did in a beautiful furnished apartment with a live-in housekeeper, eating at the restaurants where she played. With ample money, food and good warm clothes, her war had been a comfortable one, to say the least.

Then, one day a Red Cross worker contacted her and informed her that her husband was alive, in Munich and anxious to return to England. Five days later she is told her sons are known black market dealers and have been found and are being held by the Americans. Her good life is starting to tumble down. Then to her total surprise, the Russians actually issue her a travel permit and petrol coupons to drive her own car out of Russian-occupied Vienna to Munich; something she never thought would happen.

It was a slow drive to Munich. It normally takes only a day, but because the roads are packed with refugees and demobilized soldiers traveling west, the trip took two and a half days on the packed Autobahn.

As they drive through the bombed ruins to their old home on Leopold Strasse, the streets all look so different, with piles of rubble instead of grand houses. Mother glances at her two boys sharing the front passenger seat thinking to herself: How is she going to cope with these boys; they are fifteen and young men, they have been running the streets wild for years.

Will they do what she tells them? They will want to eat everything in sight. If they were in Vienna she would at least know how to find some good winter clothes for them. The Red Cross Doctor told her that her husband would probably be an invalid in a wheelchair. She will have to cope with all that too? Staring at her boys through the mirror, she thinks.

"It's going to be hard getting to know these two young men".

The car stops outside the two blackened stone columns that once supported the gates of the Lambert home. They all walk up to the big pile of burned rubble. Ken says,

"Mother, it's been picked over by everyone.
Everything is burned. We looked for photographs;
there's nothing. It's all gone, burned".

Ron puts his good hand into his mother's, the three close in a tight group and hug for a long time.

They drive to Oskar and Bo's cellar. Ken tells her where to stop the car. Mother says,
"Is that where you were living, before it was bombed?"
Ron smiles,
"No, after it was bombed... Come on and see".
They get out of the car. Ken pulls open the cellar door and beckons his mother to follow. Mother looks about the basement with a sad look on her face, picking up a little bag of carrots and three potatoes carefully arranged on the stove. Ken gathers all the things that are very precious to them and piles them on the table. Their axe saw, the big first aid kit, the date stamps, two pots and a frying pan, the pistols, and their money tin that they have kept all these years. Ken holds it up to his mother,
"Look Mother, Father gave Ron this tin before the war.
We keep our money in it".
Mother looks around the basement, then at all the stuff Ken has gathered and waves her arm across the table,
"You can't take all this with us.
We are going to see your father,
then get on an RAF plane to London".
Ron, tight lipped, says to his Mother
"Well tell us what we can take".
Mother opens the first aid kit and takes out the bottles of penicillin, then picks up the old money tin, she says,
"Take only what you can carry in those shoulder bags;
I will wait for you both in the car.
We have to get to the hospital now, come on".
She leaves and the twins stand looking around the cellar. Ken grabs their pair of bread bags and puts Ron's over his good shoulder.
He picks up the two pistols, sets the safeties and tucks them in his belt under his shirt. He puts the Tom Sawyer book and diaries into Ron's bag with their belt buckles and armbands. Both boys stand for a moment and look at their stuff; their eyes wander around the basement. Ken stuffs the compass into Ron's bag along with their well-worn Hitler Youth camp knives. Ron sits down on the bed and whispers,
"We will never see this place again, will we?
I can smell Dieter's feet and Hans here...
We made it Ken; we survived, just us two, didn't we".
"Yes I hope someone nice finds this place; it's a home".
Ken puts his arm around his brother,
"It's all right. We said we would look out for each other
and we did. We survived, didn't we?"

They hear the horn of the car outside blow just once.

The twins stand and have their last look around for a lingering moment, then turn and go.

The roads to the hospital are packed with German soldiers and refugees all on the move, all going somewhere. People pushing handcarts piled with their worldly goods. The boys feel the stares of the refugees as they sit in the comfort of the big car. Mother slams down the door locks. The back seat is stacked to the roof with her luggage. They arrive at the British Army Hospital and make their way to the wards for concentration camp victims.

Mother talks to the Sister first and goes into the ward alone.

The boys watch her through the windows in the doors.

She walks down the rows of beds looking left and right reading the names on the charts. Halfway down she stops and approaches a man who is all skin and bones, a living skeleton. He is asleep with a bottle of liquid running into his arm. The boys see her hands go up to her tearful face then to her mouth in shock as she recognizes him as her husband. She looks back at the boy's faces at the window and nods. Mother stands for a long while holding Father's hand and just looking at him and weeping.

Ken Looks at Ron and says,

"Well she had a good war, she is almost plump".

"There must have been a pile of good food in Vienna".

Ken looks through the window at his mother standing at his father's bedside,

"Ron, what are we going to say to him?"

"Not much, he looks as if he's asleep... Ken, I feel terrible.

I think I need a shot of that stuff. Give me your arm

when we go in there, I feel a bit dizzy".

Ken takes Ron's weight and whispers,

"It's the hospital; they all smell like this,

it makes you feel ill even if you're not".

After a while the nurse comes by and gently leads Mother out past the boys. Ron touches the nurse's arm and says almost casually,

"Is he going to die?"

Nurse in a broad English accent says smiling,

"No, come on, you can see him too.

But you must both be quiet.

No talking, don't wake him up.

He is asleep, he needs the rest.

He's going to be all right, in time.

Six years in a concentration camp...

Well it's a wonder he is still alive isn't it".

The boys follow the nurse down to their father's bed. They just stand there, tears welling in their eyes as they look at the bag of bones and the living skeleton that's hanging onto a thread of life. The twins look sadly at their father's face, his very deep-set eyes, darkened with years of malnutrition, drawn cheeks that are almost transparent like parchment. There is a tube from a bottle of clear liquid going into his arm that is held fast with wide surgical tape that conceals half of their father's camp number.

It had been very crudely tattooed on his arm in Dachau almost six years earlier. Ron's eyes follow another tube that comes out of the bed and goes down to a heavy glass bottle on the floor.

Ron sways a little and grabs for Ken's arm. Ken catches him and the two boys stand and hug.

Ron buries his tearful face under Ken's jacket trying to muffle and conceal his deep sobs. He is feeling very sorry for his father, thinking, poor old Dad, he must have felt so hungry too and for so long. Well it's all over now.

Ron also feels very sorry for himself. His arm hurts bad, so do his knees. He is finding it painful just to stand there. He has always been the strong leader, the one who had to always put up the brave front, comforting Ken and making all the important decisions. It seems all right now it's all over.

So he starts slowly to free himself, he begins to let go. They have made it through the war now. He has looked after Ken as his father had asked him to; his job is done. They are a family again, together.

He feels a wave of sheer relief and then a cool cloud of dizziness sweeps through him.

He closes his eyes and slowly leans on his brother letting go of that survival instinct that had kept them alive and kept him going as the leader for the past six years.

Letting go of the effort of just trying to keep standing upright.

He allows himself to slide to the floor in a faint at Ken's feet.

Ken grabs Ron's head so it doesn't bang on the floor. He bends down to cushion his brother's fall.

He feels dizzy too, the room is swimming. Ken is aware of nurses in light blue uniforms rushing about, seeing Ron lifted onto a gurney and being wheeled off down the ward.

He is aware of two nice nurses, one on each side of him walking him past his mother, her face looking scared, with tears, biting into her good fur-lined gloves.

Ken, is now sitting on a hospital bed, watching them cut Ron's uniform off his skinny body with long scissors and lay him out, taking off his old dressing.

Then he watches dreamily as big green screens are wheeled around both of their beds. A nurse with bright red hair puts her face close to Ken's and asks,

"Can you undress yourself, young man?
We are going to give you a nice blanket bath…
Come on, I will help you, then you can go to sleep
and have a nice long rest".

Ken is aware of gentle hands undressing him and feels his pistols being drawn out of his belt, he didn't care anymore, the voices of the nurses sounded distant and far away.

"Look, he's got two guns in his belt.
What are you doing with these here, young man?
We'd better get them locked away before you shoot someone".

Ken watches the doctor and nurses attend to Ron's arm, allowing himself to be sponged and bathed by the happy smiling nurse with red hair. She makes sport out of washing his dirty swollen legs, and then gently applies the soothing ointment that is wrapped by soft spongy bandages. He dozes off to a deep sleep.

Ken awakes suddenly to the sound of a food trolley and the clatter of dishes. The screens that were around their bed have gone and he looks over to Ron who is still fast asleep with bottles and tubes all around him. The ward is full of young British soldiers all in bright blue pajamas, some sitting up and reading, some looking very sick. A young nurse comes over to Ken,

"Well, you had a nice sleep".

She looks at a watch that is pinned to her breast pocket.

"Sixteen hours, now that's what I call a good sleep.
Are you hungry yet, do you need these?"

She holds up a bedpan and a bottle. Ken nods and smiles as sweetly as he can. Lunch is minced beef in gravy, mashed powdered potatoes and cabbage boiled to a light green that's almost white. Dessert is a blob of boiled rice with a dent in the top that is filled with honey.

It is devoured very quickly. A young British soldier with his arm in a sling comes over and smiles,

"Hello lad, how do you feel today?
I see you made short work of the rotten lunch.
The food in here is horrible, isn't it?"

Ken shakes his head,

"Oh no, it's wonderful.
I haven't seen honey in years.
I ate so much I'm bursting".

The soldier brings a bar of Kit-Kat chocolate out from his arm sling and offers it to Ken, but the gift is intercepted and grabbed by the ward sister, a stern buxom woman in a dark blue tight fitting uniform.

"Oh no, my lad, that's not on your diet sheet today".

She turns to the soldier, who is grinning,

"So, do you want to kill him? He's on medication.

No sweets for two weeks. I'll keep that for you for later".

Ken chats to the men on the ward and the nurses; they bring him news from the other ward. He finds out that his mother is sleeping under his father's bed on a mattress and Ron has been wheeled out and has had an operation on his arm. His father is talking and would soon be sitting up. Ken couldn't understand why he was being kept in the hospital, he felt very well. Only Ron should be in here, he thought, he's the one who's sick.

A week slips by and Ken is now enjoying his natural functions in the privacy of the bathroom, he stands looking at the white tiles that go all the way up to the ceiling. All the chrome taps and bath railings shine.

The toilet is so clean one could eat dinner out of it. He looks at the mirror and wonders how they drilled holes right through the glass without cracking it. He stands gazing at himself in the full-length bathroom mirror. He hates his naked body, but when he is dressed in the fresh well-fitting bright blue pajamas, he likes what he sees. He thinks:

"Mother would like me better

if she could see me in this outfit.

I look almost human.

The next morning Ron wakes up and calls softly for Ken. He stands over him grinning,

"Ron, you wet the bed all the time...

So they shoved that tube up your dinky.

There's a bottle on the floor.

You're lying on a rubber sheet...

How do you feel? You look much better.

They operated on you, twice you know".

The young nurse with red hair arrives and sticks a thermometer in Ron's mouth and takes his good wrist to feel his pulse,

"Well, we are looking better today. How do you feel?"

She holds up a urine bottle,

"I'm taking your catheter out today, so I want you

to use this next time you want to go, alright?

You have one good arm.

Then when you're done, press the button there.

Someone will come and take it from you".

Ken leans over and says nodding towards the nurse,

"You know Ron, she has seen us both totally naked.

She changed you and I got a blanket bath.
We should ask her to show us her things...
Ha, she has seen ours it's only fair isn't it? Ha".
The nurse stands over Ron grinning,
"Don't you be so cheeky my lad?
You might just get a smacked bottom from Sister.
She has a strong right hand".
Ken laughs,
"Ha, oh yes please,
Mm, a smack on the bottom from Sister.
What a treat, we will look forward to that.
Ron did you hear that? We are going to get
our bottoms smacked by Sister... Ha, Ha".

After two weeks Ron is told he can get up. Ken and the nurse have to teach him to walk all over again. His legs are all wobbly from the weeks he has spent in bed. The buxom ward Sister tells the twins that tomorrow they will be allowed to see their father and mother. Ken will be able to push Ron in a wheelchair through the hospital. When they get to their father's ward they notice that all the men look like living skeletons.

Their father is the only one who is sitting up, propped up on pillows. Their mother is sitting on a chair next to his bed reading the paper to him.

Father notices the two boys as soon as they come through the doors into the ward. He can't believe how much they have grown, but he does recognize them. They are his boys all right; he has no doubt about that. They come to the edge of the bed and just stand there, staring.

Ken thinks his father looks so much better than the first time he saw him. Ron holds out the old Prince Albert tobacco tin to show his father,
"Look sir, we still have it, we keep our money in it".
"Don't call me sir. I'm your father; call me Dad".
Everyone is smiling with tears welling up in their eyes. Ken wheels Ron closer to the bed; they take turns hugging. When it's Ken's turn, he is shocked just how thin and wasted his father is, hugging him he could feel all of his bones. Father says,
"Do you two play chess?"
Ken answers looking at Ron for approval,
"No, I think we have forgotten how".
"Well I can show you both again,
they have some grand chess sets in here".
The boys draw themselves closer to their father. He holds each boy's hand,
"Well we are all together now.
Your mother and I love you both more than ever.
We will have to get to know each other all over again.

When we get out of here we will go to England, and
be a family again. We'll have so many stories to tell,
we won't stop talking for years".
Ron has been studying his father's forearm, looking at his numbers.
He kicks off his slipper and shows the sole of his left foot,
"Look Dad, we got numbers too,
when we were nine at the start of the war".
Mother gets up and gently takes hold of Ron's foot then looks at Ken
who nods and kicks off his slipper too showing his numbers, mother
shakes her head sadly. The ward Sister arrives smiling,
"Come on you two, we have to break up this party.
Go back to your ward. Your mother is on duty in five minutes".
Mother fits Ron's slipper back on his foot, kisses her husband and
the two boys then she says,
"I'm working here as a volunteer, so they feed me and
they let me sleep on the mattress under your father's bed".
It's a fine day. Still dressed in the bright blue army pajamas Ken
pushes Ron in the wheelchair through the gardens of the hospital
grounds.
"So, Ron, I wonder what English schools are like.
It will seem funny going back to school.
We can't write much English, can we?"
Ron laughs,
"Well we will learn won't we? … In England"
Ken shouts out loud,
"Shit Ron, we did it, you and me we survived?"
"Yes… We bloody did"
Both boys start singing
"Oh, Auntie Nelly had a fat belly,
and a red pimple on her bum,
with a red pimple on her bum.
Oh Auntie Nelly had a fat belly,
with a big pimple on her bum, Bang…
Yuck, Ha".

At that moment a German policeman in uniform with an Iron Cross
around his neck rides an old squeaky bicycle past them. Ken laughs and
points at his flat tire, the policeman looks at them thinking they must be
British soldiers ridiculing the defeated German military and pulls a sour
face at them.
"Look Ron… Look at his iron cross… Old Iron, old iron!"
Ken runs, pushes Ron down the path, racing around the narrow
footpaths. Ron is holding onto the wheelchair with his good arm, and the
boys yell out loud in unison,

"Oh, any old iron, any old iron,
Any, any, any old iron,
You look a treat,
walking down the street,
you look all nipper,
from your napper to your feet,
dressed in gray, dressed in green,
with your father's old green tie on,
Oh... We, wouldn't give you tuppence,
for your old watch chain,
old iron, old iron.
Oh... did'l, did'l, dum, dum,
did'l, did'l, dum, dum.
Dar did'l, dum, dum... dum, dum".

EPILOGUE

The Lambert twins were discharged from the British military Hospital in Munich. Ken's feet and knees had been in a bad way, swollen due to malnutrition. Ron's gunshot wound healed clean.

The Lambert family traveled to England in August 1945, bought a house just outside London, and the boys enrolled in a technical college.

Professor Tollin the kindly old German school Principal; whose Jewish sympathies were reported to the Gestapo, perished with the Jewish teacher Herr Rosen, and the fourteen young Jewish boys in the dreaded concentration camp at Auschwitz.

Karl Kaltenbrunner and his father the captain both survived the war. Karl works on the railway as a laborer. His father was shot dead in a soured black market deal three months after the war.

Alf and Heidi left the luxurious black market dealers' apartment to run away from rival gangs. They sat out their war on Heidi's uncle's farm near Starnberg. They were married in 1952. They now own and run the beer hall that the Gestapo agent took from her late parents. They have a son and a daughter.

The Lambert's cook, her husband Max and the two housemaids were put on a train and sent back to England at the outbreak of the war.

In the summer of 1948 Ron was killed in a bicycle accident, just one month after his seventeenth birthday.

Three months later, at age seventeen and a half, Ken was drafted into the British army for his compulsory national service.

He served six years as an officer in a parachute commando regiment, and was wounded twice during the Mau Mau war in the jungles of Kenya. He was medically discharged to the regiment's reserves with the rank of Captain.

In 1954, with an army educational grant, Ken went back to Munich to attend the newly built Technical University studying engineering, electronics and cinematography.

One summer holiday, he hiked alone, back to the camp in the mountains where he and his brother with two friends had spent that summer of 1944. Carrots and potatoes were still sprouting through the overgrowth of ferns in their little garden.

That night he slept in the open, on the same spot where their tent had stood. He watched the sun set to the right of their camp, munched on the young carrots and wild asparagus and thought about his brother and friends Dieter and Hans, resolving to write this all down as a memorial to them.

There, under the big old tree that was the center of their camp, he buried some of his brother Ron's ashes. They had been compressed into the battered tobacco tin that their father had given them in 1939 when they were nine years old.

Ken had kept that tin safe all those years.

To mark the spot, he screwed a brass plate into the trunk of the tree that had provided shelter for the boys that wonderful summer.

It is deeply engraved with the names and dates of his brother, Dieter and Hans.

Ken is now married to a lawyer and has four sons. Two of his boys are twins. He enjoyed a successful career as a Motion Picture Film Cameraman in Hollywood and went on to be DP (Director of Photography) mostly with Disney. To his credit, there are works such as Foxy Lady, Flipper and The Armchair Theater. He is now retired.

Made in the USA
Charleston, SC
05 October 2015